Republicanism in Ireland

MANCHESTER
1824

Manchester University Press

Republicanism in Ireland

Confronting theories and traditions

Edited by Iseult Honohan

Manchester University Press

Published by Manchester University Press
Altrincham Street, Manchester M1 7JA, UK
www.manchesteruniversitypress.co.uk

British Library Cataloguing-in-Publication Data is available

Library of Congress Cataloging-in-Publication Data is available

ISBN 978 0 7190 7592 6 *paperback*

First published by Manchester University Press 2008

This edition first published 2016

Printed by Lightning Source

Contents

Contributors

John Doyle is Senior Lecturer in International Relations, and Head of School of Law and Government, Dublin City University. His publications include: 'Irish diplomacy on the UN Security Council 2001–2: Foreign policy-making in the light of day', *Irish Studies in International Affairs*, 15 (2004); 'Re-examining the Northern Ireland conflict', in Vassilis Fouskas (ed.), *The Politics of Conflict* (Routledge, 2007); 'Towards a lasting peace?' The Northern Ireland multi-party agreement, referendum and Assembly elections of 1998', *Scottish Affairs,* 25 (1998); 'Governance and citizenship in contested states: The Northern Ireland peace agreement as internationalised governance', *Irish Studies in International Affairs,* 10 (1999).

Garret FitzGerald is a former Taoiseach (1981–82 and 1983–87) and Minister for Foreign Affairs. He was a signatory of the Anglo-Irish Agreement 1985, and is a long-time contributor to political debate in Ireland, Britain and Europe as economist, journalist and statesman. His books include: *All in a Life: Garret FitzGerald, an Autobiography* (Macmillan, 1991); *Reflections on the Irish State* (Irish Academic Press, 2002); and *Ireland in the World: Further Reflections on the Irish State* (Liberties Press, 2005).

Tom Garvin is Professor of Politics, School of Politics and International Relations, University College Dublin and was Department Head, 1991–2005. He is author of *The Evolution of Irish Nationalist Politics* (Gill and Macmillan, 1981; 2nd edn 1983); *Nationalist Revolutionaries in Ireland* (Clarendon, 1987); *1922: The Birth of Irish Democracy* (Gill and Macmillan, 1996); *Mythical Thinking in Political Life* (Maunsel, 2001); *Preventing the Future: Why was Ireland so Poor for so Long?* (Gill and Macmillan, 2004); 'Introduction' (with Andreas Hess) to Gustave de

Beaumont's *Ireland Social, Political, and Religious* (Harvard Belknap, 2005).

Iseult Honohan is Senior Lecturer, School of Politics and International Relations, University College Dublin and IRCHSS Senior Research Fellow 2007–08. She is author of *Civic Republicanism* (Routledge, 2002), contributing co-editor (with Jeremy Jennings) of *Republicanism in Theory and Practice* (Routledge, 2005), and author of articles including 'Friends, strangers or countrymen? The ties between citizens as colleagues', *Political Studies* (2001).

Gareth Ivory has been Audience Research Manager at Radio Telefis Éireann since 2002. He was awarded a PhD in 1999 by the University of Wolverhampton for his research on 'The political parties of the Republic of Ireland and the Northern Ireland issue, 1980–1995'. His publications include 'Revisions in nationalist discourse among Irish political parties', *Irish Political Studies* (1999), and 'Fianna Fáil, constitutional republicanism and the issue of consent', *Éire-Ireland* (1997).

Jeremy Jennings is Professor of Political Theory, Queen Mary, University of London. His publications include 'Citizenship, republicanism and multiculturalism in contemporary France', *British Journal of Political Science* (2000); 'The third Democracy: Tocqueville's views of America after 1840', *American Political Science Review*, 98 (2004, co-author, with Aurelian Craiutu); and *Revolution and the Republic: A History of Political Thought in France since the Eighteenth Century* (Oxford University Press, forthcoming).

Cécile Laborde is Reader in Political Theory, School of Public Policy, University College London. Her publications include *Pluralist Thought and the State in Britain and France, 1900–25* (Macmillan, 2000); *Republicanism and Political Theory* (co-edited, with John Maynor) (Blackwell, 2008); and *Critical Republicanism* (Oxford University Press, 2008).

Martin Mansergh is TD (MP) for South Tipperary, elected June 2007. He was previously a member of Seanad Eireann (Irish Senate), and Special Advisor to the Taoiseach with special reference to Northern Ireland and the peace process. He is author of a doctoral thesis in Oxford on eighteenth-century French history, and has written extensively on Irish history and politics, including essays in *The Legacy of History* (Mercier Press, 2003). He was also a contributor to Norman Porter (ed.), *The Republican Ideal* (Blackstaff, 1998).

Margaret O'Callaghan is Senior Lecturer, School of Politics, International Studies and Philosophy, Queen's University Belfast. She is author of *British High Politics and a Nationalist Ireland: Criminality, Land and the Law under Forster and Balfour* (Cork University Press/St Martin's Press, 1994); 'The political position of women in the Independent Irish State, 1921–1970', in S. Deane, M. O' Dowd et al. (eds), *The Field Day Anthology of Irish Writing*, Vol. 5 (Field Day, 2002). She has recently co-edited (with Mary E. Daly) *1916 in 1966: Commemorating the Easter Rising* (Royal Irish Academy, 2007), and has written numerous articles on aspects of modern Irish history.

Catherine O'Donnell is Research and Evaluation Officer, Co-operation Ireland. She was IRCHSS post-doctoral fellow, Humanities Institute of Ireland, UCD, 2005–07. She is author of *Fianna Fáil, Irish Republicanism and the Northern Ireland Troubles, 1968–2005* (Irish Academic Press, 2007). She was previously research fellow at the School of Politics, International Studies and Philosophy, Queen's University, Belfast, on a joint North-South project examining the 1966 commemoration of the 1916 Rising, and contributed to the collection edited by Mary E. Daly and Margaret O'Callaghan, *1916 in 1966: Commemorating the Easter Rising* (Royal Irish Academy, 2007).

Henry Patterson is Professor of Politics at the University of Ulster at Jordanstown. His recent books include *Ireland since 1939: The Persistence of Conflict* (Penguin, 2007), and *Unionism and Orangeism in Northern Ireland since 1945: The Decline of the Loyal Family* (with Eric Kaufmann) (Manchester University Press, 2007). His current research is on the history of border Protestants during the Troubles and on the role of victims' organisations in the peace processes in Ireland and the Basque Country.

Preface and acknowledgements

The idea for this book emerged gradually while I was engaged in a number of other projects on republican theory. But it took definitive shape when I was invited by John Coakley, as Director of the Institute of British-Irish Studies in the School of Politics and International Relations at University College Dublin, to convene a conference on 'The Future of Republicanism in Ireland' under its auspices in May 2004. Some of the chapters that follow are based on papers originally presented at this conference. The remaining chapters have been commissioned for this volume.

I would like to thank John Coakley for providing this opportunity, and for his advice and support. Thanks are also owed to all the speakers, chairs and discussants at that event, and to Hazel Moloney and Kevin Howard for their contributions to its success. University College Dublin provided financial support through its conference fund.

At various stages I have benefited greatly from discussions with and suggestions from Linda Cardinal, Finbar Cullen, Christopher Farrington, Tom Garvin, Gareth Ivory, Terence Kane and Jennifer Todd. The book owes much to the patience and organisation of the editorial team at Manchester University Press.

Parts of Chapter 5 previously appeared as 'Secular philosophy and Muslim headscarves in schools' in the *Journal of Political Philosophy,* 13 (2005): 305–29. Chapter 8 appeared in a different form in Garret FitzGerald's *Ireland in the World: Further Reflections* (Dublin: Liberties Press, 2005). I am grateful to the editor and publishers for allowing these to appear here.

1 Introduction: putting Irish republicanism in a wider context

Iseult Honohan

The most common understanding of Irish republicanism since the mid twentieth century has been as a commitment to separatist nationalism – in particular the end of British government involvement in Northern Ireland – and the pursuit of this aim through a campaign of armed force. The term has been principally applied to Sinn Féin, the IRA and a range of dissidents, all of whom tended to combine this with an anti-parliamentary and abstentionist approach to electoral politics. But a republican heritage is claimed also by most of the mainstream political parties in the twenty-six counties, which has been officially a republic since 1949.

Thus the term 'republican' has a high valency in Irish politics, but just what it means be a republican in Ireland is a contested matter. Does it reflect a consistent theoretical position, or is it just a label? Almost all who claim its mantle identify the United Irishmen movement of the 1790s as the origin of the ideals of an independent Ireland and a politics unmarked by sectarian divisions. Beyond this there is considerable disagreement on both its ideas and its lineage.[1] Some have argued that it lacks any coherent meaning, or, at the worst, that it is just a synonym for Anglophobia.[2] As well as separatism and physical force, republicanism has also been associated with cultural nationalism, revolutionary austerity and an authoritarian political style. These reflect factors including its genesis in eighteenth-century movements that included revolutionaries as diverse as Jefferson and Robespierre, its growth in the age of European nationalism, the influence of an authoritarian Catholicism on its constitutional expression, and the effects of marginalisation from the exercise of power.

The nature and meanings of republicanism are a matter of particular interest at a time when Sinn Féin, the party most closely identified with the separatist version of republicanism in the last fifty years, has entered mainstream politics, engaged in the peace process leading up to the Good

Friday Agreement, and decommissioned weapons. Electoral success and the resumption of devolved government in Northern Ireland since May 2007 have brought the party once more into government in Northern Ireland. Although its electoral advance in the Republic seemed to encounter a set-back in the 2007 general election, it is not clear what the longer trend will be. These developments have been accompanied by a public process of articulating the meaning of their republicanism by Sinn Féin leaders.[3] Other political parties have repositioned themselves in response to Sinn Féin's success, and attempted to reclaim their own republican inheritance. Thus the de-escalation of politically motivated violence allowed mainstream politicians who, against the backdrop of continuing violence in Northern Ireland, had distanced themselves from the revolutionary actions of 1916 to reclaim this central part of the founding myth of Irish politics.

Debates about the meaning of republicanism in Ireland are thus not just matters of abstract speculation. Contrast the battles among the parties over the inheritance of republicanism, as described by Gareth Ivory in Chapter 6 below, with the absence of any such debate in the United States. There the Republican Party does not now trade as, nor do Democrats make counter-claims to be, *the* true republicans, despite the fact that republicanism was a key element in the American Revolution and the foundation of the United States. The status of political institutions and actors as in some sense republican is taken for granted, not a subject of contention.

This reference to the United States introduces the fact that republican ideas have broader foundations and a longer history than the conventional Irish narrative reflects. There is a significant tradition of republican ideas in Europe and beyond, and republican politics has a concrete realisation, most prominently in France. In recent years republicanism has experienced a revival in international normative political theory. It is the aim of this book to examine Irish republicanism in some depth to see if and how it fits into this broader tradition of ideas and practice. The book goes beyond the – as yet unconcluded – debate on the national question and rival claims to the republican succession. As well as analysing the character of Irish republicanism, it aims to cast light on what relevance, if any, broader republican ideas and traditions may have for Ireland in addressing the challenges of the twenty-first century.[4]

With this in mind, the authors, who include historians, political theorists, political scientists, and senior statesmen who have played important historical roles in the peace process, were asked to address the following questions:

- Has Irish republicanism constituted a specific ideology?

- To what extent has it been part of a wider republican mainstream?
- What has been the practical impact of republican ideas in political practice?
- Are there lessons to be drawn from the experience of French republicanism?
- Finally, have republican ideas any bearing on some of the political issues which are most immediate for twenty-first century politics?

Coming as they do from different disciplines, and adopting different perspectives and emphases, the authors have risen to meet this challenge. The book is in three parts, which in turn examine republicanism in Ireland historically, comparatively and with respect to contemporary political perspectives.

In this introduction, I set the scene for the chapters that follow by outlining the features of the broader republican tradition, its practical embodiment in France, its rediscovery in the history of ideas in recent years, and the force of the current international revival of republican normative theory. Finally, I draw out some of the threads of these arguments on the relationship of Irish republicanism to the wider tradition, and identify what these ideas may have to offer to Irish politics today.

The wider republican tradition

The tradition of republican thought (sometimes referred to as civic republicanism) has roots in Athens and Rome, and has been interwoven with practical politics from the Renaissance Italian city-states through the seventeenth-century English Revolution up to the American and French Revolutions of the eighteenth century.[5]

Notwithstanding common perceptions, this tradition is best understood not as requiring either *national* independence nor the absence of a monarch *per se*, but as opposing domination whether by external or internal forces, by government, individuals or sectional groups. Put more positively, it advocates realising freedom, the common good and self-government among citizens who are necessarily interdependent. The idea is that if those who are mutually vulnerable recognise that they share a common fate and can act in solidarity, they may jointly be able to exercise some collective direction over their lives.

In any discussion of the ideas of republicanism we need to note that, despite the focus on a common cluster of ideas, the republican tradition consists not of a single thread but of multiple interwoven strands – Italian, English, Dutch, American, French and Australian to name a few – each with a different twist. In addition, there have been small city-state and extensive territorial republics, and these have embodied Catholic,

Protestant, militantly secularist, radical and conservative political perspectives.

The leading classical exponents of republican theory, Machiavelli, Harrington, Rousseau and Madison, were not armchair theorists engaging in utopian speculation; they addressed immediate political problems of the self-governing Florentine city-state, the seventeenth-century English republic (or commonwealth – the first English translation of *res publica*), France, and the American colonies respectively. Their writings inspired two of the great modern revolutions in America and France.

The core elements of the classical republican tradition that evolved between the sixteenth and eighteenth centuries were first, a preference for forms of 'mixed government', neither wholly democratic nor monopolised by a sovereign. This creates a balance of social forces or institutions to prevent domination by particular, corrupt interests and to realise the common good of citizens. Secondly, freedom is guaranteed by the rule of established laws, in place of the arbitrary will of a ruler; in Harrington's words this represents 'the empire of laws and not of men' under which citizens are free not 'from the law but by the law'.[6]

Preserving this fragile freedom from the threat of external and internal power depends, thirdly, not only on good institutions, but also on developing the character of citizens, so that rather than being essentially self-interested, they develop a strong commitment to the common good. For Machiavelli, citizens who 'neither arrogantly dominate nor humbly serve' must be active, accept duties and perform both political and military service.[7] Most republicans advocated a civic militia, both to provide defence and to instill civic spirit. (Its ironic legacy nowadays is found in the USA in the constitutional right – originally the duty – to bear arms.) For the less militaristic Rousseau, still 'the better the state is constituted, the more does public business take precedence in the minds of the citizens' who should 'fly to the assembly'.[8] Since people will always experience tension between common and their individual interests – the source of corruption – some form of civic education is essential.

Finally, substantial economic inequalities pose an obstacle to equal citizenship: citizens need to be independent of the overbearing will of others – originally this implied that they should be property owners. It was then usual to exclude from citizenship those seen as naturally dependent: propertyless wage-earners and women (though, it must be said that in this respect republicans were no different from 'early' liberals). On the other hand, excessive wealth and economic inequality among citizens were seen as undermining political equality. Thus republicans were prepared to consider state intervention to limit excessive accumulation of wealth, and even to redistribute wealth among citizens, and were, in socio-economic terms, relatively radical.

By the late eighteenth century a kaleidoscope of different permutations of these ideas presented itself. Two strands in particular were important. In America, James Madison extended the theory to fit a large, increasingly commercial society. Co-author of the *Federalist Papers* and the United States Constitution, he boldly redefined a republic as government through representatives (as opposed to the direct popular rule of a democracy), and introduced separation of powers between federal and state governments as well as between branches of government. But it is less often noticed that he still emphasised the need for civic virtue in citizens and rulers: 'If there be no virtue we are in a wretched situation ... No theoretical checks, no form of government can render us secure.'[9]

A wholly different tack was taken by Rousseau, who restated the idea that republican freedom was possible only in a small participatory community, though he did not hold out much hope that this could be realised anywhere in the modern world (with the possible exception of Corsica). But he delivered a swingeing criticism of the oppression and corruption of his time. This inspired the French revolutionaries to create a large republic based on the values of liberty, equality and fraternity, and to try to realise his elusive vision of the collective sovereignty of the people (where 'each individual while uniting himself with others obeys no one but himself and remains as free as before'[10]). At this time, though less influentially, women writers, including Mary Wollstonecraft, expressed republican hopes for the improvement of society through self-rule and civic virtue to include women as equal citizens.

Irish thinkers were not without influence in this movement. The American revolutionaries were deeply influenced by the writings of Harrington, whose works had been edited by the Irish scholar and deist, John Toland, and of Francis Hutcheson, who was born in Down and taught in Dublin for ten years before going to Glasgow, where he became one of the leading moral philosophers of the Scottish Enlightenment.[11] It was in this period that the United Irishmen, following American and French example, called for the end of tyrannical rule in Ireland. Yet the scholarship of historical reinterpretation has barely mentioned Ireland, an omission strikingly emphasised by Margaret O'Callaghan in Chapter 3 below.[12]

Partly because it was discredited by the excesses of the French revolutionary terror, republicanism in the nineteenth century was eclipsed by the more prominent movements of liberalism, socialism and nationalism.[13] But it passed on significant legacies to each of these – ideas of balanced government and the rule of law to liberals, of social interdependence and the negative political effects of economic inequality to socialists, and of collective self-government to nationalists. It also had an interesting, if largely overlooked, afterlife in the work of those archetypal

liberals, Constant, Tocqueville and Mill, all of whom stressed – as well
as freedom – the importance of active citizens concerned with the wider
good of society.

But even as the vote was gradually extended to the working class and
to women, the idea of active participation was sidelined as dangerous or
impractical. And civic virtue was increasingly seen as redundant in
commercial societies. So citizenship became broader at the cost of becoming shallower. As one writer neatly sums it up, the civic, political and
urban ideal was succeeded by one that was civil, polite and urbane.[14]

In any case, traditional republicanism – and not only its Irish expression – was open to the criticisms that it is too austere and demanding of
its citizens; that its concern for the common good threatens to oppress
individuals and minorities; that its emphasis on collective self-government
may support populist majoritarianism; that it has been intrinsically militaristic and masculinist; and that its concern is focused on citizens to the
exclusion of others.

Republican ideas have had different practical legacies, each coloured
by the particular context in which they developed. At this point, before
turning to the Irish tradition, the subject of Part I, it is useful to consider
the way in which the French republic, in one sense the quintessential or
'exemplary' republic, has embodied this tradition.

France: la République une et indivisible

Part II deals with the contemporary experience of the French embodiment
of republican ideology, and the difficulties this has encountered. Despite
the appeal to 1789 and its origins in the French Revolutionary period,
Irish republicanism has been relatively little analysed with reference to
French republicanism. The latter clearly exhibits its ancestry in, and
systematic concern with, many themes of classical republicanism:
freedom, common citizenship in the political community, and civic
commitment to the common good. Thus, following an historical tradition, an official *Guide Républicain,* widely distributed in 2004, has
entries explaining the meaning and implications of values and issues such
as *citoyenneté, civisme, égalité,* and *liberté.*[15] In another sense, as becomes
clear in Jeremy Jennings's chapter here, it is a very specific realisation
that bears witness to the evolution of French history long before and
after 1789. It constitutes a discourse that has evolved in ways that reflect
the circumstances of its origin and development: its emphasis on
rationality, enlightenment, and secularism (*laïcité* – another entry in the
Guide) – as well as a strong role for the central state. It has particular
preoccupations: a principled concern with uniformity, fear of diversity
and of *communautarisme* – sectional group identity or communalism,

which seems to be understood as a greater threat than individual self-interest or corruption.

Jennings examines the evolution of republican ideology in France, and the compromises and tensions that this has involved. He identifies the distinctive features of French republicanism as: a conception of the appropriate political institutions grounded upon democracy and the sovereignty of the nation; a commitment to emancipation through a secular education system; a concern for individual rights combined with a desire to further social justice; and a specific conception of citizenship. Jennings concludes by noting questions about the viability of this French republican model, and identifying current challenges to it arising from multiculturalism, European integration and the globalisation of the economy.

In Ireland, the relationship of republicanism with religion, more specifically with Catholicism, has been a complex one. While the United Irishmen strove to include those of all faiths, state republicanism became closely connected with the Catholic Church in the twentieth century. This is in contrast to the French model which has emphasised secularism as a core republican value. That the secular character of the state and public life is to be preserved is a position central to French republicanism, but one that has experienced tensions. Cécile Laborde's chapter reconstructs the philosophical arguments that underlie the French republican model, showing how it represents a particular understanding and institutionalisation of secularism as a way to promote equality among diverse citizens – one that is comparable with the difference-blind version of egalitarian liberalism, though emphasising more strongly the autonomy of the public sphere. This chapter analyses a number of values which underlie the secular ideal in France in order to explore the principled reasons why French republicans oppose the wearing of headscarves in schools, while also suggesting that there are resources within republicanism for alternative approaches.[16]

These two chapters show the complexity of applying republican principles to practice. They reveal tensions both within French republican ideology itself and between republican ideology and practical contingencies. These give rise to disaffection and periods of civic unrest in France, as, for example, the widespread riots and car burnings in the autumn of 2005, after the death of two teenagers of North African extraction while fleeing the police, and in the spring of 2006, weeks of strikes and protests which forced the government to back down on proposals for more flexible employment contracts for young people.

But, even if particular accommodations are necessary, republicanism is the official ideology in France and is taken seriously to justify the design of political institutions, positions and public policies in a way that has been remarkably rare in Ireland.

It should also be said that French political and intellectual life has been relatively little touched by the current revival of republican ideas in normative political theory, referred to there with some reserve as '*néo-républicanisme*'.

The contemporary republican revival

Although liberalism had a sweeping victory over socialism in the global realignment of the 1990s, since then there has been a remarkable revival of republican ideas. This seems to have stemmed principally from an increasing sense of the limitations of the prevailing forms of liberalism, and the difficulties it encounters in dealing with a range of issues from global interdependence, environmental risk and inequality through ethnic and cultural diversity, political corruption and citizen alienation. This revival emphasises the need for a strong framework of law to protect freedom and the common goods shared by citizens, and for citizens to have both a sense of responsibility and the opportunity to participate in self-government.

These ideas first emerged in historical, legal and normative political theory. Republicanism was put on the theoretical map again through historical scholarship which excavated and re-identified it as a coherent tradition. A particularly important role in this rediscovery has been played by two scholars. J.G.A. Pocock outlined a continuing thread from Athens and Aristotle through Machiavelli and Harrington to the American Revolution.[17] He emphasised the ideas of political participation, civic virtue and corruption, and the historical specificity and fragility of republican politics. His work challenged a conventional view that the American Revolution was guided solely by Lockean natural right principles. Quentin Skinner traced a position with specifically Roman roots, given its classic formulation by Machiavelli, and the English seventeenth-century movement that included Harrington and Sidney. He identified at its centre a 'neo-Roman' conception of freedom, the status of independence guaranteed by legal limitations on a ruler's arbitrary domination.[18]

In the United States, republican ideas were invoked in a debate on the interpretation of the constitution and the functions of its various parts. This challenged a prevailing understanding of the constitution as primarily a set of rules to limit power, regulate competing interest groups and protect individual rights. Legal scholars highlighted the way in which the constitution has a historical and continuing role as a framework for collective self-government, based less on private interests than on deliberation on common goods. In the context of the opposition of Republican presidencies to liberal judicial activism, this implies a stronger role for the judiciary, and a more active and deliberative role for all branches of government, than a neutralist liberal model supports.[19]

Finally republican ideas have re-emerged in normative political thought. At a philosophical level, the republican revival followed a period in which political theory had been dominated by the 'liberal-communitarian debate', and appeared to some to offer a way out of the impasses at which that debate had arrived. In order to meet the criticisms of earlier accounts, contemporary theorists rearticulating republicanism for the modern world stress the importance of minimising domination, both private and political; of inclusive deliberative determination of the common good in politics; and of accommodation of diverse moral and cultural perspectives.[20] But the diversity of the historical tradition is reflected in different accounts of what republicanism means and has to offer. These approach the problems of interdependence, and integrate the cluster of values of freedom, civic virtue and participation in different ways. Thus republicans have differed on just how freedom and the common good are best realised. One strand focuses on the distinctive account of freedom as non-domination, and on minimising domination – the threat of arbitrary interference by individuals, groups or the state – and on ensuring that government promotes common rather than sectional goods. This strand has been articulated primarily by Philip Pettit. Another emphasises the importance of civic virtue or responsibility, and others emphasise that freedom further requires that people can actively participate in political decision-making and have some control over the conditions of their collective lives.[22] These last two highlight two distinct dimensions of active citizenship. All agree, however, that limiting domination requires the 'empire of law' rather than of persons, and that this involves dispersing power and creating strong mechanisms of accountability. Moreover, realising freedom and common goods cannot be achieved through creating effective institutions and laws alone, but depends on citizens who act in a public-spirited manner rather than always promoting their own private interests. So eliciting civic virtue and minimising its obverse, corruption, remain important themes. The contemporary exponents of republican theory have, in addition, attempted to show how the logic of its fundamental concerns provide a basis for disentangling it from the more authoritarian, militaristic or majoritarian variants of the past.

In their concerns about freedom republicans were early forerunners of liberalism, but they place more emphasis than liberals on realising common as well as individual goods, and on cultivating solidarity among citizens. This brings them close in another direction to communitarians, those for whom values are realised in community.[23] But what republicans are concerned with is the political community that develops over time through the interactions of citizens framed by political institutions. Thus they differ from those communitarians (including many nationalists) who see politics as expressing a pre-political community of ethnicity or shared values. While some communitarians react to contemporary problems by calling for the renewal of moral or religious purpose and community in society, the distinctive concern of republicans lie in freedom, participation in self-government and political solidarity.

The contemporary republican revival has had less to say about its socio-economic implications. But to the extent that most of its theorists identify substantial material inequalities in society as undermining equal citizenship, they offer grounds for state regulation and some level of redistribution in the name of equal citizenship, without reverting to state socialism.[24] In particular, republican thinking offers an alternative to the emphasis of libertarians or neo-liberals on individual rights, the sanctity of the market even at the cost of inequality, and the radical limitation of the role of government.

Contemporary republicans have not addressed the question of religion in great detail. But it can be said that the theory is not systematically secularist, and that some of its proponents have been concerned to accommodate religious and cultural diversity more substantially than French republicanism allows. Thus the relationship of this form of republicanism to nationalism has been debated. While all distinguish a republic in principle from an ethnic or culturally based pre-political community, some argue that a republican politics needs in practice to be supported by a liberal nationalism, which maintains a common public culture among citizens, however diverse they may be in their private lives.[25]

This revival has not been wholly academic in conception or reach. Republican theorists tend to locate themselves explicitly in a specific local context, both theoretical and practical. Many of these arguments have developed within debates about the nature and future of politics in, for example, the United States or Britain. This reflects an emphasis on the need to develop political solutions appropriate to particular contexts. Thus contemporary republican theory has expressed practical concerns with bringing government to account and dealing with corruption in political contexts from Australia to Italy.[26] And the theory has struck a chord with politicians and policy makers in a variety of contexts. Philip Pettit has been invited to Spain by Prime Minister Jose Luis Zapatero to articulate his new account of republicanism as non-domination.[27] One of its earliest philosophical advocates, Charles Taylor, has played an active part in Canadian public life, being, for example, appointed in February 2007 to a commission on a controversy over the norms that are reasonable to demand of newcomers.[28]

While republicanism approaches liberalism in one direction, it approaches communitarianism in the other. Thus, Robert Putnam, whose best-selling call for civic revival, *Bowling Alone*, emphasises the importance of participation in civil society, is often referred to as a republican.[29] He has been in demand from political leaders from Bill Clinton to Tony Blair in their concern to address the reconstruction of community and civic engagement in their countries.

Having set out the international context of republican theory and tradition, we are now in a position to address its manifestations in Ireland.

Irish republicanism: examining the tradition

The chapters in Part I offer diverging arguments on the character of Irish republicanism and its adherents, and its relationship to the mainstream European and American tradition.

Tom Garvin challenges the notion that there is any theoretical continuity in the Irish republican tradition, highlighting the heterogeneity of those who have claimed the title of republican. He identifies some continuity in an insurrectionist style and a romantic and fantasist mode of political thinking, often combined with contempt and disregard for actual political institutions. He draws attention to a gap between rhetoric and reality, reflected in the diverse positions of republicans on issues, for example, of language and religion, and their lack of focus on the institutions that might realise their republican ideals.

In Chapter 3 Margaret O'Callaghan addresses the issue of the relative invisibility of Irish republican ideas, highlighting the absence of any mention in the works of Pocock and Skinner, the scholars largely responsible for the rediscovery of the republican tradition. She questions whether this is because Irish republicanism actually has no history, and challenges the assumptions underlying its dismissal as a tradition of ideas. Comparing the influential accounts of French and Irish nineteenth-century historians of their countries' revolutionary period of the 1790s and of early republican political action, she identifies the reasons for a long tradition of denial of republican ideas in the early failure of the project, and the interest among both Protestant and Catholic historians in identifying republican movements with sectarianism and mob violence. She points to evidence that there was a greater spread of mainstream republican ideas and less ethnic nationalism in elite and popular nineteenth-century political expression than is often recognised.

A question that has to be addressed in the Irish context is the relationship of republicanism and nationalism, which have in general tended to be treated as interchangeable in historical discussions.

One way of looking at this is to see political nationalism as addressing the origin and locus of political legitimacy, while republicanism addresses more specifically the form of government and relationships of citizens. Perhaps because in Ireland the first was never finally settled fully, the second received less theoretical attention, even while a state was progressively constructed from 1922 onwards.

Certainly from the mid twentieth century onwards being a 'republican' in Ireland increasingly meant affiliation with a movement whose goal was complete independence from Britain and political unification of the island through military means. 'Nationalist' was a more inclusive category that encompassed a range of other approaches to, and flexibility in means of achieving, self-determination, from Home Rule through qualified political independence to (after 1922) accepting partition as an intermediate measure. Thus, to be a republican was to be a specific kind of political nationalist, more radical and less open to compromise.[30]

But nationalism – the idea that the Irish people constituted a natural community – had cultural, religious, and economic dimensions. To be a nationalist could mean being committed to a strong Irish identity, to the revival and public promotion of the Irish language and heritage, or to the establishment of an independent economy, which could be combined with different approaches to politics.

Neither republicans nor nationalists made the freedom or participation of individual citizens in self-government a prominent part of their thinking.

Nonetheless, at least from 1933, when Fianna Fáil came to power, republicanism had both establishment and dissident forms. The establishment form displays some of the elements of broader republicanism, such as the emphasis on the common good in the 1937 Constitution, and on public spirit or revolutionary austerity in the development of Irish social and economic independence.

In the light of the emphasis on secularism in France, one of the most notable features of Irish republicanism is its connection with Catholicism. For the first fifty years of the Irish state, in clear contrast to France, there was no clear liberal distinction between public and private culture. Parts of the 1937 Constitution envisaged an explicitly communitarian republic embodying Catholic and Irish culture in public life, tempered only slightly by the inclusion of other recognised religions. Education, funded mainly by the state, has been organised predominantly on communal religious lines. While, in a concession to minorities, the relatively few Protestant and Jewish (and latterly Muslim) schools were funded, in practice most schools were subject to the control of the Catholic Church, and constituted a semi-public realm in which a Gaelic and Catholic vision of the good for citizens was promoted. Thus the republic established under De

Valera exemplified a more communitarian and authoritarian strand of republicanism. It aimed to realise not a politically determined common good based on deliberative participation, but a pre-politically defined vision of the good for society that was shaped by cultural nationalism and a powerful institutional church.

But there were also countervailing anti-clerical – if not secularist – accounts of republicanism, which challenged the establishment account. Mark McNally has shown how Seán O'Faoláin, identifying the Gaelicising and Catholic policies implemented from the 1930s as a 'betrayal of the republic', adumbrated an alternative account that adhered more closely to the European republican mainstream.[31]

On economic and social policy, as with the mainstream and its French exemplar, Irish republicanism had both right- and left-wing expressions. Some, in the tradition of James Connolly, invoked Tone's appeal to 'the men of no property', and adopted left-wing social and economic policies, but this was by no means a universal or primary position.[32] Irish republicanism, like its European counterparts, has co-existed with a variety of social perspectives. The development of a society of small holders was no less consistent with the mainstream republican tradition than the programme of nationalisation that more radical republicans proposed.

On questions other than political independence, republicanism in Ireland constituted a rather general set of aspirations, whose adherents increasingly acted pragmatically in practice, rather than embodying specific principles that, as in France, were invoked to determine policy on education, the economy and other areas.

Reassessing republicanism in Ireland

But there has recently been a reassessment of republicanism in Ireland. Why? There seem to have been two conceptual factors at work here. On the one hand, it was clear that as the peace process evolved, Sinn Féin, the party associated most closely with physical force republicanism, had to reconsider the ideology that had been based on the achievement of complete political independence and unification through armed struggle. Since the mid-1990s Sinn Féin shifted the emphasis increasingly to electoral and parliamentary politics and rearticulated its party platform. Thus, for example, at the meeting of Sinn Féin that agreed to support the Police Service of Northern Ireland in January 2007, Gerry Adams claimed that 'Irish republicanism is about people. It's about the future; it's about a new egalitarian society; it's about the new Irish and the indigenous Irish; it's about the Proclamation of 1916 becoming a reality. So it's bigger than us; it's bigger than Sinn Féin; it's in the common good.'[33] In reaction to this repositioning, other parties reasserted their republican credentials.

On the other hand, while nationalism in its various forms was long seen as more benign than republicanism, it too became problematic in the 1980s and 1990s. Increasing involvement with Europe made an emphasis on political nationalism and sovereignty difficult to sustain. Attempts at rapprochement with the Northern Protestant tradition made the claim to incorporate Northern Ireland seem aggressively irredentist, and promoting cultural or religious nationalism seem narrow and exclusive. A long period of questioning Irish identity and whether it should be understood as based essentially on Gaelic culture, on the one hand, or on Catholic religion, on the other, led to the downplaying of nationalism itself.[34] It should be noted that this was under way well before the number and diversity of immigrants became as significant as they are now. The questioning of nationalism was further assisted by the appearance in the early 1990s of displays of an uglier side of nationalism in the Balkans, Eastern Europe and the former USSR. Thus the idea of a 'pluralist republicanism' or even a 'postnationalist' Ireland was mooted.[35] This shift in the evaluation of nationalism made possible the opening up of many exclusive institutions and practices, including – what was widely regarded as an historic moment – the opening of the GAA's Croke Park to the 'foreign' game of rugby, and, in particular, the match played against England there in February 2007.

It is in these contexts that the ideas of the wider republican tradition have been invoked, and republicanism characterised in a way that distinguishes it from exclusive nationalism. Such invocations almost all look back to Tone's claim to include all – Protestant, Catholic and Dissenter – in the republican tradition. This is seen as capable of leading towards a political form that can accommodate diversity. Indeed, Philip Pettit has suggested that one distinctive feature of Irish republicanism in the eighteenth century was a more ecumenical attitude to religion than that found in comparable movements in America, France or Britain: 'Unlike the anti-Catholic separatism that prevailed in America, and unlike the anti-religious secularism of France, Irish republican separatism of this period was not particularly hostile to Catholics, and its separatism was accepting of religion in general.'[36]

But the silence of contemporary normative republican theorists on the subject of Irish republicanism has also been noted. Despite Pettit's Irish origins, apart from a passing reference, he has only recently and briefly addressed the Irish connection.[37] There is a certain irony in the fact that one of the first contemporary attempts to apply broader republican thought to Ireland applied it to unionism rather than nationalism. This was in Norman Porter's *Rethinking Unionism*, published in 1996.[38] This outlined an account of a 'civic' unionism distinct from the cultural unionism that was itself a mirror-image of cultural nationalism. It was distinct also from a purely procedural liberal unionism that denied the systematic disadvantage that majoritarian procedures imposed on the Catholic minority. On this view unionists could and should support political unity of citizens within Northern Ireland. Richard Kearney also engaged in the clarification of historical republican ideas in order to distance them from the culturally exclusive aspects of nationalism.[39] Since then, there have been continuing attempts to rethink the application of republican ideas across a wide range of social and cultural issues in Irish society, particularly creatively by Finbar Cullen as editor of *The Republic*.[40]

An international republican-communitarian theorist has also had an impact on thinking in Irish political circles. As Taoiseach, Bertie Ahern, more explicitly than Tony Blair and Bill Clinton, acknowledged the influence of Robert Putnam's ideas on community and social capital: he invited him to speak to policy groups in Ireland on several occasions, and he cited his inspiration behind the decision to set up a Taskforce on Active Citizenship in 2006.[41]

Thus republican ideas have been taken up in a wider debate in search of what might be called a 'public philosophy' for Ireland in the twenty-first century.[42] In attempting to reconnect freedom and the common good, republican theory strikes a chord in Ireland, where widely held values of community and the common good were interpreted in an authoritarian direction and set against freedom by advocates and critics alike.[43] It has emerged at a point where society seems ready to move on from the debates between the concrete liberal and communitarian positions that polarised the Irish public in the campaigns on abortion and divorce and took up much of the 1980s and 1990s.[44] It has also appeared relevant in a period of moral reassessment of the effects of the changes that have attended the otherwise flourishing society of the Celtic Tiger economy.[45]

In Part III, approaches to republicanism in recent Irish politics are examined and analysed. The chapters here examine the relationship of different Irish political parties to republicanism, the extent to which Sinn Féin republicanism has taken a radically new turn, and the relationship between Irish and civic republicanism.

First, Gareth Ivory examines the meaning and use of republican language in public discourse and political debate in Ireland since 1970 – from early debates on historical revisionism, through more conceptual reflection on the wider sense of republicanism and its relationship with nationalism, to the continuing rearticulation and contestation of the republican heritage among political parties in the Republic. The author reconsiders the historical connection of nationalism with republicanism, and tracks the shifting discourse of republicanism in the public arena and in the major political parties who have claimed the republican inheritance, detaching it from the political violence, religious and cultural sectarianism, and social authoritarianism of which they have accused the republican movement.

Martin Mansergh re-examines Fianna Fáil's distinctive republicanism. Starting from an examination of the historical tensions in Irish republicanism since 1916, this chapter considers the relationship of 'the republican party' to the movement in Ireland. Drawing a distinction between republicanism as the ideology and tradition underlying the Irish state, inherited from the 1916 period of revolution, and republicanism as an ideology determined to reunite Ireland, today peacefully or previously by force, he compares the positions of Fianna Fáil and Sinn Féin and their capacity to deal with contemporary political and economic issues.

Catherine O'Donnell argues that the fact that Fine Gael, while known for its hostility to republicanism defined as militant anti-British separatist nationalism, long espoused the rule of law, democratic institutions and values, and their associated rights and freedoms made its position more republican in the international sense than that of other parties. Its statements and policies with respect to Northern Ireland and improving relations with Britain created the path that other parties were to follow. The current reinterpretation and rehabilitation of republicanism in Ireland has, she argues, allowed it to be more explicit about its republican credentials.

In Chapter 9, John Doyle analyses the political development of Sinn Féin as it has come to be a significant player in electoral politics in both parts of Ireland. Through examining its manifestos, public utterances and political practice, he addresses arguments that it is moving towards the centre or downplaying its nationalist project. He argues that Sinn Féin has been and continues to be republican in a sense deeper than physical force separatism, and has maintained both a civic republican emphasis on equality, political participation and activism, and its nationalist project, at the same time as allying itself with groupings that oppose corporate globalisation. He identifies a crucial future challenge for Sinn Féin as the development of policy from the perspective of a governing party, particularly with respect to the economy.

Henry Patterson's contribution reconsiders the legacy of the militant republican movement, and reassesses one of its darker sides. He examines the impact of IRA killings of members of the Ulster Defence Regiment in districts close to the Border. He argues that the republican desire to transcend sectarianism and the achievement of reconciliation depend on the acknowledgement by those in the republican movement of the character of those killings and their implications for the Protestant community.

In the final chapter Garret FitzGerald both draws on his practical experience of government and takes a more speculative approach, assessing the extent to which Irish politics does or could embody civic republican principles, He first distinguishes republicanism from anti-monarchism, and considers the historical position of republican leaders from 1916 to 1923 on this question. He goes on to examine ways in which the fundamental ideas of civic republicanism, providing for freedom and the common good and addressing the problem of corruption, might be given institutional embodiment in contemporary Irish politics, and identifies challenges this would encounter. He concludes with some reflections on the arrival of Sinn Féin republicans into a more central role in electoral politics.

A future for republicanism?

Irish republicanism has had a distinctive trajectory. It has been heavily weighted towards resisting external domination, often at the expense of other republican concerns of minimising internal domination, promoting engagement in self-government, supporting common goods, and limiting corruption. It has not been seen as a doctrine that can be systematically applied to policy in the way that French republicanism has been understood. But we may learn from French republicanism that it too has been shaped by a specific history, and that an emphasis on ideological coherence does not necessarily resolve the problems that policies are designed to address. For republicanism to contribute to Irish political life does not necessarily require rigorously following the French example; a more pragmatic and contextual approach to the application of political ideas may be desirable. Whether a less stringently assimilationist and secularist approach can be developed better to deal with Ireland's new cultural and religious diversity remains to be seen.

We can distinguish between a systematic programme of republicanism and a more fluid republican language or discourse, which may channel and influence political thinking without rigidly determining political positions.[46] Of course, the language of freedom, the common good and citizenship can be and has been used hypocritically. Political theorists are aware that any theory that becomes fashionable in practical politics is likely to be carried just as far as serves the political purposes of the time. But rather than being merely window dressing, republican theory also provides a critical edge for calling to account those who claim to represent the tradition.[47] Lying somewhere between a programme and an all-purpose rhetoric, the contemporary rearticulation of republican theory offers valuable elements of a public philosophy in its concerns with freedom as non-domination, the engagement of citizens in pursuing the common good and in self-government, and the accountability of government. In Ireland, contesting domination, whether external or internal, identifying the risks of exclusion and inequality, and maintaining a commitment to common goods such as health and social provision, the environment and cultural heritage, important in the heyday of the Celtic Tiger, become all the more urgent under more constrained economic conditions. It remains to be seen to what extent republican ideas may be able to set a standard for public life as Ireland faces the challenges of unprecedented economic, social and environmental change, increased immigration and cultural diversity, and the opportunities and pressures of globalisation.

Notes

1   See chapters in Norman Porter (ed.), *The Republican Ideal* (Belfast: Blackstaff, 1998).
2   Roy Foster, *Modern Ireland* (London: Allen Lane, 1988), where the index entry for republicanism reads: 'see Anglophobia; Catholicism; nationalism; and Irish Republican Brotherhood', p. 669.
3   For example, Gerry Adams, *Selected Writings* (Dingle: Brandon Books, 1997).
4   For treatments of the IRA and the military dimension of republicanism, see: Ed Moloney, *The Secret History of the IRA* (London: Penguin, 2003); Richard English, *Armed Struggle: The History of the IRA* (London: Pan, 2003).
5   For a more detailed overview, see Iseult Honohan, *Civic Republicanism* (London: Routledge, 2002), Part I.
6   James Harrington, *The Commonwealth of Oceana and a System of Politics* (Cambridge: Cambridge University Press, 1992 [1656]), p. 8.
7   Nicolo Machiavelli, *The Discourses* (B. Crick, ed.), (Harmondsworth: Penguin, 1983 [1531]), p. 253.
8   Jean-Jacques Rousseau, *The Social Contract* (Harmondsworth: Penguin, 1968 [1762]), p. 140.
9   James Madison, cited in Michael Sandel, *Democracy's Discontents* (Cambridge MA: Harvard Belknap, 1996), p. 132.
10 Rousseau, *Social Contract*, p. 60
11 He is also thought to buried in Dublin, in the graveyard (now a paved square) behind St Mary's Church, Mary Street.
12 Though see S.J. Connolly (ed.), *Political Ideas in Eighteenth Century Ireland* (Dublin, Four Courts Press, 2000). Also papers presented in November 2006 at an Irish Historical Studies seminar in Boston College's Dublin site, with Quentin Skinner as respondent.
13 But see Duncan Kelly, 'Reforming republicanism in nineteenth century Britain: James Lorymer's *The Republican* in context', *Republicanism in Theory and Practice* (London: Routledge, 2005), pp. 41–52.
14 J.G.A. Pocock, *The Machiavellian Moment* (Princeton: Princeton University Press, 1975), p. 64.
15 *Guide Républicain* (Paris: Delagrave, 2004).
16 For the development of alternative perspectives, see Cécile Laborde, 'Female autonomy, education and the *hijab*' CRISSP, 9,3 (2006): 351–77.
17 Pocock, *Machiavellian Moment*.

18 Quentin Skinner, *The Foundations of Modern Political Thought* (Cambridge: Cambridge University Press, 1978); *Liberty before Liberalism* (Cambridge: Cambridge University Press, 1998).

19 Cass Sunstein, 'Beyond the republican revival', *Yale Law Journal*, 97 (1988): 1539–90; Frank Michelman, 'Foreword: traces of self government', *Harvard Law Review*, 100 (1986): 4–77; 'Law's Republic', *Yale Law Journal*, 97 (1988): 1493–537.

20 See Philip Pettit, *Republicanism* (Oxford: Oxford University Press, 1997); John Maynor, *Republicanism in the Modern World* (Cambridge: Polity, 2003) and Honohan, *Civic Republicanism* respectively.

21 Pettit, *Republicanism*; Maynor, *Republicanism in the Modern World*.

22 Michael Sandel, *Democracy's Discontents* (Cambridge MA: Harvard Belknap, 1996); Adrian Oldfield, *Citizenship and Community* (London: Routledge, 1990); Bejamin Barber, *Strong Democracy: Participatory Politics for a New Age* (Berkeley: Univesrsity of California Press, 2004).

23 The wider sense of community intended by the English word communitarianism needs to be distinguished from the French sense of '*communautarisme*', which refers to sectional groups.

24 But see articles by Philip Pettit, Richard Dagger and Henry Richardson in a special issue of *Politics, Philosophy and Economics* (2006).

25 For different views on this, see David Miller, *On Nationality* (Oxford: Oxford University Press, 1995); Arash Abizadeh, 'Does liberal democracy presuppose a cultural nation? Four arguments', *American Political Science Review*, 96 (2002): 495–509; Honohan, *Civic Republicanism*.

26 'Special issue', *Australian Journal of Political Science*, 1993; Maurizio Viroli, *Republicanism* (New York: Hill and Wang, 2002).

27 Carolina Martin, 'El maestro Pettit examina al alumno Zapatero', *El Tiempo*, 5 June 2006. Available at www.princeton.edu/~ppettit/tiempo.pdf (accessed 26 February 2007).

28 www.cbc.ca/canada/montreal/story/2007/02/09/qc-reasonableaccommodation20070209.html (accessed 26 February 2007).

29 But see, e.g. Per Mouritsen, 'What's the civil in civil society', *Political Studies*, 51, 4 (2003): 650–68.

30 For a fuller treatment of Irish nationalism see Richard English, *Irish Freedom: A History of Nationalism in Ireland* (Basingstoke: Macmillan, 2006). A variety of analyses of the republican movement appear in Fearghal McGarry (ed.), *Republicanism in Modern Ireland* (Dublin: UCD Press, 2003) and Robert Savage (ed.), *Ireland and the New Century: Politics, Culture and Identity* (Dublin: Four Courts Press, 2003).

31 See Mark McNally, 'Seán O'Faoláin's discourse of "the betrayal of the Republic" in mid-twentieth century Ireland', in Iseult Honohan and Jeremy Jennings (eds), *Republicanism in Theory and Practice* (London: Routledge, 2005)

32 See, for example, Henry Patterson, *The Politics of Illusion: Republicanism and Socialism in Ireland* (London: Hutchinson Radius, 1989); Richard English, *Radicals and the Republic: Socialist Republicanism in the Irish Free State 1925–1937* (Oxford: Oxford University Press, 1994); Richard English, *Ernie O'Malley: IRA Intellectual* (Oxford: Oxford University Press, 1999).

33 www.sinnfeinonline.com/news/3178 (accessed 27 February 2007).

34 The Fine Gael leader Enda Kenny's characterisation of Ireland as a Celtic and Christian country in a January 2007 speech could revive such a debate, even if couched as an argument for the Irish capacity to understand the challenges of immigration and integrating new communities. www.finegael.ie/news/index.cfm/type/details/nkey/30416/pkey/653 (accessed 27 February 2007).

35 Richard Kearney, *Post-nationalist Ireland* (London: Routledge, 1997).

36 Philip Pettit, 'The tree of liberty: republicanism, American, French and Irish', *Field Day Review*, 1 (2005): 29–41 at p.41.

37 Pettit 'The tree of liberty'; 'Culture in the constitution of a Republic', *The Republic*, 3 (2003); 'From republican theory to public policy', *The Republic: Essays from RTE Radio's Thomas Davis Lectures*, 2005; see also Pettit, *Republicanism*, p. viii.

38 Norman Porter, *Rethinking Unionism* (Belfast: Blackstaff Press, 1996).

39 Kearney, *Post-nationalist Ireland*.

40 *The Republic*, Vols 1–3, 1999–2003 (Dublin: Ireland Institute). See also Gareth Ivory, Chapter 6 below.

41 'Harvard professor my guru since early 1990s, says Ahern', *Irish Times,* 3 September, 2005. www.ireland.com/newspaper/frontpage/2005/0903/10046 96679HM1PUTNAM.html (accessed 26 February 2007).

42 I take this term from Sandel, *Democracy's Discontents*.

43 See Pettit, 'The tree of liberty'; Iseult Honohan, 'The common good and the politics of community', *Questioning Ireland* (A. Ingram, F. Litton and J. Dunne, eds), (Dublin: IPA, 2000).

44 2007 polls indicate that 75% of Irish people support divorce in 2007, compared with the 50/49 split vote on which divorce was introduced in 1995: 'Three in four voters would now support divorce', *Irish Times*, 5 February 2007, www.ireland.com/newspaper/frontpage/2007/0205/1170363595705.html.

45 For example, Peter Clinch, Frank Convery and Brendan Walsh, *After the Celtic Tiger: Challenges Ahead* (Dublin: O'Brien Press, 2002); Fintan O'Toole, *After the Ball* (Dublin: New Island Press, 2003); David Jacobson, Peadar Kirby and Deiric Ó Broin (eds), *Taming the Tiger: Social Exclusion in a Globalised Ireland* (Dublin: New Island Press, 2005).

46 I owe the application of Pocock's distinction between republicanism as a programme and as a language in Ireland to Mark McNally. McNally, 'Betrayal of the republic', p. 80.

47 See, for example, Fintan O'Toole, 'The unreal republic', *The Republic: Essays from RTE's Thomas Davis Lecture Series* (Mary Davis, ed.), (Dublin: Mercier/RTE).

Part I
The Irish tradition

2   An Irish republican tradition?

Tom Garvin

Conor Cruise O'Brien, many years ago, wrote a mock encyclopaedia article as follows: 'Irish strategy, 1014–1945: The campaign and actions of Brian Boru, Owen Roe O'Neill, Marshal Browne, Commodore Barry, Wellington, Admiral Browne, General Sheridan, Field Marshals Alexander and Montgomery, and many others.'[1]

He went on to point out that a compilation of Irish verse-writers might look equally odd, citing the *Oxford Book of Irish Verse*, which included poems by Goldsmith, Sheridan, Emily Brontë, Fitzgerald, Wilde, MacNeice and Cecil Day Lewis. In speaking of Irish republicanism I find myself in a somewhat analogous quandary. Essentially the problem is one of continuity: not so much political continuity as intellectual or even cultural continuity. I take it for granted that there is certainly a political tradition in Ireland that is commonly labelled 'republican' and which has been around for quite a long time, certainly since the 1850s and perhaps since the 1776–89 period, as an echo of the American and French Revolutions. However, what have the following 'republican' figures got in common with each other intellectually: Theobald Wolfe Tone, John Mitchel, James Stephens, John O'Mahony, Arthur Griffith, Patrick Pearse, James Connolly, Liam Lynch, Eamon de Valera, Sean Russell, Sean Sabhat, Sean Mac Stiofáin, Professor John Kelly, Gerry Adams and Bertie Ahern? Mitchel was pro-slavery. James Stephens apparently aspired to be president-for-life (*á la* Papa Doc Duvalier of Haiti) of an Irish Republic. Griffith is certainly equally anomalous; he was, after all, a monarchist, but he was also the much-resented president of the Irish Republic in the Second Dáil from January to June 1922. Weirdly, in the logic of 'IRA constitutional history' he should be regarded as the founding father of today's IRA/Sinn Féin; actually he was not only a monarchist but also an imperialist and an advocate of a permanent partnership with Great Britain.

The anomalies mount. Tone had no regard for the Irish language and despised and hated Catholicism in true Jacobin style; in 1793 he attended the last general meeting of traditional Irish harpers in Belfast, and famously noted afterwards 'strum, strum and bedamned to you!' He also was a firm opponent of neutrality, being in favour of a solid alliance with France. A century and a half later, Russell was in favour of an alliance with Nazi Germany, and did his level best to engineer one, thereby endangering Ireland's neutrality and very political existence. He could quite logically be seen as a traitor, but there is a mutilated statue of him somewhere in Clontarf. To take a third example of Irish republican indifference to neutrality, Pearse and his comrades boasted in 1916 of their alliance with 'gallant allies in Europe'. Parenthetically, Pearse was quite happy to contemplate a Hohenzollern princeling on the throne of an independent Irish kingdom. More recently, some republicans have commonly made a fetish out of neutralism, for reasons that were partly opportunistic, partly pro-Soviet and mainly anti-American. Again, back in pre-1916 days Pearse insisted that, without the Irish language, there could not possibly be an Irish nation. In Pearsian logic, by speaking English we are actually murdering the historic Irish nation. Many of these people were not democrats in any modern understanding of the term. Even when they did adhere to democratic values, they often did so very reluctantly and commonly after they had come to the conclusion that the democratic process would have to be used to achieve 'republican' values that were often unconnected with democratic principles. 'Republican' values commonly involved some kind of moral and cultural transformation of the Irish people, a people held to be unsatisfactory from some cultural or 'spiritual' point of view. The core of the republican tradition seems to me to be nationalist, separatist, vaguely socialist and sometimes caesaro-papist. Democracy is merely optional and clearly to be subordinated to moral principle.

Two republican constitutions

Whatever about continuity with the United Irishmen of the 1790s, there does seem to be some validity to claims for a continuity of the republican tradition since the Fenian oath was first administered in Langan's timber yard in what is now Fenian Street in Dublin in 1858. This Fenian tradition was very clearly anti-monarchist, separatist and adhered to a somewhat whiggish theory of electoral democracy. Despite the cultural revivalism of John O'Mahony and others, the tradition was at that time far more concerned with separation from the United Kingdom and the establishment of an independent all-Ireland polity than with the kind of cultural authenticity espoused by the Gaelic League in Ireland after 1893 or by (say) Plaid Cymru in late twentieth-century Wales.

In 1862, John Pigot, a Fenian publicist, wrote a constitution for an independent Irish republic; versions of his ideas remained current in the fantasy world of Irish underground separatism generations later.[2] Pigot envisaged a modernised Ireland with a strong army and navy. The Fenians were keen on sea power and an American connection or even alliance. Irish-American Fenians were later to finance the *Fenian Ram*, devised by John Philip Holland, an ex-Christian Brother from Clare. This was the first serious working prototype of a submarine, and was financed by John Devoy and the American Fenians/IRB in the hope of launching an attack on the Royal Navy in the Atlantic. Pigot envisaged an alliance with either France or the United States, and envisaged that the new independent country would be able to control the western approaches and be a menace to the British Empire in various unspecified and vaguely imagined ways. He proposed a rather Bonapartist constitution, heavily influenced by American and French models. A lower chamber was to be directly elected, and the upper chamber, elected by a restricted franchise, was to elect in turn a president-for-life, presumably with James Stephens, the egomaniac Fenian leader, in mind. Executive and legislature were to be separated both legally and physically, the legislature to be situated in Athlone and the executive in Limerick. The hatred of Dublin, capital of the island and symbol of British power in Ireland, was evident and was a theme which has recurred in 'republican' thought many times. The provinces were to be abolished and replaced by nearly a dozen geographically designated cantons. The rather striking modernism and 'French' character of the document was exemplified in particular by its proposal of universal, secret, manhood suffrage and by the non-traditional character of the proposed cantons. Control over education was almost casually conceded to the various churches, in a very un-French (and un-American) but very British deviation from the general trend of the document.

Versions of these ideas surfaced regularly in IRB literature. Among the separatists the IRB appear to have been the only ones who gave serious consideration to the kinds of democratic political institutions an independent Ireland should have. In practice, all that sort of thing tended to be left to Irish Party lawyers or British civil servants, almost as though it were just a matter of housekeeping. The political institutions of the present-day Republic of Ireland owe as much to the series of Home Rule bills introduced between 1885 and 1920 as they do to Fenian ideas. This paper takes the view that the Irish Constitutions of 1919, 1922 and 1937 are more democratic than republican; all three are far more concerned with representative democracy and the sovereignty of the people than they are about the virtuous citizen or government by public and equal deliberation. The word 'republic' does not occur in any of the three documents.

Back in 1911, the IRB paper *Irish Freedom* ran an interesting and intelligent series of articles on the constitutional forms which an independent Ireland might adopt. The pseudonymous author ('Lucan') remarked that his personal preference would be for twenty years of military dictatorship by an 'Irish Cromwell', a man with 'patriotism, fanaticism, single-mindedness and clear hard courage'.[3] Failing a new Lord Protector, a democratic republic was to be preferred, with tolerance for all religions, free compulsory education, democratic representative institutions and universal suffrage including both sexes. However, university graduates, professional men, army officers, political leaders and businessmen would be entitled to extra votes. A national militia was seen as preferable to a standing professional army. Parliament would have two houses, the lower house having a six-year term and being elected by the population, the upper house being elected by those in possession of multiple votes.[4] Military service was to be universal and obligatory, the coinage was to be decimal and both English and Irish would be recognised languages.[5] Other writers in nationalist papers, most notably perhaps John J. Horgan of Cork, proposed political institutions for an independent Ireland. Horgan proposed several that actually materialised, most notably proportional representation, a modernist and hyper-democratic idea that seems to have had immediate appeal. He also proposed a second chamber which would be specifically designed to protect the rights of minorities.[6]

Electoral democracy, moderated by a bourgeois franchise, was accepted as the form an independent Irish polity should take. There were those who proposed a theocratic constitution and others who demanded a socialist republic, but they never became mainstream. There was, however, a certain hankering after a cult of the leader, understandable in a country which had had two great charismatic nationalist leaders in the nineteenth century, Daniel O'Connell and Charles Stewart Parnell. It was also comprehensible in a culture that had long possessed cults of the gallant military hero: Hugh O'Neill, Eoghan Roe O'Neill, Lord Edward Fitzgerald and Robert Emmet. Furthermore, the violence of the years after 1913 encouraged a political authoritarianism among many 'republican' separatists, which sometimes congealed into a settled and perversely idealistic contempt for democracy.

Despite all this, electoral republican democracy was to win out in most of Ireland, but in a rather qualified form. The two obvious qualifications I wish to discuss are those generated by the British monarchical system and the power system of the Catholic Church, Joyce's twin tyrants of Thames and Tiber. The ostensible cause of the Irish civil war of

1922–23 was the British insistence on all of Ireland remaining, at least in theory, within the British Empire; not only was there to be a partition of the island, but the 'free' part was to remain technically part of His Majesty's dominions. Most republicans swallowed this latter condition, but resolved to move to a true republic as quickly as possible, whether by violence or by constitutional means. By 1950, independent Ireland had gone republican in title as well as in reality.[7] The second qualification was the power of priests and bishops, exercised in an authoritarian, obscurantist and top-down fashion, and in ways that went completely against the ideas of classical republicanism. Clerical rule was secretive and the decisions of bishops commonly were imposed on a government technically responsible to the electorate rather than to clerics. As time went by, political subservience to clerical opinion waned and eventually faded away.

However, these residues of what had been the British regime in Ireland lasted long enough to leave a sneaking sense that Irish democracy was somehow incomplete, lacking or flawed. An ancient material inequality persisted during the generations after independence. The evident mediocrity of some political leaders and the obvious financial corruption of some others obscured the equally evident fact that democracy in Ireland merely reflected rather accurately the virtues and the faults of the Irish people. Irish republican democracy was clientelist, localist, secretive and sometimes pathologically short-termist because Irish people were that way. To put it rather differently, many Irish people were not really all that republican.

To some, Irish republican democracy looked too top-down, centralised and generally uncomfortably reminiscent of the centralised British state that had been constructed in Ireland in the decades after the catastrophe of the Great Famine. Some republican writers have suggested massive decentralisation or even the virtual dismemberment of the centralised Irish state and a drastic federalisation. Most conspicuous among these proposals is, perhaps, the Provisional IRA's 1974 proposal for a four-province federation in *Peace with Justice: Proposals for Peace in a New Federal Ireland*, a pamphlet published by Provisional Sinn Féin.[8] It is usually ascribed to Desmond Fennell. The document proposed a four-tier pyramid of government, with local councils at the bottom, regional councils staffed by experts and local councillors at a sub-provincial level, a democratically elected 'Dáil' for each of the four traditional provinces and a federal parliament for all of Ireland at the apex, seated in Athlone in an apparent echo of the Fenian document discussed earlier. This would involve the abolition not only of the present-day Northern Ireland and the Republic of Ireland, but also the abolition, for political purposes at least, of the thirty-two traditional counties of Ireland. Presumably these entities

were to be doomed because of their historical English or British provenance. Their abolition also flew in the face of the evident fondness for the
county as a unit of the Gaelic Athletic Association. The total disregard for
the fact that most Irish people live in towns and cities was possibly reflec-
tive of the historical fact that Irish cities are mainly of Viking or English
provenance. The idea of placing government in a small town admittedly
has certain attractions; it separates government from academia and business, and works well in the United States and worked well also in the
Federal Republic of Germany before reunification. It also would have
helped to balance the country demographically.

Ireland has become habituated to centralised government in both
parts of Ireland, and the simple fact that Irish government has been like
this for a very long time is in itself an argument against change; 'if it
works, don't fix it' is a useful adage. The reason the United States is
extremely decentralised and federal is rooted in the country's origins in an
alliance of separate colonies against an outside power. Germany's federal-
ism has analogous historical roots. Ireland's centralised system is rooted,
by contrast, in a well-meant British attempt to revolutionise the government of the country in the decades after the Great Famine by rationalis-
ing and bureaucratising a failed aristocratic system.

These two proposals for root-and-branch transformation of the Irish
political system, separated from each other by a century, have one thing
in common: a wish to destroy the actual governmental system of Ireland
in favour of a system imagined as being completely different and owing
little or nothing to previous political experience or practice. To that extent
they are both indeed revolutionary. Edmund Burke, commenting on the
French Revolution over two centuries ago, reproached the French revolutionaries for contemning everything that they had inherited, in particular
the traditional local and national assemblies which would have permitted
a reversion to the politics of compromise and negotiation. These institutions the revolutionaries had abolished.

> You had all these advantages in your antient states; but you chose to act
> as if you had never been moulded into civil society, and had everything
> to begin anew. You began ill, because you began by despising everything
> that belonged to you. You set up your trade without a capital ... respect-
> ing your forefathers, you would have been taught to respect yourselves.
> You would not have chosen to consider the French as a people of yester-
> day, as a nation of low-born servile wretches until the emancipating year
> of 1789.[9]

Burke was, of course, arguing for the wisdom of the past and the learn-
ing process of past generations to be permitted to inform the present. The

fact that most of Ireland has had a successful electoral democracy for over two generations was ignored completely by the Provisional Sinn Féin document of 1974. Despite its undoubted shortcomings, Irish democracy was very well established and the population of the Republic was unwilling to see it dismantled in favour of a system based on tiny localities and pyramids of representative bodies; the country had had such local councils (Rural District Councils) up to 1926, when they were abolished, mainly because they presided over steadily shrinking populations and had very little to do. In both parts of Ireland local government has been reshaped pragmatically to react to the fact that the country was urbanising. Going back to the four provinces, identification with which was very weak, would have been regarded as reactionary; the provinces had not been used as administrative units since the seventeenth century. Furthermore, the consent of Northern Ireland to amalgamation with the rest of Ulster and the rest of Ireland would not have been forthcoming. Again, the giving of a complete parliamentary assembly to the tiny province of Connacht would have been extravagant treatment for a small and impoverished entity in financial thrall to the rest of the Republic. Furthermore, Leinster is a questionable entity; it naturally divides into north and south ('South Leinster' and 'Greater Meath'); in early history, the distinction between Cuala and Bregia was very real, the dividing line approximating to the Dublin/Wicklow border. Dublin and Belfast would deserve statehood; Cork deserves statehood as much as Connacht from the point of view of population, and would probably agitate for it.

The unreality of the Provo proposal reflects two things: a fantasist style of thinking and an utter disregard for popular consent. There is also an absence of historical sensitivity and sociological awareness. One does not have to be a Burkean to accept that the future must be built on the past; even post-war Germany, dismembered and recovering from a horrific war and an equally horrific and murderous regime, built on its own past, a past understood in very immediate and concrete terms. The *Länder*, destroyed by Hitler, were re-established in both the eastern and western regions. Later the DDR abolished them, and significantly the dissolution of the communist regime was marked by the immediate and spontaneous reestablishment of the eastern *Länder*. Modern Germany is determinedly and happily provincial, despite the half-artificial character of some of the modern *Länder*.

Similarly, in Ireland the counties are now traditional, whatever their original provenance (They have been around since the seventeenth century, and the eastern ones are centuries older). People have county patriotisms. Everyone knows which one is the Kingdom, which one the Model County, the Rebel County, the Banner County or the County God Help Us. We all know where the Wee Six are. Dubliners, whether thought

of as Jackeens, Jacks or Dubs, have a very strong sense of local patriotism, as do the inhabitants of other Irish towns and cities. The provinces,
although of archaic provenance, are not as culturally immediate as are the
counties and towns, and Leinster, the largest of the provinces, is easily the
least immediate. Connacht is scarcely an entity at all. By contrast,
Munster and Ulster have real presences in popular culture. In fact the
provincial map of Ireland is more reminiscent of a Victorian whiskey
bottle than of anything else.

The poverty of theory

Political theory without reference to political science and its allied disciplines, sociology, history, anthropology and economics is rather like
trying to fly by flapping your arms up and down; you have the right idea,
but utterly inadequate means. That is why the intellectual descendants of
Aristotle are so important. Montesquieu, Burke and de Tocqueville all, in
their different ways, remind us that human beings must always be seen in
a social and historical context, and there are no Robinson Crusoes. Thus,
in Ireland, we are not only stuck with the counties and very little else; we
are also stuck with Northern Ireland and the Republic of Ireland. Perhaps
these two entities can be used to construct something bigger and finer
than either, but neither can be simply demolished, treated as though they
never had existed and replaced by something new and, because of that
very newness, pseudo-traditional. Neither can they be replaced by something which is neophile; 'Northwest Province' sounds a little too much
like an Irish answer to Airstrip One.

Notes

1   C.C. O'Brien, 'Irishness', in his *Writers and Politics* (Harmondsworth: Penguin,
    1976 [1965]), pp. 132–5.
2   Anonymous ('A Silent Politician'), *On the Future of Ireland* (Dublin: Harding,
    1862), passim. See T. Garvin, *Nationalist Revolutionaries in Ireland 1858–1928*
    (Oxford: Clarendon, 1987), pp. 118–20.
3   *Irish Freedom*, October 1911. On the IRB in general, a recent excellent study is
    O. McGee, *The IRB* (Dublin: Four Courts Press, 2005).
4   *Irish Freedom*, November 1911.
5   Ibid.
6   *Leader*, 5 August 1911; *Catholic Bulletin*, August 1911.
7   Tom Garvin, *1922: The Birth of Irish Democracy* (Dublin: Gill and Macmillan,
    1996); Bill Kissane, *Explaining Irish Democracy* (Dublin: UCD Press, 2002).
8   Dublin: Sinn Féin Information Office, 1974. Authorship is commonly ascribed to
    Desmond Fennell.
9   Edmund Burke, *Reflections on the Revolution in France* (Harmondsworth:
    Pelican, 1968 [1790]), pp. 122–3.

3 Reconsidering the republican tradition in nineteenth-century Ireland

Margaret O'Callaghan

If you read the extensive works of J.G.A. Pocock on anglophone republicanism, or if you look to the recent multi-volume analysis of European republicanism edited by Quentin Skinner and others, you will find virtually no mention of Irish republicanism.[1] Are we therefore to conclude that, at a serious intellectual level, it does not have a history? If it does indeed have a history, why is it so outside the realm of international scholarship? This essay seeks to begin to answer those questions primarily by reference to the nineteenth century. One of the reasons why republicanism in Ireland in the twentieth century has been so malleable and shifting a signifier, why it is so contested and unstable, is because of the intellectually denied or contested nature of its history. It is absent not just from international scholarship but from a plethora of apparently mainstream histories of nineteenth-century Ireland.

There are two ways of approaching these absences. One is through an examination of history-writing, particularly of nineteenth-century Ireland, and another is through an examination of representations of Irish political actions in the first century of republicanism's ideological reality on this island – from the 1790s to the 1890s.

One answer for the Irish peculiarity would be to suggest that successful republican projects are associated in the early and late modern period with states – either pre-existing states that were restructured through republican ideology, or colonial territories that defined themselves as states through republican ideology. The foundational connection of republicanism in Ireland with the failure of a revised state project of an independent republican Ireland in 1798, or a collapsed United Irish revolution at the end of the eighteenth century,[2] conditioned the writing of republicanism's history in Ireland – and indeed Irish history itself – throughout the nineteenth century and, arguably, into the twentieth, if not the twenty-first. In other words, the nature of Ireland's relationship with the United Kingdom, and the nature of internal relations within the island as a consequence of that relationship, framed the expression and reading of at least one version of republicanism in Ireland as sedition, and consequently conditioned its subsequent representation.[3]

Though republicanism in Ireland had roots in earlier contexts – ancient Roman, continental early modern, French revolutionary and American, with some even arguing that the commonwealth ideal had an expression in the seventeenth-century confederation of Kilkenny – at least one version of its formulation and expression from the late eighteenth century onwards was in opposition to the British connection. I cannot think of a single Irish republican post-1800 who was not an Irish nationalist, though Jacqueline Hill has argued persuasively that many of the strands in radical loyalist Dublin Protestant popular thought in the 1820s and 1830s were republican, even if their adherents did not proclaim themselves to be republicans.[4] This opens up a range of questions on the relationship between what is described as the 'patriot' tradition in eighteenth-century Ireland and classic republican virtues. Quite a lot of work has been done on the complexities of republican thinking in Ireland in the 1790s – on the individual thinking of figures like Wolfe Tone and Robert Emmet, on William Drennan and Thomas Russell,[5] on the complexities of relations in various Irish contexts from Wexford to Belfast to Roscommon, on Defenderism and its complex relations with the United Irishmen,[6] and on the cultural politics of the Scottish connection.[7] Less explored areas remain: other lines of transmission or theatres of intellectual exchange such as, for example, the intellectual curriculum of Trinity, or the trans-Atlantic republican affinities that linked Ireland's republican experiment with the post-revolutionary Albany of Thomas Addis Emmet where he presided as a senior member of the bar.[8] This acknowledgement of republicanism's complex initiatory period in Ireland does not compensate for the lack of any serious examination of its role in the transformation of early nineteenth-century Irish political culture. Do republican ideas just go away between the Union in 1801 and the Young Irelanders of the 1840s? Is Jacqueline Hill correct in seeing their existence purely in loyal dissident Protestant Dublin, unyoked from separatist ideas with which the United Irishmen had bound them? Is it important to remember that the republicanism of the United Irishmen was not initially defined by an anti-monarchism; that it so defined itself in the later 1790s in response to state repression? Do Tone and O'Connell have more in common with one another that Tone had with Davis, as Oliver MacDonagh has argued?

The lack of overt proclamation of republican separatist lines after 1798 and the Act of Union can partly be explained in terms of fear. Who were the target audience for Robert Emmet's horrendous death? His head was not displayed outside St Catherine's Church to strike terror into the Catholic or indeed Protestant lower orders. The young men of middle- and upper-class Protestant Ireland were those who were warned off by this exemplary display not to take the path of Emmet, Tone or the Sheares brothers, or hundreds of other Irish Protestants who had been republicanism's architects and popularisers in an Irish context. For the 1798 rebellion at a higher social level had been a bitter dispute within the relatively small society of professional Protestant Ireland, or even professional Protestant Dublin. Those who sentenced were frequently relatives, friends or colleagues of those that they sentenced. This was a profoundly bitter disagreement about past and future political choices within professional Protestant Ireland.

The historiography of the rebellion, or rather the propaganda wars that were conducted through the ostensible medium of history-writing about the rebellion, were partially routes through which those who had rebelled, or had sympathised with those who did, were invited to reconsider their interests in the long-term.[9] Set against the republican choices of the elite rebels was the alternative British state and Irish loyalist explanatory model of sectarianism as the key to Irish politics. This interpretation required that Irish Protestants should stick together and preferably support the Union. This was initially an internal debate within Protestant Ireland, often within families. The close connections, for example at the Irish bar, between the seditious and the destroyed, and the former friends and often relatives who condemned them, ensured that 1798 was a particularly intimate catastrophe for Protestant Ireland. It was of course also a wider catastrophe – the largest bloodiest series of battles, atrocities and killings on the island of Ireland between the wars of the seventeenth century and the present.

The republican project, as enunciated particularly by Tone, challenged the sectarian interpretation of Irish historical and political choices. It did not deny the existence of sectarianism in Ireland, but proposed a quasi-utopian project whereby the 'common name of Irishmen' could unite Catholic, Protestant and dissenter in rejection of state and popular sectarianism, the rule of party placemen, political corruption and possibly the crown. Projects of nationhood that had won in America could create a new political future for Ireland. The key tenet of Irish republicanism in its initial phase was that nationality was derived solely by birth in Ireland,[10] and fidelity to a brotherhood of free men – 'a nation not a province, citizens not slaves' in Tone's words. Breaking the connection with England was represented as a step 'to break that execrable slavery, by which, under the more plausible name of connection we have been chained for six hundred years'. The free citizen could exist only in the free nation. Republicanism was at one level a minority elite movement. At another level, through the forms and iconography, vocabulary and pasted oaths disseminated through Defenders and adopted at different levels of popular resistance movements, it had a broad political purchase throughout the country. It was vitally important in connecting the ideal of republican independence with a gamut of popular rights.

Because of the republican project's initial failure in 1798, because of the terror that preceded and succeeded it, and because of its catastrophic shadow over the next decades, we have no open separatist republican debates in these years, although we have the materials for such a history through a new reading of popular protest movements of the first three decades of the nineteenth century, which generally resisted existing exactions, resisted new state impositions and sought to redress aspects of the land system through a language of rights.[11] Ian McBride argues that the commitment of northern Presbyterians in particular to United Irish exhortations to trust Catholics had never been deep, and thus commitment to a republicanism yoked to separatism was easily dislodged after the rebellion, and it could be represented by Musgrave and others as a Catholic sectarian *jacquerie*; hence the apparent dearth of overt republicanism in Ulster after 1801.[12] Tom Bartlett's work on the Dublin Castle informers paints a different picture of northern commitment.[13] We do not yet fully understand the fate of United Irish legacies in the north. The work of the Rev. George Hill in the mid nineteenth century suggests that republicanism was more vibrant in Ulster in the nineteenth century than certain accounts would suggest. Elsewhere it is in seditious and secret spaces that republican ideas are to be found, often coded in the 'unwritten law' language of what Dublin Castle called the rural *banditti*.[14]

Oliver MacDonagh, considering genealogies and connections in nineteenth century Irish republicanism, wrote:

> For the key to his [O'Connell's] type of separatism, we must look, not to categories of nineteenth century nationalist theory, groups defined by race, religion or culture, still less to twentieth century groups defined by economic class or relationship, but to the eighteenth century radicals and philosophers. O'Connell spoke Tone's language, but not Davis's. Tone defined Irish nationalism in essentially the same terms as the framers of the Declaration of Independence had defined American. But Davis spoke 'spiritually', like Mazzini. O'Connell – it need hardly be said – would have parted company with Tone, where the turnings to revolution or secularity appeared. But for a long way he travelled the same road. For each, particular societies were essentially agglomerations of individuals; and as an individual realized himself by the assertion of his independence and the pursuit of his isolated good, so also did a collective individual, a nation. Nationality was a means of actualising one's dignity and freedom

as a human person, and a necessary means to adopt where the group with which one was associated was inferior either in law or in the estimation of the world at large. Thus the solution of the puzzle whereby the assumption that all men were essentially separate and essentially similar, and possessed essentially the same rights and worth, could end in assertions of the right of national self determination, would seem to lie in Enlightenment concepts of equality.[15]

All of this still leaves us with the problem of defining the meanings of republicanism in an Irish case, as well as attempting to chart these shifting meanings and their articulators over time. This can be begun by attempting a reconstruction of sequences of discourses about what Irish republicanism meant at different times and in different contexts.

The contested republican tradition

We do not have access to an interrogation of republicanism in Ireland in the ways in which, for example, historians have interrogated it as an aspect of the revolution and the history of the following century in France. The Irish republican tradition is primarily characterised in its first century and since by the contestation or refutation of its actual existence (as for instance in Tom Garvin's chapter in this volume)[16] and by the fact that intellectual analysis of the phenomenon did not then, and has perhaps never, passed out of contested contemporary politics.[17] Rather than be seen to facilitate that which is called republicanism, particularly in its contemporary Sinn Féin form, historians have been driven to reproduce as analysis the interpretative framework of Dublin Castle and leading Unionist and British politicians throughout the nineteenth century. In this reading, Irish republicanism cannot be taken intellectually seriously. Peasants can be transformed into Frenchmen, in some cases through republican ideology,[18] albeit of the kind characterised by Kevin Whelan as the 'republic in the village',[19] but such a transformation can never be said to characterise any Irish agrarian protestors. Tom Dunne argues in *Rebellions, Memory, and 1798* that sectarianism is the key motif of 1798, and that rebel actors in Wexford spoke in Irish in excoriation of Clann Luther, and Calvin, and deployed other macaronic languages of dispossession, retribution and sectarian attack. The truth of the latter language does not necessarily substantiate the reduction of the motives for rebellion to sectarianism. Exclusively explaining 1798 in such terms is merely the most recent example of this endlessly recurring trope of sectarianism as eternally the key to Irish history. Republicanism in this representation is always a thin veil that masks it. The coexistence of a new republican language with earlier vocabularies of resentment in Wexford in the 1790s at perceived dispossession, or settler-hatred, in both languages, may however be more usefully characterised in terms that Breandán O'Buachalla, borrowing from Raymond Williams, but working from Irish language and English language sources, has called 'the confluence ... of the "residual" with the emergent in Irish ideology in the late eighteenth and early nineteenth centuries'.[20]

Rather than seeking to deny that republicanism had any popular purchase during and after the 1790s, it might be more useful to ask why most of the nineteenth-century Irish written nationalist tradition is not notably ethnically and religiously based – if republicanism has indeed had as limited a popular purchase as certain analysts would suggest.[21]

It is easy to construct a rogues' gallery of ethnic nationalist, clericalist bigots like D.P. Moran, but more difficult to explain how the nineteenth century written nationalist tradition is manifestly at least partially republican. It is certainly not ethnically exclusivist.[22] Not all nationalist movements in nineteenth-century Ireland are republican, but a significant number of them are. The non-sectarian secular ideals of republicanism are at the centre of the public ideology of the United Irishmen, Emmet, the Young Irelanders and the under-researched mass movement that was Fenianism. There is a clear public intellectual endeavour to construct a republican tradition. Thomas Davis sought to construct an English-language genealogy for a republican line in a manner that consciously drew upon the work of Michelet and the Thierry brothers – Augustin in particular. *The Nation*, which he edited, was widely read. Its European correspondents were extensive in the range of politics and ideology that they covered, and which they invariably identified with the revolutionary generation of 1848. The editorial line consciously linked into the republican print literature of the 1790s. Two decades later Fenian publications also deployed a republican rhetoric, in particular the Fenian paper, *The Irish People*, as did *The Irishmen*, *The Shamrock*, *The Flag of Ireland* and others published by Richard Pigott and later bought by Parnell and relaunched as *United Ireland*, the prime propaganda weapon of the Land and National Leagues.

Representing republicanism in the nineteenth century

Ann Rigney, in her study of three historians of the French revolution, analyses how they embed their politics in their narrative styles.[23] She shows how Michelet, in mitigation of his own political position, narratively succeeded in rendering trivial the death of the king by the very language he uses to describe it. She shows how the slaughter of the Swiss guards can be represented in very different ways by Lamartine and Michelet. But we have no comparable study of the historical and political representations of any such key event or text in nineteenth-century Ireland.[24] We know that the significant interpretative intervention on 1798 was Musgrave's, and in many ways we have not advanced greatly beyond the Musgrave/Madden clash. In *Memoirs of the Different Rebellions in Ireland* published in London and Dublin in 1801, Musgrave, acting as a propagandist for loyalists, clearly justified Union by insisting that republicanism was a guise, and that a Catholic sectarianism, identical to 1641, was the real motive of rebellion. We now treat much of the information that Musgrave collected seriously, but his narrative techniques and the ways in which they consciously draw on earlier atrocity literature in Ireland remain unexamined. Sectarianism clearly existed, as Musgrave claimed, but then the state itself was defined by its sectarianism. Why did Musgrave seek to conceal all other variables for this one over-riding narrative device? No one denies the existence of republicanism in France because not every *sans culotte* was a *philosophe*. R.R. Madden, having returned from colonial exploits and rediscovered his nationalism as a liberal Catholic, was not, in the first extensive documentary account of the United Irishmen – *The United Irishmen: Their Lives and Times*, published initially between 1842 and 1846 – anxious, in redeeming them, to emphasise their republicanism.

The achieved Third Republic in France to some degree stabilised the republicanism of the revolution within the state, even if it did not end the French right's anti-secular impulses. In marked contrast to this, republicanism in Ireland remained and remains associated with anti-state rebellion, and, as such, was represented at the time and since in official state and officially inspired representation as barbarism, sectarianism, mindless violence or base ignorance. It is subsumed within the seditious and treasonable stereotype of Irish rebellion prevalent in the 1830s, best epitomised by Carleton's story 'Wildgoose Lodge'. There the rebellious are frozen in vice. Parodying a Freemasonry gathering or United Irish meeting, the leader of the Ribbonmen, a secret society, is represented as a hedge-school master. His savage countenance is illuminated at the ghastly alter of the Catholic chapel where he meets his dupes, men murmuring in Irish, swearing to perform an act the nature of which they do not know, while downing whiskey on the alter. They then proceed over soaking terrain to slaughter a family in their house, pitchforking a baby to death in a scene eerily reminiscent of Cruickshank's depictions of 1798.[25]

Here and elsewhere the dissemination of ideas that we deem to be republican is represented as having filtered down to the peasantry.[26] Though they are depicted as debased dupes, it is significant that they are also represented as mouthing neo-republican lines. Their fraternity is presented as a grotesque version of one of the brotherly societies, the

Freemasons, or indeed the United Irishmen themselves in their illegal, secret phase.[27] In the repeated deployment of such stereotypes in fiction, official reports, newspaper coverage and travellers' accounts, nineteenth-century Ireland is represented as a place that requires to be remade.[28] The stereotype, variants of which are advanced in cabinet discussions, House of Commons debates, police memos, letters to Dublin Castle and throughout the loyal press, presents an Irish peasantry that live in a state of brutal if devious ignorance, cocooned from ideas, print culture, the wider world.[29] One does not have to concur with Eric Hobsbawm in thinking that peasants think in a language of pure theory to recognise the extraordinary condescension of such a view. Early nineteenth-century Irish language material is redolent of the latest foreign news, events with Bolivar in South America, political argument. Most agrarian rebels were not republicans but some of them spoke a language at least partially inflected by republican rhetoric and concepts.[30] Their fraternal associations or secret societies drew upon earlier agrarian combinations but also mirrored Defender and United Irish codes and signs, as the bizarrely distorting mirror of Carleton's propagandist prose makes clear. The writing of Irish history often reproduces the language of contemporary polemic in fiction and in state analysis.

One alternative approach would be to take the written words of Irish republicans in the nineteenth century seriously. The writers of *The Nation* after 1848, when it abandoned earlier caution about republican rhetoric and fears of evoking the memory of 1798, and, in the later period, the Fenians in particular have left an abundant republican legacy.[31] Irish Famine emigrants to America did not, as Kevin O'Neill has written, 'look to eighteenth century republicanism as a point of entry into American discourse and life' for complex reasons. But they embraced the language of the American republic particularly during the civil war, which provided the impetus for the mass republican movement that was Fenianism. As O'Neill quotes the words of the poor Irish Union soldier Peter Walsh:

> In this country it is very different. Here we have a free government just laws and a Constitution which guarantees equal rights and privaleges to all Here thousands of the sons and daughters of Ireland have come to seek a refuge from tyranny and persecution at home ... Here they have an open field for industry ... Here Irishmen and their descendants have a claim a stake in the nation and an interest in its prosperity Irishmen helped to free it from the yoke of Britain ... And have rushed by thousands to the call of their adopted country ... their blood stained every battlefield of this war ... We who survive them have a double motive then to nerve us to action. We have the same national political and social interests at stake not only for ourselves but for

coming generations and the oppressed of every nation for America was a common asylum for all [*sic*].[32]

Republicanism and republicans drove the greater part of nationalism and nationalist movements in nineteenth-century Ireland. Republican ideas were widely disseminated at elite and popular levels. The Catholic Church and the state in Ireland sought to stymie the revolutionary capacity of republican rhetoric and action. Almost all public political nationalist rhetoric is conducted in a vocabulary of republican concepts of the freeman in a free polity. Irish republicanism's pervasive capacity to absorb outside influences from France and America, and constantly to remake and redefine itself in new political contexts, determined that Irish nationalism was predominantly non-sectarian and non-ethnic in the ideal, if not always in the actual.

Notes

1 See Martin van Gelderen and Quentin Skinner (eds), *Republicanism: A Shared European Heritage, Vol. 1: Republicanism and Constitutionalism in Early Modern Europe*, and *Vol. 2: The Values of Republicanism in Early Modern Europe* (Cambridge: Cambridge University Press, 2002). See J.G.A. Pocock, *The Machiavellian Moment: Florentine Political Thought and the Atlantic Republic* (Princeton: Princeton University Press, 1975). See too, proceedings of a seminar on eighteenth-century Irish political thought at the Folger Library in Washington DC in the summer of 1998, at which J.G.A. Pocock was present – published as S.J. Connolly (ed.), *Political Ideas in Eighteenth Century Ireland* (Dublin: Four Courts Press, 2000).

2 There is a vast literature on the 1798 rebellion in Ireland. For a summary of recent scholarship see Thomas Bartlett, Daire Keogh and Kevin Whelan, *The Irish Rebellion of 1798: A Bicentennial Perspective* (Dublin: Four Courts Press, 2003).

3 On the broader question of the politicisation of Irish historical representation in this and other time-frames see Clare Carroll and Patricia King (eds), *Ireland and Postcolonial Theory* (South Bend: University of Notre Dame Press, 2003).

4 For an alternative version of a specifically Protestant republicanism in 1830s and 1840s Dublin see Jacqueline Hill, *From Patriots to Unionists: Dublin Civic Politics and Irish Protestant Patriotism, 1660–1840* (Oxford: Oxford University Press, 1997). See Oliver MacDonagh's analysis of O'Connell as having more in common with the thought-world of Wolfe Tone, rather than with that of the broadly republican Young Irelanders of the 1840s: Oliver MacDonagh, 'O'Connell and Repeal, 1840–1845', in Michael Bentley and John Stevenson (eds), *High and Low Politics in Modern Britain* (Oxford: Oxford University Press, 1983).

5 Marianne Elliott, *Wolfe Tone, Prophet of Irish Independence* (London and New Haven: Yale University Press, 1989); Ruan O' Donnell, *Robert Emmet and the Rising of 1803* (2 vols) (Dublin: Irish Academic Press, 2003); Thomas Bartlett (ed.), *Theobald Wolfe Tone: Life of Theobald Wolfe Tone Compiled and*

Arranged by William Theobald Wolfe Tone (Dublin: Lilliput Press, 1998); Thomas Bartlett, *Theobald Wolfe Tone* (Dundalk: Dun Dealgan Press, 1997); James Quinn, *A Life of Thomas Russell, 1767–1803: A Soul on Fire* (Dublin: Irish Academic Press, 2001); Nancy Curtin, *The United Irishmen: Popular Politics in Ulster and Dublin, 1791–1798* (Oxford: Clarendon Press, 1994).

6   Jim Smyth, *The Men of No Property: Irish Radicals and Popular Politics in the Late Eighteenth Century* (Dublin: Palgrave Macmillan, 1992).

7   Ian McBride, *Scripture Politics: Ulster Presbyterians and Irish Radicalism in Late Eighteenth-Century Ireland* (Oxford: Clarendon Press, 1998).

8   Luke Gibbons has begun this exploration in 'Republicanism and radical memory; the O'Conors, O'Carolan and the United Irishmen', in Jim Smyth (ed.), *Revolution, Counter-Revolution and Union: Ireland in the 1790s* (Cambridge: Cambridge University Press, 2000), pp. 211–37.

9   The propaganda wars were mainly conducted through the medium of the historiography of the rebellion. See in particular Richard Musgrave, *Memoir of the Various Rebellions in Ireland* (Dublin, 1801). Its main thrust was to demonstrate the folly of those Protestant United Irishmen who had been foolish enough to ally themselves with the Catholic lower orders who, it was alleged, used the rebellion to pursue old sectarian and land grievances, and to massacre their Protestant fellow countrymen. R.R. Madden's work of the 1840s was an attempt to counter such an interpretation: *The United Irishmen; their Lives and Times* (Dublin, 1846). These historiographical wars were fought anew in 1898 and in the recent bicentenary in 1998. For conflicting contemporary interpretations see Bartlett, Dickson, Keogh, and Whelan, *The Irish Rebellion of 1798: A Bicentennial Perspective* (Dublin: Four Courts Press, 2003) and Tom Dunne, *Rebellions, Memory and 1798* (Dublin: Lilliput Press, 2004).

10 A formulation at least rhetorically adhered to by all who called themselves Irish republicans until the constitutional referendum of 2004.

11 See Thomas Bartlett, *The Fall and Rise of the Irish Nation: The Catholic Question, 1690–1830* (New York: Barnes and Noble, 1992) for the years up to 1830, including Gregory's period in Dublin Castle, fears of French invasion, the atmosphere of fear of revolt and of Napoleon.

12 McBride, *Scripture Politics*, and see too: Ian McBride (ed.), *History and Memory in Modern Ireland* (Cambridge: Cambridge University Press, 2001).

13 Thomas Bartlett, *Revolutionary Dublin: The Letters of Francis Higgins to Dublin Castle, 1795–1801* (Dublin: Four Courts Press, 2003).

14 See Galen Broeker, *Rural Disorder and Police Reform in Ireland, 1812–1836* (London and Toronto: Routledge, 1970) for an insight into the scale of Dublin Castle observation of the population. See too: Margaret O'Callaghan, 'New ways of looking at the state apparatus and the state archive in nineteenth century Ireland', *Proceedings of the Royal Irish Academy* 104c: 2 (2004): 37–56; and Heather Laird, *Subversive Law in Ireland, 1879–1920: From 'Unwritten Law' to the Dáil Courts* (Dublin: Four Courts Press, 2005).

15 McDonagh, 'O'Connell and repeal', pp. 24–5.

16 This line is most clearly stated in the work of Tom Garvin, where agrarianism and sectarianism are represented as the keys to Irish political group action. This interpretation is intensified by Conor Cruise O'Brien in his work, *Ancestral Voices*

(Chicago: University of Chicago Press, 1994). Republicanism in an Irish context is here and elsewhere represented as a garb on Catholic sectional interests – hence the particularly scornful representation of 'the Protestant republican' by those who hold this view. Dr Garret FitzGerald, former Irish Taoiseach, vehemently insisted that there was no such thing as republicanism in nineteenth-century Ireland at the UCD IBIS conference on Irish Republicanism on which this volume is based.

17   That may well also be the case in France. See Perry Anderson's series of articles on French intellectual culture in the *London Review of Books* in 2003–04, particularly in his focus on the political and historiographical consequences of key contestations in French historiography of the revolution.

18   Eugen Weber, *Peasants into Frenchmen: Modernisationisation of Rural France, 1870–1914* (Stanford: Stanford University Press, 1976).

19   Kevin Whelan, *The Tree of Liberty: Radicalism, Catholicism and the Construction of Irish Identity* (Cork: Cork University Press,1996).

20   Quoted by Peter McQuillan, *Native and Natural* (Cork: Cork University Press, 2004). See too Breandán O' Buachalla, *Aisling Ghear* (Dublin: An Clóchomhar, 1996).

21   Key nationalist texts like the Young Ireland journal *The Nation* are clearly not sectarian. The explanation of Irish popular insurrection given by Thomas Moore indicates that material, social and cultural grievances animate popular movements rather than the sectarianism that it suits the state, propagandists like Mortimer O'Sullivan, and loyalists to impute to them. See Thomas Moore, *Memoirs of Captain Rock: The Celebrated Irish Chieftain, With Some Account of his ... Written by Himself* (London: Longman, 1924) . See O'Callaghan, 'New ways of looking at the state apparatus and the state archive in nineteenth century Ireland', *Proceedings of the Royal Irish Academy* 104c: 2 (2004): 37–56.

22   Studies of the cultural nationalism in the early twentieth century repeatedly cite Moran as nationalist, clericalist and sectarian. This is deemed to indicate that Irish nationalism is invariably clericalist and sectarian, that Irish nationalism and republicanism are invariably synonymous – that, therefore, republicanism in an Irish context not really republicanism at all. For the most lucid statement of this view of Irish nationalism as ethno-sectarian, see O'Brien, *Ancestral Voices*.

23   Ann Rigney, *The Rhetoric of Historical Representation: Three Narrative Histories of the French Revolution* (Cambridge: Cambridge University Press, 2003).

24   Clare Carroll has done this for some texts from the sixteenth and seventeenth centuries in 'Barbarous slaves and civil cannibals: translating civility in early modern Ireland', in Carroll and King (eds), *Ireland and Postcolonial Theory*, pp. 63–80. Stuart Andrews, in analysing the enduring power of Musgrave's History of the Rebellion, has begun this process for nineteenth century propagandist history-writing: Stuart Andrews, *Irish Rebellion: Protestant Polemic, 1798–1900* (London: Palgrave Macmillan, 2006).

25   The most horrific visual representations of horrors allegedly inflicted by the rebels in 1798 were the work of George Cruickshank who depicted the rebels in a frame familiar to those accustomed to atrocity – story narratives of Irish Protestant experience framed through the bridge at Portadown in 1641.

26   See Luke Gibbons, 'Between Captain Rock and a hard place; art and agrarian insurgence', in Tadhg Foley and Sean Ryder (eds), *Ideology and Ireland in the Nineteenth Century* (Dublin: Four Courts Press, 1998) pp. 23–44.

27   On republicanism and freemasonry, see Jim Smyth, *The Men of No Property: Irish Radicals and Popular Politics in the Late Eighteenth Century* (Dublin: Palgrave Macmillan, 1992) for popular incorporation of elite fraternal forms and practices.

28   See Seamus Deane, *Strange Country: Modernity and Nationhood in Irish Writing Since 1790* (Oxford: Clarendon, 1997).

29   See John Wilson Croker, *A Sketch of the State of Ireland, Past and Present* (Dublin and London, 1808).

30   Samuel Clark and James Donnelly, *Irish Peasants: Violence and Political Unrest, 1780–1914* (Manchester and Wisconsin: University of Wisconsin Press, 2003).

31   For the best recent studies of Fenianism that raise questions about some of Vincent Comerford's conclusions in R.V. Comerford, *The Fenians in Context: Irish Politics and Society 1848 to 1882* (Dublin, 1985 and 1998), see Christy Campbell, *Fenian Fire: The British Government Plot to Assassinate Queen Victoria* (London: Harper Collins, 2002), the same author's *The Maharajah's Box: An Imperial Story of Conspiracy, Love and a Guru's Prophecy* (London: Harper Collins, 2000); and Owen McGee, *The IRB: The Irish Republican Brotherhood from the Land League to Sinn Féin* (Dublin: Four Courts Press, 2005).

32   Kevin O' Neill 'The star-spangled shamrock: meaning and memory in Irish America', in McBride (ed.) *History and Memory in Modern Ireland*, pp. 118–38.

Part II
French republican ideology
in practice

4   Republicanism and the French political tradition

Jeremy Jennings

In this chapter I will seek to explore a general set of questions that relate to issues of republicanism and the French political tradition.[1] Thus, I will focus upon the broad rationale of republicanism in France, the extent to which republicanism has constituted a public philosophy that has had an impact upon practice and policy, the distinctive institutional arrangements that are associated with the republic in France, before finally seeking to assess some of the tensions within French republicanism and the challenges it might face in the immediate future. At best this account will be superficial – such is the importance of republicanism within the French political tradition[2] – but I hope that my remarks might provide material for fruitful comparison with the republican tradition in Ireland.

To begin, the construction of the French nation state has been a process extending over many centuries and thus what one sees today is the result of an evolution that incorporates not just the experience of republicanism but also that of the monarchy and other important phenomena such as Bonapartism.[3] The French Republic is therefore a work of synthesis and one that builds upon centuries of self-conscious state-building and centralisation.[4] The argument, advanced most prominently in recent years by François Furet and Pierre Rosanvallon, has been that the Revolution (and therefore the Republic) did not break with the absolutist traditions of the *ancien régime* and thus that it reappropriated the attributes of royal sovereignty for itself. As a consequence, it is contended, the Republic continued the aspiration to achieve unity and social consensus at the expense of a difficulty in conceiving society as a plural entity.[5]

However, the starting point of French republican culture is the Revolution of 1789,[6] an event which led (inevitably, some would argue) to the later establishment of the First Republic and to the enunciation of the key republican principle of the sovereignty of the people, a people conceived of as belonging to a nation shorn of privilege and freed from arbitrary power and corruption. Subsequently, French republicanism was to grapple with the problem of finding an appropriate institutional form for such sovereignty.[7] Through what electoral procedures, for example, was a national will to be given voice and expression?[8] What form was government itself to take when, as was the case in 1789, there were many who believed that the republican form could not be adapted to a large modern state?[9] Specifically, it should be noted that the fervent belief in the sovereignty of the people, expressed through a popularly elected chamber, has been such as to engender a long-term hostility towards the judicial review of legislation and what is often referred to, in derogatory terms, as the 'government of judges'.[10]

The legacy of the French Revolution upon the French republican tradition has been both profound and durable. The participants in the Revolution of 1789 believed that their actions were of world significance and that the values they espoused were of universal import and application. On this view, France was the homeland of humanity and thus the French Republic was the privileged vessel through which the progress and emancipation of all humans, regardless of nationality or religion, was to be attained. If this republican universalism was for the most part addressed to foreign countries and peoples (for example, in the First World War when French intellectuals opposed German nationalism and militarism with the universal, and French, message of liberty and justice), it was frequently deployed in order to secure the deliverance of populations indigenous to France herself.

The nineteenth-century writer and historian Jules Michelet provides one of the best examples of these sentiments. A recurrent theme in Michelet's writings is the evocation of the exemplarity of the French experience. It is most vividly expressed in a chapter entitled 'Tableau de France' hidden within his account of the history of the middle ages.[11] The special genius of France, according to this description, lay in its unity and diversity and in its capacity for interaction and assimilation. 'It is', Michelet writes, 'a wonderful spectacle to regard this vast and powerful organism, where the varied parts are so skilfully related, contrasted, and connected, combining the strong with the weak, the negative with the positive'.[12] France, however, had to be seen as a whole and when it was the impression was one of unity and of a single personality. Here Michelet makes uncritical reference to the long process of centralisation and unification begun under the monarchy, commenting that 'in this way was formed the general, universal spirit of the country'. With each day, he remarks, 'the local spirit' was overcome, the influence of the 'soil, of climate, of race' gave way before that of 'social and political action'. History had overcome geography. Men had escaped 'the tyranny of material circumstances'. In this 'marvellous transformation', Michelet continued, 'spirit has triumphed over matter, the general over the particular, the idea over the real'.[13] Given this open embrace of all humanity within the republican schema, there is no more fascinating tale, as Sophie Wahnich has shown,[14] than the manner in which the universalistic aspirations of the Revolution were replaced by the denunciation of the foreigner and by what Mona Ozouf has termed a 'fraternité xenophobe'.[15] The crucial ingredient of this republican universalism, however, is that human nature is deemed to be identical and that emancipation, for individuals, communities and nations alike, is defined in terms of an escape from cultural, ethnic and historical particularisms.

How can this penchant of French republicanism for universalism be explained?[16] As Colin Jones has recently written in *The Great Nation*,[17] '[i]n many senses, the eighteenth century was France's century'.[18] The country bounced back from the gruelling wars that had characterised the final years of Louis XIV's reign and was able 'to imprint its influence on every aspect of eighteenth-century European life'. It had the largest population of any of the great powers and experienced long-term economic growth and improving living standards. Paris remained at the epicentre of the intellectual world, and, as Marc Fumaroli has reminded us, the eighteenth century was an age when Europe spoke French.[19] It was not only the language of international diplomacy but also the language of civilisation, of the arts, and of the republic of letters. To speak French, in this sense, was to be a party to the aspirations of humanity as a whole. As Jones himself acknowledges, to thus regard France in the eighteenth century as the 'great nation' does not mean that the country was without weaknesses. This was manifestly not the case. However, despite the upheaval and turmoil produced by the Revolution, at the end of the century France had succeeded in greatly extending its borders. In short, what in retrospect looked like Britain's inevitable rise to become the world's dominant power in the nineteenth century, did not look quite so certain from the vantage point of the windmill on the top of the hill at Valmy at the moment when France's revolutionary army put to rout their Prussian opponents on 12 September 1792.

It was in these circumstances, as the new regime faced both its internal and external enemies, that a new definition of the nation had quickly to be found. This definition was provided with breathtaking audacity by the Abbé Sieyès in his famous pamphlet of 1789, *Qu-est-ce que le Tiers Etat?*[20] Henceforth, the Third Estate was taken to be 'a complete nation', with the aristocracy in particular cast out unceremoniously and without regret from the body politic. Next, the representatives of the Third Estate formalised their political ascendancy not merely by redescribing themselves as 'the representatives of the French people' but also by declaring themselves to be members of the *Assemblée nationale*. The nation thus had been given unambiguous political expression and henceforth it was acknowledged that 'the principle of all sovereignty resides in the nation'.

In this way were disclosed two ideas of immense significance and importance for the republican movement.[21] The first was that the nation was a self-conscious political construct, the fruit and product of an immense act of (revolutionary) will. The second, and one soon to be made graphically explicit, was that nations possessed the right to self-determination. The latter in particular denoted a complete break with traditional international practices, although it had been presaged by the slightly earlier American example. Both were made manifest at the *Fête de la Fédération*, celebrated on the *Champs de Mars* a year to the day after the storming of the Bastille and orchestrated in such a way as to shroud the nation in a mystical halo. As Pierre Nora has written, '[t]he festival expressed the disappearance of internal frontiers, the abolition of regional disparities, the excitement associated with an act of mutual consent submitting a united France to an authority freely accepted'.[22] Just as dramatically, these same ideas were applied to those parts of the territory that had been annexed to France under the monarchy. In the so-called *serment de Strasbourg* the delegates of the national guards of Alsace, Lorraine and Franche-Comté affirmed the determination of these territories and their inhabitants to be a part of the French nation.

There is much that could, and arguably should, be said about the general manner in which over time the nation replaced God as the source of all legitimate authority. With God, although not yet dead, now deemed to be absent from human affairs, there was, it has been argued, a felt-need for a new organisational principle capable of generating loyalty amongst individual members of the community and for some this dubious role fell to the nation.[23] This was undoubtedly a European-wide phenomenon but in the case of France it has a special dimension and one that again serves to explain the universalist aspirations of French republicanism. As René Rémond has shown,[24] the idea that France was 'the eldest daughter of the Church' has deep roots in her history and served for centuries as the foundation block upon which national unity was forged. This belief, he explains, had three essential pillars: with the baptism of Clovis, France had been the first nation to convert to Catholicism; from the time of Charlemagne onwards, France had had a privileged and special relationship with the Holy See; and, as was proven by her history, France had been chosen by God to fulfil a special mission. From the latter followed a conception of France as 'the sword of God'. 'From this assurance, even when secularised', Rémond comments, 'proceeds the conviction, deeply rooted in French culture, that the actions of France are of a significance for humanity. She does not only defend her own interests, however legitimate they might be; in contrast to other peoples who are motivated by

egoistic considerations, she fights for generous causes, be they the evan-
gelisation of pagan peoples, the principles of 89, the defence of the rights
of man, the respect of international law.'[25] In short, the universalism of
French republicanism in part derives from the secularisation and appropriation of a core religious belief in the divine mission of the French
people.[26] As Naomi Schor has argued, the French Revolution, in destroy-
ing the Gallican Church, 'enabled French universalism to perpetuate and
propagate itself'.[27]

However, the forced seizure by the republicans of France's claim to
possess a providential destiny was not without cost. Specifically, the
Republic turned the Roman Catholic Church into its bitter enemy,
thereby establishing the division between what were known as Red and
Black France.[28] The reality of the two Frances was always more complex
than a simple division between clericalism and anti-clericalism would
suggest. Yet, for its part, the Church did not hesitate to portray the French
Revolution and the two military defeats by Germany in 1870 and 1940
as signs of God's displeasure at a sinful France. The secular Republic was
castigated as morally decadent and politically corrupt, as well as being
controlled by Protestants and Freemasons.[29] In their turn, the republicans
virtually excluded the Church from official versions of French history and
developed a highly disrespectful anti-clerical lexicon.[30] Whilst there were
undoubtedly moments of reconciliation between Church and Republic –
most notably the *Union Sacrée* that accompanied the First World War –
the clash between these two value systems was no better illustrated than
by the momentous struggle that surrounded the fate of the unfortunate
Captain Dreyfus.[31] If the Dreyfusard cause deployed the republican rhetoric of truth, justice and reason, its opponents rallied to the values of an
eternal France: authority and order. In 1905, after bitter and acrimonious
debate, Church and state were formally separated.[32] In subsequent years
the conflict between Republic and Church was to reappear and, although
now much abated, it still has a capacity to divide opinion (for example,
in 1984 when the issue of state funding for Catholic schools was raised,
the Church successfully mobilised mass protest against the planned
reforms).

More significantly, the clash with the Church gave rise within French
republicanism to a distinctive understanding of the strict separation
between the public and the private – religious faith, for example, is a
purely private matter – as well as to the (difficult to translate) concept of
laïcité. The latter, when expressed through law, guarantees liberty of
conscience and divorces citizenship from religious affiliation. In 1905, for
example, France ceased to define itself as a Catholic nation. By the same
token, *laïcité* also stipulates that the state must adopt a position of
public neutrality towards all private manifestations of religious faith and

practice. The state, in short, is obliged to respect religious and spiritual differences, as similarly are religious believers required to accept the republican value of mutual tolerance. Clearly, some religions find these constraints more difficult to accept than others, as indeed do some religions operate with a less watertight distinction between the realms of public and private life. The recent influx of large numbers of Muslim immigrants into France has accordingly posed a significant challenge to these core republican principles.[33] (The complex basis of French secularism is further discussed by Cécile Laborde in Chapter 5 below.)

The Revolution of 1789 made at least one other major contribution to the universalism of French republicanism: as the *Declaration of the Rights of Man and the Citizen* made plain, all French citizens were deemed to be the free and equal possessors of a set of human rights that were of universal application. These rights were defined as those of liberty, property, security and resistance to oppression. Every society in which the guarantee of these rights was not assured was said not to possess a constitution. Above all, this declaration was a pronouncement of war against the *ancien régime* and was intended to demonstrate that France was no longer the property of the monarch. The primary concern thus was to arm France against a possible return of royal despotism rather than to protect the poor against oppression by their new masters. Nevertheless, the declaration announced the new creed of the Republic and became the basis for all subsequent republican constitutions in France.[34]

Here then, in the Revolution of 1789 and in the struggles of republicans over the next two hundred years to make the Republic a reality, was a drama which produced its own powerful mythology, with its martyrs, its heroes (most notably, the people astride the barricades), and its villains (amongst whom were to be found not only the royal family, the aristocracy and the clergy but also England, cast invariably as the land of privilege and inequality and as the new Carthage).[35] Moreover, the struggle to establish the Republic upon a secure foundation was not a battle that was won overnight. The first four Republics fell in what at best can be described as ignominious circumstances, each effectively handing over power to individuals who were seen as being capable of strong leadership (in turn, Napoleon Bonaparte, Napoleon III, Marshal Pétain and General de Gaulle). The present constitutional arrangement, instituted in 1958 under the threat of military insurrection in what was then French Algeria,[36] is nominally a parliamentary democracy but such has been the extent of presidential power and the ineffectiveness of the national assembly that critics such as the eminent political scientist Maurice Duverger have not hesitated to describe the Fifth Republic as a 'Jacobin monarchy'.[37] As President Chirac's presidency limped towards its inevitable end and the political class in its entirety came to be held in low public esteem, there was talk of the need to move to a Sixth Republic.

Nor was this struggle to establish the Republic without resort to violence.[38] The First Republic in particular was forged in the cauldron of the reign of Terror,[39] and it is important to realise that for many decades the Republic was indissolubly linked to the idea of violence. In 1848, for example, at the moment of the birth of the Second Republic, writers of the stature of Alexis de Tocqueville, Michel Chevalier and Edouard Laboulaye, sought to convince the French electorate that the new Republic should be modelled upon the moderate American example rather than Robespierre's Jacobin model of the past.[40] Only when the Republic began to free itself of this association with violence was it able to appeal to a broader level of support across French society. Crucially, this republican tradition produced multiple political cultures, of which arguably the two most important are the liberal, moderate tradition of 1789 and the rights of man and the radical, revolutionary tradition of 1793 and the Jacobin Republic. Alternatively the divisions within the republican tradition could be characterised as being between realists and romantics, bourgeois and workers, right and left, or, more simply, between those prepared to compromise with the realities of political power and those for whom republicanism was a new religion and harbinger of a new society.[41]

The defining moment in this evolution was the decade of the 1870s, the decade when the Republic effectively put revolution behind it and when it accepted the institutional compromise and synthesis that, to a greater or lesser extent, still exists today.[42] The principle of the sovereignty of the nation and of the people, which for ardent republicans could only have been embodied in a single parliamentary chamber elected upon the basis of universal (male) suffrage, was tempered by the acceptance of a conservative upper chamber, the Senate, and a president with not inconsiderable powers. In this way was the support of the bourgeoisie for the Republic secured. If the squabbling about the appropriate institutional form for the Republic continued, the Republic was now perceived as the political regime that divided men least. The Republic stood for democracy but it was a democracy where a contrived balance of powers sought to ensure that the popular will of the people was never able to push the Republic in a radical direction. The sociological and electoral backbone of the Republic now became the small property owner. Note that women were denied the vote until after the Second World War, largely because republicans remained distrustful of the influence upon them of the Roman Catholic Church.

It was in the succeeding decades that the Republic established such key individual liberties as freedom of the press, the right to join a trade union and to go on strike, the right to demonstrate in public and the right of association.[43] The *Marseillaise* became the national anthem and 14 July became a national holiday. For this reason this period has sometimes been regarded as the 'golden age' of republican liberties. A less glowing picture, however, is revealed in Jean-Pierre Machelon's *La République contre les libertés?*[44] On this account, the pursuit of stability and order meant that striking workers, anarchists, religious congregations and civil servants (not to mention women) felt the full force of state repression as the fundamental liberties of certain categories of individuals were disregarded in the name of social peace. The result was growing disillusionment amongst the working-class movement and renewed hostility from the Catholic Church.

It was also in these decades that republicans refocused their ardour towards the establishment of a national educational system which would embed republican culture amongst the population as a whole. Here is a key aspect of republicanism as a public philosophy. In brief, French republicanism locates itself within the tradition of Enlightenment and of Rationalism and it was this tradition, refracted through the lens of Comtean positivism, which spawned a virulent anti-clericalism. Drawing upon the philosophy of Immanuel Kant – in effect, the official philosopher of the Third Republic – the ambition was to propagate a secular ethic of potential universal application and it was to be through the state school that this was primarily to be achieved. Henceforth it was to be by means of the educational system, rather than by resort to street fighting, that the citizen of the Republic was to attain an emancipation that derived from becoming an autonomous and rational being.[45] Moreover, it was the *instituteurs* and the professors of the Republic who were to constitute the new secular elite and who were to be called upon to act as the shock troops in the fight against the forces of darkness and reaction.[46]

The second key institution of republican pedagogy was to be the army. Here we need to take into account the sheer geographical, cultural and linguistic diversity of France in order to understand the manner in which military service was used as a way of turning peasants into Frenchman.[47] The army not only taught the raw recruits to read and write (and in many cases to speak French) but also to be patriots and defenders of the Republic. The army of France was to be that of the citizen-soldier. More than this, the France of the republican movement was always the 'great nation', the light of humanity, the source of liberty and of progress, and this message could be carried beyond the borders of France, by arms if necessary. This was never seen as a belligerent nationalism but as a form of patriotism where the interests of France and those of humanity were deemed to coincide. This logic explains not just the 'civilising mission' attributed to the French Empire but also many of the broad themes of French foreign policy to this day.[48] It also explains the continuing affection amongst many republicans in France for obligatory military service. Indeed, the decision to end conscription was only taken in 1996.

The extent of this educational optimism should not be underestimated. It has been and remains central to the political preoccupations of French republicans. The Republic was not just to be limited to a set of political institutions. The ambition was to create a republican culture that was deeply rooted in the ordinary, daily activities of the French population. The difficulty was, and remains, that of defining what that culture was and of finding the appropriate means of its transmission and expression. We get some idea of the problem if we consult the history of the humble postage stamp in France.[49] Given that the use of an image of the Head of State was not acceptable, how could the Republic be given symbolic representation? The Republic has in turn been portrayed in a variety of allegorical forms, as the expression of peace, of truth, of justice, of equality, of the rights of man, of law, of progress, of science, of commerce but also, and probably most enduringly, as the expression of the eternal verities associated with the land and a rural France. Even here, in something as seemingly innocuous as the postage stamp, we see therefore the tension between a conservative and a radical vision of the Republic. The same inconsistency and variation is discernible in the countless busts and statues of the Republic which adorn France's public squares and town halls and of which Maurice Agulhon has proved such an instructive historian.[50] If the Republic, known affectionately as Marianne, was to take on female form she has by no means always been adorned in the Phrygian bonnet of revolution or dispensed the physical bounty attributed to her by Honoré Daumier. This apprehension and uncertainty arguably remains to this day, and was vividly evident, for example, during the bicentenary celebrations of the French Revolution.[51]

The fact remains, however, that over the last two hundred years the Republic in France has been able to build up not just its own powerful mythology, constructed around key events, places, institutions and individuals, but has also painstakingly erected an impressive repertoire of values and linguistic concepts that have provided politicians, policy makers and ordinary citizens with a seemingly inexhaustible supply of alternative descriptions and visions of the Republic. No better guide to this republican galaxy is to be found than the *Dictionnaire critique de la République* published in 2002 by Christophe Prochasson and Vincent Duclert.

At the heart of this republican rhetoric is the famous slogan: Liberty, Equality and Fraternity.[52] Let us note that it was only over time that this established itself as *the* republican motto. Note too that initially there were arguments about the order in which the words were to appear. Fraternity invariably found itself something of the poor relation, its claims to attention subordinated to third place, only for it to emerge in full view with the Revolution of 1848. For the republicans of the Second Republic fraternity alone could prevent liberty from creating privilege and equality from producing oppression. But was and is the slogan a coherent one, capable of easy translation into policy and practice? The evidence would seem to suggest not. Each of these key terms has been subject to continuous redefinition. Liberty, for example, was originally seen in terms of the absence of oppression by both Church and state but under the influence of the Jacobins it became associated with the pursuit and the reign of virtue. Later, and especially in reaction to the authoritarian regime of Napoleon III's Second Empire,[53] moderate republicans sought to free the concept of liberty from these classical overtones, preferring to emphasise the importance of liberty of conscience, freedom of speech and the press, and the freedom to go about one's business as one wished. They also stressed the important liberty of the right to property. Liberty, in short, came to be defined as the liberty of the individual and of the bourgeois property owner. The republican Left, especially in the guise of the once-powerful French Communist Party (PCF) which successfully married French republican traditions to Soviet Marxism, the tricolour to the red flag, has never accepted this definition.[54] More recently, the claims for recognition on the part of France's religious and ethnic minorities have posed a further challenge to this restricted definition of liberty.

More generally, how can the recognition of the right to liberty, understood as the right to do anything that is not injurious to others, be allied to the republican value of equality? Here again the debate has been long standing, especially as it was quickly recognised (and long before it received its famous analysis by Alexis de Tocqueville) that the primary motor of the French Revolution was a passion for equality.[55] Equality was originally understood as an end to aristocratic privilege and thus in terms of civil equality, an aspiration powerfully symbolised by the abolition of the feudal order in the summer of 1789. Today the principle of equality is enshrined in Article 2 of the Constitution of the Fifth Republic. From this, it follows that the law of the Republic accepts no distinctions on the grounds of birth (or indeed of race or religion). Citizens are equal in terms of rights (including political rights) and in terms of equal access to public office or employment, but in practice this has not been translated into social and economic equality. Equality thus is understood in formal terms as an equality of rights and acts as a principle of non-discrimination rather than as a motor for radical change that permits the legislator to secure either an equality of opportunity or an equality of outcome.

Again it is important to understand that this reading has not gone unchallenged in recent years. Is the reliance upon an equality of rights, it is asked, sufficient response to the continued under-representation of women to positions of elected office[56] or to the so-called 'new inequalities' that have arisen as a result of high unemployment and large-scale immigration?[57] Should an equality of rights be jettisoned in favour of a real equality of opportunity? Indeed, should the term 'equality' be replaced by calls for equity and parity (especially with regard to gender issues). Just as controversially, should France for the first time contemplate a policy of positive discrimination as a means of overcoming the undoubted disadvantages suffered by its ethnic minorities? As it stands, clear policies of reverse or positive discrimination are not allowed, although the right-wing president elected in 2007, Nicholas Sarkozy, bravely challenged this republican taboo.

Part of the argument is that the very slogan Liberty, Equality and Fraternity has become both meaningless and misleading. It is hypocrisy, critics argue, for example, to believe that France is a country which provides equality of access to higher education and health care, despite the republican rhetoric to the contrary. How then has the republican impulse towards fraternity been integrated, if at all, into this vision? Fraternity's high water mark within the republican pantheon was in 1848, when with the birth of the Second Republic it attained an almost messianic dimension. The Republic, it was announced, would be a social republic or it would not exist. With the repression of the June days this optimism was quickly dissipated but what remained – and what remains today – is the belief that the Republic must aspire to achieve social justice. The promise of the Revolution has to be realised. That aspiration has sat uneasily beside what has amounted to the social conservatism of many of the governments of the Republic. By the end of the nineteenth century it had been transposed into the doctrine of *solidarity*, a doctrine which emphasised not just the rights but also the duties of individual citizens, not the abolition of classes but the mutual bonds that existed across classes.[58] In the opinion of one of its advocates, Celestin Bouglé, *solidarisme* attained the status of being 'the official philosophy of the Third Republic'.[59] The mood for national renovation that followed the liberation of France in 1944 led to the formal inclusion of many social rights into the constitution of the Fourth Republic as well as the nationalisation of large sectors of private industry and banking. Republicanism now turned to creating the welfare state. Today, however, it is this French 'social model' that not only lends distinctiveness to French republicanism but which, its critics argue, is in need of reform.[60]

In summary, the ideology of French republicanism has been subject to considerable internal tension, if not contradiction. One area of relative consistency and unanimity, however, has been the distinctive conception of citizenship that has consistently informed republican thinking and practice (and which is still very much in evidence today).[61] The literature on this topic is truly vast, so what follows is at best a superficial sketch of this central theme in French republican thinking.[62] The guiding thread is that it is citizenship rather than race, ethnicity or religious affiliation that defines membership of the political community. As an ideal this has various components: the citizen is a member of a national, rather than a local or particularistic, community towards which he or she is expected to display an element of civic pride and fidelity; the citizen is possessed of both rights and obligations towards this community and should therefore recognise the merits of both reciprocity and social solidarity; the citizen is expected to participate actively in its political life (to vote, to be well informed about public matters, etc); the citizen is expected to display the moral characteristics appropriate to life in such a national community (through the payment of taxes, national military service, etc). In this context, the French themselves speak of the republican value of *civisme*. In contrast, behaviour by the citizen which displays racism or what is referred to as *communautarisme* (attachment to a particular community) are regarded as examples of *incivisme*.[63]

Arguably the clearest (and most persuasive) recent account of this conception of citizenship has been provided by Dominique Schnapper, now a member of the French Constitutional Council. Schnapper's central idea is that the Republic is to be conceived as a 'community of citizens'.[64] Crucially, Schnapper distinguishes the nation from the ethnic group, seeing the former solely as a political entity. She is thus able to argue not only that the nation is 'more open to other than all forms of ethnicity' but also that cultural homogeneity is not necessary for the Republic to exist. 'In return', she tells us, 'it is a necessary condition for the existence of the nation that its citizens accept the idea that there exists a political domain independent of their particular interests and that they must respect the rules governing its operation'. The Republic defines itself as 'an attempt through citizenship to transcend particularistic adherences', be they biological, historical, economic, social, religious or cultural. In short, according to this conception of citizenship, membership of the political community is open to all those who are prepared to accept its rules and values, irrespective of birth. It rests upon the possibility of political and cultural integration.[65]

What, finally, of the challenges faced by the French republican tradition? And what of its capacity to adapt to new circumstances or issues? First, we should recognise that republicanism has long felt itself to be under challenge. The late nineteenth-century philosophical dominance of neo-Kantians such as Renouvier and Vacherot was displaced by Henri Bergson, and to the point that Julien Benda in his famous text of 1927, *La Trahison des clercs*, denounced a whole generation of French writers for their abandonment of universalism and their embrace of a nationalistic particularism. After the Second World War, the twin movements of decolonisation and feminism (as articulated by Frantz Fanon and Simone de Beauvoir) portrayed republican universalism as a form of white, male domination. Moreover, it has long been argued that the institutions that foster republican integration have for some time ceased to work efficiently. The inter-war years, for example, characterised by both economic and political crises, did little to enhance the prestige of republican political institutions and severely challenged the assumption that, within the Republic, it was possible for ordinary people to succeed and to climb the social ladder. Nevertheless, in the situation of ideological meltdown that followed the disintegration of the Soviet Bloc and the emergence of a recognisably global, free-market economy, there took place a remarkable resurgence of republican sentiment and reassertion of republican values. Cast adrift from her traditional moorings and wounded by the deceptions of the present, France seemed to turn in upon herself and to find comfort in what at times amounted to a nostalgic reaffirmation of a golden age of republicanism.[66]

Today the challenges to republicanism come in various forms. One is to suggest that republicanism as an ideology is no longer capable of motivating the electorate. Another is to suggest that the Republic has not delivered on its promises, that the Republic is a charade. Still another is to suggest that as a political form the Republic has long been tarnished. Instead of the sovereignty of the nation all that remains is government by self-serving elites; instead of democratic institutions there is only Presidential power. Many of these criticisms are of long standing. As proof of the decline of the republican model, people turn to the evidence provided by dwindling electoral turnout and the growing willingness to vote for extremist parties of either the left or the right (cruelly exemplified by the presence of Jean-Marie Le Pen in the second ballot of the 2002 presidential elections as well as by the willingness of large numbers of left-wing voters to lend their support to Trotskyist candidates in the first ballot). They cite mounting levels of crime, violence, homelessness, social fragmentation, and an increasingly individualistic attitude amongst the French population as proof that republican acculturation no longer works.[67] Of recent years both the press and the bookshops have been full of examples of such republican doom and gloom, the pervading sense of pessimism not aided by the highly public humiliation of losing the 2012 Olympic bid to a self-consciously multicultural London.[68]

Beyond this there are a series of other challenges. I shall briefly allude to three of these. The first I shall simply describe as the multicultural challenge.[69] As we have seen, the republican conception of citizenship rests upon the possibility and desirability of integration.[70] For decades this model proved to be highly successful, the Republic fruitfully integrating generations of Poles, Italians and Jews from central and eastern Europe. But, the argument goes, faced with large-scale Muslim immigration, such a goal is today neither possible to attain nor desirable to achieve. So conceived, integration becomes either a form of discrimination and oppression or an impossible dream. To accept such an argument, however, would be to jettison the humanistic, rationalist vision of republicanism. It would also entail the abandonment of the community of citizens and its replacement by the politics of identity. For a decade or more, debate about this issue has all too frequently focused upon the highly symbolic issue of the wearing of the veil by Muslim girls in French state schools. Hard-line republicans have consistently advocated a position of non-compromise and in effect it was this stance that won the day when, in 2004, a law was passed banning all overt displays of religious affiliation from state schools. The protests this new law evoked were as nothing compared with the general conflagration that engulfed the suburbs of most of France's major towns and cities in the late autumn of 2005. To date, although there has been no shortage of commentary and analysis, there has been no general agreement about the causes of the widespread looting and car-burning that night after night filled French television screens and left politicians searching for effective responses. Poor housing, high levels of unemployment amongst young males of immigrant backgrounds, or straightforward negligence on the part of the state, usually figure high on the list of explanations.[71] Significantly, commentators disagree about whether traditional republican strategies should be abandoned to meet what effectively amounts to the ghettoisation of significant sections of France's urban population.[72] There was however no evidence of doubt in the words of President Jacques Chirac. In his television address to the nation on 14 November 2005, he recognised not only that what was at stake was 'our policy of integration' but also that the 'profound malaise' of which recent events were a sign, could only be responded to by remaining 'faithful to the values of France'. To those 'daughters and sons of the Republic' presently expressing their anger, he reaffirmed that 'the duty of the Republic was to offer to each and everyone the same opportunities', specifically with regard to employment. To that end, however, France could not 'compromise' its basic principles of equality and solidarity. Discrimination, in short, would not be met by positive measures such as job quotas. 'We belong', he told his audience, 'to a great Nation, as shown by her History but also by the principles upon which she is founded. A Nation which radiates across the world.' That the principal light shining from France across the world at that moment was the glow of thousands of burnt-out cars and public buildings seemed not to have diminished President Chirac's faith in old republican mantras.

Next comes the challenge of Europe and of European integration. For all its universalistic pretensions and aspirations French republicanism has focused upon a vision of a national community. It is to this community that the citizen owes his or her loyalty; it is within the sphere of the republican nation state that the citizen is called upon to play an active role. In an environment where loyalties are becoming increasingly transnational and where an increasing number of problems require crossnational solutions, can such a conception of citizenship transcend the nation state or is it increasingly redundant? Again, the omens do not look especially promising. In May 2005 the French electorate voted decisively to reject the proposed EU constitution in a referendum that amply demonstrated the depth of anti-EU sentiment, thereby bringing the European project to a shuddering halt. From that moment the right-wing government headed by Dominique de Villepin did not hesitate to clothe itself in the rhetoric of economic patriotism and national champions (or to celebrate the revival in fortunes of the French football team).

The third challenge I will simply identify as being that of globalisation. The point here is simply this. The French Republic has built up a distinctive model of both social provision and economic management which to date has remained remarkably impervious to the demands of economic liberalisation of the last three decades. The state in France retains a strong presence within the economy; it employs approximately 30 per cent of the working population; it spends somewhere in the region of 50 per cent of GNP; and remains the provider of generous pensions and other social benefits. Two problems can be identified here. The first is that the French economy is being out-performed by many other rival economies (including that of Ireland) whilst mounting public debt is reaching what will soon be unsustainable levels. Remember that France has persistently been in breach of European Central Bank regulations with regard to both its public-sector borrowing requirement and its national debt. High levels of long-term unemployment and relatively low levels of economic growth are just two of the most obvious manifestations of recent economic failure.[73] The French model, in short, is coming under increasing pressure from the global economy. For some, if not for all, reform or perish looks to be the only alternative. But reform will pose a fundamental challenge to the republican ideal of social solidarity. Secondly, there is an argument that the French social model is no longer fit for purpose. French academics, amongst others, seem to react instinctively against any adverse commentary upon the French social model by foreign observers, but they would do well to consult a recent analysis provided by Canadian Timothy B. Smith, entitled *France in Crisis: Welfare, Inequality and Globalisation since 1980*.[74] Smith charges that globalisation is used as 'the big excuse' for France's difficulties (the reality is that they are home-grown and the result of political failure) and that the language of solidarity is a cloak for the defence of corporatist self-interest amongst public-sector workers. The French social model, he contends, has done little to tackle persistent inequalities and protects the privileges – or 'rent-seeking' – of those 'inside' the system. Public-sector pensions, largely funded by the tax payer, constitute by far the largest item of government expenditure. Moreover, the French welfare state does not serve the interests of immigrants, young people, and women. As Smith writes: 'The French welfare state is a middle-and upper-middle-class welfare state, not a working-class welfare state. It is a pensioners' state, not a pro-youth state. It is a protection system for those already employed, not a full-employment state. It is concerned to protect jobs, not in allowing or helping the market to create (and destroy) them in the first place.'[75] In short, beneath the French Republic's rhetoric of solidarity lies only the self-interest of those either in work or enjoying the benefits of a state pension.

What resources are available within French republicanism to respond to these challenges? Here it is not possible to reach a definitive verdict. I would however suggest that there is evidence to suggest that republicanism can respond to the challenge of ethnic and religious diversity in a constructive and innovative way. The establishment of educational priority zones would be one such example. The question would be just how far republicanism could and should go on this road of compromise. On Europe, clearly much will depend upon the evolution of the European community itself, but again it does not seem to be beyond the bounds of possibility that something resembling a republican conception of citizenship could be transposed upon a European framework. Indeed, this might be the very thing required to give a sense of belonging to the citizens of a multiethnic and multinational Europe. On the issue of market pressures to reform, I am less optimistic about the ability of French republicanism to respond. The demonstrations in the spring of 2006 (largely organised by students) were not only a major humiliation for the governing right-wing coalition but also seemed to testify to an unwillingness on the part of the electorate to contemplate even minor reforms. It is hard to know how the French state will be able to square the circle of poor economic performance and generous social provision. My guess, in other words, is that it is less the challenges of Europe or of multiculturalism that might derail republicanism in France but straightforward financial realities.

Notes

1   For a general account see Claude Nicolet, *L'idée républicaine en France* (Paris: Gallimard, 1982).

2 See Sudhir Hazareesingh, *Political Traditions in Modern France* (Oxford: Oxford University Press, 1994), pp. 65–97.

3 On the latter see Sudhir Hazreesingh, *The Legend of Napoleon* (London: Granta Books, 2004).

4 It has long been recognised that the reality of French state-building and centralisation is more complex that the rhetoric of Jacobinism would have us believe: for a short examination of this issue see Yves Mény, 'The Republic and its territory: the persistence and the adaptation of founding myths', in Sudhir Hazareesingh (ed.), *The Jacobin Legacy in Modern France* (Oxford: Oxford University Press, 2002), pp. 183–95.

5 See in particular Pierre Rosanvallon, *Le Modèle politique français: La société civile contre le jacobinisme de 1789 à nos jours* (Paris: Seuil, 2004).

6 For what might be called the pre-history of republicanism see Johnson Kent Wright, 'The idea of a republican constitution in Old Régime France', in Martin van Gelderen and Quentin Skinner (eds), *Republicanism: A Shared European Heritage Vol. I: Republicanism and Constitutionalism in Early Modern Europe* (Cambridge: Cambridge University Press, 2002), pp. 289–306.

7 See Serge Berstein and Michel Winock (eds), *L'Invention de la démocratie* (Paris: Seuil, 2003).

8 See in particular Patrice Gueniffey, *Le Nombre et la Raison: La Révolution française et les élections* (Paris: EHESS, 1993). Gueniffey's conclusion is that during the French Revolution electoral procedures were designed not to reflect a variety of opinion but the rational expression of consensus.

9 See Jacob Levy, 'Beyond Publius: Montesquieu, liberal republicanism and the small-republic thesis', *History of Political Thought* XXVII (2006): 50–90.

10 See John Bell, *French Constitutional Law* (Oxford: Clarendon Press, 1992).

11 'Tableau de France' in Michelet, *Oeuvres complètes, Vol IV: Histoire de France* (Paris: Flammarion, 1974), pp. 331–84.

12 Ibid., p. 381.

13 Ibid., p. 384.

14 Sophie Wahnich, *L'impossible citoyen: L'étranger dans le discours de la Révolution française* (Paris: Albin Michel, 1997).

15 Mona Ozouf, 'L'idée républicain et l'interprétation du passé national', *Annales* 53 (1998): 1075–87.

16 See Pierre Bouretz, *La République et l'universel* (Paris: Gallimard, 2000) and Naomi Schor, 'The crisis of French universalism', *Yale French Studies* 100 (2001): 43–64.

17 Colin Jones, *The Great Nation: France from Louis XV to Napoleon* (London: Penguin, 2003).

18 Ibid., p. xiii.

19 Marc Fumaroli, *Quand l'Europe parlait Français* (Paris: Fallois, 2001). For a succinct statement of what was taken to be the superiority and acknowledged universality of the French language see Antoine de Rivarol, *De l'Universalité de la langue française* (Paris: Bailly, 1784).

20 On Sieyès, see William H. Sewell, *A Rhetoric of Bourgeois Revolution: The Abbé Sieyès and What is the Third Estate?* (Durham and London: Duke University Press, 1994). According to Sewell, Sieyès's pamphlet 'not only set forth the

essential principles adopted by the new state – the destruction of all privileges, the establishment of national sovereignty and equality before the law – but elaborated the political strategy by which the political revolution was accomplished', ibid., p. 7. Reference can here be made to a similar text to that of the Abbé Sieyès, Charles-Philippe-Toussaint Guiraudet's, *Qu'est-ce que la nation et qu'est-ce que la France?* (Paris: EDHIS, 1991 [1789]). Guiraudet wanted to argue that France should not be seen as being composed of Estates and Provinces but simply as a physical space inhabited by an 'aggregation' of twenty-five million individuals. It is interesting to note that Guiraudet makes constant comparison with the English example. The English case should not be copied because it would reintroduce hereditary power but he does concede that in England the counties at least (unlike their provincial counterparts in France) do not have the pretension to see themselves as 'distinct States'. The whole emphasis of the text, in other words, falls on overcoming the 'imagined divisions' which separate the French as individuals from one another.

21 On these developments see Jacques Godechot, *La Grande Nation: l'expansion révolutionnaire de la France dans le monde de 1789 à 1799* (Paris: Aubier, 1956).

22 Pierre Nora, 'Nation', in F. Furet and M. Ozouf (eds), *Dictionnaire critique de la révolution française* (Paris: Flammarion, 1988), p. 806.

23 Possibly the clearest statement of this argument can be found in Conor Cruise O'Brien 'Nationalism and the French Revolution', in Geoffrey Best (ed.), *The Permanent Revolution: The French Revolution and its Legacy 1789–1989* (London: Fontana, 1988), pp. 17–48. O'Brien speaks of the 'Spinoza effect': 'the vacuum created by the disappearance of belief in a personal God, and the need to fill that vacuum'. The literature in English alone on the subject of nations and nationalism is vast. Anthony Smith in particular has produced a considerable body of literature on this subject.

24 René Rémond, 'La fille aînée de l'Eglise', in Pierre Nora (ed.), *Les Lieux de Mémoire*, Vol. III (Paris: Gallimard, 1984), pp. 4321–51.

25 Ibid., p. 4335.

26 For an examination of one consequence of this faith in the special mission of France see Tony Judt, *Past Imperfect: French Intellectuals, 1944–1956* (Berkeley and Los Angeles: California University Press, 1992).

27 Schor, 'The crisis of French universalism', p. 44.

28 See Douglas Johnson, 'The two Frances; the historical debate', in Vincent Wright (ed.), *Conflict and Consensus in France* (London: Cass, 1979), pp. 3–10. More generally see Pierre Birnbaum, *'La France aux Français': Histoire des Haines Nationalistes* (Paris: Seuil, 2006).

29 See Maurice Larkin, 'Fraternity, solidarity, sociability: the grass roots of the grand Orient de France (1900–1926)', in Hazareesingh (ed.), *The Jacobin Legacy*, pp. 89–114.

30 See Jacqueline Lalouette, *La République anticléricale* (Paris: Seuil, 2002).

31 See Vincent Duclert, *Alfred Dreyfus: l'honneur d'un patriote* (Paris: Fayard, 2006).

32 See Dominique de Villepin (ed.), *1905, la séparation des Eglises et de l'Etat* (Paris: Perrin, 2004) and Jacqueline Lalouette, *La Séparation des Eglises et de l'Etat* (Paris: Seuil, 2005).

33 See, for example, Pierre Birnbaum, *The Idea of France* (Hill and Wang: New York, 1998), pp. 207–79; Joseph Macé-Scaron, *La Tentation communautaire* (Paris: Plon, 2001); Jeanne-Hélène Kaltanbach and Michèle Tribalet, *La République et l'Islam* (Paris: Gallimard, 2002); Manuel Valls, *La Laïcité en face* (Paris: Desclée de Brouwer, 2006); Régis Debray, *Ce que nous voile le voile* (Paris: Gallimard, 2004); and Patrick Weil, *La République et sa diversité: Immigration, intégration, discriminations* (Paris: Seuil, 2005).

34 See Jacques Godechot (ed.), *Les Constitutions de France depuis 1789* (Paris: Flammarion, 1995) and Lucien Jaume (ed.), *Les Déclarations des droits de l'homme* (Paris: Flammarion, 1989).

35 See Norman Hampson, *The Perfidy of Albion: French Perceptions of England during the French Revolution* (Houndmills: Macmillan, 1998).

36 See Michel Winock, *L'agonie de la IVe République: 13 mai 1958* (Paris: Seuil, 2006).

37 See Bernard Chantebout, *La Constitution française; propos pour un débat* (Paris: Dalloz, 1992).

38 See Jean-Clément Martin, *Violence et Révolution: Essai sur la naissance d'un mythe national* (Paris: Seuil, 2006).

39 See most recently David Andress, *The Terror: Civil War in the French Revolution* (London: Little, Brown, 2005) and Jean-Clément Martin, *Violence et Révolution: Essai sur la naissance d'un mythe national* (Paris: Seuil, 2006).

40 Marc Lahmer, *La Constitution Américaine dans le débat français, 1795–1848* (Paris: L'Harmattan, 2001).

41 See Pamela Pilbeam, *Republicanism in Nineteenth-Century France 1814–1871* (London: Macmillan, 1995).

42 See Serge Berstein, 'Le modèle républicain: une culture politique syncrétique', in Berstein (ed.), *Les Cultures politiques en France* (Paris: Seuil, 1999), pp. 113–43. For a clear expression of the political logic that informed this compromise see Paul Lacombe, *La République et la liberté* (Paris: Le Chevalier, 1870) and Ernest Duvergier de Hauranne, *La République conservatrice* (Paris: Germer-Baillière, 1873). The contrary position, that of the disillusioned republicans, is seen in Louis Blanc, *Histoire de la Constitution du 25 fevrier 1875* (Paris: Charpentier, 1882).

43 See Jean-Marie Mayeur, *Les débuts de la IIIe République 1871–1898* (Paris: Seuil, 1973), pp. 108–10.

44 Jean-Pierre Machelon, *La République contre les libertés?* (Paris: Presses de la Fondation Nationale des Sciences Politiques, 1976). This is not a view fully shared by Philip Nord. If he accepts that 'French republican culture concealed a hidden, authoritarian self', operating with what he terms 'certain exclusions', he nevertheless contends that in the areas of education and civil liberties the achievements of the Third Republic in this period were considerable. '[T]he Third Republic', he argues, was 'a democratic regime that sprang from and then nurtured a resurrected civil society': see Nord, *The Republican Moment: Struggles for Democracy in Nineteenth-Century France* (Cambridge, MA: Harvard University Press, 1995), pp. 246–53. See also Pierre Rosanvallon's fascinating discussion of these issues in *La démocratie inachevée: Histoire de la souveraineté du peuple en France* (Paris: Gallimard, 2000), pp. 313–35.

45 See Mona Ozouf, *L'école de la France: Essais sur la Révolution, l'utopie et l'enseignement* (Paris: Gallimard, 1984); Yves Deloye, *Ecole et Citoyenneté* (Paris: Presses de Sciences Po, 1995); Katherine Auspitz, *The Radical Bourgeoisie: The Ligue de l'Enseignement and the Origins of the Third Republic 1866–1885* (Cambridge: Cambridge University Press, 2002).

46 See for example Venita Datta, *Birth of a National Icon: The Literary Avant-Garde and the Origins of the Intellectual in France* (Albany, NY: State University of New York Press, 1999).

47 See Eugen Weber, *Peasants into Frenchmen: The Modernisation of Rural France 1870–1914* (London: Chatto and Windus, 1979).

48 See Véronique De Rudder, Christian Poiret, and François Vourch, *L'Inégalité raciste. L'Universalité républicaine à l'épreuve* (Paris: PUF, 2000) and Nicolas Bancel, Pascal Blanchard and Françoise Vergès, *La République coloniale: Essai sur une utopie* (Paris: Albin Michel, 2003).

49 Alain Chatriot and Michel Coste, 'Les Timbres-Poste', in Vincent Duclert and Christophe Prochasson (eds), *Dictionnaire critique de la République* (Paris: Flammarion, 2002), pp. 972–7.

50 Maurice Agulhon has produced three studies: *Marianne au combat: L'imagerie et la symbolique républicaines de 1789 a 1880* (Paris: Flammarion, 1979); *Marianne au pouvoir: L'imagerie et la symbolique républicaines de 1880 a 1914* (Paris: Flammarion, 1989); and *Les metamorphoses de Marianne: l'imagerie et la symbolique républicaines de 1914 a nos jours* (Paris: Flammarion, 2001).

51 See Steven Laurence Kaplan, *Farewell, Revolution* (Ithaca: Cornell University Press, 1995), 2 vols.

52 Michel Borgetto, *La Devise "Liberté, Egalité, Fraternité"* (Paris: PUF, 1997) and Mona Ozouf, 'Liberté, égalité, fraternité', in Nora (ed.), *Les Lieux de mémoire*, Vol. III, pp. 4353–88.

53 See Sudhir Hazareesingh, *Intellectual Founders of the Republic: Five Studies in Nineteenth-Century French Political Thought* (Oxford: Oxford University Press, 2001).

54 See Jeremy Jennings, 'Communism', in C. Flood and L. Bell (eds), *Political Ideologies in Contemporary France* (London: Pinter, 1994), pp. 52–72.

55 For example, this had earlier been the view of both Germaine de Staël and Henri Saint-Simon.

56 See, for example, *Sur le principe d'égalité* (Paris: La Documentation française, 1998).

57 See Jacques Donzelot, *Face à l'exclusion: le modèle français* (Paris: Esprit, 1991); Pierre Rosanvallon, *La Nouvelle Question Sociale: repenser l'Etat-providence* (Paris: Seuil, 1995); Pierre Rosanvallon, *La Nouvelle Critique Sociale* (Paris: Seuil, 2006); Alain Renaut, *Modèle social: la chimère française* (Paris: Textuel, 2006).

58 See for example Léon Bourgeois, *Solidarité* (Paris: Armand Colin, 1896). On the philosophy of Solidarity see Jean-Fabien Spitz, *Le Moment Républicain en France* (Paris: Gallimard, 2005).

59 Celestin Bouglé, *Le Solidarisme* (Paris: Giard et Brière, 1907), p. 1.

60 Timothy B. Smith, *France in Crisis: Welfare, Inequality and Globalisation since 1980* (Cambridge: Cambridge University Press, 2004).

61 See Alain-Gérard Slama, 'L'Etat sans citoyens', *Pouvoirs*, 84 (1998): 89–98 and Marc Sadoun, 'L'Individu et le Citoyen', *Pouvoirs*, 94 (2000): 5–17.

62 See however Sophie Duchesne, *Citoyenneté à la française* (Paris: Presses de Sciences Po, 1997).

63 French republicanism has a long tradition of providing manuals intended to instruct the individual citizen on appropriately republican forms of behaviour. For the latest example, see *Guide Républicain: L'idée républicaine aujourd'hui* (Paris: Delagrave, 2004).

64 Dominique Schnapper, *La Communauté des citoyens: sur l'idée moderne de nation* (Paris: Gallimard, 1998).

65 See here Schnapper's earlier work *La France de l'intégration* (Paris: Gallimard, 1991). For a more recent statement of Schnapper's views in English, see 'Making citizens in an increasingly complex society: Jacobinism revisited', in Hazareesingh (ed.), *The Jacobin Legacy*, pp. 196–216.

66 A recent expression of these sentiments would be André Bellon, Inès Fauconner, Jérémy Mercier, and Henri Pena-Ruiz, *Mémento du républicain* (Paris: Fayard, 2006).

67 Michel Winock, 'L'intégration fonctionne-t-elle encore?', *L'Histoire* (229) 1999, pp. 58–61.

68 Fairly typical of the genre are the following texts: Nicolas Baverez, *La France qui tombe* (Paris: Perrin, 2003); Jacques Julliard, *Le malheur français* (Paris: Flammarion, 2005); Pierre Lellouche, *Illusions Gauloises* (Paris: Grasset, 2006); Nicolas Baverez, *Nouveau monde, Vieille France* (Paris: Perrin, 2006).

69 For a broader discussion of this theme see my 'Citizenship, republicanism and multiculturalism in contemporary France', *British Journal of Political Science*, 30 (2000): 781–95.

70 The best account in English remains Adrian Favell, *Philosophies of Integration: Immigration and the Idea of Citizenship in France and Britain* (Houndmills: Macmillan, 1998). See also Vincent Viet, *La France immigrée: Constructions d'une politique 1914–1997* (Paris: Fayard, 1998). There is no shortage of material examining this theme.

71 See Hugues Lagrange and Marco Oberti, *Emeutes Urbaines et Protestations: Une singularité française* (Paris: Sciences Po, 2006); Véronique Le Goaziou and Laurent Mucchielli, *Quand les banlieues brûles ... Retour sur les émeutes de novembre 2005* (Paris: La Découverte, 2006); Yann Moulier Boutang, *La Révolte des banlieues ou les habits nus de la République* (Paris: Editions Amsterdam, 2005).

72 See the discussion organised by *Le Monde*: 'Des cités à la cité', *Le Monde*, 3 March 2006.

73 See Alain Lefebvre and Dominique Méda, *Faut-il brûler le modèle social français?* (Paris: Seuil, 2006).

74 Smith, *France in Crisis*.

75 Ibid., p. 22.

5　Theorising French republican secularism

Cécile Laborde[1]

There is no single model for the proper role of religious institutions and beliefs in a republic. The identity of the Republic of Ireland was historically forged around the mobilising force of Catholicism. The American Republic rejected European-style official establishment and embraced religious pluralism. The French Republic, for its part, opted for a more radical separation between state and religion, the outcome of decades of conflict with the hegemonic Catholic Church. As a result, French secularism – or *laïcité* – is often suspected of harbouring an anti-religious, intolerant and illiberal prejudice, as betrayed recently by the polemic over the law banning religious signs (particularly Muslim headscarves) in schools. This piece shows that – on one interpretation at least[2] – French republican secularism is compatible with liberal principles of religious freedom and toleration. Relegating religion to the private sphere and establishing a non-sectarian, neutral public sphere is shown to be one effective way of guaranteeing the free exercise of religious freedoms for all and to secure common membership in an egalitarian political community transcending particular beliefs and allegiances. The republican doctrine of separation, therefore, furthers the liberal principles of freedom of religion, equality of respect and state neutrality. However, *laïcité* offers a distinctively *republican* interpretation of the requirements of liberal neutrality. It endorses a more expansive conception of the public sphere than liberalism, as well as a thicker construal of the 'public selves' which make up the citizens of the Republic. So, crucially, state schools are seen to be part of the public sphere and pupils, as potential citizens, are required to exercise restraint in the expression of their religious beliefs. The ban on Muslim headscarves in schools, on this view, helps protect the neutral public sphere from religious interference and secure a system of equal religious rights for all. In other words, limits on the exercise of religious liberties in the public sphere are necessary conditions for the maintenance of a system of equal liberties for all. The key difference between liberal secularism and republican *laïcité* is that the latter makes greater demands on state institutions (in terms of abstention and non-discrimination) and on its citizens (in terms of restraint).

Laïcité, like many doctrines of separation between state and religion, contains both an *institutional doctrine of separation*, which outlines what separation means for governmental institutions, and a *doctrine of conscience*, which prescribes norms of conduct both for religious organisations and for individual citizens.[3] When applied to state schools, the separation doctrine and the doctrine of conscience have combined to justify banning on religious signs in schools.

Laïcité as a separation doctrine

On 11 December 1905, republicans in power abolished the Concordat which, since 1801, had regulated the relationships between the French state and 'recognized religions' and had, in practice, entrenched the political and social power of the dominant Catholic Church. The first two articles of the 1905 Law of Separation between Church and State read:

> Article 1. The Republic ensures freedom of conscience. It guarantees the free exercise of religions.
> Article 2. It neither recognises nor subsidises any religion.

The principle of separation between church and state has since been recognised as a quasi-constitutional principle, and is implicitly referred to in Article 1 of the 1946 Constitution, according to which 'France is an indivisible, *laïque*, democratic and social republic'.[4] The 1905 Law of Separation embodies a classical ideal of liberal separation between state and religion, underpinned by an individualistic and egalitarian conception of justice as best pursued through state abstention from religious affairs. In order to clarify the sense in which the Separation Law embodies an ideal of egalitarian justice as state neutrality, I identify four strands that make up the separation doctrine: (i) libertarian, (ii) egalitarian, (iii) agnostic and (iv) individualistic.[5] When combined, they are shown to lend themselves to a conception of (v) formal, rather than substantive, equality between religions. French *laïcité*, in this sense, tallies with liberal principles of formal equality before the law and 'the privatisation of differences'.[6] Where, however, *laïcité* slightly diverges from such egalitarian liberalism is in its republican emphasis on (vi) the strict preservation of the autonomy of the secular public sphere, which is regulated by (vii) an independent ethics, and more expansively constructed than standard liberal understandings would allow.

(i) A libertarian principle

The state permits the practice of any religion, within limits prescribed by the requirements of public order and the protection of basic rights. It neither promotes nor combats particular religious beliefs, and refrains from interfering in the internal affairs of religious institutions. The principle of religious freedom was first (ambiguously) asserted during the 1789 Revolution: in the wording of Article 10 of the Declaration of the Rights of Man, 'no-one should be persecuted [*inquiété*] for their opinions, even religious ones'. A century later, the principles both of religious freedom and religious pluralism were entrenched by the Third Republic: the 1905 Law of Separation graphically symbolised the removal of state control of religion, and the recognition of the pluralist structure of background religious institutions in civil society.

The principle of religious freedom is 'libertarian' in the narrow sense that it chiefly requires that the state *refrain* from interfering in religious affairs. Thus Article 1 of the 1905 law ('the republic *guarantees* the free exercise of religions') is typically understood by official republicans not to mandate positive state aid to religions: the exercise of religious freedoms should simply not be unduly constrained or burdened by the state. Religions should be allowed to flourish in the private sphere without state interference, according to the zeal and organisational capacities of their adherents and the appeal of their dogma. Only in particular cases should the state provide financial aid to support the exercise of religious freedoms. For example, the 1905 law authorised the public funding of chaplaincies in 'closed' institutions such as the army, prisons and boarding schools, so as to guarantee rights of religious exercise to those physically unable to attend normal religious services. But this is a rare justifiable exception to the general principle of state abstention. On the whole, therefore, the combination of the provisions of Articles 1 and 2 of the 1905 Separation Law is not deemed to generate a conflict of principles similar to that between the 'non-establishment' and the 'free exercise' clause of the First Amendment of the US Constitution.[7] In American jurisprudence, the protection of the 'free exercise' clause sometimes requires relaxing the 'establishment' clause, by compelling the state to step in positively to guarantee that adequate provision is available for the exercise of (notably minority) religious rights. French official republicans generally opine that non-establishment and state abstention are in themselves sufficient guarantees of the free exercise of religious freedoms.

(ii) An egalitarian principle

Minimally understood, the egalitarian principle requires that the state does not give preference to one religion over another: the equality referred to here is equality between believers of all faiths. This goes beyond the libertarian principle, as the state can theoretically allow unlimited religious freedom and still treat some religions preferentially. Thus French republicans typically refer to the 'weak establishment'[8] of the Anglican Church as falling short of the egalitarian principle.[9] Even though religious freedoms and religious pluralism are fully protected in the United Kingdom, establishment in itself confers material and symbolic privileges to adherents to the majority confession. In France, under the Concordat, throughout the nineteenth century, Catholicism was similarly recognised as 'the religion of the great majority of the French' (without, however, being the official religion of the state), a status which conferred benefits unavailable to the other 'recognised religions', Protestantism and Judaism. The 1905 law aimed to place all religious institutions on an equal plane.

Naturally, equality between all religions essentially meant the abolition of the privileges of the dominant church. However, strong hostility to the Separation Law by the Vatican, and reluctance by French Catholic authorities to implement it, led republicans to make a number of concessions (notably allowing free use by Catholics of state-owned churches).[10] Such historical compromises, however, are not deemed to generate obligations on the part of the state to extend such benefits to religions, such as Islam, which were not present on French soil (at least in mainland France) in 1905. They are seen as minor, historically contingent, infringements of the separation principle. For example, free use of state-owned religious buildings was only possible because Church property belonged to the state in the first place. Today, to allow public support towards the construction of Muslim mosques, for instance, would violate the spirit and the letter of the law, which postulated that, *from 1905 onwards*, all religions would be treated identically – none would be subsidised by the state. Therefore, official republicans urge the strict respect of the separation principle and reject the idea of the 'historical compensation' of Islam as incoherent and spurious.[11] In the words of a recent official report, 'drawing on the principle of equality, the *laïque* state grants no public privilege to any religion, and its relationship with them is characterised by legal separation'.[12]

(iii) An agnostic principle

This third principle, understood minimally without reference to its theological connotations, implies that the state should neither favour nor disfavour religion as such: it should be 'agnostic' – neutral by ignorance – vis-à-vis the respective claims of believers and non-believers. This is often contrasted to the American situation where, in spite of official non-establishment, a diffuse religious culture permeates public institutions.

For French official republicans, when the state introduces religious practices and symbols into its institutions, even of a theistic nature (for example, when it requires state officials to swear belief in God), it implicitly puts pressure on non-believers to conform, and therefore fails to treat them with equal respect. Only a fully secular public culture can adequately respect liberty of conscience, understood as permitting 'free adhesion to a religion and the refusal of any religion.'[13] The 1905 law explicitly put an end to the official recognition of the 'social utility of religion' recognised by the Concordat. Public culture did not need to rely on transcendental foundations: for the first time, the possibility of a fully secular public morality was adduced. Steps towards the secularisation of the public sphere had already been taken in the 1880s. For example, communal cemeteries were secularised: religious signs such as crosses were removed and only discreet symbols were allowed on individual tombstones. Religious marriages are ignored by French law: only civil marriages have legal validity. Exemption from military service may be granted on non-religious conscientious grounds. The agnostic principle, in sum, requires the state not to single out religious believers for special treatment, and to ensure that the public sphere is bereft of potentially exclusionary religious references and symbols. The 'naked public square' best expresses the ideal of equality between all citizens.

(iv) An individualistic principle

The individualistic principle stipulates that (i) individuals should be treated identically by the state, 'with no distinction made on the basis of origin, race or religion' (Article 2 of the 1958 Constitution) and (ii) if rights are attributed to groups, they should not override the individual rights of their members. Principle (i) is the core of 'difference-blind' liberalism, which provides each individual with a uniform set of rights regardless of her culture, identity or beliefs.[14] The French state goes as far as forbidding the collection of statistics about racial origins or religious affiliation. The use of ethnic categories (such as 'White', 'Black' or 'Arab') is banned in official discourse, and there are no reliable official statistics on the number of Catholics, Protestants, Jews and Muslims in France. The ban on religious classification graphically symbolises the refusal to allow 'morally irrelevant' religious affiliation either to confer a benefit or impose a burden on individual citizens. Principle (ii), which asserts the primacy of individual rights over group rights, should be qualified, notably in relation to religion. Religious institutions are not merely aggregates of private individuals: they are inevitably communal institutions which generate their own set of duties and obligations for their members. An overly individualist construal of religious organisation (one, for example, which would require churches to be democratically organised) would clearly undermine the whole point of religious freedom, which entails respect for church autonomy. Thus the 1905 Law recognises the hierarchical structure of the Roman Catholic Church.

Yet it is undeniable that the official republican reading of *laïcité* is strongly influenced, on different levels, by the wider individualistic philosophy of the 1789 Revolution, which strongly asserted both principle (i) and principle (ii). The 'emancipation' of Jews provided an early, paradigmatic model of the individualistic model of citizenship which was substituted for the mosaic of corporate laws inherited from medieval society. In the famous words of *député* Clermont-Tonnerre, 'Jews must be refused everything *qua* nation, and granted everything *qua* individuals ... They must no longer constitute a political body or order in the state: they acquire citizenship individually'.[15] Thus the French government recently requested a 'reservation' of Article 27 (on minority rights) of the International Covenant on Civil and Political Rights, on the grounds that 'France is a country in which there are no minorities, and where the chief principle is non-discrimination'. Hence the rejection of group rights: individual rights such as religious freedom, freedom of speech, association and so forth are sufficient to ensure that individuals are free to practice their religion and express their cultural identities in the private sphere, without express public recognition. Multiculturalism – the public recognition of collective identities and the attribution of special rights to communities – is castigated as a return to the mass of anomalies and special cases that entrenched privileges and inequalities under the *Ancien Régime*.

(v) A principle of fairness

In what sense, then, does the separation doctrine articulated in the last four sections embody an ideal of fairness? The difference-blind and abstentionist neutrality of the state is fair to individuals because it treats them identically, regardless of their particular faith, identity and affiliations. Official republicans deny that a situation in which religious groups fare differently under a neutral state is inherently unfair. The state establishes fair background conditions – a religiously neutral public sphere – and lets the cards fall where they may, as it were, instead of pursuing the chimerical objective of achieving 'equality' between religious groups – whatever this means. Such arguments were recently reiterated in response to a Muslim request that public authorities exceptionally subsidise the buildings of mosques, to remedy the radically insufficient provision of adequate Muslim religious facilities. What would be unfair would be for public authorities to treat Muslims differently from other religious groups – for example, to refuse to grant planning permission for the building of mosques to local Muslim communities. But as long as the Republic guarantees to Muslims the full and fair application of the law, republicans should not worry about how successful particular religious groups are in translating into specific outcomes the equal set of opportunities offered to them.

Thus far, I have spelt out the implications of the separation doctrine as a doctrine of formal equality. So far, we might say, so liberal. For *laïcité* closely resembles the anti-multiculturalist, egalitarian liberalism recently defended by Brian Barry.[16] There are, in addition, two further features which make *laïcité* a distinctively *republican* interpretation of liberalism, influenced by Rousseauist Jacobinism and refined by the founders of the Third Republic. The reluctance to grant public recognition to differences – religious or cultural – appears all the more tough-minded in light both of the relative 'thickness' of the public sphere in France and the claim by the state to embody an independent secular ethics. Both combine to make the 'public' identity of citizenship an expansively constructed identity, and one that is more discrepant from the 'private' identity of citizens than liberals would allow.

(vi) A homogeneous public identity

All separation doctrines are founded on a distinction between the public and the private spheres; what distinguishes *laïcité* is the relatively expansive construal of the former in relation to the latter. This should be related to the French 'state tradition'.[17] Many historical factors combined in France to ensconce the view that 'the state' stands for a homogeneous, autonomous public domain: the Roman-law influenced doctrine of state sovereignty elaborated after the religious wars of the sixteenth century, the struggles of the absolutist monarchy to shake off the domination of the Vatican, the need to forge national unity out of disparate regional, corporate, and religious traditions, and the emergence of a central bureaucracy with a distinctive mission and ethos. The Rousseau-influenced revolutionary hostility to intermediary groups and 'factions' – associated with privileges, divisiveness and corruption – shaped a view of republican democracy as unitary, permanently fragile and under threat. The public sphere was to be protected from the interference of particular loyalties, identities or groups, lest it allow the 'general will' to disaggregate into myriad conflicting private wills.

It is, however, the struggles of the state to establish its political hegemony against a domineering Catholic Church still wedded to the pre-revolutionary order that shaped most deeply the expansive and unitary *laïque* public sphere in the nineteenth and early twentieth centuries. With *laïcité* and the separation of the religious and political spheres, the republican state partly took over the spiritual mission previously pursued by the Catholic Church. As republican philosopher Charles Renouvier lucidly foresaw in 1872, 'let us be aware that the separation between Church and

State signifies the organisation of the moral and educational state'.[18] Hence the central importance of education to *laïcité*. If the Republic was to create 'citizens' out of 'believers', it had to engage in a strong formative project, aimed at the inculcation of the public values of democratic and egalitarian citizenship, and introduce an alternative set of civic symbols into the public sphere, so as to lead citizens to endorse a robust public identity capable of transcending more particular religious, cultural and class loyalties.[19] What was, then, this public identity based upon?

(vii) An independent public ethic

Charles Taylor has suggestively argued that a project of identifying shared political values that all citizens can endorse, whatever their particular *comprehensive* conceptions of the good, is at the heart of the tradition of western democratic secularism. He identifies three 'modes of secularism': first, the 'common ground' approach, based on converging but religiously derived precepts of morality shared by all Christian sects; second, the 'independent ethic' approach, seeking to abstract from religious beliefs altogether and rely on general features of the human condition. He argues that both approaches are unsuited to contemporary pluralist societies, the first because of its narrow Christian roots, and the second because of its hidden secularist bias. Rawls's 'overlapping consensus' approach seems to him to be a third, truly 'free-standing' conception which can nonetheless be endorsed from a variety of – both secular and religious – perspectives.[20]

It has been rightly suggested that 'French republican secularism is the clearest expression of the second, 'independent ethic' mode of secularism'.[21] In 1910, leading republican Ferdinand Buisson claimed that France was the only country that had tried to found a morality outside of religion and of metaphysics.[22] The French tradition of the autonomy of the state, complemented after the Revolution by the republican ideal of a self-governing people democratically establishing the terms of its political constitution, strongly rejected the 'heteronomy' involved in subjecting political authority to religious institutions, transcendental foundations and revealed truth.[23] More specifically, *laïcité* as an ethic independent of religion, based on reason and conscience, had roots in the Enlightenment search for a natural religion and in nineteenth-century attempts to establish the scientific foundations of morality.[24] Jules Ferry, the main promoter of *morale laïque* as the public philosophy of French schools, argued that such morality was 'neutral' in the sense that it was distinct from 'those high metaphysical conceptions ... over which theologians and philosophers have been in discord for six thousand years'. Instead, it appealed to 'a moral truth superior to all changes of doctrine and all controversies'. This truth was compatible with – though not derived from – traditional moral views, what Ferry called 'the good old morality of our fathers'.[25]

As Marcel Gauchet has suggested, the aim was to 'encompass all religions without doing violence to them, from a superior viewpoint', a project which he contrasts to American-style 'civic religion' and its 'common-ground' strategy of finding a theistic 'lowest common denominator'.[26] To put the point differently, *laïcité* was a kind of 'second-order' secularism, a set of rational, moral values upon which a variety of 'first-order' comprehensive views, including religious ones, could converge. Like contemporary liberals, French republicans believed that one could be a religious believer in the private sphere and a citizen in the public sphere. However, because of the particularly robust conception of civic identity endorsed by republicans, the demands of citizenship were fairly stringent ones, as I shall suggest in the next section.

Laïcité as a doctrine of conscience

Laïcité as a doctrine of conscience prescribes norms of conduct for religious organisations, in terms of their internal 'laicisation' (§1) and for individual citizens, in terms of religious restraint in the public sphere (§2).

(i) The 'laïcisation' of religions

The chief obligation that the separation doctrine imposes on religious groups is to respect the law, renounce all claims to political power, and refrain from intervening in public debate in partisan fashion. Historically, *laïcité* was essentially an anti-clerical doctrine in this sense. Throughout the nineteenth century, the Church had used its social power – notably its monopoly of primary education – to preach anti-republican, royalist doctrines, and only accepted republican institutions slowly and reluctantly: while Catholics had tactically 'rallied' to the Republic in 1892, it was only in 1945 that the Assembly of Cardinals and Archbishops of France publicly accepted *laïcité*, as entailing both religious freedom and the 'sovereign autonomy of the state in temporal matters'.[27] Renouncing clericalism and accepting religious pluralism were not, however, the only concessions that French religions made to the laïque order: they also profoundly transformed their doctrine, practices and institutions, in three main ways.[28] First was the privatisation and individualisation of religious life – a most difficult and protracted adjustment as far as the Catholic Church was concerned. With *laïcité*, it was relegated to the status of a private institution with no legitimacy in public debate and reduced visibility in social life. *Laïcité* implicitly fostered a view of religious life as a discrete and personal activity, a view which notably looked with suspicion at forcible attempts at religious conversion and 'proselytism'. The second major transformation forced onto religious believers was the revision of their dogmas, chiefly to allow the primacy of state laws over religious prescriptions. Thus Jews, often presented by French republicans as a model of successful laicisation of religion, had in the early nineteenth century reinterpreted a number of religious obligations (for example, family law, dietary prescriptions) to facilitate their accession to citizenship, according to the principle *Malkhuta dinah* (the country's law is the law).[29] The third transformation was thus the 'nationalisation' of religions, their recognition that believers must show full allegiance to the French state, not to foreign-based religious authorities. Gallicanism – the early monarchical effort to 'nationalise' the French Catholic Church – was rooted in the long-standing suspicion that 'those *messieurs* [the Jesuits] are not from France, they are from Rome'.

Drawing on those historical examples, official republicans argue that, just as traditional religions have made significant efforts to adapt to the framework of the *laïque* state, so should more recently established ones such as Islam. The suspicion is that Muslims, in contrast to Catholics, Jews and Protestants in the past, may be unable or unwilling to reform their religion in order to ease the tension between their civic and their religious identities. There is – they argue – a tension between Islam and *laïcité*, first, because of the seeming absence of separation between spiritual and temporal spheres in Islam (Islam is an all-embracing communal identity, which makes it difficult for believers to distance themselves from their religion to act as full members of democratic society); second, because of the universal scope of Islam (membership of the *Umma* – the universal community of believers – overrides national citizenship) potentially creating a conflict of loyalties between civic and religious allegiances; and third, because of the proselytising proclivities of Islam, which threaten the fragile social peace historically achieved through enforced religious restraint.

Further, relationships between the French state and the Muslim community are made difficult by the internally divided and disorganised nature of the latter. French *laïcité*, for all its commitment to the separation of Church and state and its 'privatised' and 'individualised' construal of religion, has always relied on state recognition of centralised religious authorities, which act as representatives of French Catholics, Jews and Protestants and legitimate interlocutors to the government. Since the 1980s, efforts have thus been made to set up a representative Muslim Council, seen as one important step towards the creation of a truly 'French Islam' (one less dependent on foreign states). The paradox is that the French state, while avowedly respecting and even encouraging the self-organisation of Muslims, discreetly sought to entrench the authority of moderate, *laïque* leaders over the Muslim community. The neutral state, therefore, is not totally indifferent to the structure of religious communities or to the content of their doctrines. In particular, it favours the 'laïcisation' of Muslim organisations along lines already followed by Catholics, Protestants and Jews. In addition to the demands it makes of religious organisations, laïcité also makes specific demands on individuals, especially in the public sphere.

(ii) Religious restraint in the public sphere

In recent Anglo-American liberalism, debate has focused on the question of the legitimacy of religious argument in public debate. When citizens engage in public reasoning, to what extent should they bracket off their comprehensive conceptions of the good, and notably their religious beliefs? In France, while similar issues have arisen in relation to censorship, abortion and bioethics, they have been quite marginal, given the prima facie suspicion of religious arguments in public debate. More attention has been paid to the question of the legitimacy of the expression of religious faith by state agents. Laïcité postulates that only if the public sphere is kept free of all religious symbols can it treat citizens equally. This puts stringent limits on the expression of religious beliefs by public functionaries. Official republicans insist that a line be drawn between 'freedom of conscience' and the 'expression of faith in the public sphere'.[30] It is not always legitimate for citizens to 'make use of a private right in public':[31] in the public sphere, the value of religious freedom must be balanced against other values derived from the principle of laïcité as neutrality. The first is that of equal respect of citizens as users of public services. This implies, of course, that no discrimination can be made between citizens on grounds of religion, gender or race. But public services must also display outward signs of neutrality: they must be seen to be neutral. Thus public agents have a 'devoir de réserve' (obligation of restraint): they must not display any sign of religious allegiance, so as to show equal respect to all users of public services. Thus French law has been very strict about banning religious symbols in public services. On 3 May 2000 (the Marteaux decision), the Conseil d'Etat reasserted that 'the principle of laïcité puts limits on the right [of state agents] to express their religious convictions while engaged in public functions'.[32] Recently, for example, a Muslim tax inspector was prevented from wearing a headscarf while on duty. While there have been debates in other countries about the compatibility of state uniforms with religious dress,[33] in France, the ban on the wearing of religious symbols by public agents is an uncontroversial one and applies regardless of whether state agents must wear official uniforms or not (as in the case of tax inspectors). The second laïque value which can override duties of faith is that of the state's interest in the application of a uniform rule to all its agents. Thus exemptions from the normal rules of organisation of public service to allow functionaries to perform duties associated with the exercise of their religious duties (daily prayers, weekly day of rest) are granted parsimoniously by administrations and courts. What is called in France 'the ethos of public service', in sum, imposes fairly stringent limits on the exercise of religious freedoms in the *laïque* public sphere.

Laïque schools and republican citizenship

It is in state schools that the doctrine of *laïcité* has found its fullest application. Given the centrality of education to the republican project, it is in that area that the obligations both of the state and of citizens (*laïcité* as separation doctrine and *laïcité* as doctrine of conscience) apply most strictly. The educational laws of the 1880s are, with the Separation Law of 1905, the building blocks of the institutional architecture of *laïcité* in France. The ideals of *laïcité* were fully implemented in state schools nearly twenty years before formal separation of Church and state, an indication of the utmost urgency with which republicans considered educational reform. The primary objective was to take primary education out of the hands of the Catholic Church. Schools were to be *civic* institutions whose chief mission was to 'create citizens' imbued with the republican ethos; this mission could be achieved only if schools were *neutral* towards religious and other particular allegiances.

Schools, then, were central to the *civic* project of the Third Republic. The monopoly on primary education enjoyed by the Catholic Church meant that most children were socialised into a culture that was anathema to the liberal principles of 1789. Where religiously controlled schools had taught deference towards traditional authorities, tolerance of natural and social inequalities, and encouraged cultural and political divisiveness, republican schools would promote principles of equality, mutual respect, and national unity. The republican school, therefore, was a microcosm of republican political society: within its walls, children would learn to become citizens, a shared public identity that transcended their local, cultural and religious affiliations. A law of 1884 established the principle of free and compulsory primary education both for boys and girls. All were to be subjected to a nationwide uniform curriculum. Throughout the country, republican schools competed with parish churches as the symbolic focal point of village life, and teachers were dispatched from their training colleges with a proud sense of the importance of their civilising mission, that of making 'peasants (and Catholics) into Frenchmen'.[34] The state's interest in education is constructed expansively: schools are seen as paradigmatically public spaces, not as extensions of the family or local community. In contrast to the conception prevalent in Britain, for example, where schools are broadly responsive to the needs and demands of local communities, sometimes along religious and cultural lines, in

France, the 'detached school' is seen as promoting specific civic values which cut across communal divisions.[35] Civic education, which affirmed the independent ethic of *laïcité*, was substituted for religious education in schools in 1882, and all children were taught about basic principles of universal morality, the great principles of the 1789 Revolution, and their rights and duties as citizens of the French Republic. State schools were openly anti-monarchical and pro-republican: as Ferry put it, republicans could not, lest they give up on their civic mission altogether, promise political neutrality. The one thing they could promise, he said, was religious neutrality.

The religious *neutrality* of schools was achieved through the scrupulous avoidance of any reference to religion in the content of education, and the removal of any religious signs such as Christian crosses from classrooms. While this was denounced as an openly anti-religious affront by many Catholics, republicans insisted that the fact that schools refrained from either endorsing or criticising religious values meant that they could be truly inclusive and respect the diversity of private beliefs; in the words of the 1884 law, they could be open to all 'with no distinction made on the basis of opinion or religion'. Ferry insisted that teachers be sanctioned if they disturbed the 'fragile and sacred conscience' of children or offended parental beliefs. Here are his precise instructions, as he laid them down in a famous *Letter to Teachers* in 1883:

> The republic stops where conscience begins ... When you propose a precept or maxim, ask yourself if you know a single honest person who could be offended by what you are going to say. Ask if the father of a family ...could in good faith refuse his consent to what he would hear you say. If yes, refrain from saying it; if no, speak out [...[You are in no way the apostles of a new religion.[36]

The purpose of public education was to diffuse a corpus of objective knowledge, while neutralising all 'partisan' or 'metaphysical' opinions. It was crucial that schools be neutral in this sense, as attendance was compulsory, intake was mixed, and young children were particularly vulnerable to external influence and indoctrination. Furthermore, because the purpose of civic education was to foster a sense of civic commonality and mutual respect between children, it was crucial that schools be insulated from the divisive sectarianism that threatened to tear apart civil society. This conception of the school as a 'sanctuary' was further entrenched in the 1930s when, to counter the rise of fascist and communist propaganda, the government explicitly banned all forms of political or religious 'proselytism' in state schools. In the – almost Arendtian – words used in a recent official report, as children in a republic are 'expected to live together beyond their differences', schools must be 'protected from the furore of the world'.[37]

Naturally, teachers have a special duty to embody this neutrality of the state: the *'devoir de réserve'* applies to them more strictly than it does to other public agents. There is, for example, a *prima facie* incompatibility between the function of primary school teacher and any ecclesiastical function. While teachers cannot be discriminated against on grounds of their private religious beliefs, they should not express them in schools. Thus a Versailles administrative court recently ruled that the wearing of a Muslim headscarf by a teacher was in breach of *laïcité*, as it would violate the freedom of conscience of the children entrusted to her care. Her religious rights were limited by the state's interest in the preservation of a non-sectarian, non-discriminatory public square. What then, of pupils? Although no such stringent demand of religious restraint applies to *users* of public service who do not represent the neutrality of the state in an official capacity, republicans argue that state-school pupils are no ordinary users of an ordinary public service. Because schools are miniature 'communities of citizens', where pupils learn the principles of *public* citizenship, the principles of toleration of civil society do not apply with full force in them, and *laïcité* makes demands of religious restraint on pupils too.[38] Thus official republicans believe that the ban on ostensible signs of religious belief (such as Muslim headscarves, Jewish yarmulkas and large-sized Christian crosses) in schools helps further five central values of the secular philosophy of *laïcité* I have elucidated in this piece: the preservation of a shared, non-sectarian public sphere; the distinction between the private and the public identities of individuals; equality before the law and non-discrimination; universal civic education in common schools; and the guarantee of equal religious rights for all.[39]

This argument has not gone unchallenged in France. Other *laïque* republicans have protested that the ban undermines the very values that *laïcité* was supposed to protect: religious freedom (the point of school neutrality is to guarantee, not limit, pupils' freedom of conscience), equality as non-discrimination (the ban on religious signs discriminates against Muslims for whom veiling is a religious obligation) and civic inclusion (the ban in practice leads to the exclusion of veiled girls from state schools). Those republicans are committed to the principles of secularism, but do not believe that they justify forbidding pupils from wearing religious signs. Yet others have criticised the ban in the name of a more radical challenge to republican secularism itself. *Laïcité*, they argue, is a sectarian doctrine, an ideological chimera, or an anachronistic residue. *Laïcité* is sectarian because the expulsion of religion from the public sphere falls short of the ideal of neutrality: it fails to treat believers and non-believers with equal respect and is biased in favour of the latter.

Laïcité is ideological because, in practice, the separation between state and religion is far from complete in France, and Catholic culture still pervades public life, if often in hidden ways. This makes it all the more crucial to ensure that religious minorities, such as Muslims, are not indirectly discriminated against: secularism should be reconceptualised, not as an unreachable ideal of separation between state and religion, but as a practice of even-handed treatment by the state of all religions. *Laïcité*, finally, is castigated by some as an anachronistic residue of a naively scientist age, and deemed unsuited to a world where religious groups legitimately aspire to participation in public life, especially as rationalist secular principles are unable to give guidance on the most pressing ethical issues of the day. On this view, secularism should be given up entirely, and the public role of religions wholeheartedly recognised. The debate about the headscarf ban, therefore, has sparked a profound and multifaceted reconsideration of the principles and practices of *laïcité*. Whether the flaws of republican secularism, as it is currently conceived and applied in France, justify jettisoning its liberal and egalitarian principles in favour of an uncertain politicisation of religious identities remains, however, to be seen.[40]

Notes

1 An extended version of this piece has appeared as 'Secular philosophy and Muslim headscarves in schools', *Journal of Political Philosophy*, 13 (2005): 305–29. I am grateful to the editors for permission to reprint. In preparing this version, I have greatly benefited from the invaluable editorial work and substantive comments of Iseult Honohan.

2 For an elucidation of the 'anti-religious', 'feminist' and 'communitarian' strands of republican laïcité, see Cécile Laborde, 'On republican toleration', *Constellations: An International Journal of Critical and Democratic Theory*, 9 (2002): 167–83.

3 Here I follow Robert Audi, 'The separation of Church and State and the obligations of citizenship', *Philosophy and Public Affairs*, 18 (1989): 259–96.

4 *Laïque* is the adjectival form of *laïcité*.

5 The first three are adapted from Robert Audi, 'The separation of Church and State'.

6 See, notably, Brian Barry, *Culture and Equality* (Cambridge: Polity, 2001).

7 For stimulating reflections about this conflict, see Harvard Law Review Note 'Developments in the Law: Religion and the State', *Harvard Law Review*, 100 (1987): 1606–781.

8 Veit Bader, 'Religious diversity and democratic institutional pluralism', *Political Theory*, 31 (2003): 265–94, at p. 269.

9 Jacques Zylberberg, 'Laïcité, connais pas: Allemagne, Canada, Etats-Unis, Royaume-Uni', *Pouvoirs*, 75 (1995): 375–2, at pp. 42–3.

10 For details, see Alain Boyer, *Le droit des religions en France* (Paris: Presses Universitaire de France, 1993), pp. 125–40.

11 Jeanne-Hélène Kaltenbach, Michèle Tribalat, *La République et l'Islam. Entre crainte et aveuglement* (Paris: Gallimard, 2002), p. 118 ; Daniel Licht, 'La triade médiatique: ignorance, bienveillance, complaisance' in Charles Zarka (ed.), *L'Islam en France*, special issue of *Cités*, March (2004): 341–5, at pp. 343–4.

12 Stasi report, at http://medias.lemonde.fr/medias/pdf_obj/rapport_stasi_111203. pdf (8 pages, accessed 6 October 2005). The Stasi Commission, named after its president Bernard Stasi, was convened by President Jacques Chirac in the summer of 2003 to give advice on whether Muslim schoolgirls should be allowed to wear headscarves in state schools.

13 Henri Pena-Ruiz, *Dieu et Marianne: Philosophie de la laïcité* (Paris: Presses Universitaires de France, 1999), p. 138.

14 For a recent statement, see Barry, *Culture and Equality*.

15 Cited in Danièle Lochak, 'Les minorités et le droit public français: du refus des différences à la gestion des différences', in Alain Ferret and Gérard Soulier (eds), *Les minorités et leurs droits depuis 1789* (Paris: Harmattan, 1989), pp. 111–84, at pp. 111–12.

16 However, the refusal to recognise the existence of 'minorities' and to accept that religious freedom is more than a 'negative' liberty which merely requires state abstention for its proper enjoyment would be seen as too uncompromising even by egalitarian liberals such as Barry.

17 Kenneth H.F. Dyson, *The State Tradition in Western Europe: A Study of an Idea and Institution* (Oxford: Martin Robertson 1980); Pierre Rosanvallon, *L'Etat en France. De 1798 à nos jours* (Paris: Seuil, 1990) and for a comparative analysis of French and British concepts of the state, Cécile Laborde 'The concept of the State in British and French political thought', *Political Studies*, 48 (2000): 540–57.

18 Marcel Gauchet, *La religion dans la démocratie. Parcours de la laïcité* (Paris: Gallimard, 1998), p. 47.

19 Yves Deloye, *Ecole et citoyenneté. L'individualisme républicain de Jules Ferry à Vichy* (Paris: Presses de la Fondation Nationales des Sciences Politiques, 1994).

20 Charles Taylor, 'Modes of Secularism', in Rajeev Bhargava (ed.), *Secularism and its Critics* (Delhi: Oxford University Press, 1998), pp 31–53.

21 Bhargava, *Secularism and its Critics*, 'Introduction', p 17.

22 Cited in Phyllis Stock-Morton, *Moral Education for a Secular Society: The Development of* Morale Laïque *in Nineteenth Century France* (New York: State University of New York Press, 1988), p. 174.

23 See the stimulating analyses of Gauchet, *Religion dans la démocratie*, pp. 31–60.

24 Stock-Morton, *Moral Education*; Jacqueline Lalouette, *La République anti-cléricale: XIX-XXème siècles* (Paris: Seuil, 2002), pp. 142–60, 227–61. For anthologies of *laïcité*, see Guy Gauthier, Claude Nicolet (eds), *La laïcité en mémoire* (Paris: Edilic, 1987), and on republican philosophy generally, see Claude Nicolet, *L'idée républicaine en France (1789–1924): Essai d'histoire critique* (Paris: Gallimard, 1982).

25 Cited in Stock Morton, *Moral Education*, p. 99.

26 Gauchet, *Religion dans la démocratie*, p. 51.

27 Boyer, *Le droit des religions*, p. 65.

28 Of course, many of these changes may not be due to *laïcité* itself, but to the broader secularisation of western society; yet given the particularly strict conception of the separation of politics and religion and the robust conception of citizenship enforced by the French state, they were more profound and painful there than elsewhere.

29 Martine Cohen, 'L'intégration de l'Islam et des musulmans en France: modèles du passé et pratiques actuelles', in Jean Baudouin, Philippe Portier (eds), *La laïcité, valeur d'aujourd'hui? Contestations et renégotiations du modèle français* (Rennes: Presses Universitaires de Rennes, 2001), pp. 315–30, at pp. 316–18.

30 Pierre Mazet, 'La construction contemporaine de la laïcité par le juge et la doctrine', in Baudouin and Portier (eds), *La laïcité, valeur d'aujourd'hui?*, pp. 263–83, p. 270.

31 Gauchet, *Religion dans la démocratie*, p. 84.

32 Cited in Stasi report, p. 2.

33 See, for example, the debate about the wearing of Sikh turbans by the Royal Canadian Mounted Police.

34 Eugen, Weber, *Peasants into Frenchmen* (Stanford: Stanford University Press, 1976).

35 See Meira Levinson, 'Liberalism versus Democracy? Schooling Private Citizens in the Public Square', *British Journal of Political Science*, 27 (1997): 333–60, and on 'detached schools', see her *The Demands of Liberal Education* (Oxford: Oxford University Press, 1999), pp. 65–82.

36 Jules Ferry, 'Lettre aux instituteurs' (27 November 1883), reprinted in *Pouvoirs*, 75 (1995): 109–16, at p. 111 and passim.

37 Stasi report, p. 7.

38 Catherine Kintzler 'Aux fondements de la laïcité scolaire. Essai de décomposition raisonnée du concept de laïcité', *Les Temps Modernes*, 527 (1990): 82–90.

39 For a more detailed argument to this effect, see Laborde, 'Secular philosophy and Muslim headscarves in schools'.

40 I develop these arguments, and offer a revised theory of republican secularism, in my *Critical Republicanism* (monograph under preparation for Oxford University Press).

Part III
Republican ideology
in contemporary Ireland

6 The meanings of republicanism in contemporary Ireland

Gareth Ivory

The weave of nationalism and republicanism in Ireland has bequeathed a complex political and historical legacy.[1] Add to this the flexible, and frequently interchangeable, use of the terms 'nationalist' and 'republican' among Irish political parties, the electorate, journalists and academics – not to mention the backdrop of several decades of political violence in Northern Ireland – and confusion reigns. The seminal event for republicans of every political hue in contemporary Ireland is the insurrection of Easter Week 1916. Ownership of what 1916 means both politically and historically is keenly contested, however. Taoiseach Bertie Ahern's decision to reinstate a military parade to commemorate the ninetieth anniversary of the Easter Rising in 2006 prompted much criticism from political opponents. The charge – rejected by Fianna Fáil –was that the event was conceived so as to shore up Fianna Fáil's republican flank against the Sinn Féin electoral threat. Before the celebrations, the sequence of events that led up to 1916 was explored by many commentators. The underlying debate centred on whether the insurrection was legitimate or not, and whether a democratic mandate was retrospectively conferred on the events of Easter Week following the Sinn Féin electoral success in 1918.

Among the positive assessments, former Fine Gael Taoiseach Garret FitzGerald argued that his father (who was in the General Post Office during Easter week 1916) and his friends believed that 'only a rising could rekindle the almost extinguished flame of Irish nationalism'.[2] Fianna Fáil TD and MEP Eoin Ryan (grandson of Jim Ryan, also in the GPO) argued that his grandfather and his contemporaries in the wider nationalist community saw 1916 as 'one step in a campaign ... to bring self determination into all aspects of Irish economy, culture and politics'.[3] Dermot Keogh asserted that 'those who took part [in 1916] defy simplistic categorisation'[4] while Diarmaid Ferriter pointed to many different groupings 'excluded from the prevailing political establishment ... [who] were working hard to undermine what they identified as a prevailing smugness within the status quo'.[5] Fianna Fáil Senator, Martin Mansergh highlighted the fact that 'the ideal of sacrificing one's life for a cause was ubiquitous in the Europe of the First World War ... [and] that the notion of blood sacrifice was about the few dying for the many'.[6] Noel Whelan argued that the Rising was one of the seminal events that led to Irish independence, adding that 'if the 1916 Rising has become the most prominent of these events, then that is, in part, because parties across the political spectrum can claim a particular affinity to it'.[7] Tom McGurk highlighted difficulties in celebrating the 1916 Rising since the civil war as 'the Invisible Republic – declared in 1916, sworn allegiance to in the first Dáil and abandoned by the Treaty – continued to haunt Irish politics', but concluded that, in the context of the 1998 Belfast Agreement, 'it has been deemed once again safe to let the ghosts of 1916 loose in time for the ninetieth anniversary'.[8] Tim Pat Coogan and Eamon Phoenix drew attention to the inspiration the 1916 leaders took from anti-Home Rule loyalists, and the fact that the arming of the Ulster Volunteer Force during 1913 was supported by the leader of the British Conservative Party, Andrew Bonar Law.[9]

Contributions from critics of the 1916 Rising were less numerous in the Dublin-based print media. Ruth Dudley Edwards argued that 'there was no moral justification for the calamitous 1916 Easter Rising' adding 'we should be ashamed of our President, our Taoiseach and every other person who praises the people in 1916 who took the first steps on the bloodthirsty, ruthless, terrorist trail'.[10] Paul Bew wrote 'the truth is that 1916 did play a vital role in creating modern Ireland. It led to independence but also endowed the country with an economic and social philosophy which condemned it to material failure until Seán Lemass had the courage to change its course in the 1960s'.[11] Separately, he wrote that the 1956 celebrations of the Rising were tinged with embarrassment, in the light of the contrast between current realities and the fact that 'the revolutionaries had argued that a mix of political sovereignty, nationalist economic policy and, radical agrarian policy and compulsory Irish in the schools would produce a Gaelic speaking nation of twenty million'.[12]

There was a consensus that the events of Easter Week 1916 had a profound effect on Irish history and that the key political demands were self-determination and sovereignty. Perhaps, however, 1916 might be better described as a 'nationalist' rather than a 'republican' uprising or insurrection. Taking a long view, the ideals of 'republicanism' have traditionally been invoked in Ireland to articulate feelings of alienation and marginalisation by those who perceive themselves as distant from the exercise of political power, disadvantaged socio-economically and disillusioned with the trajectory of the political realities of their epochs. Adherents of republicanism in the Irish context have existed on both sides of the left-right political axis.[13] In many instances however, the use of republican ideas and the philosophical discourse surrounding them in Ireland can be seen as a tool designed to redress adverse political realities, both real and perceived. Yet since the mid-1990s, there has been a broader discussion among politicians, journalists and academics about both the meaning of republicanism from a philosophical perspective and how this perspective may inform Irish politics.

The key concern of this chapter is to examine debates over the meaning and ownership of republicanism as they have evolved in contemporary Irish public and political life. These debates emerged first in the context of conflicting interpretations of Irish history and the role of armed struggle in bringing about independence. Thus the point of departure is an analysis of the impact of revisionism in Irish historiography on public debates. Next, the chapter focuses on the interaction of republicanism and nationalism at a more conceptual and philosophical level and the re-evaluation of republican themes. Finally the usage of republican language and ideas by Irish political parties is outlined.

Revisionism in Irish historiography

1986 saw the publication of a short essay by the Irish (and Oxford-based) historian Roy Foster, assessing contemporary historiography and the teaching of Irish history. This was but one of several essays, articles and books published from the late 1980s that contributed to the controversy surrounding 'revisionism' in Irish history. Broadly speaking 'revisionists' challenged the established view that Irish history was to be seen as an eight-hundred-year oppression of a monocultural Irish nation by the British, ended only by revolutionary action leading to an independent Ireland. The article, entitled, 'We are all revisionists now' highlighted the central concern of historical 'revisionism' as 'a desire to eliminate ... the retrospectively "Whig" view of history'. Part of this project would challenge historical myths about the nature of British influence in Ireland, as economic, social and political forces operating across the islands over the last few centuries were subjected to rigorous analysis.[14]

Professional historians who contributed to this debate highlighted that, in the Irish context, 'revisionism' took different forms over time and pre-dated the outbreak of the troubles in Northern Ireland, that it was not a uniquely Irish phenomenon, and that the new analyses frequently came from historians based outside Ireland.[15] Here the argument was that these professional historians were working to the norms of European and international historiography, away from the strictures, inherited and politico-social, encountered by their Irish-based colleagues. Predictably, perhaps, there was a certain edge to the debate in Ireland.

Critics of revisionism reacted strongly to what they perceived to be the complete abandonment of the traditional interpretation of the history of the Irish nation and the struggle for independence. For example, Desmond Fennell challenged the construction of a new 'moral interpretation' of Irish history, which sought to determine degrees of 'rightness' and 'wrongness' in the nature, course and play of Anglo-Irish relations in the past. He asserted that 'revisionism' was a concerted policy that sought to discredit the motivation, style and achievement of the Irish republican tradition, namely a sovereign independent Republic, and claimed that the 'armed struggle' of the Provisional IRA motivated and enabled the Irish political elite to jettison Irish republicanism as an ideology and, with it, its direct links with traditional Irish nationalist ideology, the goal of self-sufficiency having already been abandoned by the late 1950s.[16]

While publications during the 1960s and 1970s make it clear that 'revisionist' approaches to Irish historiographical analysis predated the 1980s, the intensity of the debate on the implications of 'revisionism' within the local Irish context was at its most raw in the 1980s.[17] Commenting in 2004 on revisionism, which he had referred to in 1987 as 'an intellectual fashion of the last twenty years or so, with as yet no adequate counterweight to it', Martin Mansergh suggested that

> Since then, a sort of Hegelian synthesis has been achieved. Traditional nationalist interpretations of Irish history were challenged by revisionism. Both have since been superseded by post-revisionism. The same process is reflected in the Good Friday Agreement – the squaring of circles. The philosophy underlying it is a mixture of the traditional and the revisionist, but it certainly is not solely or mainly revisionist. We have transcended that debate, and I would tend to be happier with the way things are now.[18]

Revisionists sought to challenge established orthodoxies and to expose nationalist myths by pointing to the history of political diversity on the island, by asserting that two identities and allegiances exist, and by contending that both had to be acknowledged, recognised and respected in any comprehensive political settlement in Ireland.

Reconsidering the relationship of republicanism and nationalism

A similar process of re-evaluation saw a revival of interest in the nature and legacy of republicanism in Ireland after 1995. Against the backdrop of the emerging Northern Ireland peace process, leading up to the bicentennial celebrations of the 1798 United Irishmen Rising and the signing of the Good Friday Agreement in April 1998, new themes and debates emerged. New philosophical debates on civic republicanism facilitated stripping nationalist mantra from republican principles. In a manner similar to the debate on 'revisionism', the meaning of republicanism in Ireland became the subject of debate among politicians, academics and journalists.

The provocatively entitled edited volume *The Republican Ideal*, published in 1998, was the first in an emerging focus of re-evaluation and analysis. It saw contributors writing of the need to 'regain', 'reclaim' and 'revisit' this ideal. Competing interpretations of republicanism were presented; three of the contributors, Martin Mansergh (Fianna Fáil), Mitchel McLaughlin (Sinn Féin) and Des O'Hagan (Worker's Party) defined themselves as republicans. However, the points of departure for their analyses differed. The contributing editor, Norman Porter, sought to tease out and disaggregate rhetorical overlaps between republicanism, nationalism and nationality.[19]

Two years later Finbar Cullen, editor of the journal, *The Republic*, challenged the lack of clarity in the use of the terms nationalism and republicanism, and argued for their separate evaluation.[20] He argued that nationalism is 'an ideological force' that 'developed as a response to real political circumstances and served particular interests'. He contended that the communities upon which nations and nationalities are built exist prior to self-imagining by nationalists. For Cullen, emerging nationalisms reinforce inequalities and injustices present within national communities, as gender, ethnicity, sexuality and class are not the primary concern of nationalism. Crucially, nationalist imperatives inhibit structural change within national communities. By contrast, republicanism, which places the emphasis on sovereignty of the people and good government in the interests of the common good, is a political programme with a different set of fundamental concerns. Cullen suggested:

> The republican principles of democracy, citizenship and internationalism challenge the usurpation of nation and nationality as principles by nationalism. Attaching rights and obligation to a common citizenship leads to more open and democratic outcomes than attaching them to nationality. The democratic allocation of sovereignty in the republic means that each person has a right to be self-determining and to a share in government. And the purpose of this is to advance the common welfare of the people. Nationalism, however, collapses all these rights into the rights of the nation. The right of the nation to be self-governing is placed above the right of each person to be self-governing, and the welfare of the nation which usually means the interests of the dominant

section, is placed above the common welfare of the people. Finally, the internationalism of republicanism challenges the inward focus of nationalism. It also challenges the nationalist idea that interests can be confined within national boundaries.[21]

While there is considerable merit in disentangling the concepts, one might also wonder how they have become to be intertwined at all, and what has been the legacy of that interconnection in the Irish context. I want here to briefly examine 'republicanism' and 'nationalism' at a historical level to highlight how, as political ideologies, they address different political concerns, develop independently of one another, and thus can and ought to be discussed separately. Republicanism, crystallising in the Italian city-states and the Atlantic revolution of the eighteenth century, can be thought of as addressing forms of government and advocating a self-governing citizenry; nationalism, growing through the nineteenth century, as addressing the characteristics of the citizenry, and advocating ethnic or cultural homogeneity. What is of critical importance is which comes to dominate when the two ideologies interact.

At a theoretical level, republicanism can be defined as a political system where rule is in the interests of all the citizens rather than in the interests of an autocracy or oligarchy. Sovereignty is vested in the entire citizenry; attention to the interests of the citizenry by the citizenry is therefore essential. The unhindered pursuit of the interests of citizens can be achieved only in an independent republic. The imposition and establishment of a republic by force of arms is countenanced because the resulting state affords the only means whereby complete human freedom can be achieved. Active participation by citizens in the political life of the republic supports and fortifies it, while a willingness to protect the republic against external threat is a duty of citizenship. The realisation that interests are inextricably linked to the welfare and vibrancy of the republic prompts active involvement in public affairs. Moreover, complete human freedom is achieved through active participation in public affairs: the freedom desired by citizens has both individual and communal aspects. In the modern era, participation requires that representative government be subject to a system of checks and balances as well as public accountability so that the public or common good can be preserved. Finally, citizens of the republic are deemed equal while their individual rights are protected against excessive state power.

Nationalism, by contrast, draws on a wide variety of factors and processes including ethnicity, the impact of modernisation, class-dominated and state-centred perspectives and uneven economic, political and cultural development within regions.[22] In addition, different factors across separate historical eras and geopolitical situations account for the emergence of nationalism.[23] As a political force, it dates from the early nineteenth century and was associated, at least initially, with reactions to the imperialism of revolutionary France. As a political principle, and, in the classic formulation, it demands that the political and national unit be congruent with ethnic and political boundaries. The evidence suggests, however, that nations and nationalisms can survive in the absence of securing an independent nation-state.[24] Frequently cultural distinctiveness – be that in linguistic, religious or ethnic terms – is the critical feature of nationalism. Nationalism can be conceived of as a cultural phenomenon whereby political mobilisation around the nationalist banner is a response to perceptions within a culturally distinct group that the erosion or destruction of the particularisms of their cultural life are likely without structures that explicitly protect and defend their desire for cultural self-determination.

A 'republican-nationalist' synthesis might suggest that any struggle for independence would be predicated on and defined by the republican principles, and that the nation – in whose name that struggle had been fought – is subordinate to these principles. The primary function of a Republic is to provide for structural and institutional arrangements wherein a political community can organise for the pursuit of the 'common good'. Republicans would be concerned to ensure that rule is in the interests of all citizens but their primary loyalty would be to the Republic once established. Republicans may also be nationalist (or socialist) but their republicanism would have separate theoretical, conceptual and political motivations. Having established a republic and recognising that their interests and welfare are inextricably linked to its survival, republicans would be concerned to defend and protect the Republic against both external threats and internal corruption. A complication arises if strong nationalism and nationalist sentiments are present within a newly founded Republic as it is likely that the Republic will have strong specific resonances reflecting the characteristics of a vibrant nationalism. In effect, the republican concern to protect the newly constituted Republic may reinforce, either inadvertently or deliberately, the defence of nationalist characteristics, whereas the retention and maintenance of such specific nationalist characteristics ought not to be the central concern for republicans.

By contrast, a 'nationalist-republican' synthesis would attach greatest significance to the nation and the nationalism which underpinned the struggle for an independent Republic. It would facilitate the implementation of the specific political goals – typically a desire to establish an independent state – of the host nation, acknowledge the benefits of a republican political structure and ensure that the political system in the newly founded Republic reflects and defends the nationality, national sentiment and fervour out of which the state was born. In this scenario, it is the interests of the nation which would determine the character of the Republic. The principal concern for 'nationalist-republicans' would be to guarantee and safeguard the interests of the nation over and beyond the interests of citizens. However, when there are competing interpretations over what constitutes the 'nation' or indeed how it was constituted, it becomes much less clear how precisely the interests of the nation are to be determined.

In the Irish case, selective ethno-cultural and religious considerations came to characterise the political nationalism which emerged after 1937, while at the same time, political debate about the character of the Irish nation, the nature of Irish identity and treatment of the national (ethno-cultural and religious) minority was inhibited. The critical point in relation to the two schema discussed is that the concerns of republicanism and nationalism can be treated independently of one another. This is important for considering the Irish case. Frank Callanan, considering the changing usage of the terms 'nationalism' and 'republicanism' from the late nineteenth century until the 1916 Rising, argues that the 1916 leader Patrick Pearse preferred to use the nomenclature 'nationalist' or 'separatist', rather than 'republican' prior to the insurrection, so as to ensure that 'the republic to be proclaimed was his own creation'.[25] He concludes that 'the uses of the terms nationalist and republican have never been altogether fixed or exact, and have been determined by an intersection, shifting across time, between ideology and convenience of designation'.[26] Moreover, Norman Porter argues that 'even benign nationalism has the potential to turn ugly and ... to play the dominant role in any relationship with republicanism'.[27]

Broader debates on republicanism

Among the themes identified in a broader debate that emerged are: the narrow meaning of republicanism in Ireland hitherto; explicit acceptance of the failure to deliver on the 1916 vision, and whether and how republicanism can be relevant in the contemporary world of Ireland in the twenty-first century. While it is outside the scope of this article to review all these themes in depth, some key contributions are identified here; the existence of a growing body of literature on the subject of republicanism is in itself noteworthy.

The Ireland Institute, founded in 1996, has provided a forum for politicians, academics and journalists to voice their opinions on the issue of republicanism. It has set itself the objective of providing an 'active intellectual environment for the study, discussion and promotion of Irish republican thought through historical and cultural research'.[28] An early address to the Institute saw the feminist historian Mary Cullen calling for a 'vigorous and broad based public debate about the meaning of republicanism today' on the basis that 'the most striking feature of what public discussion there is around republicanism is its poverty'.[29] Since 2000, the Institute's journal, *The Republic*, has addressed themes including: republicanism as an ideal in contemporary Ireland; republicanism as a body of ideas about politics and society; and the role of culture in a republic.[30] The editor, Finbar Cullen, suggested that the issues facing modern Ireland 'will not be answered by appeal to dogma or preconception' arguing that 'it is time to confront our anti-intellectualism and to begin to develop an authentic Irish approach to ideas and ideology'.[31] Encouraging both political and philosophical debate is clearly fundamental to the Institute.

In the context of increased globalisation and the rapid growth of transnational governance, Liam O'Dowd asked a fundamental question: 'whether the republican ideal can or should survive in the new world order and within Ireland in particular'.[32] As a republic is a bounded territorial political community, within which popular sovereignty, self-determination and democracy take primacy, clearly this is no longer the central political unit in an era where increased levels of technical and functional governance as well as global strategies adopted by multinational corporations predominate. The emerging reality of 'a 'permanent' form of governance dominated by officials and specialist agendas associated with capital accumulation and Ireland's role in the EU' is inimical to the traditional republican ideals of sovereignty, citizenship and accountability. O'Dowd argued that the new era requires an 'updated republican ideal' where, for example, expanded powers of parliamentary scrutiny 'might expose the arbitrary power' of global corporations. As deliberative or participatory democracy becomes the norm and supplants representative democracy, outcomes could be assessed in the context of equality of citizenship.

The former IRA hunger striker, Tommy McKearney, presented another perspective on Irish republicanism. Lamenting the 'baleful influence of catholic nationalism' upon Irish republicanism, he believes 'contemporary conditions make the attainment of a secular republic more feasible than before' for radical Irish republicans.[33] He argues that 'Irish republicanism must root itself in a radically progressive theory and system of government', that it must be a 'living, vibrant philosophy' by adjusting to changing events and must 'answer the questions posed not by its enemies but by the demands of the present day'. He reflected on earlier republicans, how they outlined 'programmes that were contemporary to their era' adding that while 'they were correct in their epoch [this] cannot mean that they have left us with all the answers to the present period'.[34] He argues that although the cause of past republicans has been similar,

'the states they envisaged were very different' and posts an intriguing
assessment of republicanism in Ireland

> Throughout the past two centuries, *The Republic* has been a vehicle for
> certain sections of Irish people that have felt mistreated, politically impo-
> tent and unable to gain redress through conventional parliamentary
> means ... In a real sense, *The Republic* is the goal of Irish people in revolt
> and it becomes a serious possibility if it ever turns out to be the Irish
> people in revolt ... At the end of the day, *The Republic* is a paradigm
> rather than a concrete legal entity.[35]

In 2003/04, RTÉ Radio broadcast several essays as part of the Thomas
Davis Lecture Series on the topic of 'The Republic'. Themes ranged from
conceptual analyses to evaluations of key individuals and events critical
to Irish republicanism. One contributor, Iseult Honohan, spoke of the
revival of republican ideas in the 1990s, following the victory of liberalism over socialism and the resulting global realignment. In the context
of the contemporary world, she suggested that republicanism offers
perspectives on limiting market excesses, redressing political apathy
among citizens, rekindling community solidarity and providing for a
citizenship based on civic interdependence rather than ethnic or cultural
commonalities.[36]

There is a growing acceptance that the 1916 ideals have yet to be
realised. For example, at the state funerals in October 2001 for Kevin
Barry and his comrades who were executed during the War of Independence, Cardinal Cahal Daly spoke sharply of the failure across eighty
years to deliver social justice in Ireland. He argued that the purpose of
1916 was to achieve freedom for the sake of social justice, a purpose
which was clear in the Proclamation and the Democratic Programme
adopted unanimously by the first Dáil, and he concluded that 'we are still
very far from having turned the noble rhetoric into reality, or translated
the songs of freedom into life experience for our poor and their children,
our aged, our homeless, our refugees; or into equality of opportunity for
dwellers West of the Shannon or West of the Bann, or for people in sectors
of urban blight, whether in Dublin or Cork, in Belfast or Derry. There is
still a vast accumulation of unfinished business to be done.'[37]

Another contributor to the Thomas Davis Lecture series, *Irish Times*
columnist Fintan O'Toole, reviewed the confusion that existed in Ireland
for much of the twentieth century relating to the idea of 'the Republic'.[38]
He identified four forces – arguably five, if economic inequality is
included – that have constrained the emergence of a pure republic in
Ireland. First, the control (spiritual and temporal) enjoyed by the Catholic
Church cut against an open dialogue between citizens on individual

freedoms that might be expected within a republic. Secondly, the legacy of a secret and self-appointed cabal 'claiming to act on behalf of the Irish Republic has tended to discredit the idea of republicanism' and preserved the notion that the Irish state is somehow incomplete. Thirdly, the corruption perpetrated by sections of the political and business elites, and progressively exposed from the mid 1990s, is anathema to true republicanism. Fourthly, the emerging notion that the state is an entity in itself 'with interests of its own that are not necessarily the same as the public interest' is highlighted. O'Toole's verdict is that these limitations are being addressed, though work to ensure the removal of these constraints is a continuing task. He concluded his analysis with the following challenge:

> The great weakness of republican thinking has always been its struggle to connect a notion of political equality in which each citizen has the same weight in the determination of the public good, with the reality of economic inequality in which some citizens obviously carry more weight than others. The Ireland that has emerged over the past decade is one in which there has been greater prosperity, but also an ever widening gap between rich and poor. This imbalance of power cannot be disconnected from the public realm ... Republican democracy has to be given a content that goes beyond the nature of political institutions and that content has to centre on equality.[39]

Irish political parties and republicanism

These intellectual debates have to some extent been mirrored in debate on the meaning of republicanism among Irish political parties. Contributions from political representatives, North and South, highlight the fact that the main parties in the Irish nationalist tradition recognise a necessity to engage in debate on this matter. This debate has taken two forms. Initially, the focus here too was on the meaning of republicanism in an Irish context, with specific reference to its historical legacy. Against the backdrop of the peace process, narrow interpretations that shackled previous exchanges have consciously been cast aside. Increased references to the inner republicanism of each of the main Dublin-based political parties since the mid/late 1990s not only rehabilitated republicanism as the activity of its physical force variant diminished, but also reflected the importance that each of the Irish political parties attached to retaining, and, to a certain extent, reclaiming the legacy of republicanism from Sinn Féin. Party political debates are noteworthy for a general awareness of the narrowness of previous definitions of republicanism; a growing acceptance of the existence of many interpretations of Irish republicanism;

determined efforts to advance more acceptable definitions; an enthusiasm for exploring the differences between republicanism and nationalism; an implicit acceptance of the failure to deliver on the 1916 vision; a growing focus on citizens and citizenship when conceptualising republicanism; and a broadening of basic republican principles to include socio-economic issues.

Irish party perspectives on republicanism in the 1980s must be seen within the prevailing political climate. Continuing high levels of violence in Northern Ireland, an almost complete alienation of the nationalist minority from political structures in Northern Ireland, compounded by the British government's handling of the 1981 IRA hunger strikes, set the broad political context. More specifically, electoral support in Northern Ireland for the IRA hunger strikers slowly translated into support for Sinn Féin, as the voting power of this community block – typically referred to as the republican community – was stirred into electoral activism. This electoral threat from the Irish physical-force nationalist tradition prompted the SDLP, the moderate nationalist party in Northern Ireland, to lead a political initiative to establish a nationalist consensus on the Northern Ireland issue, while simultaneously eschewing political violence as a *modus operandi*. The spectre of electoral support for Sinn Féin across the island of Ireland proved critical to persuading the other Irish nationalist parties to participate in the New Ireland Forum initiative of 1983–84. The initiative brought together political representatives from Fianna Fáil, Fine Gael, Labour and the SDLP and invited participation from other interested groups and individuals. However, it failed in its ultimate objective, namely, to establish an agreed nationalist consensus on the political way forward for Northern Ireland. One explanation, attributing this to the personal and political rivalry between the the Fianna Fáil leader, Charles Haughey and the Fine Gael leader and then Taoiseach, Garret FitzGerald, ignores the very real and deep differences in the nationalist perspectives offered. Haughey had overseen a significant 'greening' of Fianna Fáil policy on the Northern Ireland issue upon becoming party leader and Taoiseach in December 1979. Eighteen months later, Fianna Fáil was denied an overall majority by two IRA hunger strikers elected to Dáil Éireann in the 1981 general election. In such a climate, Haughey was unlikely to endorse what might be perceived to be a moderate nationalist perspective. Realpolitik dictated public utterances on the issue of republicanism during the mid 1980s.

The publication of the New Ireland Forum Report in May 1984 and the diplomatic initiatives that led up to the 1985 Anglo-Irish Agreement prompted intense political debate. Taking the lead, Garret FitzGerald challenged those interpretations of republicanism in which it had become synonymous with an exclusively defined Irish nationalist tradition, arguing that such a definition left Irish republicanism open to the charge of creating second-class citizens of those outside the tradition. Instead he argued for a 'pluralist' republican tradition – one which embraced all Irish people in their diversity.[40] This ideal was not a new departure for FitzGerald; it had provided the essential underpinning for the launch in 1981 of his 'constitutional crusade' when he saw his job as persuading 'the Irish people to adopt the principles of Tone and Davis'.[41]

In the months before the signing of the Anglo-Irish Agreement on 15 November 1985, Charles Haughey contended that the Irish republicanism to which his party gave allegiance was 'the political embodiment of the separatist, national tradition that is central to the freedom and independence of the Irish nation' and that this required an adherence to the 1916 Easter Proclamation, the 1919 Declaration of Independence, Articles 1, 2 and 3 of the 1937 Constitution, and the 1949 Dáil Declaration against the partition of Ireland.[42] He argued vociferously against the Agreement and stressed that his party acted as 'the moral barrier against a violent and abhorrent form of nationalism' – a clear reference to Sinn Féin and the Provisional IRA.[43] Haughey's perspective on the Northern Ireland issue was not shared by all his party colleagues. While he survived three revolts against his leadership of Fianna Fáil during 1982–83, animosity continued to exist between him and several leading members of the party.

The most prominent of these was Des O'Malley, who represented a more moderate position on the issue, and was by then a dissident Fianna Fáil backbench TD. In particular, O'Malley openly challenged the Fianna Fáil interpretation of republicanism under Haughey's leadership. During a Dáil debate in February 1985 he made his subsequently famous 'Standing by the Republic' speech claiming that 'republican' was perhaps 'the most abused word in Ireland today', consisting primarily of 'Anglophobia'.[44] This explicit criticism of his party leader led to his expulsion from Fianna Fáil. Within the year he had established a new political organisation, the Progressive Democrats.

In July 1986, Tánaiste and Labour party leader Dick Spring felt obliged to reaffirm his republican credentials, indicating that 'the essence of that republicanism is uniting Irish people', while tracing its philosophical development 'through Tone and Emmet to the Young Irelanders, through Parnell and Connolly'.[45]

By far the most notable feature of these views is the invocation of nationalist icons, although it is significant that different political leaders took refuge with different sets of dead patriots and different nationalist events. Moreover, any reference to the central role of citizens is absent.

Fast forward a decade. The stalemate of Northern Ireland politics eased slightly in the early 1990s.[46] John Hume, leader of the SDLP from 1979 to 2001, and Gerry Adams for Sinn Féin sought to establish an agreed position on the Northern Ireland issue. Away from public view, Irish and British diplomats drafted what became the Downing Street Declaration of December 1993. The nuanced constitutional balance achieved in this Declaration, the prospect of a pan-nationalist political initiative (the Forum for Peace and Reconciliation), and the reversal of Irish government policy of twenty-five years, which had aimed at the political isolation of Sinn Féin, encouraged the IRA to declare its August 1994 ceasefire. The Fianna Fáil-Labour government gave way to the 'Rainbow' Coalition of Fine Gael, Labour and Democratic Left in November 1994. Political momentum on the Northern Ireland issue was maintained under the new Taoiseach, John Bruton, with the completion of the Joint Framework Documents by the Irish and British governments in February 1995. A further change of government in Dublin in 1997 saw the return of Fianna Fáil to power – on this occasion with the Progressive Democrats as coalition partner. In London too, eighteen years of Conservative governments ended as Tony Blair's 'New Labour' romped home in the 1997 Westminster election. Despite the collapse of the IRA ceasefire in February 1996, an opportunity for kick-starting the Northern Ireland political process presented itself in late summer 1997 when the IRA declared its second ceasefire. Nine months later, in April 1998, the multiparty talks at Castle Buildings in Belfast concluded with the Good Friday (Belfast) Agreement. Referendums, North and South endorsed the deal that had been struck. Elections to the new Assembly in June 1998 opened up the possibility of meaningful politics in Northern Ireland.

Contributions made by politicians demonstrate the significantly different tone and perspectives offered from the late 1990s onward. For example, speaking at the 1998 Fianna Fáil Ard Fheis, Taoiseach Bertie Ahern accepted that the Fianna Fáil conception of republicanism was 'perhaps too narrow in the past' and that 'true Republicanism has been about building, sustaining and developing a successful Irish parliamentary democracy'.[47] Speaking at the Humbert Summer School in August 1998, just days after the Omagh bombing, Ahern stated that 'republicanism is … about moving on, neither handcuffed to our history, nor heedlessly fugitive from it'.[48] Séamus Brennan, the minister with responsibility for overseeing the 1798 commemorations, argued that republicanism 'is always and only about creating a society free of in-built constraints to the achievement of the full potential of all its citizens',[49] while John Hume asserted that 'true republicanism is not about flags and emblems … It is about establishing inclusive political institutions to which all sections of society can give their allegiance. In a genuine Republic, all citizens can play a full role in determining the future of that society.'[50] At the annual Wolfe Tone Commemoration in Bodenstown in 2000, Ahern recognised aspects of republican heritage within each of the political parties, including the 'constitutional republican' credentials of the SDLP, and argued that Fianna Fáil's mission 'is to develop and strengthen throughout the island a modern democratic and constitutional republican tradition'.[51]

The republicanism espoused by Sinn Féin has also undergone reappraisal.[52] Speaking at the Institute for British-Irish Studies at University College Dublin in December 2000, Mitchel McLaughlin acknowledged the 'narrow sense' in which the term 'Irish republicans' was used and called for a 'broader definition', embracing all who are committed to the complete freedom of the Irish people. He argued strongly for building 'a real coalition between republicans in the broadest sense' and affirmed 'the vision of the Irish Republic that we [Sinn Féin] seek encompasses all of Ireland and its entire people. It involves social and economic equality as well as political freedom. It values the Irish language and Irish culture while embracing cultural diversity in Ireland and internationally.'[53] Subtle changes within Sinn Féin thinking have been observed since the late 1990s with the promotion of 'universalisable first principles' in Sinn Féin statements – typically democracy, justice, equality and freedom, and perhaps even a certain ambiguity as regards the traditional political objective of Irish unity.[54] Marking the centenary of the birth of Sinn Féin in 2005, Gerry Adams identified inclusiveness and equality as core to republican concerns for citizens in Ireland stating that the members of his party

> want a national republic which delivers the highest standards of services and protections to all citizens equally, guaranteeing parity of esteem and equality of treatment, opportunity and outcome ... The republic Sinn Féin wants to build requires an accessible and responsive democracy, recognising and upholding basic human, civil and political rights. It would vindicate equal rights and promote social equality. It would promote economic equality through the exercise of social and economic rights. It would accept that these rights are not only indivisible, but in the interests of all.[55]

In February 2006, the leader of the Sinn Féin party in Dáil Éireann, Caoimhghín Ó Caoláin, reiterated that 'many of the promises of the [1916] proclamation of which we have spoken have yet to be achieved'.[56]

For the Irish Labour Party too, the issue of republicanism was the focus of renewed interest. In September 1999, the leader, Ruairí Quinn, outlined his 'ten pillars for a real Republic'. Central to his prescription was 'a constitutional guarantee of fundamental social and economic rights for every citizen; full employment and guaranteed participation in a vibrant enterprising economy for every worker ... [and] the active promotion of a pluralist and tolerant civic culture to ensure equal rights for all minorities, particularly as we move from being a predominantly homogenous to a multi-cultural society'.[57]

Philosophically at least, Fine Gael still appears to be in the shadow of Garret FitzGerald vis à vis the debate on the meaning of republicanism. Perhaps there is less incentive for them to enter the debate when the Fine Gael appraisal of the themes and concerns identified in the 1980s – specifically the need for pluralism – has won broad acceptance across the political spectrum in Ireland. However, in 2003, Fine Gael senator and party spokesman on Northern Ireland, Brian Hayes highlighted republican themes underpinning the actions of the Cumann na nGaedheal governments from 1922 to 1932. Parliamentary democracy in the fledgling Irish state was established; the Constitution of the Irish Free State was enacted; civilian control over the army was secured; a new, unarmed police force was founded and an independent permanent civil service open to all on a meritocratic basis was created. Fundamentally, the transition of power from Cumann na nGaedheal to Fianna Fáil in 1932 confirmed these achievements. He made the following observation on Irish republicanism of 1916:

> The Proclamation of 1916 was a revolutionary document that all Irish people could subscribe to ... Republican principles must be at the heart of all political parties in a Republic, however the real dividing point between parties, comes not from Republicanism, but whether a party is Socialist, Social Democratic, Conservative, liberal, Christian Democratic, Green or Nationalist in perspective. That is ultimately where the difference lies. The reality is that those who founded this state came from various political and social backgrounds. It was clear that one thing above all else bound them together; the demand for Independence ... there was always a real division amongst those who fought for our independence and the idea that one single agreed position on social issues was accepted, is a good deal wide of the mark.[58]

Hayes's contribution is particularly interesting: without indicating where precisely he, or his party, are positioned on whether socio-economic rights fall within the meaning of republicanism, he identifies how the imperatives for the men and women of 1916 were such as to lead them to set aside these socio-economic concerns at that critical moment in Irish history.

Among the Progressive Democrats, Michael McDowell has made several strongly worded interventions on the meaning and legacy of republicanism. He has also identified the importance of socio-economic issues, arguing that 'the values of a Republic are based upon the maintenance of a healthy tension between the civil, political and economic rights of the citizen, on the one hand, and the aspirations of the community as expressed through a majority, on the other'. This creative tension 'depends fundamentally on the creation of a system of civil and political fundamental rights, and upon the functioning under the rule of law of democratic institutions to discharge legislative, executive and judicial functions, and upon a deep seated individual and communal commitment to the resolution of difference by reference to democratic and liberal principles'.[59] In addition, McDowell has a highly state-focused analysis that centres on existing constitutional structures as well as a measure of political expediency. Prior to the 2002 general election, and with the backdrop of the emerging electoral challenge of Sinn Féin in the Republic of Ireland, he analysed the implications of republicanism for Irish voters. He stated that Ireland was an independent sovereign democratic Republic and that the Irish Constitution contained the framework of that independence, that sovereignty, and that democracy. He highlighted that Article 9 of the Irish Constitution described 'loyalty to the State' as a fundamental duty of all citizens and that election to Dáil Éireann was confined to citizens. He asserted that the powers of government in the state were the exclusive monopoly of the organs of the state established under the Constitution, that the sole power to raise a military or armed force is vested in the Oireachtas and that the sole power of administration justice is vested in the courts. He concluded,

> These provisions make it clear that no person who owes an inconsistent loyalty to any other body or group has a moral or constitutional right to seek election to Dáil Éireann. No person who owes a loyalty to any armed or military forces other than those maintained by the Oireachtas has the moral or constitutional right to seek election to Dáil Éireann … A vote for a candidate in Dáil Éireann who owes no loyalty to the State, or who subjugates that loyalty to the State to loyalty to a paramilitary organisation, is a clear and unequivocal breach of our fundamental duty as citizens to give our loyalty to our independent, sovereign, democratic Republic.[60]

Following the themes developed by John Hume, the current SDLP leader, Mark Durkan, has argued that the SDLP is 'a party of true republicanism'. He, too, challenges narrow interpretations of Irish republicanism and stresses that republicanism in Ireland 'must not be allowed to become a synonym for narrow nationalism'. Instead

> [I]t must be a by-word for the relentless pursuit of equality, for the unflinching defence of social justice and the pursuit of unity, peacefully and by democratic consent … The responsibility of Republicanism must

not just be about the national security we provide to the wider country, but also the social security we provide to young mothers, to children, to senior citizens. It must not just be about erecting standards on flagpoles, but ensuring the most progressive standards for all our people. It must not just be about reducing political divisions but overcoming social divisions as well.[61]

This brings us back to discussions in the context of the 2006 commemoration of 1916. In the light of efforts to capture the broader sense of republicanism, it is noteworthy that, despite the increasing emphasis placed on the notion of citizenship within 'republicanism', that this received hardly any attention from those contributing to these discussions. The exception to this was the speech by Bertie Ahern at the opening of the commemorative exhibition on the Rising at the National Museum, where he stated that:

> Citizenship cannot be delegated or outsourced. Citizenship comes with duties as well as rights ... In this Republic, we are citizens, not subjects. And, it is as citizens that we remember our past, reconcile our differences and renew our hope for the future. Our civic duty calls on us to look beyond our purely private roles and rights as consumers to our active roles and responsibilities as citizens. Active citizens shape strong societies. The more we involve ourselves in shaping our society locally, the more our society nationally will reflect and meet our needs. Society is not abstract. It does not belong to others. It is the sum of our actions and our choices as citizens.[62]

A year earlier, in April 2005, Ahern indicated that he intended to establish a Taskforce on Active Citizenship. Six months later, he announced terms of reference for this Taskforce and in April 2006 he announced its membership. The final report of the Taskforce was published in March 2007 – it was launched by the Taoiseach, Bertie Ahern.[63]

Conclusion

The meaning of republicanism has been, and arguably still is, contested by Irish political parties, albeit current debates are more about the nature of the republican vision and looking forward, rather than being entrapped by the particular historical legacy of nationalism and republicanism in Ireland. Since the mid 1990s there has been an effort to distance the republican ideal from the concerns of nationalism be they moderate or militant. At its most abstract, arguments can be made for the complete disassociation of nationalism from republicanism. However, to understand citizens in a republic devoid of national characteristics or historical legacy seems unreal. National characteristics evolve and are challenged over time by contemporary dilemmas that change across the generations. Legacies have the capacity to entrap in the past as well as free for the future. Both will always exist. Yet political representatives and other interested individuals are agreed that republicanism is relevant in Ireland and more generally in the contemporary world.

The key concern of this article has been to examine changing contemporary meanings of republicanism in Ireland. Heated exchanges over the interpretation of Irish history have given way to more philosophical understandings of republicanism as an ideal as well as how best republican principles can be given practical application. The increased use of the term 'citizen' by political representatives from each of the main Irish political parties is the clear indicator of a changing emphasis that itself points to very particular meanings in the Irish context hitherto. Secondly, from the beginnings of Garret FitzGerald's 'constitutional crusade', Fianna Fáil, Labour, Sinn Féin, the Progressive Democrats and the SDLP have been determined to present political visions framed within the context of republicanism. While differences remain, the visions offered have moved beyond considerations of political structures. Increasingly, the demarcation rests on the issue of whether socio-economic rights come within the remit of republicanism, with perspectives seeming to depend on where a political party lies on the left-right political axis. Republicanism in Ireland has been framed and championed by nationalists since independence. This has inhibited the emergence of the more typical political axis in the western world. Contemporary debates on the meaning of republicanism have the capacity to move the Irish party system towards a politics divided more sharply on socio-economic issues.

Notes

1   The views and observations contained in this article are expressed in a personal capacity.
2   *Irish Times*, 12 April 2006.
3   *Irish Times*, 13 April 2006.
4   *Irish Examiner*, 11 April 2006.
5   *Irish Examiner*, 10 April 2006.
6   *Irish Times*, 15 April 2006.
7   *Irish Examiner*, 15 April 2006.
8   *Sunday Business Post*, 16 April 2006.
9   *Irish Independent*, Weekend Review, 15 April 2006; *Irish News*, 17 April 2006.
10 *Irish Independent*, Weekend Review, 15 April 2006.
11 *Irish Times*, 15 April 2006.
12 *Irish Examiner*, 14 April 2006.

13   Brian Hanley, 'Change and continuity: republican thought since 1922', in *The Republic*, 2 (2001): 92–103 (Dublin: Ireland Institute).

14   Roy Foster, 'We are all revisionists now', *Irish Review*, 1 (1986): 15, at p. 2.

15   D. George Boyce and Alan O'Day, '"Revisionism" and the "revisionist" controversy', and D. George Boyce, 'Past and present revisionism and the Northern Ireland troubles', in D. George Boyce and Alan O'Day (eds), *The Making of Modern Irish History: Revisionism and the Revisionist Controversy* (London: Routledge, 1996).

16   Desmond Fennell, *The Revision of Irish Nationalism* (Dublin: Open Air, 1989) pp. 65–9.

17   The best overview of these works is D. George Boyce, 'Past and present revisionism'.

18   'In the service of the State history', *History Ireland*, 12: 3 (Autumn 2004): 43–6, at p. 44.

19   Norman Porter (ed.), *The Republican Ideal: Current Perspectives* (Belfast: Blackstaff, 1998).

20   Finbar Cullen, 'Beyond nationalism: time to reclaim the republican ideal', *The Republic*, 1 (2000): 7–14.

21   Finbar Cullen, 'Beyond nationalism', pp. 13–14.

22   James Goodman, *Nationalism and Transnationalism: The National Conflict in Ireland and European Union Integration* (Aldershot: Avebury, 1996), pp. 11-33.

23   Benedict Anderson, *Imagined Communities: Reflections on the Origins and Spread of Nationalism* (London and New York: Verso, 1983). See also Peter Alter, *Nationalism* (London: Edward Arnold, 1989), pp. 92–124.

24   For example, consider the multinational character of the British nation, the ethnically diverse Swiss political nation, the Polish nation – until 1918 straddling three empires – and the Kurds, currently distributed across four states.

25   Frank Callanan, '"In the name of God and of the dead generations": nationalism and republicanism in Ireland', in Richard English (ed.), *Ideas Matter: Essays in Honour of Conor Cruise O'Brien* (Dublin: Poolbeg, 1998), pp. 109–22.

26   Ibid., p.121.

27   Norman Porter, 'Introduction: the republican ideal and its interpretations', in Porter (ed.), *The Republican Ideal*, p. 18.

28   See www.republicjournal.com/institute/institute.html (accessed 12 January 2007).

29   Mary Cullen, 'The meaning of republicanism: a debate', www.irelandinstitute.com/MaryCullen.htm (accessed 18 April 2001).

30   www.republicjournal.com/ (accessed 12 January 2006).

31   Finbar Cullen, 'Old ideas for a democratic future', *Fortnight*, April (2001): 18–19.

32   Liam O'Dowd, 'The changing world order and the republican ideal in Ireland', *The Republic*, 1 (2000): 22–39, at p. 22.

33   Tommy McKearney, 'Republicans should be neither Catholic or nationalist', *The Other View*, 2 (Autumn 2000): 9–10, at p. 10 (Belfast: Mill Print).

34   Tommy McKearney, 'Republicanism in the 21st century', *Fourthwrite*, 1: 3 (March 2000) www.fourthwrite.ie/issue1alt3.html (accessed 12 January 2006).

35 Tommy McKearney, 'Whither the republic?' *Fortnight* (February 2001) :18–19.

36 Iseult Honohan, 'Reclaiming the republican tradition', in Mary Jones (ed.), *The Republic* (Cork: Mercier Press, 2005), pp. 25–41.

37 Homily by Cardinal Daly at the state funeral for Kevin Barry and comrades, 14 October 2001. See www.ireland.com/newspaper/special/2001/kevinbarry/index.htm (accessed 12 January 2007).

38 Fintan O'Toole, 'The unreal republic', in Jones (ed.), *The Republic*, pp .88–101.

39 Ibid., pp. 100–1.

40 *Irish Times*, 4 March 1985.

41 *Irish Times*, 28 September 1981.

42 *Irish Times*, 1 April 1985.

43 *Dáil Éireann Reports*, Vol. 361 (col. 2599), 19 November 1985.

44 *Dáil Éireann Reports*, Vol. 356 (col. 277), 20 February 1985. A similar point had been addressed forty years earlier, by the Fianna Fáil Minister for Lands, Seán Moylan, when he responded to the charge that Irish hated the the British by saying: 'We hate those English evils that Dickens pilloried; we detest those English pretences that Thackeray portrayed; we abhor the pious impostures which Trollope laid bare, not because we regard them as English, but because we recognise them as evil, and because we saw their vicious results made manifest in our own country in an English imposed poor law and judicial system; in the development of a slavish snobbery; in our remembrance of a tithe imposed, at worst, to create well paid sinecures for churchmen who were no churchmen, and, at best, to support a Church which was the mere appandage of an alien aristocracy.' But reading those literary masters, he said, 'they got, too, an understanding of the fact that there was in England a depressed and outlawed class, that there were in England, too, men of high courage and honourable resolve, and discovered that there, too, lived a people like their own, with whom they could live in friendly sympathy'. *Irish Times,* 13 February 1946.

45 *Irish Times*, 14 July 1986.

46 Despite the stalling of the Brooke-Mayhew political initiative of 1991–92.

47 Address by Bertie Ahern at the 63rd Fianna Fáil Ard Fheis, 22 November 1998.

48 Bertie Ahern, 'A cradle of possibilities', in John Cooney and Tony McGarry (eds), Peace in Ireland: Humbert Bicentenary Papers (Dublin, Humbert Publications, 1998) pp. 14-22 at p. 22.

49 Seamus Brennan, 'Republican challenges for today's Ireland', in Cooney and McGarry (eds), *Peace in Ireland*, pp. 50–5, at p. 53.

50 John Hume, '1798 to 1998: lessons for the future', in Cooney and McGarry (eds), *Peace in Ireland*, pp. 4–13, at p. 9.

51 Speech by the Taoiseach, Bertie Ahern, at the Annual Wolfe Tome Commemoration, Bodenstown, Co. Kildare, 15 October 2000, at www.fiannaFáil.ie/ (accessed 18 October 2000).

52 The article contributed to this volume by John Doyle supports this claim.

53 Mitchel McLaughlin, 'Redefining Irish republicanism', Address to the Institute of British-Irish Studies, University College Dublin, 4 December 2000 (Institute of British-Irish Studies, UCD, Working Paper Series 5).

54 Jennifer Todd, 'Nationalism, republicanism and the Good Friday Agreement', in Joseph Ruane and Jennifer Todd (eds), *After the Good Friday Agreement –*

Analysing Political Change in Northern Ireland (Dublin: UCD Press, 1999), pp. 49–70.

55   Gerry Adams, *The New Ireland: A Vision for the Future* (Brandon: Dingle, 2005) pp. 37–8.

56   RTÉ Television, Prime Time, 9 February 2006 available at www.rte.ie/news/2006/0209/primetime.html (accessed 12 January 2007).

57   Ruairi Quinn, 'The way forward', *Labour News* (Dublin, November 1999), special edition.

58   Brian Hayes, 'Ireland, republicanism and Fine Gael', Address to Ireland Institute, 10 April 2003, at www.finegael.ie/news/index.cfm/type/details/nkey/22835/pkey/653 (accessed 12 January 2007).

59   Michael McDowell, 'Time to reclaim the true notion of republicanism', *Sunday Independent*, 25 February 2001.

60   'Stand by the Republic: reject Sinn Féin', press release, Michael McDowell, 25 February 2002.

61   Mark Durkan, 'Address to The Ireland Institute', 27 February 2003, at http://www.sdlp.ie/media/speeches/prdurkanirelandinstitute.shtm (accessed 12 January 2007).

62   *Irish Times*, 10 April 2006.

63   For full details on all aspects of the work of the Taskforce on Active Citizenship, see, www.activecitizen.ie (accessed 3 December 2007).

Fianna Fáil and republicanism in twentieth-century Ireland

Martin Mansergh

Every so often, the full title, Fianna Fáil: the Republican Party, is the subject of false alarms, with the report that someone somewhere in the organisation has decided that the Republican Party subtitle, which often appears in small print, should be dropped, presumably for fear it may alienate a section of voters. A revisionist takeover, perhaps? The alarms are groundless, because, if there is one thing that has united different leaders of Fianna Fáil, and certainly all the ones I have worked with, it is the conviction that republicanism is the most important element that unites the party, regardless of an otherwise wide left-right spectrum of views on economic, social and socio-moral questions, not to mention foreign policy.

The dual name of the party is revealing, if one comes to reflect on it. Contemporary use of the name 'Fianna Fáil' dates from the time of the Volunteers prior to 1914. It was the name of a short-lived bulletin edited and largely written by Terence McSwiney for supporters of the Cork Volunteers who were against Redmond's call to rally to the side of the British Empire in the opening stages of World War I. It was, he explained, the name of the ancient soldiers of Ireland. Shortly before the party's foundation, it also featured in the altered opening line of the Irish version of Peadar Kearney's *The Soldier's Song*, which became the national anthem. It had previously been used in a seventeenth-century poem by a Tipperary Dominican priest, Pádraigin Haicead, who 'bestowed' the description Fianna Fáil on the weary soldiers of Eoghan Roe O'Neill after their victory at Benburb in 1646.[2] The name reaches back also therefore to the traditions of confederate Ireland at a formative stage of Catholic nationalism.

Cardinal O Fiaich pointed out that the first modern use of the term 'republic' in Ireland was not by the Cromwellians, but by Eoghan Roe O'Neill in 1627 in a letter to King Philip III of Spain,[3] seeking to recover both independence and ancestral lands under Spanish protection. Notwithstanding this interesting reference, and other historic roots in classical and seventeenth-century republicanism and the Enlightenment, documented by A.T.Q. Stewart in his book *A Deeper Silence*,[4] Irish republicanism, as we recognise it today, dates from Wolfe Tone and the United Irishmen and from the period of the American and French Revolutions.[5]

There is a certain latent tension, and not just in the case of Fianna Fáil, between nationalism and republicanism. Nationalism is about cultural and, to varying degrees, ethnic identity, though not necessarily in an exclusive sense, combined with political patriotism. Republicanism conceptually is about the democratic rights of citizens and the form of the state. The republican project in Ireland in the 1790s was conceived as being universalist and inclusive, though not including women, no more than in France or the United States, which also excluded slaves. It was about substituting for Protestant, Catholic and Dissenter the common name of Irishman, and not about reifying different religio-national community identities. When historian and Irish honorary consul in Antibes, Dr Pierre Joannon, wrote to me following the Good Friday Agreement to say that it was certainly not republicanism in the French sense of 'the Republic one and indivisible', he was undoubtedly correct, and Garret FitzGerald's father Desmond FitzGerald for one would have been deeply relieved.[6]

Irish republicanism, given a new lease of life by the survivors and successors of Young Ireland in the Irish Republican Brotherhood, faced a situation by the 1860s, where the divide on religio-national lines, which did not clearly exist in the 1790s, had hardened. Charles Kickham, who was an incorrigible romantic about the Volunteer unity of 1782, ruminated sadly: 'When Freedom's sun rises over an enfranchised Irish nation, there will be no flag with Dungannon inscribed upon it lifted to the light.'[7]

With the progress of reform and democracy, the strength of the nation grew. But it faced the problem of wringing independence from a resistant and often contemptuous imperial power. It not merely did not have substantial help or participation from what became the Unionist minority of the population concentrated in north-east Ulster, but faced active resistance. Repeated attempts to broaden the base by Parnell, by the literary revival, and by the revolutionary movement itself made very little impression on the Ulster Unionist bedrock.

Garret FitzGerald has commented recently on the very different values that pertained nearly a century ago. Many people today find it difficult to disassociate republicanism from violence. Yet, quoting from an article by Canadian scholar Gary Peatling in a recent issue of *Études Irlandaises*, a graphic example of the opposite stereotype was provided by

Lord Northcliffe, owner of the London *Times*, in 1914, when he told a transatlantic audience: 'The Scotch-Irish are by nature better equipped for work than for talk. They have never taken the trouble to put together their case before the world, preferring to depend for what they believe to be their liberty on abundance of rifles, ammunition and machine guns. The Irish of the South, on the other hand, are fine orators and admirable writers ... easy, charming, versatile, poetical, but unpractical.'[8] This was the 'romantic Ireland' that Yeats and many others believed in 1913 was 'dead and gone', a serious misjudgement that does not impair marvellous or resonant poetry.[9] Indeed, from Walter Bagehot to Northcliffe, the Prussians were often the point of comparison for the Ulster Protestant community.[10] 1916 and the following years changed all that, literally.

There was always a tension between ideals and realities. An independent Ireland should ideally have been a united one, but in practice it was the creation of the people in the parts of the country that were overwhelmingly of one religious and political tradition. In the North of Ireland, there was an explicit identification of Nationalism with Hibernianism, which may have consolidated what there was as a minority, but it did not make the options any easier for them in the majoritarian culture that prevailed amongst Ulster Unionists and Nationalists throughout Ireland alike. Whereas the 1916 Proclamation spoke of 'cherishing all the children of the nation equally', the 1919 Declaration of Independence made no pretence of inclusion. It referred to 'we the elected representatives of the ancient Irish people', and baldly stated that the Irish people have never ceased to repudiate foreign usurpation, clearly leaving any class of a unionist as aliens outside the fold, if not part of the English garrison.

As we know, one of the mainsprings and justifications of the Irish revolution was the cultural revival, and, certainly at an ideological level, the political, economic and cultural ideals of Irish-Ireland were common to both sides of the civil war divide. Notwithstanding republican excommunication, outside of a few individuals, there was little trace of the anticlericalism that was once more evident among the Fenians and even some of the Irish Parliamentary Party in the 1880s. Thomas Davis's and Michael Davitt's views on separation of Church and state were quietly discarded.[11]

The parties of independent Ireland had to come to terms with the fact, and they had already been adjusting to it for some time, that the new state would be confined to twenty-six counties. While aspiring or claiming to cover the whole island, the state was overwhelmingly the work of the Irish people, mainly of one tradition, and mainly South of the border, though not exclusively so.

With regard to remaining minorities, Cumann na nGhaedheal, and later Fine Gael, sought to appeal to ex-Unionists, while Fianna Fáil appealed to Protestant and even Jewish nationalists. The Constitution of 1937 was an amalgam of different influences, with distinctive Irish and Catholic values interwoven with a wider liberal democratic and Republican heritage.

In using the term 'republican' in an Irish context, in a different sense to 'nationalist', one must not be too schematic, either North or South. While subscribing to a certain formal separation of Church and state, Irish republicanism has not in practice been a civic secularism, but pretty much an overlay of Irish nationalism in the island as a whole. This has led to the exhortation given by one Irish foreign minister that Northern nationalists should take the United Irishmen rather than Defenderism as their model.[12] Defending and promoting the interests of one's electorate, and consolidating an often contested political base, rarely leaves much room for unreciprocated magnanimity or generosity. That has been largely the position between communities within the North, who are often accused of playing the zero sum game, and between North and South.

Republicanism is not the exclusive property of any one party. The three main parties have roots connecting them back to 1916, though they have grown other roots since. The Progressive Democrats (PDs) were formed, after a notable 'I stand by the Republic' speech by Des O'Malley,[13] which gave it a liberal, pluralist content on lines also promoted by Garret FitzGerald in the course of his constitutional crusade. As Minister for Justice, Michael McDowell, calling on his impeccable political pedigree, promoted the republican ideals and traditions of his grandfather, Eoin MacNeill, the better to castigate modern-day Sinn Féin. Nevertheless, even with such caveats, two parties in particular lay constant emphasis on their republican character, Fianna Fáil and Sinn Féin.

Here it is important to draw another distinction between republicanism as the ideology and tradition underlying the Irish state, inherited from the 1916-21 period of revolution, and republicanism as an ideology determined to reunite Ireland, today peacefully, or previously, in Sinn Féin's case, by force.

As I have more than once experienced, it is quite possible to attend an old IRA commemoration where the speaker has focused entirely on the struggles of an early generation and the achievements of independent Ireland, and omitted all reference to the situation in Northern Ireland.

For the first generation, the task was completing Irish independence. De Valera acknowledged that a republic existed in 1945, some time before it was declared by John A. Costello in 1949.[14] The paradox was that complete political independence was accompanied by a trade dependence on Britain amounting to 90 per cent, or 95 per cent, if Northern Ireland is included.

Seán Lemass saw his primary task as securing the economic independence of Ireland, and doing away with the abject social conditions that existed before independence. He emphasised, as many of his successors have done, the social dimension of republicanism and the importance of equality of opportunity. In retirement, he was the only former leader of Fianna Fáil to have become an avowed European federalist, something more commonly found amongst Fine Gael leaders.[15]

Fianna Fáil appears to outsiders as something of an anomaly that does not easily fit into left-right categories. I acknowledge that the same argument has been made on behalf of Fine Gael and the PDs. Republicanism does or can subsume many of the more positive qualities of socialism, without getting too involved in the dogmas of state ownership, though as a matter of pragmatism many state companies were acquired or set up by Fianna Fáil governments, including the most recent Bord Gáis Eireann takeover of Dublin Gas in 1987.

On the socio-moral plane, progress since the late 1980s has been made mainly by consensus between the main parties. There are still competing instincts internally in both of them, between those whose priority is to reflect and project Catholic values versus the liberal modernisers.

While there are parallels in terms of longevity in office with the Swedish Social Democrats and the Canadian Liberals, Fianna Fáil also has much in common with founding independence movements, such as the Indian Congress Party and more recently the African National Congress or indeed the Gaullist movement, which survives more in the institutions of the Fifth Republic than in the fractured parties of the French right. All four movements were associated with a towering figure, who was not only the political leader of a liberation struggle, but who also subsequently shaped national political life. Nelson Mandela's speech writer in the early 1990s, Raymond Suttner, has pinpointed the conceptual difference between a political party and a national movement, as the ANC and the other examples have perceived themselves to be, while acknowledging that there is no absolute distinction. A national movement is one that believes in popular power, not just representative democracy.[16] This is reflected in Irish circumstances not only in the direct democracy of constitutional provisions for referendums, but also in active civic participation through many channels, and political programmes directed primarily for the benefit of the population at large.

It has been remarked in India that 'the monolith of the Congress Party has given way to the reality of Coalition politics'.[17] Fianna Fáil also succeeded, though somewhat bumpily in the beginning, in making the difficult jump from being the champion of single-party government to accepting the reality of coalition. It also, in a different way, governs in social partnership with some of the main blocs in society: trade unions, employers, farmers, and some of the community and voluntary sector. While not providing perfect industrial peace, such a constructive approach nonetheless limits the scope for social conflict.

Fianna Fáil would not until comparatively recently have described itself as a *constitutional* republican party. At a theoretical level, up to 1970, it was considered that the Irish state did have the right to use force, unlike private (paramilitary) armies. Some of the Blaney-Lynch differences between 1968 and 1970 centred on this.[18] Political and ideological divisions hampered the party's freedom of manoeuvre, in a way that ceased to be the case in recent years.

In the 1970s and 1980s, key political initiatives like Sunningdale and the Anglo-Irish Agreement emanated primarily from Fine Gael and Labour coalitions.

Close involvement in the advent of the peace process restored Fianna Fáil to a central position in this key subject area. Policy became a synthesis of republicanism as traditionally understood and the more liberal revisionist strain of thought. This is reflected, for example, in the new Articles 2 and 3. Fianna Fáil was a barrier to significant growth in support for militant republicanism after a brief setback during the Hunger Strikes, but also acted as a bridge to bring militant republicans into mainstream politics, drawing on its own and older traditions in the South.

With the success of the peace process, Sinn Féin, having achieved a victory over their Social Democratic and Labour Party (SDLP) rivals in the North, has begun to mount a serious challenge to several parties in the South. Rhetorical denunciations are likely to have only limited effectiveness in stemming its rise.

The Sinn Féin critique likes to portray this state as a 'corrupt Republic'. It need not be so, and, as has been pointed out, there are even worse things than corruption. Their appeal to the somewhat rebellious instinct among the young is not to be underestimated.

I was much struck by the reprint in the *Irish News*, courtesy of Eamon Phoenix, of a de Valera speech in 1935 at a national turf-cutting competition near Portarlington, attacking the get-rich-quick mentality among new industrialists:

> It is only by strict honesty, keeping to bargains, scrupulously fulfilling contracts and being on time with orders that we can succeed in business ... If we are going to be self-sufficient, we must have a very high standard of commercial morality. If I were to be asked what is the greatest benefit that can be given to our people by our Schools, I would say that it is by

teaching the simple virtues of truth, honest and fair dealing, with one another.[19]

Not everything about the first generation of independent Ireland is worthy of rejection.

The past twenty years have been both the best and worst for the party, best in terms of national progress and substantial political achievement, worst in terms of electoral erosion and potentially catastrophic political scandal, the Taoiseach Bertie Ahern's leadership being vitally important in its contribution to the first and its mitigation of the second. In all-Ireland terms, however, Fianna Fáil carries slight baggage, compared with Sinn Féin, and therefore has, along with other parties here, a vital role to play in building North-South confidence. Alternative government combinations, the availability of which is desirable from a democratic choice point of view, have to demonstrate that they would be able to maintain economic confidence as well.

Notes

1 Fianna Fáil (closed down by censorship, December 1914). Incomplete set available, National Library of Ireland.

2 'Séadnadh Mór', cited in Peter Beresford Ellis, *Hell or Connaught! The Cromwellian Colonisation of Ireland 1652–1660* (Belfast: Blackstaff, 1975), p. 111.

3 Tomás O Fiaich, 'Republicanism and separation in the seventeenth century', reprinted in *The Republic*, 2 (2001): 25–37.

4 A.T.Q. Stewart, *A Deeper Silence: The Hidden Origins of the United Irishmen* (London: Blackstaff, 1993).

5 For example, Seán MacDiarmada, one of the signatories of the 1916 Proclamation, when asked why they had proclaimed a republic, cited the examples of France and America. 'The former, he stated, had been a firm friend of Ireland for generations, while millions of Irish people had played a central role in the development of the latter.' Gerard MacAtasney, *Seán MacDiarmada. The Mind of the Revolution* (Manorhamilton: Drumlin Publications, 2004), p. 155.

6 *The Memoirs of Desmond FitzGerald 1913–1916* (London: Routledge and Kegan Paul, 1965), p. 103: A subordinate officer in the GPO had taken to dating notes '1st (or 2nd etc) Day of the Republic ... And that method of dealing seemed to associate the Rising with the French Revolution, an association that was utterly repugnant to me.'

7 'Undivided Ireland' (1862), in *The Valley near Slievenamon – A Kickham Anthology*, compiled by James Maher (Kilkenny, 1942), p. 155.

8 Gary Peatling, 'Unionist identity, external perceptions of Northern Ireland, and the problem of Unionist legitimacy', *Éire-Ireland*, 39, 1&2 (Spring/Summer 2004): 225.

 9   'September 1913', *The Collected Poems of W. B. Yeats* (London: Macmillan, 1963), pp. 120–1.

10   'The ultimate end of terrorism', *The Economist*, 23 November 1867. *The Collected Works of Walter Bagehot*, edited by Norman St John Stevas, (London: The Economist, 1974), Vol. VIII, pp. 89–92.

11   For Davitt's views on Church and state, see F. Sheehy-Skeffington, *Michael Davitt, Revolutionary, Agitator and Labour Leader* (London: T. Fisher Unwin, 1908). Reprinted 1967, with an introduction by F.S.L. Lyons. See especially pp. 190–223.

12   Dick Spring, Minister of Foreign Affairs, 1993–97.

13   Speech on the Family Planning Amendment Bill, 20 February 1985, Dáil Debates, Vol. 356, cols 276–85.

14   Nicholas Mansergh, *The Unresolved Question: The Anglo-Irish Settlement and Its Undoing 1912–72* (New Haven and London: Yale University Press, 1991), pp. 319–22.

15   See Martin Mansergh, 'The Political Legacy of Seán Lemass', *The Legacy of History for Making Peace in Ireland* (Cork: Mercier Press, 2003), pp. 330–53.

16   Remarks made at Delhi Policy Group meeting, 28 November 2006, proceedings to be published in due course.

17   Reba Som, *Gandhi, Bose, Nehru and the Making of the Modern Indian Mind* (New Delhi: Penguin/Viking, 2004), p.7.

18   Martin Mansergh, 'Political Legacy of Seán Lemass', pp. 350–3 and 403.

19   'On This Day: May 6 1935', *The Irish News*, 6 May 2004.

8   Fine Gael – a republican party?

Catherine O'Donnell

Introduction

Originating from the founding party of the state, Fine Gael has historically stressed the protection of the state, democratic values, law and order
and citizen rights. In doing so Fine Gael has articulated a number of ideas
and principles understood to be synonymous with a wider republican
tradition which, as many of the other contributors to this collection have
commented, emerged from Italian city-states and the American and
French Revolutions of the eighteenth century. This republican tradition
stressed the ideals of liberty, equality, fraternity and collective sovereignty
and, as Gareth Ivory explains in Chapter 6, concerned itself with forms of
government and advocated a self-governing citizenry. Irish republicanism
of the 1790s is seen to have been very much inspired by French and American republicanism. This chapter seeks to explain why Fine Gael, despite
having much in common with the wider international republican tradition, has not enjoyed a public image as a republican party in the Irish
context. It suggests that much of this has to do with the particular way in
which republicanism has been defined in twentieth-century Ireland. The
chapter also considers Fine Gael's changing relationship with republicanism since 1998.

Led by William T. Cosgrave after the deaths of Arthur Griffith and
Michael Collins in August 1922, Cumann na nGaedheal concentrated its
efforts on consolidating the new Irish state, and did so with the support
of the Catholic hierarchy.[1] The party's pragmatic and conservative image
was thus established early on. In contrast, Fianna Fáil, led by Eamon de
Valera, appeared to provide a radical alternative. Having maintained
power in formative periods of the Irish state, Fianna Fáil placed republicanism central to its ethos and electoral advance by using it as a justification for the party's economic and social policies.[2] Thus republicanism in
twentieth century Ireland was defined by Fianna Fáil's ability to use it as

a legitimating and distinguishing force. Because of Fianna Fáil's success in setting the key components of republicanism in twentieth century Ireland it is impossible to discuss Irish republicanism, or Fine Gael's relationship with republicanism, without reference to Fianna Fáil.

Irish republicanism became identified with an anti-British nationalism (used to justify the economic war of the 1930s), the expression of the right of the Irish to national self-determination and an anti-partitionist position (seen most clearly since the Troubles). IRA violence has also meant that Irish republicanism has often been viewed as undemocratic. In Ireland nationalism and an anti-partitionist position were key components of republicanism, and as a result distinguishing between nationalism and republicanism is difficult in the Irish context. Therefore a party's position on Northern Ireland has been seen as a key indicator of its republican credentials. Republicanism in Ireland, largely defined by the way in which it was articulated by Fianna Fáil (and Sinn Féin), has been summed up as 'a shorthand term for insurrectionist anti-British nationalism, usually, but not invariably, combined with a rather vaguely expressed preference for political democracy, representative institutions, and human rights'.[3] Defined in these terms, Fine Gael, prior to 1998, would not be defined as republican. Indeed it was unwilling or unable to articulate its key principles as republican even though these principles identified the party with a wider republican tradition. Fine Gael, like Fianna Fáil, emphasised the eventual unity of Ireland with complete independence and nationhood on the international stage. Fine Gael also stressed the defence of democratic principles, the protection of the state and rejected militant action in the pursuit of its aims. The view of Fine Gael as not republican was reinforced by the party's decision, influenced from the late 1960s onwards by Garret FitzGerald and Donegal TD, Paddy Harte, to refrain from using anti-partitionist language in favour of a position which concentrated on the principle of consent and a pluralist society prior to unity.

In the post-Good Friday Agreement period a general redefinition of republicanism by Fianna Fáil (and Sinn Féin) to incorporate ideas more traditionally advocated by Fine Gael has altered how republicanism is understood in contemporary Ireland. Republicanism, in the Irish context, now resembles a position closer to that normally associated with Fine Gael than with Fianna Fáil. Fianna Fáil now stresses democratic values, unity by consent and constitutional means as central to its understanding of republicanism. This has allowed Fine Gael to apply the label 'republican' to the terms which it has always advocated and therefore argue that it is a 'republican' party. The Fine Gael position now fits, not only the wider international understanding of republicanism, but also the definition of Irish republicanism in the new post-Good Friday Agreement context.

Fine Gael now argues that the ideological reformulations enshrined in the 1998 Agreement represent a general conversion to the party's position. It is thus even more pertinent that the Fine Gael position be considered when attempting to understand modern Irish republicanism. This chapter will examine the Fine Gael position and detail how the party has reaffirmed its relationship with republicanism in recent years.

Section One shows that, while Fine Gael advocated ideas associated with a wider international understanding of republicanism, prior to 1998 the party's position was not seen as republican in the Irish context. This was due to the party's emphasis on values which were not seen as synonymous with Irish republicanism: the protection of the state, democratic values and the rights and freedoms afforded by democracy. Fine Gael's prioritisation of these principles had implications for the party's position on Northern Ireland during the Troubles. It is also the rationale behind the party's recent self-appointed function of defending the state and Irish democracy from any dangers which it perceives to be inherent in the peace process. Section Two examines the party's position in relation to British-Irish relations and considers the way in which Fine Gael has stressed a constructive and active implementation of political ideals. Section Three assesses the form and development of ideas within Fine Gael since the start of the Troubles in Northern Ireland. Fine Gael's traditional image as less republican than its main rival party, Fianna Fáil, is understood in the context of the party's position in these key areas.

The chapter concludes by explaining how Fine Gael's position, centred around the achievement of a united Ireland within the context of excellent British-Irish relations, brought about by constitutional means and the protection of the democratic values of the Irish state, can now, in the context of a redefinition of Irish republicanism generally by Fianna Fáil and Sinn Féin, be more easily termed by the party as 'republican'. Fine Gael is now happy to apply the term 'republican' to its traditional values and content to assert itself as a republican party.

Fine Gael and the defence of democratic values

Irish republicanism's ambivalent support for democracy has been the subject of much debate. Like Tom Garvin, Richard English and Patrick Maume have stressed the undemocratic nature of Irish republicanism.[4] They were referring not only to the militant campaign which republicans have utilised at different points to advance the ideal of the Republic but also to the way in which they have deliberately ignored the expressed will of the majority. Others such as Joost Augusteijn have, however, argued that while republicans have had an 'ambiguous' relationship with democracy, their objectives have been democratic.[5] He illustrates that it is

possible to view republicans as 'rejecting the circumstances within which
the democratic will of the Irish is expressed' but still remaining democratic in their outlook.[6] Garvin does concede that Irish republicans are
'not invariably' vague on democratic principles, and indeed, for Fine
Gael, there is no ambiguity. Its members have continuously stressed the
party's clarity on the issue of democracy. Guarding the democratic system
of the state is a central form of ideological expression for Fine Gael and
its prioritisation of democratic values and the protection of the state have
historical foundations. The policies of the Cumann na nGaedheal government from 1921 onwards are often credited for the survival of democracy
in Ireland.[7] Present day Fine Gael members are keen to revive memories
of their party's involvement in the consolidation of Irish democracy.[8]
Former Fine Gael Taoiseach, John Bruton, has pointed to the important
contribution by Cumann na nGaedheal to 'put the state on a firm constitutional foundation' and enable the country to 'emerge[d] from the
violence and lawlessness of the Civil War'.[9] The importance of democratic
values and the protection of democratic structures in Ireland have
remained with the party and have informed the party's strident rejection
of IRA violence throughout the Troubles in Northern Ireland. In turn Fine
Gael's strong position on democracy has been central to its endorsement
of the Good Friday Agreement. Fine Gael leader, Enda Kenny, has stated:
'Fine Gael supports the Good Friday Agreement because the principles
underpinning it are the same principles that my party has enunciated and
defended since its foundation. Quite simply, we have always stood for a
settlement based on reconciliation, mutual respect, democracy and power
sharing.'[10]

He has reiterated the 'rejection of violence and commitment to
democracy' as key principles underpinning the party's support for the
Good Friday Agreement.[11] While supporting the Agreement and the peace
process, Fine Gael has been keen to distance its position from militant
republicanism. For example, former Fine Gael leader, Michael Noonan,
has spoken of the party's ability, in the aftermath of the Good Friday
Agreement, to view nationalism as a 'true badge of honour' but emphasised that this was not always the case: 'For too long, nationalism has
been confused with militant republicanism as displayed by the IRA and
others who claimed to be fighting for Ireland. We should, however, never
forget that extreme nationalism can be detrimental to our country's interests and we should always be careful not to let pride in the nation blind
us to the twin threats of racism and isolationism'.[12]

Kenny has also sought to highlight the distinction between his party's
position and the republicanism espoused by Sinn Féin:

> One hundred years after the founding of the original Sinn Féin Party, the
> current users of that title dishonour the memory of the founding fathers

of Sinn Féin through their association with the IRA and its criminal network ... A political party with clear links to organised criminality, defenders of suspected beneficiaries of the proceeds of such criminality are not inheritors of the legacy of [Arthur] Griffith or [Michael] Collins. They undermine the vision and aspirations of constitutional republicans and corrupt the political process that they previously refused even to recognise. Today's Sinn Féin shares nothing but the wording of the Party founded by Griffith and none of the true Republican idealism of Collins. If today's Sinn Féin wants to be fully accepted as an exclusively democratic Party then all links with criminality have to be severed.[13]

Fine Gael's consistent rejection of an anti-democratic element within Irish republicanism is clear. The party has sought to protect the image of nationalism from harm caused to it by its association with militant republicanism, as seen in Michael Noonan's statement above. In the post-Good Friday Agreement era, Fine Gael has sought to remind the public of the damage which it argues has been caused by those who took on the republican label while espousing the use of violence,[14] and to reclaim the more positive aspects of Irish republicanism. Fine Gael has stated that it could never contemplate support for a violent campaign, given the importance that it attaches to the democratic state, democratic ideals and the rights and freedoms that the state can offer. Fine Gael senator Brian Hayes has summed up the values cherished by the party:

> The values that underpin our modern State with a rational legal system of government are inherently Republican values. The right of the people to determine their own government. Universal suffrage. Free speech. Rule by the majority. Respect and accommodation of minorities. Free and fair elections. The separation of powers between the executive and the courts. A written constitution. Civilian control over the army. The concept of Citizenship.[15]

Enda Kenny has also spoken of the need to redefine modern republicanism in such terms and to distance it from its image of 'the bomb and bullet' and make a more positive link between republicanism and the community. In doing so, Ireland can move towards the establishment of a 'civic republic' which 'upholds and practises true republican traditions – freedom, pluralism, justice, equality, brotherhood.' In Kenny's view, reformed ideals of republicanism and the Republic have the potential to deliver 'a real chance to revive the moral and spiritual dimensions of democracy, to renew our "society", to actively support our hardworking people in the lives they live day-to-day'.[16] Fine Gael's attempts here to lead the debate as to how to ensure that republican ideals maintain a relevant and constructive position within contemporary Ireland are influenced by

the preference which the party has given to a positive and active implementation of political ideals (as discussed in the next section).

We have seen how Fine Gael's consistent defence of democracy
informed the party's stance in relation to the IRA's campaign as well as its
endorsement of the Good Friday Agreement. In addition, this has caused
the party to assume responsibility for ensuring that the current peace
process does not forego democratic principles. As a result, Fine Gael has
periodically questioned the current peace process and Sinn Féin's position
within it. While Fine Gael has been willing to support an arrangement
involving Sinn Féin in government in Northern Ireland, it has clearly
stated that it not endorse Sinn Féin in government in the Republic since,
according to the party, that would entail an assault on the democratic
values and structures of the state. Fine Gael members have claimed that
damage would be caused to 'all that is decent about our state' if Sinn Féin
were to be in government in the Republic.[17] Enda Kenny has been clear
that his party 'will have no truck with Sinn Fein in Government' and the
reason for this relates to the need, in his view, for Sinn Féin 'to complete
its journey to full democracy'.[18] Senator Brian Hayes praised Fine Gael's
work since the foundation of the state 'to secure the legitimacy of this
state' and claimed that suggesting putting Sinn Féin in government and in
charge of the affairs of the state 'is an insult to the legitimacy and good
standing of this Republic'.[19] Jimmy Deenihan, Fine Gael TD for Kerry
North, has argued that Fine Gael has played an important role, under
John Bruton and now under Enda Kenny, in raising questions about IRA
decommissioning and Sinn Féin's involvement in criminality with a view
to ensuring that that 'peace process will succeed fully'.[20]

Fine Gael believes that its defence of democratic values is shared by
its supporters.[21] This is the rationale for its firm objection to the possible
early release of the IRA members responsible for the killing of Garda Jerry
McCabe in June 1996. Fine Gael TD, Bernard Allen, argued that Sinn
Féin should support the forces of law and order in both the Republic and
Northern Ireland. Rejecting the possibility of any deals between Fianna
Fáil and Sinn Féin on speaking rights for northern representatives in the
Oireachtas and on the killers of Garda Jerry McCabe, Allen claimed
that 'Fine Gael established the democratic institutions of this State, and
we will not allow them to be undermined in any way'.[22] Likewise, the
Fine Gael leader, Enda Kenny, objected to the suggestion that the government might negotiate the early release of the IRA prisoners responsible for
the death of Garda McCabe in return for progress on IRA decommissioning.[23] Speaking in the Dáil, he claimed that the 'republican movement
has corrupted the process in this country'.[24] Similarly, he has stressed the
need for Sinn Féin to prove its conversion to democracy by breaking all
links with criminality and assisting the operation of law and order.[25] Fine

Gael TD for Cavan-Monaghan, Seymour Crawford, argued in April 2005 that Fine Gael's advocacy of democracy was at the core of the party's contribution to the peace process and the Good Friday Agreement, and he called for a similar acceptance of democratic principles by all other parties: 'It is time for not only clear thinking but clear action with every-one following the road of debate and democracy, firstly supported by Fine Gael through the Sunningdale Agreement, Anglo Irish Agreement, the Framework Document and culminating in the Good Friday Agreement.'[26] Fine Gael's spokesperson on justice, Jim O'Keeffe, made a similar point in the aftermath of the Northern Bank robbery in Belfast in December 2004, when he called on Sinn Féin to accept the rule of law.[27] Nevertheless, despite these misgivings about Sinn Féin, Fine Gael has given its support to the peace process, and has done so because it sees it as a process, however slow it might be, that involves bringing Sinn Féin to a point where it will fully accept the democratic principles and ideological stand-points long advocated by Fine Gael.

Fine Gael, British-Irish relations and active politics

Fine Gael's defence of democratic ideals has led the party consistently to challenge the IRA's violent campaign since the start of the Troubles. Such an unwavering position on the IRA has led to a public perception of hostility to republicanism in contrast to Fianna Fáil, who espoused repub-lican rhetoric and appeared more sympathetic to removing what they identified as the causes of IRA violence.[28] Thus Fine Gael does not fit Garvin's definition of republicanism as generally vague on support for democracy, and equally it does not fit his description of republicanism as 'insurrectionist anti-British'. In fact Fine Gael's image as non-republican in Ireland has been compounded by its long-standing advocacy of good relations with Britain.[29] The Cumann na nGaedheal party emphasised the need for strong links with Britain. One of Fine Gael's founding members and former party leader, James Dillon, strongly advocated the establish-ment of durable relations across the British Isles as a mechanism for true reconciliation on the island. Speaking in the Dáil in 1933, Dillon argued that when partition was ended, membership and participation in the commonwealth could deliver the 'truest form of freedom'.[30] A similar recognition of the need for favourable British-Irish relations was alluded to by the Fine Gael Taoiseach in the Inter-party government, John A. Costello, when in 1948 he introduced the Republic of Ireland Bill to the Dáil. Costello explicitly explained his intentions in relation to this Bill. The measure, he stated, was 'not designed nor was it conceived in any spirit of hostility to the British people or to the institution of the British Crown ... not [one] intended to be destructive or to have any centrifugal effect upon another nation or nations, and particularly those nations that form the Commonwealth of Nations'.[31] In fact, Costello saw the declaration of Ireland as a republic as designed to 'achieve a greater measure of friendship and goodwill than has ever existed in the long and tragic association between Great Britain and Ireland. We want to increase that friendship and that goodwill.'[32] Costello stressed that the Bill was not intended to adversely affect relations with Britain or lessen the state's relationship with the nations of the Commonwealth.[33] Speaking in 2004, Fine Gael's Gay Mitchell referred to the building of relations with other states, such as members of the Commonwealth, and in a more recent context, within the European Union, as providing the basis for the true fulfilment of the nation's independence.[34]

This emphasis on relations with Britain and the other Commonwealth countries can be seen to have originated from Arthur Griffith's original advocacy of a dual monarchy as the basis of relations between Ireland and Britain.[35] The connection with Britain remains an important tradition within the modern Fine Gael party.[36] Even though the Fine Gael leader from 1977 to 1987, Garret FitzGerald, offered only a minimal treatment of the circumstances of the link with Britain in the event of the political reunification of Ireland,[37] both as Minister for Foreign Affairs in 1973 (Sunningdale Communiqué) and Taoiseach in 1985 (Anglo-Irish Agreement), he formalised an British-Irish approach to the search for a solution in Northern Ireland.[38] Thus the establishment and maintenance of favourable relations with Britain has been central to Fine Gael policy on Northern Ireland. Again this has differentiated Fine Gael from the other main republican voices in Fianna Fáil and in Sinn Féin, in particular, who were consistently critical of the British government throughout the 1970s and 1980s.[39]

Fine Gael's support for relations with Britain and traditional eschewing of anti-partitionist rhetoric is linked to the party's preference for an active approach to the pursuit of the goals of unity and complete independence from Britain. Fine Gael contends that, unlike Fianna Fáil which, it alleges, has chosen simply to make political capital from its republican language, it has always sought to promote a positive brand of politics. This was referred to by Costello in his speech to the Dáil in the debate about the Republic of Ireland Bill in 1948. Costello hoped that the declaration of a republic would 'take the gun out of Irish politics and bring about unity and domestic concord in our lives'.[40] He stressed that the purpose of the bill was to be 'constructive' for both domestic and foreign relations and not 'for the purposes of vote catching or for the purposes of evoking again the anti-British feeling which has been such fruitful ground on which politicians have played for many years past'.[41] We have already seen how Fine Gael has emphasised the positive contribution made by

Cumann na nGaedheal to the establishment of democracy in Ireland. Fine Gael also claims that it has maintained a constructive and active approach to solving the Northern Ireland problem. Accusing Fianna Fáil of 'petty bluster' in relation to planned 1916 commemorations, Enda Kenny stressed his party's willingness to 'put the country's interests over the party's interests' and referred specifically to the following examples as 'huge contributions' to 'the cornerstones of independent Ireland in the 20th century': 'W.T. Cosgrave's presiding over the birth of Irish democracy (1922–32), John A. Costello's declaration of a Republic (1949), Liam Cosgrave's leading Ireland into the United Nations (1957) and Garret FitzGerald's signing the Anglo-Irish Agreement (1985).'[42]

Brian Hayes has referred to Fianna Fáil's willingness to use the issue of Northern Ireland with the intention to 'whip up tribal fears to win votes' whereas Fine Gael have preferred to enunciate new positions which have influenced policy and which are now accepted by Fianna Fáil.[43] Michael Noonan has also claimed that the seeds of the peace process lay in Fine Gael's early and unilateral support for the principle of consent.[44] Jimmy Deenihan has described the level of interest in Northern Ireland and desire to help find a solution there on the part of Fine Gael members. He has argued that Enda Kenny, if Taoiseach, would be 'enthusiastic and energetic about driving very proactive policies' particularly on North-South issues.[45] Former SDLP and Fine Gael member, Austin Currie, intimated that the party's proactive involvement in attempts to find a solution for Northern Ireland made the offer to him to run as a Fine Gael Dáil candidate an appealing prospect.[46]

Fine Gael ideas since the Troubles

Throughout the course of the Troubles, Fine Gael sought to lead and direct the debate on Northern Ireland.[47] Central to this was the development of new and challenging ideas on the subject of Northern Ireland, unionists and British-Irish relations. This project was heavily influenced by the prominence given to Northern Ireland by former Fine Gael Minister for Foreign Affairs and Taoiseach, Garret FitzGerald. This project was embraced by the wider party and this is seen clearly in the statements by former Fine Gael TD for Donegal North East and spokesperson on Northern Ireland, Paddy Harte. Harte complemented FitzGerald's arguments by advocating the development of positive relations with Protestants in Northern Ireland, with the subject of a united Ireland relegated to a future date if so decided on by Protestants.[48] Speeches by Harte from the start of the Troubles clearly favoured the principle of consent and the establishment of a more pluralistic society in the Republic. As early as 1972, Paddy Harte talked about the need for 'the foundations of a new and just society' to be assured before unity could take place.[49] He argued that 'reunification is not yet on the agenda and we in the Republic have many changes to achieve before it will even be acceptable for debate by the most moderate of Unionist. Nothing short of a completely new Constitution leading in the direction of a Pluralist Society will be sufficient as an initial step on our part.'[50] Harte consistently argued that 'Ireland united must mean the total acceptance of the policies, the cultures, the traditions and the religious beliefs of all Irish people and the freedom to express and practice these things in a natural way. Unless this is accepted Irish unity is a myth and an illusion and Irish nationhood can never be gained'.[51] Harte's views paralleled those of Garret FitzGerald who stressed the need for a more pluralist republic as a prerequisite to unity[52] and, as Taoiseach, set about the completion of a 'constitutional crusade'.[53] He outlined his party's policies for government as including 'the creation of a pluralist society as a basis upon which to build a new relationship between North and South'.[54] Recommending constitutional change in the Republic, FitzGerald made the connection with eighteenth-century republicanism when he said 'we need to review our Constitution for our own sake. We have to do this for one purpose, to give us a Constitution which would reflect the pluralist ideal which underlies all true republicanism and has done so ever since Tone first gave it expression.'[55] Thus Fine Gael periodically invoked eighteenth-century republicanism as a legitimating mechanism for its policies, but generally had little success in attempting to define Irish republicanism in its terms prior to 1998.

Fine Gael's Alan Shatter argued that the Republic's ability to legislate for and debate policies not supported by the Catholic Church was 'symbolic of our capacity to translate the verbal commitment to a pluralist republic'. He spoke of the need to be conscious of unionist perceptions of their ability to legislate when debating policies and accused Fianna Fáil, 'the party that project themselves as the one and only true Republican party', as being willing to sacrifice relations with unionists 'for the sake of political opportunism'.[56] Former Fine Gael leader, Michael Noonan, described the twin pillars of Fine Gael thought on Northern Ireland as based around an acceptance of the principle of consent and a recognition that 'there's an obligation to try to accommodate difference by having a more pluralist society down here'.[57] On the other hand, Fianna Fáil under Charles Haughey claimed that constitutional change in the Republic should only happen as part of the negotiation process for unity, not prior to it.[58]

In addition to recognising the need for a more pluralist society in the Republic before Ulster unionists would contemplate unity, Fine Gael also differentiated itself from Fianna Fáil by promoting the principle that unity could only come about through consent. This principle was endorsed by the party in 1969[59] and reiterated as policy since then.[60] In contrast Fianna Fáil historically emphasised the Irish right to national self-determination. This claim was expressed by Fianna Fáil founding leader, Eamon de Valera,[61] and reiterated by later leaders such as Jack Lynch.[62] Sinn Féin President, Gerry Adams also referred the republican campaign as one 'for national self-determination'.[63] Fine Gael's language on Northern Ireland over the course of the Troubles concentrated on the principle of consent. Fine Gael's references to self-determination are a recent phenomenon and a result of the principle's central inclusion in the Good Friday Agreement rather than an internal party initiative. Statements by former Fine Gael leader, Michael Noonan, and former Fianna Fáil Taoiseach, Albert Reynolds, reflect well the parties' contrasting views about where priority rests in the relationship between the principles of consent and self-determination. Noonan referred to the way in which the Fine Gael party debated the principle of self-determination 'in the context of a majority [consent]'.[64] Reynolds stated that acceptance of the principle of consent was paramount but only 'provided that, as long as the principle of consent was parallel with and part of self-determination … fine, that what we needed'.[65] So while Fianna Fáil debated how the principle of consent could be accepted without prejudice to its long-held claim of national self-determination, Fine Gael debated how the concept of self-determination could be reconciled with its long-held advocacy of the principle of consent.

Conclusion

When examined closely Fine Gael has much in common with Fianna Fáil on Northern Ireland. While the parties' short-term policies have differed they have both always cited a united Ireland as a long-term policy objective and have highlighted economic obstacles as a main impediment to Irish unity.[66] However, Fianna Fáil, which emerged from the anti-Treaty wing of Sinn Féin and regularly used anti-partitionist language, monopolised the republican label and successfully defined republicanism in the Irish context in the twentieth century. In contrast, Fine Gael has been seen as less nationalist[67] and because of the centrality of nationalism to Irish republicanism, the party has had its republican credentials frequently questioned.

Those who looked in on Ireland with a knowledge of republicanism as it is understood in the wider international context could have believed it odd that Fine Gael was not seen as republican. This is because, as this chapter has illustrated, Fine Gael has historically afforded a high importance to the protection of the state, democratic principles and structures, and the rights and freedoms offered by the state; many of these values are shared by mainstream republicanism. However, these values have not been associated with twentieth-century Irish republicanism, and the principles which Fine Gael in fact emphasised have been seen as contrary to Irish republicanism. We have seen how Tom Garvin and others have noted a number of core tenets central to Irish republicanism, traditionally identified with an anti-British feeling, anti-democratic positions, an emphasis on self-determination and a militant separatist agenda.

The 'non-republican' values, advocated by Fine Gael, included building and maintaining good British-Irish relations, eschewing the militant tradition, and emphasising the principle of consent rather than the pursuit of self-determination. Fine Gael has also traditionally seen itself as elucidating a constructive and positive political agenda, not one that is used for electoral purposes. Ensuring the continued relevance of nationalism and republicanism in everyday life in modern Ireland remains a significant policy objective for the party.

In the post-Good Friday Agreement period the context for assessing republicanism in Ireland has been altered significantly. Fianna Fáil now accepts the principle of consent[68] and has sought to redefine Irish republicanism as 'inherently democratic'. Bertie Ahern reflects this new Irish republicanism: 'We value religious liberty and practice religious tolerance. Our success in Ireland is based on democratic republicanism and is inspired by the principles of equality and fraternity.'[69] Fianna Fáil's long-standing endorsement of the 1916 Rising may have raised questions in the past about the party's commitment to constitutional rather than militant republicanism but the party now emphasises that 'The 1916 Proclamation was an explicitly democratic and egalitarian vision'.[70] Ahern has also stated:

> It is often forgotten that the Easter Rising only took place, after the democratic wishes of the Irish people for a large measure of self-government had been systematically frustrated for over 30 years, indeed back to the time of the Repeal Movement under Daniel O'Connell. The Proclamation looked forward to election by universal franchise of a sovereign Irish Government and the creation of a new constitutional order that would be wholly Irish, and not British, and that would cherish all the children of the nation equally.[71]

Thus our understanding of republicanism in the Irish context has clearly undergone significant change. It has broadened to incorporate many of the principles traditionally articulated by Fine Gael. Fianna Fáil and Sinn Féin now articulate a republicanism that displays many similarities with the position traditionally expressed by Fine Gael. In the context of a general redefinition of republicanism in modern Ireland the party's position is more easily portrayed as republican. Fine Gael has been content to adopt the new definition of republicanism and apply the republican label to its traditional values and assert itself as a republican party. In the aftermath of the Good Friday Agreement Fine Gael has been keen to stress its nationalist tradition and desire for unity.[72] The key components of the Fine Gael position have largely remained constant, but the redefinition of Irish republicanism as a result of the Good Friday Agreement of 1998 mean that it is now possible for Fine Gael to articulate itself and its traditional values as 'republican'.

This has not yet altered the public perception of Fine Gael as less nationalist or non-republican. This is mainly because the memory of Fine Gael as less vociferous than Fianna Fáil in making anti-partitionist statements or in attacking the British government remains. Nevertheless the party seeks solace in its belief that its traditional defence of democratic principles, unity by consent and a pluralist society are now key components of the wider Irish republican lexicon.

Notes

1   R. Fanning, *Independent Ireland* (Dublin: Helicon, 1983), p. 18.

2   R. Dunphy, *Richard, The Making of Fianna Fáil Power in Ireland 1923–1948* (Oxford: Oxford University Press, 1995), p. 8; See also J. Prager, *Building Democracy in Ireland: Political Order and Cultural Integration in a Newly Independent Nation* (Cambridge: Cambridge University Press, 1986), pp. 194, 205.

3   T. Garvin, *1922: The Birth of Irish Democracy* (Dublin: Gill and Macmillan, 1996), p. 11.

4   R. English, '"Paying no heed to public clamor": Irish republican solipsism in the 1930s', *Irish Historical Studies*, 28: 112 (1993): 426–39; P. Maume, 'The Ancient Constitution: Arthur Griffith and his intellectual legacy to Sinn Féin', *Irish Political Studies*, 10 (1995), 123–37.

5   J. Augusteijn, 'Political violence and democracy: An analysis of the tensions within Irish republican strategy, 1914-2002', *Irish Political Studies*, 18: 1 (2003): 17.

6   Augusteijn, 'Political violence and democracy', p. 20.

7   R. English, *Irish Freedom: The History of Nationalism in Ireland* (London: Macmillan, 2006), p. 327; Garvin, *1922: The Birth of Irish Democracy*.

8   Interview with Senator Brian Hayes, Fine Gael, 21 September 2006. Both the former Fine Gael Taoiseach, Dr Garret FitzGerald, and Fine Gael TD, Jimmy Deenihan, paid tribute to the work which they believed was done by Cumann na nGaedheal in the 1920s in building the foundations of Irish democracy at an event to mark the eightieth anniversary of the party's foundation in April 2003. See press release by Fine Gael on 6 April 2003 available at www.finegael.ie/news/index.cfm/type/details/nkey/20940 (accessed 4 April 2007).

9   Speech by John Bruton TD, former Taoiseach, at a meeting of the Officer Board of the Meath Constituency Executive of Fine Gael, 8 September 2003, in the

Ardboyne Hotel, Navan, available at www.finegael.ie/news/index.cfm/type/
details/nkey/21101 (accessed 1 May 2007).

10   Speech by Enda Kenny at the Forum for Peace and Reconciliation, 27 November
     2002, available at www.finegael.ie/news/index.cfm/type/details/nkey/22254
     (accessed 1 May 2007).

11   Speech by Fine Gael Leader, Enda Kenny TD, during the statements on Northern
     Ireland in Dáil Éireann, 18 October 2006, available at www.finegael.ie/
     news/index.cfm/type/details/nkey/29528 (accessed 3 May 2007).

12   Michael Noonan, Fine Gael press release, 15 March 2002, available at www.fine-
     gael.ie/news/index.cfm/type/details/nkey/21551 (accessed 1 May 2007).

13   Speech by Enda Kenny, 16 October 2005, at Collins 22 Society Launch available
     at www.finegael.ie/news/index.cfm/type/details/nkey/26780 (accessed 11 April
     2007).

14   For example, Senator Brian Hayes has referred to the party's role in raising Sinn
     Féin's and the IRA's track record on this while continuing to support the peace
     process. Interview with Senator Brian Hayes, Fine Gael, 21 September 2006.

15   Speech by Senator Brian Hayes to the Ireland Institute, 10 April 2003, available
     at www.finegael.ie/news/index.cfm/type/details/nkey/22835 (accessed 10 April
     2007).

16   Speech by Fine Gael Leader, Enda Kenny TD, to the Young Fine Gael 20th
     National Conference, 13 November 2004, available at www.finegael.ie/news/
     index.cfm/type/details/nkey/24896 (accessed 10 April 2007).

17   Senator Brian Hayes, *Sunday Independent*, 17 October 2004.

18   Fine Gael Press Release, 7 January 2006, available at www.finegael.ie/news/
     index.cfm/type/details/nkey/30211 (accessed 11 April 2007).

19   Speech by Fine Gael Senate Leader, Senator Brian Hayes, to the Fine Gael
     Constituency Executive of Kerry North in Listowel, 9 September 2005, available
     at www.finegael.ie/news/index.cfm/type/details/nkey/26587 (accessed 11 April
     2007).

20   Interview with Jimmy Deenihan, TD Fine Gael, 25 October 2006.

21   Interview with Senator Brian Hayes, Fine Gael, 21 September 2006.

22   Speech by Fine Gael Foreign Affairs Spokesperson, Bernard Allen TD, during the
     Private Members' Debate on Irish Unity, Dáil Éireann, 2 November 2005, avail-
     able at www.finegael.ie/news/index.cfm/type/details/nkey/26896 (accessed 11
     April 2007).

23   *Dáil Éireann Debates*, Vol. 596, Col. 27, 26 January 2005

24   *Dáil Éireann Debates*, Vol. 596, Col. 27, 26 January 2005.

25   Speech by Enda Kenny, 16 October 2005, at Collins 22 Society Launch available
     at www.finegael.ie/news/index.cfm/type/details/nkey/26780 (accessed 11 April
     2007).

26   Seymour Crawford, 7 April 2005, available at www.finegael.ie/news/index.cfm/
     type/details/nkey/25729 accessed 13 April 2007.

27   Fine Gael's spokesperson on Justice, Jim O'Keefe, *Sunday Independent,* 2 January
     2005.

28   See C. O'Donnell, *Fianna Fáil, Irish Republicanism and the Northern Ireland
     Troubles, 1968–2005* (Dublin: Irish Academic Press, 2007).

29 English, *Irish Freedom*, p. 320.
30 As quoted in M. Manning, *James Dillon: A Biography* (Dublin: Wolfhound Press, 1999), p. 69.
31 *Dáil Éireann Debates*, Vol. 113, Col. 348, 24 November 1948.
32 *Dáil Éireann Debates*, Vol. 113, Col. 350, 24 November 1948.
33 *Dáil Éireann Debates*, Vol. 113, Col. 353, 24 November 1948.
34 Speech by Gay Mitchell TD, MEP, at Humbert School, 24 July 2004, available at www.finegael.ie/news/index.cfm/type/details/nkey/24304 (accessed 10 April 2007).
35 English, *Irish Freedom*, p. 259.
36 Interview with Senator Brian Hayes, Fine Gael, 21 September 2006.
37 See G. FitzGerald, *Towards a New Ireland* (Dublin: Gill and Macmillan, 1972) p. 158.
38 See G. FitzGerald, *All in a Life: An Autobiography* (Dublin: Gill and Macmillan, 1992).
39 For example, Fianna Fáil leader in the 1980s, Charles Haughey, criticised the 'massive British military, political and economic support' given to unionism which, he argued, meant unionists did not 'show any real interest in dialogue, let alone peace and reconciliation'. Presidential address to Fianna Fáil Ard Fheis, 31 March 1984, Fianna Fáil Archives, University College, Dublin, P176/788.
40 *Dáil Éireann Debates*, Vol. 113, Col. 378, 24 November 1948.
41 *Dáil Éireann Debates*, Vol. 113, Col. 348, 24 November 1948.
42 Comments by Enda Kenny, TD, 13 April 2006, on the Taoiseach's speech at the opening of the 1916 Rising exhibition at Collins Barracks, Dublin, available at www.finegael.ie/news/index.cfm/type/details/nkey/28002 (accessed 3 May 2007).
43 Interview with Senator Brian Hayes, Fine Gael, 21 September 2006.
44 Interview with Michael Noonan, TD Fine Gael, 5 October 2006.
45 Interview with Jimmy Deenihan, TD Fine Gael, 25 October 2006.
46 A. Currie, *All Hell Will Break Loose* (Dublin: O'Brien Press, 2004), p. 383.
47 In a speech to the Fine Gael Ard Fheis, 20 May 1978, Paddy Harte, then Fine Gael TD, said 'The challenge facing Fine Gael leadership is to continue to guide southern opinion in the correct direction towards Irish nationhood and to involve the Party at all levels throughout the Republic in promoting better understanding of the complexities of Northern Irish life'. Copy of speech in author's possession. Senator Brian Hayes has also referred to the way in which Fine Gael has influenced thought on Northern Ireland since the start of the Troubles, led particularly by Garret FitzGerald. Interview with Senator Brian Hayes, Fine Gael, 21 September 2006.
48 Interview with Paddy Harte, 29 January 2007.
49 Paddy Harte, then Fine Gael TD, speaking in Dundalk 3 February 1972, copy in author's possession.
50 Paddy Harte, then Fine Gael TD, speaking at University College, Dublin 21 November 1972, copy in author's possession.
51 Paddy Harte, then Fine Gael TD and spokesperson on Security and Northern Ireland, speaking in Limerick, 4 October 1978, copy in author's possession.
52 FitzGerald, *Towards a New Ireland*, pp. 142–57.
53 P. Mair, 'Breaking the nationalist mould: The Irish Republic and the Anglo-Irish

Agreement', in P. Teague (ed.), *Beyond the Rhetoric: Politics, Economics and Social Policy in Northern Ireland* (London: Lawrence and Wishart, 1987), p. 97.

54 *Dáil Éireann Debates*, Vol. 337, Col. 577, 1 July 1982.

55 *Seanad Éireann Debates*, Vol. 96, Col. 184, 9 October 1981.

56 *Dáil Éireann Debates*, Vol. 356, Cols 204–5, 19 April 1985.

57 Interview with Michael Noonan, TD Fine Gael, 5 October 2006.

58 See T.R. Dwyer, *Short Fellow: A Biography of C.J. Haughey* (Dublin: Marino, 2001), p. 204.

59 See 1969 Fine Gael Document on Northern Ireland reproduced in Paddy Harte, *Young Tigers and Mongrel Foxes: A Life in Politics* (Dublin: O'Brien Press, 2005). Interview with Jimmy Deenihan, Fine Gael TD, 25 October 2006.

60 See Fine Gael policy document *Ireland: Our Future Together* (Dublin: Fine Gael, 1979), p. 4; Interviews with Michael Noonan, TD Fine Gael, 5 October 2006, Jimmy Deenihan, TD Fine Gael, 25 October 2006.

61 See, for example, quote in D. Fitzpatrick, *The Two Irelands 1912–1939* (Oxford: Oxford University Press, 1998), p. 28.

62 See coverage of press conference given by Jack Lynch at the Irish Embassy, London, 30 October 1968, *Irish Press*, 1 November 1968.

63 As quoted in R. Bourke, *Peace in Ireland: The War of Ideas* (London: Pimlico, 2003), p. 25n11.

64 Interview with Michael Noonan, TD Fine Gael, 5 October 2006.

65 Interview with Albert Reynolds, former Fianna Fáil Taoiseach, 8 August 2003.

66 See O'Donnell, *Fianna Fáil, Irish Republicanism*, pp. 42, 197–200, FitzGerald, *Towards a New Ireland*, pp. 63–85, 161–6. Also interview with Jimmy Deenihan, TD Fine Gael, 25 October 2006.

67 A view referred to in Mair, 'Breaking the nationalist mould', p. 82.

68 See K. Hayward, 'The politics of nuance: Irish official discourse on Northern Ireland', *Irish Political Studies*, 19: 1 (2004).

69 Speech by the Taoiseach, Bertie Ahern, at the Wolfe Tone Commemoration, Bodenstown, County Kildare, 17 October 2004, available at http://cain.ulst.ac.uk/issues/politics/docs/dott/ba171004.htm (accessed 16 May 2007).

70 Speech by the Taoiseach, Bertie Ahern TD, at the opening of the Constance Markievicz Exhibition in Lissadell, Sligo, 30 March, 2007, available at http://www.taoiseach.gov.ie/index.asp?locID=558&docID=3332 (accessed 16 May 2007).

71 Speech by Bertie Ahern at the Arbour Hill Commemoration, Dublin, 24 April 2005, available at http://cain.ulst.ac.uk/issues/politics/docs/dott/ba240405.htm (accessed 16 May 2007).

72 As seen in the statements by party members quoted in this chapter and also in interviews with Senator Brian Hayes, Fine Gael, 21 September 2006, Jimmy Deenihan, TD Fine Gael, 25 October 2006.

9 Republican policies in practical politics: placing Sinn Féin in a European context

John Doyle

Introduction

Sinn Féin is the party most associated in public discourse with the term 'republican' in Ireland. It is also a party whose public rhetoric relies heavily on concepts at the core of the debates on contemporary civic republicanism. However, previous incarnations of the party have engaged in a static constitutionalism and an almost mythical idea of 'the Republic', and the party's opponents view its rhetoric as skin deep – overlaying a more fundamental authoritarianism. As Sinn Féin is experiencing a period of significant development and growth, these contradictory images of the party need to be analysed. Therefore, without denying the legacy of republican thinking in other Irish political parties, this chapter analyses the contemporary meaning of republicanism as represented by the Sinn Féin party (North and South), which emerged from the 'abstentionist' split with elements of its old leadership in the late 1980s.[1]

Sinn Féin's own self-image is that its historical roots lie in the republican ideal of the French Revolution – as interpreted by the United Irish Movement of 1798 and also by the republican and socialist thinking of James Connolly in the pre-1916 period.[2] Sinn Féin's own projection of its political ideology draws on a number of strands from these sets of political ideas. From the French revolutionary tradition Sinn Féin employs ideas of equality, secularism and, in the Irish context, independence from Britain and Irish unity. It would therefore follow that the party would have a focus on the common good and communitarian ideals – mixed with the language of the 'national' interest or the 'national' community. From Connolly the party derives a more explicit commitment to socialism and social justice and an anti-imperialist international position. From these revolutionary traditions and more directly from its own extra-parliamentary past, the party has a focus on political participation and activism, in politics as practice, even *praxis*, rather than as a purely elite-driven process.

The current developments within Sinn Féin represent an interesting study of wider relevance beyond Ireland. Its left-wing rhetoric, its electoral growth and entry into government in Northern Ireland, its high levels of activism and its strong nationalist agenda seem, at first glance at least, to represent a counter tendency in contemporary European politics. Wider debates within international relations and comparative politics ask a number of interesting questions which help us place modern Sinn Féin in a broader and international context. Firstly, the relationship between globalisation and nationalism is a debate with obvious relevance. Where is Sinn Féin placed in a typology of European nationalist parties and how does it articulate its nationalism in an era of globalisation? Secondly, the 1990s can be characterised as seeing a rush to the centre by many parties of the broad left, as they sought to win wider support after the crises caused by the perceived failure of Keynesian economics in the 1970s, and the fall-out of the collapse of Soviet style communism. Traditional 'republican' values of the left such as equality were sidelined, in this context, as individual and consumer rights were promoted as the basis for a new individualistic citizenship. As it grows, is Sinn Féin following this trend? Thirdly, has the peace process or the growth of the party led to a weakening of its policy on Irish unity? Finally, declining voter turnout and low levels of engagement with mainstream political parties are now a feature of most wealthy democracies. Parties with a high level of voluntary activism are a rarity – largely confined to those with low levels of support. As Sinn Féin grows, is it leaving behind its activist based extra-parliamentary past?

To clarify the issues involved, this paper examines four interrelated aspects of the party's current political strategy: How does the party deal with the – at least potentially conflicting – pressures of republican thought and nationalist ideology in an era of globalisation and in the context of rising xenophobia in Europe? Has the peace process moderated Sinn Féin's fundamental position on the question of Irish unity? Has the party moved to the political centre as it has grown? Has the tradition of activism and participation within the party declined since the IRA cease-fires, as a new generation of members join?

Globalisation and nationalism

As a nationalist party Sinn Féin faces particular challenges in an era of globalisation and European integration. Critics of nationalist political movements – in particular authors such as Hobsbawm and Kaldor – have placed nationalism in opposition to cosmopolitanism and global fraternity, indeed at times in opposition to modernity itself.[3] How has Sinn Féin sought to reconcile its nationalism with its republicanism and internationalism in this regard?

Despite the tendency in the critical literature to treat all nationalist parties as variants on the Milosevic regime in Serbia, at least three types of 'nationalist' party can been seen in Europe at present.

Clearly there are 'nationalist' parties in Europe of the far-right, for example the *Front Nationale* or the British National Party, who reject the concept of a non-ethnic national identity, and who have sought to mobilise on a platform of racism, playing on communities' fears in a period of societal change. While it lacks the trappings of fascism, the British Conservative Party is in many respects a state-nationalist party of this tradition, with an increasing proportion of their political platform now devoted to issues of migration, British (or indeed English) national-ism and anti-European Union rhetoric.[4]

This is not the only model of politically organised nationalism in Europe. The Scottish National Party and the moderate Catalan and Basque nationalists[5] have provided a more civic oriented model of nation-alism which is capable of a positive engagement with citizenship in a multi-ethnic society. This group clearly does not belong to the far right. They vary in their political ideology and in their commitment to economic equality but tend to take a positive view of European integration, at least since the 1980s, and a reasonably benign view of globalisation.[6]

Thirdly there are those who have placed their nationalism in the context of the anti-corporate globalisation movement asserting a nation-alist vision in contrast to the centralising tendencies of globalisation and regional integration. Sinn Féin seeks to place itself in this context. It is an active participant in the 'anti-globalisation' movement. The party calls for the cancellation of Third World debt, increased development aid and the introduction of the Tobin Tax, and Sinn Féin MEP Bairbre de Brún addressed the World Social Forum in Porto Alegre, Brazil in January 2005 on the issue of privatisation and globalisation. The party also remains highly sceptical of European integration, opposing the centralising tendencies of EU law-making and accusing the EU of prioritising market integration over social equality.[7]

On migration – the key defining issue for right-wing nationalist parties in Europe at present – Sinn Féin has explicitly rejected an ethnic model of republicanism. They, along with the Green Party, were the first political party to oppose the Irish government's plans for a referendum limiting the right to citizenship, and immediately announced they would campaign for a NO vote.[8] The party's manifestos for elections at all levels North and South since 2001 contained explicit anti-racist elements. In addition they called for an amnesty for asylum seekers already within the system and for the right to work,[9] and for the retention of an automatic right to Irish citizenship for children born in the country. The party has also had a strong position on the rights of the Irish traveller community since at least the 1980s, and calls for the recognition of travellers as an ethnic group.[10] Even if critics of the party are dismissive of their policy rhetoric, there is no doubt that Sinn Féin does not campaign on a far-right vision of nationalism, but aligns itself publicly with anti-racist organisations.

On the wider issues raised by the public debates on globalisation, Sinn Féin is highly critical of the global economic system and of the dominant role of the USA, despite the considerable significance which they attach to a strategic involvement with the United States – with Irish American groups, Congress and the Administration – regarding the peace process. The party was very active in the anti-war movement on Iraq – providing speakers for all of the major rallies and opposing the use of Shannon airport by the US military; and they have a highly critical position of US foreign policy in the Middle East in particular.[11] Inevitably these policy positions are used against them in the USA, but there is no evidence that the party has sought to distance itself from these policies or reduce their profile. Neither is there any evidence that the party feels itself under pressure to do so from its support base.

There was, for example, considerable debate about Gerry Adams's visit to Cuba in 2001 and his very public and friendly reception by Fidel Castro. Supporters of the peace process in the US Congress were very vocal in their attacks on the visit.[12] Despite this, Sinn Féin not only proceeded with the visit, but promoted it heavily via their press office. Furthermore they also went ahead with a visit to the Basque country in January 2002, despite the collapse of the peace process there.[13] The 2002 general election manifesto showed no sign that the party was concerned that their position on Cuba was a problem for them, and they explicitly called for an end to the United States embargo of Cuba.[14]

The one area in this regard where the party's policy is clearly in a state of flux is with regard to the European Union. On issues of social protection and regulation Sinn Féin is clearly closer to Berlin (or indeed Paris) than Boston. In a neo-liberal era the EU has the scale to avoid being dragged in a rush to the bottom, even if the current Lisbon agenda has elements of that economic model in its strategic vision. Sinn Féin is unclear however as to whether it would welcome a more consciously social democratic EU even if such were possible, or whether it would see such a move as a violation of national sovereignty (even if in reality small states have never been able to exercise such sovereignty in a global economy).

For example, the party's 2004 EU manifesto said that the Lisbon Agenda mid-term review in 2005 should

> end the almost exclusive focus on competitiveness and privatisation and refocus on the original balance with sustainable economic development, full employment and social protections

and later said

> increased tax-take from 'more and better jobs' must result in better provision of public services such as healthcare, education, and transport – the Lisbon Agenda must work towards setting minimum standards for state provision and must not result in any erosion of public services.

However it then went on to say that 'Sinn Féin MEPs will campaign for the restoration of economic sovereignty', that 'member state governments should retain complete control over taxation policy and strategy' and that the primacy of member states to develop their own economic policy must be re-instated'. The party is very clear that EU competition policy should be amended to allow individual member-states to use more state aid to industry and allow more proactive public-sector enterprises. They are less clear however as to whether EU policy should allow an individual state to pursue a policy of very low taxation, low labour costs, poor labour standards and low social services and still have full access to the EU market place. Certainly they seem to oppose the imposition even of social protection from Brussels.

Similarly, on issues of European security, Sinn Féin is very explicit in opposing any military role for the EU whatsoever. It opposes the use of regional organisations for peacekeeping except under explicit UN mandates. It does call for UN reform but does not engage with the debate on what should be done if UN reform does not happen. It simply says that military power and defence should be left to individual states and peacekeeping to the UN. It does not engage with the debate as to whether a counter-weight to US military capacity in the limited arena of crisis management and peacekeeping would be a positive development globally as a balancing force with a more multilateral ethos. EU security and defence policy, indeed EU common foreign and security policy, is simply dismissed as another attempt to form a superstate with military capacity.

If Sinn Féin's critique of globalisation and European integration is vague at times it is perhaps no more so that the 'anti-global capital' movement more generally. As the party grows they will be forced to develop more explicit and specific policies, which deal with the contradictions in their approach to the EU and which tackle thorny questions such as the impact on Irish farmers of a fairer trade regime for the poorest countries in the world. However, whatever policy weaknesses and contradictions there may be, Sinn Féin is clearly not an ethnic-nationalist party in the model of the European right. They have a clear anti-racist position and call for a softening of immigration laws, not further restrictions. They have sought to wed the party's politics to the global anti-establishment movement, most explicitly in opposition to the war in Iraq, but also on global trade, the environment etc. They have also pursued this agenda even when other party priorities around the peace process might have led to a softly-softly approach towards the US administration.

Moving to the centre?

Sinn Féin's public support base has radically increased since the 1994 IRA ceasefire. It continues to grow within Northern Ireland, but seemed to hit a plateau in the 2007 general election in the Republic (discussed further below). For details see Tables 9.1 and 9.2.

As Sinn Féin has grown and become more successful we might have expected to see the party shift towards the centre in its political perspectives. Without rejecting the importance of other dimensions, policy on Irish unity and issues of economic policy, public services and social inclusion have been important elements of Irish party competition. Sinn Féin has represented the strongest nationalist position on Irish unity, and has also, since the 1980s, articulated a strongly leftist rhetoric on economic and social policy. If there is a tendency to moderation in their political programme, it ought to be most visible on these two domains.

There is, however, very little evidence that Sinn Féin has moved to the centre in its broad political perspective as its support has grown. Michael Laver, in an expert survey of party policy positions, measured Sinn Féin's policy position on a range of economic, social and environmental scales.[15] The party was placed furthest to the left on economic policy – measured as a policy commitment to public spending (compared with all still existing parties) – both in 1992 (before the ceasefires) and again in 1997. In an update of this survey in 2002–03 the party was actually placed further to the left by respondents in terms of this policy dimension.[16] Interestingly, when academic experts are asked to label parties as 'left wing', the Greens become the most left-wing party, despite the Green Party's traditional disavowal of the term.

'Expert' surveys are obviously reliant on the views of the academics concerned. In Laver's 2002 study, the respondents, when asked to compare the parties in totality to their own position, put Sinn Féin on average the furthest away (a score of 15.69 out of 20, marking that party furthest from the respondent's own views). This was interestingly (from

Table 9.1   *Elections in Northern Ireland – % support for Sinn Féin*

2007	2005	2004	2003	2001	1999	1998	1997	1996	1992
Ass.	Gen.	EU	Ass.	Gen.	EU	Ass.	Gen.	Forum	Gen.
26.2	24.3	26.3	23.5	21.7	17.3	17.6	16.1	15.5	10.0

Key: Ass. – Assembly; Gen. – General

Table 9.2   *Elections in the Republic of Ireland – % support for Sinn Féin*

2007	2004	2002	1999	1997	1994
General	EU	General	EU	General	EU
6.9	11.1	6.5	6.3	2.6	3.0

the point of view of studying academics themselves rather than political parties) second only to the Progressive Democrats and Fianna Fáil at an average score of approximately thirteen each.[17] The results from Laver's study are, moreover, confirmed by other sources. For example, the *Irish Times*, in its coverage of Sinn Féin's manifesto launch for the 2002 general election in the Republic of Ireland, ran two headlines: 'Sinn Féin plans higher taxes for rich and businesses' and 'Party lays out surprisingly detailed left-wing vision'.[18]

An analysis of the Sinn Féin manifestos provides a rich source of material, as the party has fought a very large number of elections in recent years – general elections in 1997, 2002 and 2007 in the Republic of Ireland; Northern Ireland Assembly elections in 1998, 2003 and 2007; Northern Ireland Forum elections in 1996; Westminster elections in 1997, 2002 and 2005; EU Parliament elections (North and South) in 1994, 1999 and 2004; in addition to local council elections. It is beyond the space limitations of this chapter to provide a comprehensive content analysis of the manifestos over time or to make comparisons with those of other European left-wing parties. However, a few key points are clear from an analysis of the texts.[19] Firstly, there is a strong consistency over time – there has been no discernible policy shift as measured on a left-right axis in the economic and social arena. There is a strong and traditional left-wing framework to the manifestos which promotes greater public spending in areas such as education, health and housing, advocates stronger local government, environmental protection and rural regeneration and which prioritises social inclusion and equality. For example, the party calls for universal health care, free at the point of use, and increased capital gains taxes, and focuses on greater levels of public spending over tax cuts.[20] Secondly, there are often quite detailed 'community-level' policies, often reflecting the party's involvement in localised campaigns on issues such as waste incinerators, housing and drugs. Thirdly, the macro-economic frameworks in particular are occasionally highly generalised. They have become a little more specific over time – perhaps in response to the growing number of elected representatives and to the party's brief experience in government in Northern Ireland. However, they remain much less specific than the community-level policies, in particular in crucial areas such as taxation, fiscal policy and industrial development.

Apart from their focus on the peace process and Irish unity, discussed in the next section, the party's strongest macro-ideological framework is provided by the concept of 'equality'. The party has also begun to use the language of 'equality' as encapsulating its political programme in recent years. They have used the phrase 'Building an Ireland of equals' as their overall policy document and as a manifesto title in 2002; 'A budget for an Ireland of equals' as their pre-budget submission 2003; 'Governing equally for all' as their programme for government in the North; and 'An Ireland of equals in a Europe of equals' as the title of their EU manifesto in 2004; the 2007 manifesto sub-heads refer to 'Equal access to world class public services', etc. Just as Sinn Féin promoted the word 'peace' in their rhetoric during the early 1990s, they now use the concept of equality as a macro-frame. This is consciously linked to redistribution of wealth nationally and to concepts of global equality. It is also clearly a concept based on equality of outcomes, not just a legalistic 'equality of opportunity'. Many of the current senior party leadership became politically active around the time of the civil rights protests in the 1960s, and the weakness of early 'fair employment' policy, based on ideas of 'equality of opportunity' without targets and timescales for change, has had an impact on party policy. Sinn Féin was also very involved in the US-based 'McBride Principles' campaign on fair employment and in agitating for strengthened fair employment legislation in the late 1980s. This led to significant policy discussion within the party as to what was required to alter the underlying higher rates of unemployment in the nationalist community, and these perspectives now influence wider equality policy around issues of gender, race and class.

Clearly Sinn Féin has not been tested in government in the Republic of Ireland and has had a very limited experience in the North. There is also clear evidence of a high level of pragmatism in the party's actions. For example, the party opposed public-private partnership funding models in education, but Martin McGuinness, as minister for education in Northern Ireland, did not block the building of new schools in public-private partnership projects where the alternative would have been no building at all. Likewise party councillors have voted for estimates, including service charges on some councils where the alternative was abolition, despite opposing them as a form of taxation.

While the party's economic policy is framed in a highly generalised way as prioritising greater social equality, it lacks specifics in many key areas and has in some respects not moved on from their policies in the 1980s. While the logic of the party's spending plans requires an increase in taxation levels (from some sector of society), the party leader Gerry Adams was very reluctant to be specific in a pre-election address to the Dublin Chamber of Commerce in 2004, and the party's last general election manifesto for the Republic of Ireland promised only a review. This will be a pivotal point in the party's development and will determine their medium-term commitment to radical republican ideology.

The 2007 general election in the Republic was a disappointing result for Sinn Féin, by their own admission. Their vote only marginally increased from the 2002 result, despite a widespread belief, supported by pre-election polls, that they would do much better. The reasons for their poor result are complex and include factors outside of the party's own control. The election saw the lowest level of support for small parties and independents in many years – with an aggregate loss of sixteen seats – the Green Party also failed to make any gains and the Socialist Party lost its only seat. The final weeks of the campaign saw a very singular focus on the formation of a government and the selection of Taoiseach. The Labour Party's decision to enter a pre-election pact with Fine Gael, reduced that choice effectively to two blocs, and all those outside those two blocs saw their position marginalised.

There are, however, issues specific to Sinn Féin that may explain at least part of their poor result. There was a lot of media coverage in the final week of the campaign of the party leader's relatively poor performance in two high-profile television appearances. As the peace process has settled down and the era of conflict receded, media interviews shifted from their traditional focus on the IRA and we saw the first detailed discussion of the party's wider economic policies. The criticism of Adams's TV appearances focused on his perceived weaknesses on the detail of tax and economic policy – reflecting not his personal ability as a TV performer but the relatively underdeveloped nature of the party's policy in this area, as discussed above. While there were many attacks from its opponents on the party's left-wing rhetoric and some confusion over its policy on corporation tax, it was the lack of clarity and lack of depth of analysis in its economic policy rather than the extent of its left-wing vision which was at issue and which may have damaged the party.

Sinn Féin entered a power-sharing government in Northern Ireland in May 2007, with Martin McGuinness taking the post of Deputy First

Leader, and the party also gained three other senior ministerial posts. At the time of writing it is, however, too early to analyse the impact of being in government on the party's economic and social policy. Partly this is a question of time, but in addition because the Northern Ireland executive does not have full fiscal authority, Sinn Féin can continue to demand significant public spending without being required to develop a complementary tax policy. The lack of development of party policy on economics is therefore a much more telling problem in the South than it is in the North.

Clearly we cannot know what Sinn Féin would do in a future coalition government in the Republic where they had full fiscal powers, not yet available in Northern Ireland. However what is clear is that they have not, to date, abandoned previous left-wing economic policies as part of their strategy to win new voters. Their recent success is not based on or linked to a moderation of the party's social and economic policies.

Nationalism and Irish unity

The second broad area where the issue of policy moderation needs to be examined is the question of Irish unity. Literature on comparative peace processes has raised the question as to whether militant parties involved in peace processes are 'entrapped' by the process, effectively diluting their original demands as part of the inevitable compromises in political talks. Hard-line positions on core values are a crucial mobilisation tool in periods of intense conflict, but in a period of compromise and negotiation they may be abandoned. In the Irish context, Paul Bew has suggested that, by accepting the principle of consent, Sinn Féin and Irish nationalism more generally has effectively abandoned the demand for Irish unity in all practical respects in return for internal reform within Northern Ireland and North-South links.[21] This is also the premise of Ed Moloney in his recent history of the IRA when he characterises the 1998 Agreement as a trade-off, with unionists getting constitutional security and nationalists getting justice and reform.[22] It is clear that the majority of Ulster Unionists are not at all certain that the constitutional future of Northern Ireland is secure within the UK, and do not accept that issues of internal reform are so readily separated from and traded for constitutional security.[23] There has been less exploration of where Sinn Féin sees its current position on Irish unity.

This raises a related question about the nature of Sinn Féin in particular as a party operating in two separate jurisdictions with different competitors in the two party systems and, to some extent at least, different priorities among their potential electorates. It is suggested in Brian Feeney's otherwise excellent historical study of Sinn Féin that the party operates two different political programmes – with a focus on Irish unity, British injustice and human rights issues in the North, and a focus on community politics and social and economic issues in the South.[24] An analysis of Sinn Féin manifestos in recent elections suggests that, despite this being a common perception, it is not actually the case. All manifestos issued by the party in recent years have had wide-ranging content. In all manifestos issued in the North a clear majority of the documents related to social, environmental and economic issues not directly linked to the question of partition and related human rights issues. The 2003 Assembly election for example has sixty pages out of ninety-three covering social and economic issues not directly related to the conflict, the peace process or Irish unity. An analysis of press releases issued by Sinn Féin in November 2003 (the month of the Assembly election) shows a very wide range of issues raised.[25] Presumably the party focused in press releases on those issues they thought were crucial to mobilising and winning votes, and this indicates that the party press office (at least) believes that a wide range of policies are important to their voters and potential voters. Also in that election, considerable coverage in the *Irish News* and statements issued by their nationalist rivals the SDLP concerned the performance of the two Sinn Féin ministers Martin McGuinness and Bairbre De Brún.

Likewise manifestos issued in the South generally begin with and devote considerable space to Irish unity and related human rights questions. In fact the nature of the content on Irish unity actually became more specific between the 1997 and 2002 elections, and the 2007 manifesto again began with a substantive section on what should be done to advance progress towards Irish unity. In addition to promoting the party's role in the peace process, the 2007 manifesto calls for a Green Paper on Irish unity, the creation of a minister of state with responsibility for coordinating all-Ireland aspects of each department's work, and representation from Northern Ireland to be introduced in the Houses of the Oireachtas. To see the party as essentially two separate political projects is to misunderstand their political programme in the South. The development of the peace process and its relative success is not seen by the party as an irrelevancy in Dublin's working-class communities, but as a positive addition to Sinn Féin's community activism and social radicalism. The peace process gives the party a 'can-do' image at a time when the ability of politics to deliver is questioned by many. The attacks on Sinn Féin's relationship with the IRA may lose them some votes but is also used to promote the party's anti-establishment image. Martin Ferris TD was the focus of very intense media attacks for his previous arrests for IRA gun-running and was also accused of being involved in attacks on drug dealers and criminals, but he went on to be easily elected in 2002 and re-elected in 2007. The challenge for Sinn Féin will be to hold and increase this support base when the high-profile coverage and novelty of the peace process recedes.

In broad terms Sinn Féin are also tapping into a key element of Irish political culture – and in practical terms they are winning votes from the more nationalist supporters of Fianna Fáil and Labour. The electoral appeal of Sinn Féin's nationalism in the Republic of Ireland is however hard to quantify. Opinion polls asking voters to rank the most important issues in a given election do not necessarily capture long-term ideological and cultural influences of nationalism. For example, a person asked to identify the most important issues in a given election may well say 'health' if that is the dominant media debate, even if they personally always vote Sinn Féin because of their nationalist stance. Two recent political events not directly related to Sinn Féin's electoral successes also suggest an ongoing electoral relevance for issues around Irish unity and nationalism.

In the 1997 presidential election campaign there were very strident attacks on the subsequent president, Mary McAleese. It was suggested that she was close to Sinn Féin and therefore an unsuitable candidate. As she had previously stood for election for Fianna Fáil while living in Dublin, and was a public supporter of the SDLP while living in Northern Ireland, the attacks were seen by many commentators as raising a question mark over the suitability of any northern nationalist to hold the office. The nature of these attacks was rejected by a majority of the public,[26] and the high-profile debate was the beginning of McAleese's climb in the opinion polls.[27] The 1997 general election also saw the highest percentage of respondents highlighting Northern Ireland as the most important issue in the general election in recent years – and this, along with the questioning of Fine Gael's ability to manage the peace process, a potentially key issue for marginal and floating voters in that election was enough to make a difference in a tight election.[28] Certainly the two major candidates in the following Fine Gael leadership race sought to position themselves in the Peter Barry or even Michael Collins mould of constitutional nationalism, rather than the more neutralist tradition (as between nationalism and unionism) advocated by John Bruton as leader. Indeed in the 2002 general election Fine Gael went to considerable lengths to avoid any public disagreement with the government on Northern Ireland policy and effectively neutralised it as an issue.[29]

Certainly the Sinn Féin leadership is committed to the peace process. In that regard that is a clear moderation from previous positions while the IRA campaign was ongoing. However the party is equally committed to the pursuit of Irish unity, and it sees that as important to its political project in the Republic as well as Northern Ireland. Its manifestos, press releases and website clearly prioritise the party's role in the peace process and their commitment to Irish unity. There clearly is a relationship between the party's electoral growth and the IRA ceasefire and peace process, but Sinn Féin continues to see the pursuit of Irish unity as the central core of their political programme and their appeal.

Participation and activism

The literature on political parties across Western Europe highlights a reduction in recent years in levels of political participation, electoral turnout, voluntary activism and a shift to smaller, full-time professional, media-oriented parties, where membership is largely a formal affair involving a limited practical commitment to work for the party other than at election time.[30] Media coverage of Sinn Féin's election campaigns, especially the 'colour' pieces on individual candidates canvassing, often refer to the Sinn Féin 'machine' and to the large numbers of party activists working for the party – many of them travelling from the Republic to Northern Ireland and vice versa when an election is taking place in only one jurisdiction.[31] There is also a more general awareness of the party's high-profile community activism. The extent of this activism and its divergence from wider European trends of reduced participation has been not been examined rigorously, but anecdotal evidence from interviews with party members suggests that members have a very high level of activism. They attend regular cumann (branch) meetings (usually weekly), they typically take part in at least one other piece of activity per week – such as a protest, attending a community meeting or involvement in local campaigns and groups. The scale of activity of some members is very intense. It is not that other parties do not have hard-working officials and elected representatives (they obviously do). What is different however is that this level of activism is visible in 'ordinary' party members in Sinn Féin.

The other interesting result from this work was the scale of internal party activity designed to provide forums for members, and in many cases more active supporters to meet with members of the party leadership to discuss party strategy and the peace process. Interviews with figures from the leadership and journalistic accounts of the peace process attest to the scale of the effort put in by the party to running what they call 'republican family' meetings. These have taken place throughout the country at every major juncture of the process and give the party leadership a very strong sense of what their support base is willing to take in terms of political compromise, while allowing party members and supporters a regular channel for debate, and allowing the party leadership to explain the process and their strategy to their support base. These were consciously intended to avert the types of splits which Sinn Féin has experienced historically.

Finally, Sinn Féin's Ard Fheis (party conference) is also unusual for the influence it still has on party policy. While inevitably used by the leadership to maximise positive coverage, it retains for party members its constitutional function of making policy. The nature of the debates and the number of motions passed at a typical Ard Fheis reflect an institution with significant power and authority. It is also not unusual for the Ard Fheis to reject leadership perspectives on at least one issue per year.

Conclusion

Responding to the four questions asked at the beginning of this paper, it is clear that Sinn Féin has explicitly rejected an anti-immigrant, xenophobic form of nationalism. It is consciously seeking to place its nationalism in the context of the anti-globalisation movement, bringing together its previous anti-colonial rhetoric with the concerns of the modern global solidarity movement, such as fair trade and development, anti-racism and the environment. However, unlike many of the organisations in the broad anti-global capital movement, Sinn Féin is also a political party with significant influence on some local councils and with a brief experience of government in Northern Ireland. It remains to be tested in how this broad political approach could be reflected in the more concrete policy programmes required by a political party.

Secondly, Sinn Féin continues to place a high priority on Irish unity in its political campaigning and publicity North and South. Signing up to the Good Friday Agreement has not resulted in Irish unity being de-prioritised in its publicity and manifestos. Rather the peace process seems to have given Sinn Féin a platform – for a period at least – to promote their longer term political project. Irish unity therefore remains a central mobilising project for the party.

Thirdly, on social and economic equality, the party's rhetoric remains left-wing in its focus and emphasises a commitment to a high level of equality in society. It also uses the language of 'equality' as its central macro-policy framework. There is no evidence of a rush to the political centre. The party faces a challenge, however, as it grows to develop in particular more specific economic policies, which could deliver such equality. This will be a challenge, especially if the party is involved in pragmatic coalition government formation at national or local level

Fourthly, the party has retained a high level of party activism and participation by members and even supporters in the activity and internal meetings of the party. It seems to have maintained this level of voluntary commitment from 'ordinary' party members even as the number of its elected representatives grows.

Notes

1 In 1986 Sinn Féin voted at its Ard Fheis (Annual Conference) to contest general elections in the Republic of Ireland and to take their seats if elected, reversing a traditional policy of 'abstentionism' going back to the 1920s. This decision led a small group of mainly older members including the previous party leader Ruairi O Bradaigh to leave the party. The vast majority of Sinn Féin members and almost all its wider public base continued to support the mainstream party.

2 www.sinnFéin.ie/introduction (accessed 26 June 2008).

3 E.g. M. Kaldor, *New and Old Wars: Organised Violence in a Global Era* (Cambridge: Polity, 1999); E.J. Hobsbawm, *Nations and Nationalism since 1780: Programme, Myth, Reality* (Cambridge: Cambridge University Press, 1992).

4 See www.conservatives.com (accessed 26 June 2008).

5 Specifically Convergència Democràtica de Catalunya (CDC) in Catalonia, and the Partido Nacionalista Vasco in the Basque Country.

6 See for a discussion M. Keating, *Nations Against the State: The New Politics of Nationalism in Quebec, Catalonia and Scotland* (Basingstoke: Palgrave, 2001).

7 See Sinn Féin's EU Election Manifesto 2004. pp. 27–8.

8 See www.sinnFéin.ie/news/detail/4839 (accessed 26 June 2008).

9 E.g. 2001 Westminster manifesto and 2007 Irish general election manifesto.

10 See Sinn Féin (2001) *Many Voices, One Country: Cherishing All the Children of the Nation Equally: Towards an Anti-racist Ireland*, and 2004 Local Government manifesto.

11 For example Sinn Féin, *Building an Ireland of Equals* (manifesto for the general election in the Republic of Ireland, 2002).

12 *Belfast News Letter*, 24 December 2001; *Irish News*, 17 December 2001.

13 *Belfast News Letter*, 26 January 2002.

14 Sinn Féin, *Building an Ireland of Equals*.

15 M. Laver, 'Party Policy in Ireland 1997: results from an expert survey', *Irish Political Studies* 13 (1998): 159–70.

16 M. Laver (2003), unpublished data, made available to author by Michael Laver.

17 Other parties were ranked as follows, Fine Gael 11, Green Party 8.7, and Labour 6.88.

18 *Irish Times*, 8 May 2002.

19 They are all available on www.sinnFéin.ie.

20 Sinn Féin, *Building an Ireland of Equals*.

21 E.g. *Irish Times*, 15 May 1998.

22 E. Moloney, *A Secret History of the IRA* (London: Penguin, 2002).

23 J. Doyle, '"Ulster like Israel can only lose once": Ulster unionism, security and citizenship from the fall of Stormont to the eve of the 1998 Agreement', Working Papers in International Studies, 2003: 8 Dublin City University www.dcu.ie/~cis/research/publications.php (accessed 26 June 2008).

24 B. Feeney, *Sinn Féin: A Hundred Turbulent Years* (Dublin: O'Brien Press, 2002).

25 All their press releases are archived on their website.

26 In an *Irish Independent* IMS poll 28 October 1997 (a paper traditionally sympathetic to Fine Gael and hostile to Sinn Féin), 64% of all respondents, and just

over including half of those identifying themselves as FG voters, rejected the attacks on McAleese.

27 For an account see J. Doyle, 'The Irish presidential election', *Irish Political Studies*, 13 (1997): 135–44.

28 See MRBI/*Irish Times* poll, reproduced in 'Irish Political Data 1997', *Irish Political Studies*, 13 (1998): 239–40. For an analysis of opinion polls on this issue see M. Marsh and R. Sinnott, 'The behaviour of the Irish voter', in M. Marsh and P. Mitchell (eds), *How Ireland Voted 1997* (Boulder, CO: Westview Press, 1999), pp. 151–80.

29 See J. Doyle and E. Connolly, 'Foreign policy and domestic politics: a study of the 2002 election in the Republic of Ireland', *Irish Studies in International Affairs*, 13 (2002): 151–66.

30 See Issue 10: 4 (2004) of the journal *Party Politics*, especially P. Seyd, and P. Whiteley, 'British party members: an overview', *Party Politics*, 10: 4 (2004): 355–66.

31 E.g. *Irish Times*, 4 April 2002.

10 The republican movement and the legacy of the Troubles

Henry Patterson

Irish republicanism has been notorious for its internal divisions and feuds, but one unifying belief has been that it is part of a broader republican mainstream founded on ideas of the popular sovereignty of free, equal and self-governing individuals. Its founding fathers, the Belfast Presbyterians who in 1791 founded the Society of United Irishmen, had sought to achieve civil rights for Catholics and reform of parliament through the union of the different religious denominations on the island. But, as Richard English points out, in the crisis-ridden Ireland of the 1790s the United Irishmen allied themselves with the Defenders, a Catholic agrarian secret society which was sectarian, anti-English and anti-settler. English notes the result: 'there was a great tension between Defenderist, sectarian Catholic politics and the initial United Irish ambition to transcend such dynamics'.[1]

Any adequate appreciation of Irish republicanism must recognise the genuineness of the aspiration to transcend sectarianism and ethnic particularism while acknowledging the sad historical reality that the actual periods when republicanism did achieve significant popular support were ones when the movement was deeply affected by the underlying sectarian dynamics of Irish society. This chapter is written by an historian and will focus on one of the most controversial aspects of the recent IRA campaign. It does not do so to ascribe a solely sectarian motivation to the IRA or to deny the historical injustices out of which the campaign emerged. Rather its purpose is to argue that the undoubted republican desire to transcend sectarianism can only be realised by the movement coming to terms with its own implication in actions that were perceived by its victims as motivated by ethnic hatred.

Narratives of the Troubles

The return of devolved government to Northern Ireland on 8 May 2007, coming as it did after the IRA's long-delayed final agreement to go out of business in 2005, can be seen as a very clear indication that the republican movement has entered a radically new phase in its history. The qualitative distinctiveness of this period was most obvious in the various media appearances of Dr Ian Paisley and the Deputy First Minister, Martin McGuinness. These were characterised, to the chagrin of some of Dr Paisley's most fervent erstwhile disciples, by smiles and general bonhomie. Of course, it was inevitable that republicans would integrate the new dispensation into a traditional narrative where the new northern executive would be gradually knitted more and more into an all-Ireland tapestry as the hitherto 'fearful' and 'disoriented' unionists gradually accommodated themselves to the inevitability of unity. However, the subsequent general election in the Republic of Ireland, where Sinn Féin failed to win any new seats, and lost one of its existing ones, was a major setback. It was one important indication that if hard-line unionists had had to accommodate the reality of Sinn Féin's powerful electoral mandate in Northern Ireland, republicans might have to rethink the over-optimistic vistas of a republican government presence on both sides of the Border which would make Sinn Féin's 'all-Ireland' agenda unstoppable.

The result was a sharp warning to a movement that was in clear danger of being, in Stalin's terms, 'dizzy with success'. Such hubris was understandable, for, since the first IRA ceasefire in August 1994, the peace process had put the republican leadership at the centre of attention for the British and Irish governments and earned the respectful consideration not only of the Clinton White House but also of its Republican successor. Irish republicans were supremely successful in integrating the peace process into a broader narrative of their own ability to show leadership and take risks for the process of conflict resolution. Although this narrative and its more po-faced articulation inevitably infuriated the movement's many critics, it succeeded in accumulating significant moral and political capital for the movement. Thus Tony Blair's key aide, Alastair Campbell, though from time to time exasperated by the prevarications of the republican leadership on the decommissioning of IRA weapons, has made clear his admiration for the courage and political skills of Gerry Adams and Martin McGuinness while being much less sympathetic to the concerns and problems of the Ulster Unionist leader, David Trimble, who was seen as lacking the leadership qualities and political imagination of republicans.[2] Whether these judgements were at all fair or adequate is not particularly relevant to the fact that his was the common perception of key players in London, Dublin and Washington. They fed into a broader consensus in nationalist Ireland that, whatever their past, it was Adams and McGuinness who were the true 'statesmen' of the peace process, relegating even key figures like John Hume and Seamus Mallon to the margins.

One of the most remarkable achievements of the Irish republicans since the IRA's ceasefire of 1994 has been in the propagation of what threatens to become the dominant narrative of the causes of political violence during the Troubles. This narrative depicts the Irish process as one of a number of international examples of situations where a long war between entrenched colonial or settler interests and various oppressed groups has been brought to an end through negotiations between former combatants which address the issues of discrimination and structural inequality that generated the original conflict. This narrative is widely accepted in the media and parts of academia. However, unlike other struggles for national liberation in Africa and Latin America, it was the self-designated 'anti-imperialist' force that killed far more victims of the Northern Irish Troubles than did state forces. According to McKittrick et al.'s monumental study of deaths during the Troubles, *Lost Lives*, republicans were responsible for 58 per cent of the deaths between 1966 and 2003 and the Provisional IRA for 48 per cent, while the British Army was responsible for 6.5 per cent, the Royal Ulster Constabulary for 1.4 per cent and the Ulster Defence Regiment for 0.2 per cent. Even if we were to accept the republican claims of widespread collusion between state forces and Protestant paramilitaries, and add 50 per cent of Protestant paramilitary killings to those for which the security forces were allegedly responsible, we would still come up with a figure of around 17 per cent.[3]

The hegemony of a particular narrative of the Troubles has been one of the reasons for the widespread unease with the process amongst the Protestant/Unionist community in Northern Ireland. As a result, the ending of the Troubles with the IRA cessation of violence and the Belfast Agreement of 1998, although it has removed the most destructive forms of ethnic conflict in Northern Ireland, has not ushered in a period of cross-community reconciliation. The 'war' has, in part, been transferred into a clash of conflicting narratives of 'who was to blame' for the Troubles and in particular for its thousands of victims. There has been much talk of a possible Truth and Reconciliation Commission on South African lines being established. But, as Roy Foster has noted, the South African body declared that 'factual and objective truth' was not enough in a traumatised society: other forms of 'social or dialogue truth' or 'healing truth' needed to be added.[4] As he implies, there remains a major research agenda for contemporary historians to try to provide that factual and objective truth without which this dreadful period will largely remain the province of ethnic entrepreneurs ransacking it for their conflicting political projects.

The Border dimension

Most of the existing research on the IRA, like most research on the Troubles, is heavily dominated by studies that either focus on the urban areas of Belfast and Derry, or treat Northern Ireland as a single unit for analysis. This has meant that the distinct experiences of rural and Border areas, apart from the city of Derry, have been neglected. This chapter is part of a broader research project which aims to examine in detail the relation between ethno-national mentalities, religion and political violence in the Border areas of Northern Ireland: Fermanagh, Tyrone, Armagh and Down from 1969 to 1994 when the IRA declared its first ceasefire. These predominantly rural areas were the sites of some of the highest rates of violence during the Troubles.[5] They were also areas where the Protestant population, the majority in Northern Ireland as a whole, were often a minority. Fermanagh and Tyrone had been, along with the city of Derry, the sites of gerrymandering and discrimination during the years of Unionist control of the Northern Ireland state. Their Protestant populations were preoccupied with the perceived demographic threat from the Catholic community and expected their politicians to practise a politics of communal defence through control of the allocation of public housing and jobs.[6] Catholics in these areas had hoped at the time of partition to be included in the new Irish state and living so close to their co-religionists in the Irish Republic, were particularly incensed about the 'artificiality' of partition. These were also areas with strong communal memories of the seventeenth-century plantation of the county and the expropriation of the Gaelic and Catholic landowners by new English and Protestant settlers. Protestants ended up with the best land, Catholics were pushed out to the hilly and more marginal areas. As a journalist noted of south Fermanagh in 1980: 'The fact that Protestants hold much of the best land is a source of some resentment among the Catholics. "This is an area of disadvantaged land, bad land", a Catholic resident explained, "Where you get good land you tend to get them [Protestants]. They have maintained their advantage over the years".'[7]

The IRA campaign in Fermanagh

The focus here is on County Fermanagh in the south west of Northern Ireland. Prior to the Troubles, although historical memories and political and national identities were deeply divided in the county, day-to-day living was usually relatively amicable and harmonious. As the Irish travel writer, Dervla Murphy, noted of Fermanagh even during the early years of the Troubles, there was little 'to flaw the impression of a traditional rural community going about its daily tasks in a contented neighbourly way. A Protestant lends medicine for a sick Catholic cow, a Catholic fetches a spare part for a broken Protestant tractor, everybody goes to the funeral of an Orangeman who always spoke out against the fiddling of the electoral register'. But she adds that there would be a 'fuss' if 'any member of either community breaks an unwritten sectarian law'.[8] These 'laws' included no inter-marriage and no selling of land to the 'other sort'. Unionists often refer nostalgically to the pre-Troubles period as one in which they and their Catholic neighbours got on well, often claiming that Catholics were happy to come out and watch their neighbours as they paraded in their Orange regalia. This mythology of a prelapsarian Ulster functions to allocate sole blame and responsibility for the Troubles to nationalist demagogues and the IRA.

In reality much of the common coinage of internal Unionist and Orange discourse in the pre-Troubles period related to the always-present Catholic threat, in particular the alleged clerically supported strategy of 'peaceful penetration': buying up Protestant land and businesses.[9] Similarly many Catholics who would have not supported violence nevertheless continued to see Protestants as interlopers and partition as a continuous affront. There had been significant IRA violence in the county during the War of Independence and the period immediately after the creation of the northern state in 1921, and, during the 1956–62 campaign, the IRA had concentrated its activities in Border counties. Its most famous raid: the attack on Brookeborough RUC station in January 1957, in which Sean South and Fergal O'Hanlon were killed, occurred very close to one of the areas most affected by IRA attacks during the Troubles: south Fermanagh.[10] However, most of the victims of IRA attacks during the 1920s and the 1950s had been members of the state's police force killed in gun battles with groups of IRA men. The leadership of the IRA during the 1956 campaign made the decision that the part-time militia, the 'B' Special Constabulary, would not be targets. A participant in the campaign described the thinking behind this decision:

> They [the IRA] couldn't shoot a 'B' Special. There were 10,000 of them marching on the roads every night the IRA people sitting in a ditch waiting for an opportunity to hit the RUC and the British Army which were the armed people that they were fighting against, and they couldn't even fire a shot at a 'B' Special because the Specials were seen as ordinary Protestant people, mostly Protestant workers, getting a few shillings for marching around. Now there was no socialism or anything involved in the 1956 campaign ... but they were Protestant people and very much Irish and we had no campaign against the Protestant people.[11]

There is some evidence that this decision was not popular with local IRA men but it seems to have been effective as no 'B' Special was killed or wounded during that campaign.[12]

The 'B' Specials were abolished in 1970 as part of the reforms imposed by the British government on the Unionist regime as a result of the civil rights movement. The Specials were replaced by the Ulster Defence Regiment (UDR). This was to be a regiment of the British Army although, unlike any other regiment, it was to be recruited only within Northern Ireland. It was planned that the regiment would aim to recruit a significant number of Catholics and initially a considerable number of Catholics did join. However a number of factors led many of these to resign whilst the supply of Catholic recruits dried up. Most of the command staff of the UDR were former 'B' Specials, as were many of the rank and file and this could create an antagonistic atmosphere for Catholics. This 'chill factor' was added to by the reluctant British decision to support the Unionist government's introduction of internment without trial in August 1971 and the disaster of 'Bloody Sunday' in Derry on 31 January 1972, when British paratroopers shot dead thirteen people during a civil rights demonstration. The Provisional IRA also set out to intimidate and murder Catholic members. The result was that by the end of 1972 Catholics made up 3.7 per cent of the total.[13] The regiment was also accused of being infiltrated by Protestant paramilitaries and its members of having colluded in the assassination of Catholics. Even more common was the claim that UDR men regularly abused Catholics at vehicle check-points and while they were searching properties.[14]

In Fermanagh, where many Protestants had been members of the 'B' Specials, they now joined the part-time UDR and the RUC Reserve, activities which they could combine with their day-to-day occupations as farmers, factory workers, postmen, delivery men and shopkeepers. The Provisional IRA had targeted the UDR from the regiment's inception. The IRA's depiction of the UDR was of an organisation of 'state sanctioned armed sectarian thugs'.[15] This description was included in an article in the republican movement's weekly paper, *An Phoblacht/Republican News* (*AP/RN*), 'UDR in the firing line', which reported the following incident that occurred in South Fermanagh on 5 February 1980: 'A UDR man was shot dead by IRA volunteers during the evening. He was ambushed at Edenmore on the road to Kinawley.'

The same incident is described in McKittrick et al.'s *Lost Lives*:

Alexander Abercrombie, UDR, Protestant, 44, married, 4 children, farmer. A part-time corporal, his body was slumped over the steering wheel of his tractor where he had been shot by the IRA on a remote part of his farm near Kinawley, about five miles from the county Cavan border. He was found by his brother who had gone to the farm to look for him when he had not returned for a meal.[16]

AP/RN's description of the killing was typical in its minimalism and its failure to mention that the UDR man was not in uniform and was performing his occupation when he was shot. The campaign against the UDR in Fermanagh had been going on since the early 1970s and most of its victims were part-timers who were killed when they were off-duty. Thus, on 21 September 1972, Thomas Bullock, a UDR man and a farmer was shot together with his wife at their farm at Killynick, Aghalane. They were watching TV when the gunmen attacked. According to a journalist's account, 'Mrs Bullock was shot in the chest at the front porch and the gunmen stepped over her dead body and went inside where they shot her husband several times in the head and neck'.[17]

In 1972 the UDR regiment based in Fermanagh lost six members, four of them on their farms along the Border. Another ten were wounded. Four farm families with UDR members in the Garrison area had to sell their land and animals and move to safer areas.[18] So brutal and shocking was the murder of the Bullocks that it was claimed that the Provisionals had called off their campaign against off-duty members of the UDR.[19] If such a decision was ever made, it did not prevent John Bell, another part-timer, being shot dead on 22 October, when a car in which he, his father and his brother were travelling to an out-farm owned by the family was ambushed by three IRA men who opened fire from behind a hedge.[20]

However, over the next seven years only one more UDR man was killed in South Fermanagh. The reasons for this are not clear, but it may in part reflect the fact that the leadership of the movement in the early and mid-1970s was dominated by southern republicans many of whom had been involved in the 1956 campaign and who may have had qualms about the attacks on UDR part-timers. The leadership's policy document *Eire-Nua* (1971) had set out constitutional structures for a federal Ireland, which they saw as being aimed at attracting Protestants to the republican project.[21] However some of the up-and-coming Northern Provisionals saw this document as unnecessarily conciliatory towards the Unionist community. They were also disenchanted with the Southern-dominated leadership because of the disastrous 1975 ceasefire that the leadership had negotiated with the British under the mistaken impression that the latter were intent on withdrawal from Northern Ireland.[22] In fact the British had used the ceasefire to get rid of the politically embarrassing policy on internment and also to introduce the policy of 'Ulsterisation': reductions in the overt presence of the regular British Army and turning over greater responsibility for security to the locally recruited forces of the RUC and UDR.[23] It is also possible that the weakening of IRA discipline and structures during the ceasefire had undermined its capacity to continue with its campaign in Fermanagh in the mid-1970s.

When Gerry Adams and his northern compatriots challenged the leadership of the southerners from the mid-1970s, one of their targets was *Eire Nua* and what was seen as its failure to appreciate the totally reactionary and 'colon' nature of Ulster unionism. The 'Long War' strategy developed by Adams and his comrades in the late 1970s accepted that it could take up to two decades of armed struggle to break Britain's will to remain in Northern Ireland, and in the interim one of the main functions of the armed struggle was to 'keep the pot boiling': to keep Northern Ireland on London's political agenda. Adams was particularly concerned to ensure that no deal was developed between the Ulster Unionists and the moderate Nationalists of John Hume's Social Democratic and Labour Party (SDLP) which would have marginalised republicans. As one Tyrone republican explained to the journalist Ed Moloney, the killing of UDR men 'stops the Unionists doing a deal with the SDLP'.[24] It was also the case that 'Ulsterisation' by cutting down on the number of British soldiers available as targets meant the Provisionals had an added incentive to target the RUC and UDR.

The establishment of Adams's hegemony in the republican movement at the end of the 1970s coincided with an intensification of attacks on the UDR in Border areas. South Fermanagh was particularly affected. Protestants were a minority in this area which had many miles of Border with the Irish Republic; this was crossed with scores of roads which left it, in the words of the Ulster Unionist Party leader, James Molyneaux, 'wide open' to Provisional attacks launched by IRA units based in the Republic.[25] The *Irish Times* journalist David McKittrick visited Newtownbutler, one of the main towns in the area, in June 1980, when local Protestants were acutely aware of the IRA threat. So far that year three members of Galloon Parish Church had been killed. One was a police reservist, Robert Crilly, aged sixty, who was shot in January. In April Victor Morrow, a former UDR man aged sixty-two, was shot dead outside his home, and in June, Richard Latimer, a part-time member of the UDR, was shot dead inside his hardware shop in the main street of the town. As McKittrick noted of the position of UDR members in the area, 'They seem to be sitting ducks. They are armed with legally-issued weapons for their personal protection but still the Provisionals can pick them off almost at will.'[26]

Fermanagh had traditionally been a bastion of Ulster Unionist Party strength, but the fears and resentment caused by the IRA campaign encouraged the populist Protestant politician, the Reverend Ian Paisley, to begin regular visits to the county to try to establish a presence for his Democratic Unionist Party. He was loud in his protests about IRA 'genocide' and, to the dismay of local Ulster Unionists, publicly encouraged the notion that if the British government did not take action by the closure of all but the main cross-Border roads, Protestants should take whatever steps were necessary to protect themselves. On 23 June 1980 over 7,000 Protestants from all over Fermanagh came to Newtownbutler for a rally addressed by Paisley and Molyneaux, and organised by the Fermanagh United Protestant Action Group for the Defence of Family and Home. The response of *An Phoblacht/Republican News* to the rally was revealing:

> Paisley and Molyneaux are distorting the attacks on crown forces into 'Genocide against the Protestant people', an allegation which immediately collapses upon inspection. Only last week the Church of Ireland Primate, Dr John Armstrong, whilst expressing concern about killings in the area, stated that 'it is difficult to find evidence of a plan to eliminate Protestants'.[27]

AP/RN also quoted from an editorial on the killings in the *Irish Times*: 'The Provos kill them because they donned a British uniform and participated in the war against the IRA.' But the editorial was more critical of the IRA campaign than this extract implied and if we read the full text of the Archbishop's interview, we find:

> In south Armagh and Fermanagh 54 Protestants had been killed. Many students from border areas at Queen's University Belfast were seriously worried about the safety of their parents and other relatives. The chaplains at Queen's had been in communication with him about these students who are in a ferment of fear. Their studies are being upset. They get their Chaplains to ring to see if their parents are safe.[28]

Asked if there seemed to be a terrorist plan to kill Protestants or intimidate them so much that they would be compelled to move to other areas, he said 'there seemed to be a disturbing pattern in the killings. Sometime the person killed would be the natural successor to the farm, like an elder son. It is difficult to find evidence of a plan to eliminate Protestants. The only evidence is that so many people have been killed.' It seems that what the Archbishop was saying that there was no evidence that would stand up in a court of law – a common problem of democratic states dealing with terrorist movements.

The republicans also omitted this section of the *Irish Times* editorial: 'To the Unionist community along the Border, they [the UDR men] are husbands and fathers, often the mainstay of Protestant families. They do what their community by and large expects in joining the UDR … the loss of men folk is a blow to the heart of any community.'[29]

The IRA in Fermanagh condemned the organisers of the Newtownbutler rally for 'attempting to create mass sectarian strife in Northern

Ireland ... we will not allow anyone to turn the war of national liberation against the Brits into sectarian strife'. However, their declaration that 'Fermanagh people have nothing to fear because of their religion' would not have reassured many Protestants when they read: 'The only people who need fear are those who wear the British uniform or who associate with the collaborationist forces in maintaining the British occupation.'[30] The death penalty for 'association' hung over a large proportion of Fermanagh Protestants, many of who had members of the security forces in their families and whose Unionism made them de facto 'collaborators'. Protestants in the county also knew that resignation from the UDR or RUC reserve was no guarantee of safety. Thus on 17 April, Victor Morrow, a former member of the UDR, was shot dead 150 yards from his home on his way to work on the night shift of a factory in Lisnaskea. *AP/RN* had this to say of the killing:

> A founder member of Britain's sectarian militia, the UDR and a former member of the even more infamous 'B' Specials was shot dead by the IRA on the evening of 17th April. He was ambushed by the IRA on the Newtownbutler to Clones Road. The local IRA commander pointed out that their intelligence indicated that the dead man had been active member of the UDR in contradiction to media references to his recent resignation from the regiment.[31]

In fact the victim had retired from the UDR a year earlier. Perhaps he should have taken the advice of the local IRA who, in a statement, said that those who wished to resign from the UDR and RUC or had recently done so 'can have their names taken off the list of targets if they make their position know through republican contacts or clerics'.[32] But killings of former UDR and RUC men continued, and it would be one of these that caused the IRA to announce that its Fermanagh unit had been 'stood down' in January 1989. Harry Keys, a former member of the RUC Reserve, was shot twenty-three times by the IRA while sitting in his car with his girlfriend outside her home in County Donegal in the Republic.[33]

Ethnic cleansing?

The use of the term 'ethnic cleansing' in relation to the violence in these areas has been controversial. Ian Paisley used the term 'genocide' for the IRA killings in Fermanagh in the early 1980s. It was inevitable that for nationalists this language was objectionable, as it was not used by Unionists with reference to the killings and expulsions of Catholics from workplaces and residential areas in parts of Northern Ireland where they were the minority.

In existing academic analysis there is little use of the term.[34] In what is the main work on the human cost of the Troubles the sole reference is a fleeting one: 'some would argue that a process of "ethnic cleansing" of Protestants from the Border areas of Tyrone and Fermanagh has taken place over the years.'[35] It has been left to journalists to take the term seriously.[36] Because most of the victims of IRA violence were members of the security forces it has been easier for the deaths to be depicted as part of a broader essentially 'strategic' conflict between republican paramilitaries and the state.[37] The most recent academic history of the Provisionals by Richard English mentions the campaign against the UDR in county Tyrone as contributing to 'sectarian war'. He places the campaign in the context of the British state's 'Ulsterisation' policy, quoting an interview with the Tyrone republican Tommy McKearney offering:

> [v]ery bitter criticism of the British state in Ireland, that it has used locals to police the situation, with all the problems that that creates ... [In County Tyrone] we struck at the British state. But by 1975/1976 – and that is where I would still feel angry with the British state in its policy of Ulsterisation- –once they had decided to bring the regulars out of the front line and put the RUC and the UDR up front, if we, the IRA or the UDR ... In terms of pure, practical military position, its not possible to overlook a substantial section of your enemy ... the people that insisted on the primacy of the UDR and the RUC was not the IRA, it was the British government.[38]

In his conclusion, where he attempts to subject republican justifications for armed struggle to critical analysis, English is circumspect in his judgement on the campaign's effects on relations between Northern Ireland's two communities:

> Another key point concerns the effects of IRA violence on sectarian division. For even if the organisation has intended to avoid sectarian warfare – and it seems fair to acknowledge, for example, that the IRA could easily have carried out far more simply sectarian killings than it has done – that does not mean that its campaign has not had a divisive effect in some respects.[39]

How circumspect should we be about the use of the term ethnic cleansing? It is true that more Protestants could have been killed and more Protestant businesses bombed and destroyed. The process of attacks and intimidation was clearly not of Balkan proportions. But this in itself does not rule the term out. This chapter takes as its theoretical point of departure Michael Mann's innovatory comparative study of ethnic cleansing,

The Dark Side of Democracy. Here he warns us that 'murderous ethnic cleansing is not primitive or alien. It belongs to our own civilisation and to us.' He adds that 'ordinary people are brought by normal social structures into committing murderous ethnic cleansing and their motives are much more mundane'.[40] If we look at his general theses aimed at explaining these atrocities then we can easily identify Fermanagh as fulfilling one of his key factors: 'the danger zone of murderous ethnic cleansing is reached when movements claiming to represent two fairly old ethnic groups both lay claim to their own state over all or part of the same territory.'[41] But he also notes that 'going over the brink' is most likely where 'the state exercising sovereignty over the contested territory has been factionalised', i.e. full-blown ethnic cleansing occurs when the pre-existing state has disintegrated. Though Border Protestants claimed to have been left at the mercy of the IRA, the fact that many more were not killed owes much more to the continuing capacity of the British state to resist terrorism than to the 'warrior's honour' of the Provisionals.[42]

It was also limited by political ambitions of the political wing of the republican movement, Sinn Féin, when it emerged as a serious challenger to the SDLP for the political leadership of Northern Ireland's Catholics in the 1980s. From the mid-1980s Gerry Adams was also attempting to build a pan-nationalist alliance with the SDLP and Fianna Fáil, the dominant party in the Irish Republic. The purpose of this alliance was to put political pressure on the British government for a shift in its Northern Ireland policy. The Fermanagh Provisionals became an embarrassment when they carried out the bombing of the Enniskillen Remembrance Day ceremony in November 1987 in which eleven Protestants were killed. Undaunted, they continued to provide Adams with more occasions for hand-wringing when, in March 1988, they shot dead Gillian Johnston, a twenty-one-year-old shop worker, while she was sitting in a car with her fiancé. The IRA admitted to a mistake, but claimed that the real target was a family member who was in the UDR. The RUC said there was no connection between the family or her fiancé and the security forces. When the same unit set off a bomb in a school bus near Lisnaskea, aimed at the driver, a part-time UDR man, but injured school children,[43] and then went on to kill Harry Keys, the potential political costs of such activities to Sinn Féin resulted in its disbandment.[44]

In an interview with the *Observer*'s Irish correspondent, Mary Holland, in June 1988, Adams said that it would be 'vastly preferable' for the IRA to target British soldiers rather than the RUC and UDR: 'when a British soldier dies it removes the worst of the agony from Ireland. It also diffuses the sectarian conflict because Loyalists don't see the killing of British soldiers by the IRA as an attack on their community.'[45] This is the nearest the President of Sinn Féin has ever come to recognising what the

IRA inflicted upon Protestants in Border areas of Northern Ireland. As Roy Foster noted of Adams's autobiography, 'the bombing of shopping centres, the boycotting of Protestant business and the effective ethnic cleansing of Protestant communities from rural areas'[46] do not feature. A more honest evaluation was given by a member of the IRA's Army Council in an interview in 1990: 'The Unionists too are victims of partition. There are Protestant families in Tyrone who have had six in one family killed. I understand that they will remain bitter for a long time: they will probably never integrate into a unitary Irish state.'[47]

There is no doubt that many Provisionals then and now would forcefully deny that their campaign in Fermanagh was a form of ethnic cleansing. As we have seen, most of the Protestants killed were in the security forces, and Fermanagh did not experience the wholesale forced emigration of Protestants that occurred in West Cork during the War of Independence (1919–21) and which Peter Hart has chronicled.[48] Yet that the killings struck at the Protestant community's morale, sense of security and belonging in the area is undeniable. It was being made clear to them that they could continue to live in Fermanagh but on terms defined by the republican movement. That this prospect appalled more than Protestants and Unionists is clear from the following quotation from an editorial in the *Fermanagh Herald*, the county's nationalist newspaper. It was provoked by the killing of a part-time UDR man in County Down:

> To the Republicans the UDR is little better than the armed wing of the Unionist junta ... It seems a waste of time to keep pointing out how each killing adds its own little pool of bitterness to the vast sea already created by the Troubles. How many tens of thousands must there now be in this small state, who can hardly care anymore about how it all ends, their lives shattered beyond repair? How hollow to them, must sound the pleas for peace and reconciliation, for goodwill and working together, for abjuring the past to build a new society?[49]

The question of how to deal with the history of the Troubles has emerged as a topic which all the parties in Northern Ireland's new government have a commitment to address while at the same time it contains an obvious potential to destabilise its still fragile political structures. Some influential commentators have suggested that a line be drawn under the past to allow the new dispensation to establish itself. This happened in Spain where, after the death of General Franco, a *'pacto de olvido'* (pact of forgetting) was agreed by the new socialist government that feared that addressing the issues of Franco's victims would destabilise its relationship with the armed forces and police. But the pact has come under increasing criticism from the families of Franco's victims, and the

Socialist government introduced a '*Ley de memoria historica*' (law of historic memory) in 2007 to attempt to deal with the issue of repressed remembrance.[50] Apart from the lessons of the Spanish experience of trying to forget the past there is also the fact that the British government has already agreed a series of inquiries into a number of high-profile instances of state violence, it is unlikely that a policy of ignoring the victims of paramilitary organisations will be acceptable.

Dealing with the past

The republican movement faces a major challenge in how it responds to these issues. It is difficult to demand that the British state provide information on its role in the conflict as part of the process of reconciliation and confidence building and ignore the role that republicans played in many of the darkest episodes of the Troubles. In July 2002 the IRA issued a statement of apology to the relatives of 'non-combatants' killed in the course of its operations.[51] From the republican perspective many of the Protestant victims in Fermanagh were part of the state's security apparatus and thus 'legitimate targets'. But as the quotation from Gerry Adams given earlier hints, it may be possible for republicans to accept that from the perspective of the embattled communities of Border Protestants, the killings of UDR personnel were a direct assault on their very presence in this part of Northern Ireland. The unionist narrative of 'ethnic cleansing' may be an extremely contestable one intellectually, but that it speaks to the deeply felt experience of these communities is undeniable. A republican willingness to confront this part of the movement's history would be a powerful contribution to reconciliation. It would also represent evidence that there remains substance to the republican aspiration to transcend sectarianism. However, the prospects for such a settling of accounts with the past do not appear promising. *An Phoblacht* continues to run a regular feature 'Remembering the Past' which focuses with pride on key events and personalities in the IRA's campaign. Recent examples have been articles on the 'Loughgall Martyrs': the IRA men shot dead by the SAS when they attempted to attack an RUC station in 1987, and the IRA's shooting dead of three RUC men in the centre of Newry in July 1986.[52] The republican movement's radical shift in military and political strategy which has seen it jettison armed struggle, give de facto recognition to partition, and recognise policing and judicial structures in Northern Ireland make it extremely difficult to contemplate any form of historical revisionism about its campaign. For such an openness to critical historical reflection would raise the profoundly disturbing question of why so much death, injury and trauma was necessary to attain a settlement that was not fundamentally different from the Sunningdale Agreement of

1973. Nevertheless, there may be some basis for a degree of optimism that, as part of a full accounting of the North's contested past, republicans will deal with this dire aspect of their history. The willingness of the leader of the DUP to consider a republican proposal for a 'conflict transformation centre' on the site of the prison hospital at the former Maze prison where the IRA hero Bobby Sands died on hunger strike in 1981 was one of the more positive developments associated with the new government in the North. Paisley's position, at odds with views of some of his colleagues, was justified by the acceptance by republicans that the centre would also deal with the IRA killings of prison officers. If such openness to the damage, hurt and trauma caused by the IRA campaign can be built on then it would make a powerful contribution to reconciliation in the North.

Notes

1 Richard English, *Irish Freedom: The History of Nationalism in Ireland* (London: Pan Macmillan, 2006), p. 93.
2 Alastair Campbell, *The Blair Years* (London: Hutchinson, 2007).
3 David McKittrick et al., *Lost Lives: The Stories of the Men, Women and Children Who Died as a Result of the Northern Ireland Troubles* (Edinburgh and London: Mainstream, 2004), p. 1534.
4 R.F. Foster, *The Irish Story: Telling Tales and Making It Up In Ireland* (Oxford: Oxford University Press, 2001), p. 185.
5 Michael Poole, 'The geographical location of political violence in Northern Ireland', in J.Darby et al., *Political Violence: Ireland in a Comparative Perspective* (Belfast: Appletree; Ottawa: University of Ottawa Press, 1990), pp. 76–7.
6 See Henry Patterson, 'In the land of King Canute: Border Unionists and Unionist politics 1945–1963', *Contemporary British History*, 20:4 (2006).
7 'Protestants in NI Border town want the Border sealed', *Irish Times*, 23 June 1980.
8 Dervla Murphy, *A Place Apart* (London: Devin-Adair Publishers, 1978), p. 64.
9 See Patterson, 'In the land of King Canute'.
10 Some indication of the significance of the Brookeborough raid was its immortalisation in two very popular ballads: *The Patriot Game* and *Sean South of Garryowen*. The best account of the raid in its local context can be found in Peadar Livingstone, *The Fermanagh Story* (Enniskillen: Cumann Seanchais Chlochair, 1969), pp. 384–6.
11 Tomas MacGiolla, quoted in Sean Swan, 'The Official Republican Movement: From Ceasefire to Ceasefire 1962–72', PhD, University of Ulster, 2006.
12 Enda Staunton has claimed that the claim that the 'B' Specials were not targeted 'does not stand up to examination' and points to an IRA statement in September 1958 that in future the Specials would be regarded as 'legitimate resistance targets': see his *The Nationalists of Northern Ireland 1918–1973* (Dublin: Columba Press, 2001), p. 225. Yet this was two years into the campaign and implies that they were not targets up until then. By this time the campaign had

been effectively defeated and it is difficult to explain the lack of Special casualties unless they had been excluded from the list of targets during the height of the campaign.

13 John Potter, *A Testimony to Courage: The Regimental History of the Ulster Defence Regiment* (Barnsley: Pen & Sword Books, 2001), p. 67.

14 Chris Ryder, *The Ulster Defence Regiment: An Instrument of Peace?* (London: Methuen, 1991), pp. 151–85.

15 'UDR in the firing line', *An Phoblacht/Republican News*, 9 February 1980.

16 McKittrick et al., *Lost Lives*, p. 820.

17 Ibid., p. 267.

18 Potter, *A Testament to Courage*, pp. 73–4.

19 McKittrick et al., *Lost Lives*, p. 285.

20 Ibid., p. 285.

21 Henry Patterson, *The Politics of Illusion: A Political History of the IRA* (London: Serif, 1997), p. 181.

22 Paul Bew and Henry Patterson, *The British State and the Ulster Crisis: From Wilson to Thatcher* (London: Verso, 1985) pp. 78–88.

23 M.L.R. Smith, *Fighting for Ireland: The Military Strategy of the Irish Republican Movement* (London: Routledge, 1995), p. 142.

24 Ed Moloney, *A Secret History of the IRA* (London: Penguin, 2002), p. 338.

25 David McKittrick, 'Protestants in NI town want the Border sealed', *Irish Times*, 23 June 1980.

26 Ibid.

27 *An Phoblacht/Republican News*, 28 June 1980.

28 *Irish Times*, 19 June 1980.

29 'Down what road?', *Irish Times*, 25 June 1980.

30 *An Phoblacht/Republican News*, 28 June 1980.

31 *An Phoblacht/Republican News*, 26 April 1980.

32 *An Phoblacht/Republican News*, 28 June 1980.

33 McKittrick et al., *Lost Lives*, p. 1157.

34 But see an interesting questioning of the term in Graham Dawson, *Making Peace With the Past? Memory, Trauma and the Irish Troubles* (Manchester and New York: Manchester University Press, 2007).

35 M. Fay, M. Morrisey and M. Smyth, *Northern Ireland's Troubles: The Human Costs* (London: Pluto Press, 1999), p.147.

36 See Carlo Gebler, *The Glass Curtain: Inside an Ulster Community* (London: Hamish Hamilton, 1991) and Susan McKay, *Northern Protestants: An Unsettled People* (Belfast: Blackstaff, 2000).

37 Fay et al., *Northern Ireland's Troubles*, p. 133 and B. O'Duffy and B. O'Leary, 'Violence in Northern Ireland 1969–89', in J. McGarry and B. O'Leary (eds), *The Future of Northern Ireland* (Oxford: Oxford University Press, 1990).

38 Richard English, *Armed Struggle: A History of the IRA* (London: Pan, 2003), p. 174.

39 Ibid., p. 372.

40 Michael Mann, *The Dark Side of Democracy: Explaining Ethnic Cleansing* (Cambridge: Cambridge University Press, 2005), pp. 3–9.

41 Mann, *The Dark Side of Democracy*, p. 6.

42 Michael Ignatieff, *Warrior's Honour: Ethnic War and the Modern Conscience* (London: Holt, 1999).
43 Moloney, *A Secret History of the IRA*, p. 341.
44 McKittrick et al, *Lost Lives*, p. 1120.
45 Moloney, *A Secret History of the IRA*, p. 337.
46 Foster, *The Irish Story*, p. 182.
47 'The men of war promise third violent decade', *The Independent*, 29 September 1990.
48 Peter Hart, *The IRA and its Enemies: Violence and Community in Cork, 1916–1923* (Oxford: Oxford University Press, 1998) pp. 273–92.
49 *Fermanagh Herald*, 24 January 1981.
50 See Giles Tremlett, *Ghosts of Spain: Travels Through a Country's Hidden Past* (London: Faber and Faber, 2007), pp. 69–95.
51 Agnes Maillot, *New Sinn Fein Irish Republicanism in the Twenty-First Century* (London: Routledge, 2005), p. 161.
52 http://www.anphoblacht.com/features/2007-07-26 (accessed 28 July 2007).

11 Civic and Irish republicanism

Garret FitzGerald

I understand civic republicanism to be about a pluralist state marked by the public engagement of its citizens in the interest of the common good. But because of the shape that Irish history took – and despite all the pieties about Wolfe Tone and Thomas Davis – it is not easy to get Irish people to relate to this concept of republicanism.[1]

The truth is that Irish unicultural nationalism, preoccupied as it has been with its post-Gaelic Catholic ethos – which has since the nineteenth century been the prevailing political ideology of the majority in our island – and dominated by local and sectional issues rather than by the common good of Irish society as a whole, is not only different from, but in these key respects fundamentally opposed to civic republicanism. I would add that the preoccupation of Irish 'republicanism' for historical reasons, with opposition to monarchical forms in their own right rather than in terms of the actual role of these forms in the process of governance has also had a distorting effect by greatly narrowing the focus of Irish republicans.

Because the British made their monarchy a powerful symbol of their rule, and even after the First World War sought to use it to maintain what they called the 'unity of the Empire' (that is, continued British influence over the now self-governing Dominions), Irish nationalists were perforce anti-monarchist. This made them republicans in the limited constitutional sense of the word, but not necessarily civic republicans.

This greatly narrowed the Irish concept of republicanism, distracting attention even further from civic republicanism. Within the Irish state, this issue has happily been dead for more than half a century, but it is not dead in Northern Ireland, where it has continued to be an issue in the minds of many people – positive for some, negative for others.

The problem of the use of the monarchy to assert some kind of continued British involvement in Irish affairs was tackled, with consider-able if not complete success, in the negotiations with the British on the

1922 Constitution. As a result, the Irish Constitution of 1922 differed from those of all other Dominions in, for example, eliminating the Crown from domestic roles such as summoning and dissolving government – these roles being left in the Irish case to the new parliament itself.

The Crown thus remained in the Constitution for external purposes only, and the British sought, largely unsuccessfully, to use this to limit the Irish government's role in foreign affairs. But the British were eventually forced, principally by Irish diplomacy at the League of Nations and at successive Imperial Conferences, to abandon these efforts, which they finally did by enacting, in 1931, the Statute of Westminster. This issue had, however, contributed to the outbreak of a civic war, and, because of the anti-monarchist preoccupations of Irish republicanism, it has never been easy to get Irish people to relate to the concept of classical republicanism.

For a short period in the 1790s (and, less strikingly, at certain points in the nineteenth century) Irish republicanism was, at least theoretically, inspired by French-style republicanism: it was momentarily secular and anti-confessional as well as nationalist. In a very attenuated form, that tradition survived to the 1916–21 period. It is there in the 1916 Proclamation and in the Democratic Programme of 1919.

Although a republic had been proclaimed in 1916, this did not reflect as absolutist a commitment to this particular form of government as people now are inclined to believe. Rather, it reflected the practical reality that the only way in which Irish independence could be expressed at that time was by declaring a republic. This fact was attested to by my father, Desmond FitzGerald, who wrote that, when Patrick Pearse and Joseph Plunkett discussed with him this matter in the GPO during the Rising, they thought that in the only circumstances in which a Rising could possibly succeed, (i.e. with German support and a German victory in the War), Ireland would inevitably become a monarchy – as of course were all European states at that time, except France and Switzerland – probably with the Kaiser's sixth son, Prince Joachim, as king. That conversation is recorded in my father's 1913–16 fragment of autobiography, written during the 1940s, and was confirmed by Ernest Blythe's recollection of a discussion he had with Bulmer Hobson, secretary of the Volunteers.

The idea that these accounts should be dismissed – as for example, Martin Mansergh has sought to do[2] – because they might be used by partisan opponents of 1916 to discredit the Rising is simply antihistorical. Of course, Pearse and Plunkett were not *advocating* such an outcome – they did not wish it – but they were realists who knew that if the Germans won the war, following a successful Irish Rising, Ireland would suffer the same monarchical fate as had Bulgaria, Romania and Albania, and as the Germans sought to impose on Lithuania and Finland two years later. Pearse and Plunkett tried to make the best of it, by suggesting that the German prince might marry a Catholic (they clearly did not know that he had married a Protestant five weeks earlier), and that, being a German, he would want to bring his children up as Irish rather than English speakers.

It does Pearse and Plunkett no credit to try to perpetuate a myth – and I use this word deliberately – that they were unrealistic fantasists who thought that the Germans would allow a republic in Ireland, when in fact these two leaders of the Rising were hard-headed patriots, fully aware of the realities of the world they lived in, and concerned to make the best of those realities.

That myth of republicanism as being somehow incarnate in 1916 has been sedulously fostered, but in fact that was not what people felt at the time. In my father's papers, there is a letter from Erskine Childers to him written in March 1918, in which Childers asserts that 1916 had not been about creating a republic, but about self-determination. Childers added that he would be happy with self-determination within the Empire, remarking that he thought my father would also be satisfied with that. Childers was tragically executed as a republican by the government of which my father was a member in 1922.

There is further evidence of openness to forms of government other than a republic in Eamon de Valera's request to Arthur Griffith before the Treaty negotiations of 1921 to 'get me out of the straight-jacket of a republic' – and, of course, in de Valera's view that, if his objective of external association with the Commonwealth was secured, it would then be for the Irish people to decide the form of state they wanted, whether a republic or a monarchy.

We know, of course, that in the end the anti-monarchist version of nationalism prevailed here, strengthened perhaps by the collapse of so many empires and monarchies in 1918, and the consequent emergence of many republics in Europe. Given the importance the British still attached to their monarchy – their emphasis on it as the lynch-pin of their empire, in fact – and the extent to which British forces were referred to by them as the Crown forces, this Irish nationalist reaction against monarchy was probably inevitable. For very many Irish nationalists the huge symbolic importance that the British at that time attached to their monarchy automatically converted monarchy into a powerful 'anti-symbol'.

It must also be said that, quite apart from visceral Irish objections to the monarchy as a British symbol, objectively the British version of monarchy, as distinct from what is now the Continental version, is not compatible with the kind of society or political structures delineated by classical republicanism. The absence of any constitutional constraint upon the actions of the British parliament, which at least in theory is endowed with absolute power, derives from an antique and indeed medieval theory of the role of the monarch, which has survived in Britain and nowhere else.

I want to turn now to the issue of theory and practice and to address the classical concept of the republic. I feel that we should perhaps call civic republicanism *res-publicanism*. It has nothing to do with whether you have a president or a monarch, or a fully constitutional king, or queen, or grand duke. It can indeed be argued that the Scandinavian monarchies of Denmark, Sweden and Norway, and perhaps also the Netherlands, come nearer to being republics in the classical sense of the word republicanism, than does a republic such as France, which still has an executive head of state.

Even today, a monarch may indeed be more effective as a uniting force than an elected president, usually a superannuated party politician. Moreover, in certain times and certain places, like Spain, a monarch may be better placed than such a president to safeguard the state and human rights against attempts to destabilise democracy, as King Juan Carlos was able to do a quarter of a century ago, or as the king in Italy did in 1943 to get rid of a discredited dictator.

The real issue is not – as some in Ireland may be tempted by our curious version of history to believe – whether a state is headed by a monarch or a president, but rather the extent to which, under whatever kind of head of state, the citizens of a state are permitted or encouraged to play an active part in public affairs, or instead are marginalised by the political system and accorded little role or influence in the way that society develops, or are so uninterested in the state, or so lacking in sense of civic duty that they are unable to help create and sustain a genuine *res publica*.

The alternative to representative government, *viz.* participatory democracy, involving theoretically active, united and virtuous citizens, was discredited by the French Revolution. The form of democracy that we have today is thus representative democracy, which, it has to be said, does not of itself create the kind of *res publica* that the classical concept involves.

Of course, in our State, an element of direct democracy exists in a particular form: referendums. We have referendums for changes in the Constitution. We could even have them, in certain circumstances, if the government and parliament wished to get a public view on a proposed law, although government and parliament have never in fact chosen to do this.

It should be noted that there are two sides to referendums. We in Ireland think of them as very democratic. We feel that the people should have the final decision in changing the Constitution in any way, because it is their Constitution, not parliament's. We are more republican in this way than some other republics in Europe where parliament can change the constitution by a two-thirds majority.

There could also be a popular right of constitutional initiative, through which citizens can propose changes in the Constitution without the involvement of parliament. We had that in our first Constitution, but when Fianna Fáil threatened to use it to start a process, as a result of which the people might have voted for something which would have been in breach of the 1921 Treaty, and therefore undermined our constitutional position in international law, the government of the day secured parliamentary authority to abolish the initiative. For a period after the enactment of the 1922 Constitution, such a power to amend the Constitution was temporarily vested in parliament.

Many people see a referendum as the ultimate exercise in democracy, but you have to realise that other countries – such as Germany, with its experience of a dictator who used referendums to consolidate his position and to rally people in support of him – have a different view of them. This German experience would have made it impossible to secure agreement at European level in what might seem to many to be a logical process by which to adopt a European Constitution, *viz.*, by the peoples of Europe as a whole voting together – accompanied perhaps by a simultaneous double-majority system, with the individual states also voting.

The issue that needs to be addressed thus seems to be to be how to ensure that, with the type of representative government with which our history and culture have endowed us, we might secure the promotion of the public good, shaped by wide-ranging deliberation amongst citizens – which of course is what the concept of the classical republic involves.

The problems which seem to me to impede the emergence of such a society are two-fold: the danger that elected representatives may be tempted to use for private advantage the positions to which they have been elected, and may resist any popular curb on these arrangements, and the danger that the citizens themselves may lack concern for the common good.

On the first of these issues, our parliament has over recent decades set up a system, and has structured itself, and endowed itself with resources, and created posts, which seem to me to go beyond what the citizens would wish to see. The people might, for example, think that there are far too many ministers of state, many of them without much to do. (As Taoiseach, I could never find jobs of any consequence for more than seven or eight ministers of state; the rest seemed to me to be superfluous, but I had to give them the jobs otherwise I could have lost parliamentary support.) And then you have all the chairmen and chairwomen of Dáil committees – the proliferation of which, in the last twenty years particularly, worries me because only some of these committees seem to be really needed. Once this scale of patronage has been introduced, I doubt whether any future Taoiseach could, or would wish to, rein it in. The absence of any checks on what may be seen as parliamentary abuses seems to me to be a weakness in our exclusively representative democracy.

The second question is whether the Irish people have the capacity and willingness to 'work' a genuine republic. Our society has some good features, which we all enjoy and from which we all benefit. The Irish people are warm, outgoing, hospitable, and they network well with each other and with people from other countries. We tend to be successful in our relationships with other people for that reason. But Irish people also tend to be intensely localist, clearly having great difficulty in thinking in terms of the good of the country as a whole, as distinct from that of their own locality.

In government at times I was driven to despair as to whether there were even as many as 1,500 people in the country – a figure I arrived at quite arbitrarily! – who were actually interested in Ireland, as distinct from their bit of Ireland. Localism makes it very hard to govern the country. Perhaps it is the fact that we got our local government in 1898 and our own government only twenty-four years later in 1922, that has created problems for us ever since – although I feel that these problems may in fact be much more deeply rooted than that in our history.

Many people still have almost tribalist loyalties to their extended family, which impede loyalty to a wider common good. There is little sense of duty – of a duty to contribute financially through taxation, or by way of active political involvement in the process of government. In recent decades all of this has been illustrated quite dramatically in the form of such phenomena as widespread public tolerance of tax evasion, continued support at local level of politicians who have been demonstrated to have broken laws enacted by the Oireachtas, large-scale support for a politically motivated decentralisation of the public service that threatens the cohesion of our system of government because it suits people in local areas, as well as the operation of local government to favour individual clients of politicians at the expense of the environment.

It is true that when irrefutable evidence eventually emerged of financial misbehaviour by some politicians at both national and local level, this did evoke, eventually, a negative public response, at least for a period. But the revelation of involvement in tax evasion by local politicians seemed to evoke no loss of support for them at local level; instead, their exposure seems to have been widely seen as a form of martyrdom inflicted on them by external forces emanating from an alien metropolis!

The issue of tax evasion has always seemed to me to illustrate dramatically a substantial absence of a sense of civic duty in Ireland. For it has to be accepted that tax evasion is the only means by which a citizen can steal from the poorest in the land – because taxes not paid by the well-to-do necessitate additional imposts upon the whole tax-paying class, including the very poor, who, of course, pay VAT and excise duties, even when their poverty exempts them from income taxation.

Yet this form of stealing from even the poorest in the land has been practised here by a remarkably high proportion of self-employed people. This is especially the case in rural areas: 85–90 per cent of the people on the list of tax evaders now published quarterly are from outside Dublin. It is now clear that the amount of taxes to be retrieved may eventually run to several billion euro. No one could have been unaware of the existence of this practice, even if few realised just how widespread it was. Yet in my long life I never heard a sermon preached on this evil.

Moreover, we know from the Oireachtas inquiry into the behaviour of the banks, that, when I introduced the deposit interest retention tax, as a means of tracking down such evasion, the application of the system – enacted by the Dáil in response to a decision taken by my government – was undermined for a whole decade by a countermanding instruction on enforcement, issued by an unidentified civil servant in the Revenue Commissioners. This civil servant, with unbelievable arrogance, took it on himself to decide that this was not a good decision of the government and should not be enforced in the way that had been provided for.

It is also notable that a number of journalists have repeatedly sought to mitigate the practice of tax evasion, to the point of seeming to justify it. They have done this on the quite extraordinary grounds that, due to the mishandling of the public finances at the end of the 1970s, for a period tax rates were raised to a higher level – and that this entitled people to decide for themselves how much tax they should pay, setting aside the authority of the state and of the parliament elected by the people.

Against this background of widespread rejection of the duties of citizenship by a significant proportion of the better-off part of our population, the task of government in Ireland is clearly an extremely difficult one. And it is now evident that some at least of those engaged in the process of government itself were themselves corrupted by the adverse public climate in which they had to work and the lack of any sense of civic morality that might have restrained them. Iseult Honohan is, I believe, right in contending that corruption is *the* primary political problem, although it is never generally recognised as such in our state.[3]

Turning away from that unpleasant side of politics, how might civic republicanism be best promoted? Allowing citizens to contribute in a way that they feel counts would help to shape the common good by wide ranging deliberation. Political parties provide a channel for such engagement. A 1969 poll carried out professionally on behalf of the Labour Party showed that at that time about 6 per cent of the adult population were members of political parties. I think that figure today would be considerably less – perhaps 2–3 per cent. I am not sure, however, that party membership provides an adequate channel for participation in politics by citizens – although, at its best, the party system may be a useful sounding board for those who determine party policy.

A process that I found very useful, after I became Leader of Fine Gael in 1977–78, was the organisation of open public meetings. In my first tour of the country, a total of 25,000 people turned up at these public meetings, including many people and public representatives of all the other parties who came to listen and to question. In all, I had the benefit of about one thousand comments or questions, which alerted me to the preoccupations of the people in various parts of the country. Curiously this practice has not been followed by other political leaders, who have preferred to meet only the members of their own party around the country. Our political system is very inward looking in this respect. It does not look outwards towards citizens in general.

A recent striking exception to this was the decision by a minister of education to arrange twenty meetings around the country to discuss educational issues, a number of which I and others interested in education attended at the minister's request. Although teachers' union representatives used the occasions to promote some aspects of their own agenda, the meetings certainly highlighted some educational issues that were foremost in the minds of an interested public.

Other routes through which the public can communicate their concerns are of course the correspondence columns of the newspapers, and, most striking of all, through that special feature of contemporary Irish culture, daytime radio talk shows. Through this latter medium, governments in particular, and politicians in general, have, particularly since the mid 1980s, been made instantly aware of current public political concerns and are frequently put on the spot to justify their actions – or inaction.

In her book, *Civic Republicanism*, Iseult Honohan sees nationalism as involving a sense of collective identity, whereas republicanism rests on political recognition of multiply reiterated interdependence and membership of a shared public culture, rather than a culture of ethnicity, and also involves equality of recognition amongst heterogeneous citizens. Shared cultural values are, she suggests, the outcome of political interaction, provisionally embodied, open to change, and developing towards a cosmopolitan citizenship from the bottom up, through an increasing web of relationships. I think she is correct in saying that a genuine republic has an ethical community within a moral boundary.

Such a republicanism is clearly preferable to liberalism in its economic form and to nationalism. I think she is right in saying that liberalism is too thin and also lacking in a moral basis; indeed, one might go so far as to say it is amoral. Nationalism excludes or even oppresses others who are not within its frame of reference as nationals of the state. In this part of Ireland since the late 1950s there has emerged a growing concern to create here a state that would have the capacity to embrace all sections of the Irish people, a concern that I have actively shared. This has involved, for some decades past, challenging the kind of single-ethos state that my generation inherited from a troubled past – a state in which anyone who was not a Roman Catholic, and a practising Catholic at that – or who did not share the Gaelic heritage of the majority of Irish people, was regarded as insufficiently Irish and even as not being Irish at all.

Those who challenged the divisive doctrines of this uniculturalism and who sought to create a genuine republican basis on which to build an inclusive Irish community for the whole island were often treated by the apostles of the ultra-nationalist faith as some kind of traitors to the republican cause. I vividly recall some of the reactions – I would say sectarian reactions – evoked by a radio interview I gave as Taoiseach in 1981 on the subject.

The arrival of Sinn Féin IRA into a more central role in our electoral politics has raised certain issues about the relationship of republicanism and political violence. As others have argued, the fact is that people will judge Sinn Féin by what they are now, and what they are involved in doing now rather than in the past. It is, nonetheless, difficult for many of us of an older generation to accept them. Sinn Féin need to understand that it is not easy for people who for decades were struggling to make this a multicultural republic and who found that process being gravely damaged by violence – often sectarian violence – to forget those actions.

I will never forget the occasion when twelve IRA men raided a Protestant home in County Monaghan, threw the Bible in the fire – as an indication of their sectarianism – and then shot down in a nearby field a Protestant senator of this state who was coming to visit his fiancée at the house. It is not easy for someone with that recollection to accommodate to the situation where Sinn Féin are becoming part of our political system.

But I accept it; I have from the beginning favoured the peace process and have supported it. But there is a heavy price to be paid. And we should not be expected to be enthusiastic about some of the people coming in to the system at this stage. We have the duty to ensure that they have the opportunity to come in, but we also have had a duty to make sure they did not get into government in any form unless and until they have ended all the violence – latterly directed solely against their own community. We have had to insist on that. We would have been wrong to have set any other criteria or to have placed any other obstacles, or to have allowed our memory of the past to have influenced us to try and prevent the completion of the peace process.

Revulsion against IRA violence in Northern Ireland has helped our people to move towards a multicultural ethos, which has brought us a little nearer to a genuine civic republicanism.

Notes

1 An earlier version of this chapter appeared in G. FitzGerald, *Ireland in the World: Further Reflections* (Dublin: Liberties Press, 2005).
2 See Chapter 7 in this volume.
3 I. Honohan, *Civic Republicanism* (London: Routledge, 2002).

Index

Note: 'n.' after a page reference indicates the number of a note on that page.

Lightning Source UK Ltd.
Milton Keynes UK
UKOW05f0319060417
298475UK00006B/172/P

South African keywords:
The uses and abuses of political concepts

SOUTH AFRICAN KEYWORDS
The uses & abuses of political concepts

edited by

EMILE BOONZAIER & JOHN SHARP

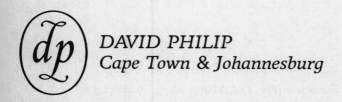

DAVID PHILIP
Cape Town & Johannesburg

First published 1988 by David Philip, Publisher (Pty) Ltd, 217 Werdmuller
Centre, Claremont 7700, South Africa

ISBN 0-86486-100-1

© David Philip, Publisher 1988

Printed by Clyson Printers (Pty) Ltd, 11th Avenue, Maitland, Cape

Contents

List of contributors

Emile Boonzaier *MA (Cape Town)* is Lecturer in Anthropology at the University of Cape Town

Sandra Burman *BA LLB (Cape Town) D Phil (Oxon)* is Director of the Socio–Legal Unit, University of Cape Town

At Fischer *MA (RAU)* is Lecturer in Anthropology at the Rand Afrikaans University

Mamphela Ramphele *MB ChB (Natal) Dip PubH (Rand)* is Senior Research Officer of the departments of Anthropology and Paediatrics and Child Health at the University of Cape Town

John Sharp *BA(Hons) (Cape Town) PhD (Cantab)* is Associate Professor of Anthropology at the University of Cape Town

Peter Skalník *MA (Leningrad) PhD (Prague)* is Senior Lecturer in Anthropology at the University of Cape Town

Andrew Spiegel *MA (Cape Town)* is Lecturer in Anthropology at the University of Cape Town

Robert Thornton *MA PhD (Chicago)* is Associate Professor of Anthropology at the University of Cape Town

Kees van Der Waal *MA (Pret) DLitt et Phil (RAU)* is Senior Lecturer in Anthropology at the Rand Afrikaans University

Martin West *MA PhD (Cape Town)* is Professor of Anthropology at the University of Cape Town

Preface

We have written this book to help students, and people outside the universities, to analyse the nature of the society in which we live. Our experience over the years has been that South African students struggle to examine certain key concepts critically, and to reorientate their thinking away from the conventional meanings of these concepts. We know this only too well, because most of us were also schooled and socialised in South Africa, and have also had to come to terms with the same preconceptions. This book is the outcome of our struggle in this regard, and we hope that it will assist others to traverse the same ground, and, in turn, to subject our conclusions to critical scrutiny.

Some of our fellow academics, in anthropology and related disciplines, will no doubt say that many of the arguments put forward in this book have been made before elsewhere. This is indeed true, but we believe that there are two strengths to the present discussion. One is that a whole range of related concepts is dealt with in one volume, rather than being scattered across diverse sources. The other is that the various chapters in this book pursue a relatively consistent argument; in the past we have often found that other authors (particularly of introductory textbooks) use the concepts discussed below in ways that are internally inconsistent.

Our title purposely recalls the very excellent book by the late Raymond Williams, although readers familiar with that work will find the format of our discussion differs substantially from his. On the other hand, we would like students, and others, to be able to use this book in much the same way that we have used, and still use, the original *Keywords:* as a source of reference to specific concepts, and as a text which one can read out of general interest.

We have tried to write this book in a way which makes the analysis accessible to students in anthropology and other social sciences. We believe, however, that there are many people outside the universities – in commerce and industry, communications, the media, education, and community service – who want to know how some of the key concepts of South African politics are used and abused in various arguments about the nature of our society, and who recognise that their ability to distinguish good sense from nonsense is hampered by the paucity of critical discussion to which they are exposed.

Like all other arguments which use these concepts, this book is a political statement. Our view is that it iṣ still necessary in South Africa to give some attention to basics. There is a growing number of studies which indulge in more or less far-fetched analogies between South Africa and other sites of conflict elsewhere in the world, and proffer elaborate solutions to the country's problems. Their authors are, apparently, convinced that they have discerned the 'realities' of the present situation and are therefore competent to talk about South Africa's prospects. We argue, however, that many of them are confused about the basic concepts which they deploy to describe South Africa. It seems reasonable to suggest that prophets who have little critical grasp of these concepts' meanings may well be false. South Africa needs fewer experts with final blueprints, and more ordinary people who understand what they and others actually mean when they begin to think and talk about the fundamentals of the society.

As editors, we wish to thank our fellow contributors for their wholehearted cooperation in the planning and execution of this book, and for the promptness with which they met our various deadlines. Drafts of most of the chapters were presented to the post-graduate seminar of UCT's anthropology department, and at the Conference of South African Anthropologists in September 1987; we are grateful to those who contributed to the discussion of these papers. We also thank Caroline White, Julia Segar and Boet Kotze for their particular contributions, Chris McDowell for preparing the index, and Russell Martin of David Philip for his encouragement and painstaking attention to detail.

EMILE BOONZAIER and JOHN SHARP

Introduction:
Constructing social reality
JOHN SHARP

This book is a critical examination of conventional beliefs about the nature of South African society. To many South Africans it is self-evident, a matter of common sense, that the society consists of different racial and ethnic groups, each of which forms a separate community with its own culture and traditions. It is believed that such groups actually exist objectively in the real world, and that there is nothing anybody can do to change this.

We take issue with this notion, arguing that all these groups, and the bases on which they are supposedly constituted, are social and cultural constructions. They are representations, rather than features, of the real world. They comprise the ways in which a portion of South African society tries to tell itself, and others, what that world is like. In other words, they are an interpretation, instead of a mere description, of reality. Any interpretation depends on the identity, beliefs, knowledge and interests of the people doing the interpreting, as much as on the characteristics of the objects being interpreted. It follows from this that different races and ethnic groups, unique cultures and traditions, do not exist in any ultimate sense in South Africa, and are real only to the extent that they are the product of a particular world-view.

How do we arrive at a heresy of this nature?

Anthropologists and others

Most of the contributors to this book are anthropologists by profession, and all have some anthropological training or expertise. Many of us have done field research in South Africa, which means that we have come into close contact with people who fall into all of the officially recognised classifications. One of the striking results of this contact is the finding that although there are many people who hold to the conventional view about South African society which was spelled out above, there are many more who do not.

The latter do not see themselves as members of one of a series of groups which are differentiated by race and culture, or, if they do, they regard such a grouping as an external imposition rather than as a basic statement of their own identity. Many people see their identity in terms that are either more inclusive or more exclusive than the notion of fundamental racial or ethnic groups implies: they may see themselves as part of a very general category of 'the oppressed', for instance, or as members of a particular local community such as a rural village. In addition, many do not try to claim that they have a single, basic identity (as the conventional model presumes must be the case); on the contrary, they recognise that their self-definitions are situational, and that they can be different things in different contexts.

Our experience as anthropologists leads us to realise that there are different interpretations of the 'reality' of South African society. We believe that this realisation is of fundamental importance, and try in this book to explain why this should be so. The explanation does not simply take the form of attempting to pit one model of South African social reality against another in an effort to prove that the conventional view, or any other view, is wrong. On its own, such an exercise would beg an important question: wrong for whom and under which circumstances?

Still less, in the same vein, do we try to speak for the people on whom the conventional view is imposed. They are capable of speaking for themselves, and are, indeed, deeply engaged in doing so at present in a variety of ways. In this regard we are mindful of the trenchant words of the French anthropologist Sperber: 'Anthropologists have neither the authority nor the competence to act as spokesmen for the people who have tolerated their presence, and even less to give the world professional guidance in moral or political matters' (1985: 5).

Our objective is more modest. We aim to bring an awareness of the existence of diverse representations of South African society to bear on the question of how one can know or say anything correct or useful about its nature and composition. This issue can be posed in another way: one cannot assume that any representation of the society is a straightforward description of its real nature, because each representation is a political statement which includes the assumptions and intentions of the people who make it. How then, given this situation, does one avoid the spineless relativism which says that since all views are firmly held by someone, and since no-one is setting out deliberately to lie, all views are equally worthy and contain at least a modicum of truth? The important analytical point is to know why people in different positions in the society hold the particular views that they do. Once one has understood the historical and strategic reasons for the salience of particular views, then one is in a better position to assess their correctness (and, indeed, their moral defensibility). Our approach most certainly does not mean that we believe that all interpretations of South African society are equally valid or legitimate.

In addressing these questions we shall give most attention to the conventional representations, in terms of racial and ethnic groups and unique cultures, because these are the views of the people who currently hold power in the country. Indeed, it is the fact that they are propagated by the powerful which makes these representations conventional: those who hold power are able, at least in some respects, to impose their conventions on others. The logic by which the powerful construct their visions of social reality is therefore a particularly important topic for critical scrutiny.

There is, however, a further reason for the concentration, in this book, on conventional ideas about the concepts mentioned above. It is that these ideas have for a long time been part of the intellectual armoury of anthropology itself. The current understanding of human culture as a sum of disparate cultures is, as Thornton explains below, a notion which emerged and flourished in Romantic and Modernist thinking in the nineteenth and twentieth centuries in Europe and North America. This notion has, therefore, its own history, and it is instructive to inquire into the circumstances in which it came to prominence. One of these circumstances was the growth of anthropology as an intellectual discipline.

At the start of the twentieth century the founders of modern anthropology introduced the idea of rigorous fieldwork into the discipline – the requirement that anthropologists should go to distant parts of the world to see 'what it was really like' there for themselves. Prior to this there had been extensive reliance on second-hand information as to the nature of human diversity, derived from reports collected by travellers or missionaries to far-flung places. The founding anthropologists, who included such names as Malinowski and Radcliffe-Brown (both of whom had links with South Africa), wanted to make their discipline more respectable and scientific, and this led them to place a premium on personal inquiry through fieldwork. They suspected that the reports of untrained travellers were biased by their preconceptions about 'primitive' or 'savage' society.

In contrast to this, the first modern anthropologists judged their own efforts at fieldwork (at 'participant observation', in the jargon they created) to be an objective recording of reality, on the basis of which they would be able to discover scientific laws of social and cultural behaviour. Such laws could be uncovered by a careful comparison of different forms of behaviour, and would, by definition, be immutable, true for all times and places, and independent of the assumptions and prejudices of the lay public.

In order to compare, however, they had to know what to compare. The basic units for comparison were, the anthropologists decided, the bounded groups of people which comprised the different societies into which humanity was divided. Each society was unified by the fact that it possessed its own culture; each culture was the way of life of a particular society. With this notion in place, it was possible to compare the forms of religious or political or economic behaviour characteristic of different societies and cultures, in order to see what was general to all humanity or specific to particular contexts.

In many ways this project was an admirable one, and several generations of anthropologists followed its path, producing rich and detailed accounts of other societies and cultures, even though they were unable to formulate so much as one law of human behaviour that was universal. It is only in more recent times that anthropologists have begun to ask questions about the reasons for their failure.

An argument which is now made (Crick, 1976; Rabinow and Sullivan, 1979; Sperber, 1985; Ardener, 1985) is that the early aim of seeing 'what was really there' was always unrealistic. The founding anthropologists were not, and could not be, the kind of neutral, dispassionate observers they claimed to be. In fact, when they suggested that the basic units for anthropological comparison were discrete societies defined by the possession of unique cultures, their thinking derived not so much from the facts of the situation they observed in Melanesia or Africa, as from European notions of the constitution of social groups. They were heavily influenced by the Romantic idea of 'national' communities of common 'blood and culture' – an idea which, when first expounded in Germany, represented not an existing fact, but an aspiration for the political unification of all German-speakers.

In point of fact, of course, none of the European nation states has ever comprised an entity which actually corresponded to the Romantic vision, and the latter is easily recognised as a myth, an 'invented tradition' that has been used by national elites to cultivate feelings of loyalty and patriotism in their followers (Hobsbawm, 1983). When the anthropologists took this notion into the field, outside of Europe, they too were inventing tradition. They did not merely report what they saw, but offered an interpretation of it. Their interpretations were simplifications of a complex reality, made in terms of concepts and categories with which they were familiar. Hence the neatly bounded 'tribal' or 'traditional' societies, composed of kith and kin who shared common beliefs, values and social practices, were, in large measure, the anthropologists' invention.

Their invention had, however, two effects. One was that it served to confirm the myths about the nature of European social and political divisions: the rest of the world was shown to be organised into groupings which were recognisably similar to, although much simpler than, the modern nation states. Evolutionist thinking claimed that the latter had developed out of these simpler groupings in selected areas, such as Europe. The whole exercise was therefore, in some measure, a self-fulfilling prophecy: a vision of Europe was confirmed by a

European vision of others.

The second effect was that the others were, in due course, influenced by the European myths. Ranger (1983) has shown how indigenous people in colonial Africa set about the invention of 'tribes' after the fashion understood by the Europeans: since the Europeans held power in colonial countries, and since they expected to find groups which accorded with their preconceptions, ambitious local leaders often sought to present them with political demands in terms they could, supposedly, recognise. This process, by which the representations of the dominators are assimilated by the dominated, and pressed into service in their dealings with the former, is one which is dealt with in several of the chapters that follow: it is an important theme in the politics of contemporary South Africa.

The point of these strictures about early anthropologists is not to suggest that they failed to perform their analytical task properly. We are not saying that they should have discovered objective truths about the nature of the social world, and that they should be condemned for failing to do so. Nor are we saying that their 'failure' to find out what social groups 'were really like' is one of the causes of the contemporary problems in situations like South Africa. This would suppose that there was one unassailable truth about the nature of South African society, which, if it could be discovered, would put an end to political conflict.

There are few grounds for supposing that such a positivist ambition is anything other than a holy grail. If one continued to hold it one would, indeed, simply persist in the fundamental error of the early anthropologists. This is because we can now see, admittedly with the benefit of considerable hindsight, that their mistake lay in not recognising that the knowledge and values of early twentieth century Europe were important in shaping their interpretations of other parts of the world. Anthropology was a dialogue between what anthropologists knew and believed and what they observed, and it remains in this position today. Hence there can be no final, definitive account of society or culture. Anthropologists can never have the last word on the people about whose lives they profess expertise.

Anthropology has taken a very long time to relieve itself of the self-imposed burden of positivism. The view that it is an interpretative study has, however, gained ground slowly, and opened up new opportunities for anthropologists. One has been the possibility of reappraising the discipline's past, and admitting that its earlier fascination with neatly bounded societies and cultures has played a significant role in moulding popular, conventional thought – not only in Europe and North America, but also, and perhaps particularly, in areas such as South Africa. Indeed, conventional thinking about 'culture' is much in debt to positivist anthropology (Asad, 1973).

This is one of the themes dealt with in many of the chapters that follow. It has also guided the selection of concepts to be discussed: we have chosen to look at terms which have figured large in the preoccupations of anthropologists, and are also fundamental to conventional discourse about South African society. By doing so we are able to suggest that the conventional wisdom mirrors the error in early anthropology. This conclusion is not in the least surprising if one recognises that the anthropological discourse and the discourse of domination in South Africa are both products of European positivism, and of the particular view of 'the others' which this approach inspired in European thinking. And it is only on the basis of self-examination that anthropologists have any grounds for a critical scrutiny of the conventional approach to understanding South Africa.

The changing discourse of domination

One reason that we question the conventional views of South Africa is, as already explained, the history of our own discipline. Another is internal to the conventional views themselves. The latter comprise a particular reading of a series of terms, some of which (such as race, tribe and ethnic group) were identified above. These concepts, and others of similar provenance, are related to each other by the manner in which they are commonly understood. We argue that, given this understanding, they constitute a discourse about the nature of South African society, which reveals the logic and serves the interests of those who wield power. They form, in other words, a discourse of domination in South Africa.

The discourse does not, of course, present itself in these terms. On the contrary, the claim is made that it is an objective description of the fundamental nature of the society, which is not subject to human intervention or revision. But if the latter were true, one could legitimately expect that the discourse itself would be constant over time: if one is describing a self-evident and unchanging reality, the terms of the description do not need to be altered. In fact, however, as Thompson (1985) and others have noted, the discourse of domination has been far from static. It has been revised several times in the course of the twentieth century: concepts which once had prominence have lost ground and been supplemented with or indeed supplanted by others.

The fact that these revisions have occurred is, in itself, a strong indication of the representational nature of the discourse of domination. Moreover, a close consideration of the sequence and timing of the revisions provides insight into the social factors that shaped the way in which the dominant representations of reality have been constructed. This theme is taken up in several chapters in this book, and the way in which the chapters are ordered also gives some indication of the discourse's development in the twentieth century.

There are, we argue, three recognisable phases in this discourse, each of which can usefully be identified by reference to a key concept. The first phase, which spanned the first half of the century, saw the dominance of the idea of 'race': in this period the conventional view was that the South African population was divided into separate races. These races were conceived as natural units, and as distinct from each other in both physical and cultural terms.

Thompson (1985) has written eloquently about the use of the idea of 'race' in South African political mythology. His exposition makes several valuable points. It shows that this form of thinking had a very long history, persisting from the seventeenth century until well into the twentieth, and that it was extremely widespread. While racism was an important element in the world-view of the Dutch settlers in South Africa, it was not confined to them. Thompson provides considerable evidence that it was shared by British observers of the country and by English-speaking South Africans. Racism was, indeed, a general mode of European thought which was carried to all corners of the earth, and was deeply ingrained in both scientific and popular consciousness. Until the Second World War, therefore, South African racism was by no means a unique phenomenon.

An important implication of the dominance of the idea of 'race' in South Africa was that, for a long time, the African population was conceived as a largely undifferentiated mass. Until 1948, says Thompson, 'the stress was still on races as populations with common qualities, rather than on differences within each race' (1985: 96). Thus although it was recognised that Africans in South Africa belonged to several different 'tribes', it was often argued that these were (relatively recent) offshoots from a single group with uniform racial and cultural characteristics. A great deal of scholarly effort, in the nineteenth and early twentieth centuries, went into speculative reconstruction of the common origins of the African population.

One of the striking developments in the dominant discourse in South Africa after the war was the growing lack of concern with historical inquiry. This was manifest, for instance, in a picture of more-or-less timeless subdivisions within the African population. No longer was the latter a single 'race', divided politically into different 'tribes'; henceforth it was seen to comprise a series of fundamentally 'separate ethnic groups, each with its own language, legal system, life-style, values and socio-political identity' (*South African Yearbook*, 1976, cited by Thompson, 1985: 199).

The point is that, beginning in the 1950s, the concepts 'race' and 'tribe' were supplemented by a new vision of 'ethnic groups' and 'nations' as the basic building blocks of South Africa. This does not mean, of course, that all references to 'race' disappeared, or that the period witnessed any real decline in racist thinking or practices on the part of the dominant stratum in the society: it is perfectly possible to be racist without stressing, or indeed even using, the term 'race'. But the new emphasis in terminology did mark a change of some significance, and it is important to understand something of the context in which the change was made.

The immediate context was, as Thompson explains, the development of the policy of apartheid after the National Party victory of 1948. The earlier policy of segregation had not required any major disaggregation of the African population, since the aim was merely to separate black from white. Segregation was a viable option only as long as the principle that white should dominate black was accepted internationally. Apartheid was, at least in part, the National Party's response to the widespread questioning of this principle in the aftermath of the Second World War. In due course the policy came to involve an attempt at internal decolonisation, by granting Africans a greater say in the running of the various 'homelands' within South Africa. The vision of a fundamentally divided African population, comprising discrete 'ethnic groups' and proto-'nations', was functionally necessary to the policy of apartheid, since it provided a rationale for allocating people to their respective 'homelands'.

In a sense, as has often been said, this policy was social engineering on a grand scale. Even a most cursory glance at the various historical accounts of the African population revealed the artificiality of the groups and boundaries which were constructed by fiat: hence the lack of any real interest shown in the past by the discourse of domination in the second half of the century. Speculations about the common origins of the African 'tribes' were largely replaced by flat assertions that each ethnic group constituted an organic entity which was, and (by implication) always had been, different from the others (as, for example, in the Tomlinson Commission Report, UG.55-1955: 14).

The fact that 'race' remained of fundamental importance in the apartheid period is clearly illustrated in such legislative provisions as the Prohibition of Mixed Marriages Act (1949), the Population Registration Act (1950), and the Group Areas Act (1950). On the other hand, the addition of the concepts of 'ethnic group' and 'nation' created greater scope for ideological manoeuvre. Thompson illustrates this in wry fashion, observing that when Africans were seen as one 'race', the accepted view was that South Africa's whites formed two groups (Afrikaners and English-speakers) which were hostile to each other. But after Africans were divided into separate 'ethnic groups', the formerly discrete white groups were fused, in conventional wisdom, into one 'nation'. The chief characteristic of the discourse of domination has always been, as Thompson says, its malleability.

At the end of his book, Thompson argues that P. W. Botha's

government places 'far less reliance on mythological legitimation' (1985: 240) than did those of his predecessors since 1948. The suggestion is that the ruling National Party, after nearly forty years in power, has become the political home of the white middle-class, both Afrikaans and (increasingly) English-speaking, and that the class interest it now represents has no particular concern with the older conceptions of rigid racial or ethnic groups. Since 1976, in particular, it has been fighting to survive in power, rather than to impose an elaborate ideological blueprint on the country.

There is much truth in these observations, but the contention that the discourse of domination has disintegrated into pragmatic survival-ism, and that the 1980s mark an end-of-ideology era, is open to question. It is certainly correct that the discourse of domination has become more fragmented than in the past: there is a significant movement, with a different class base, to the right of the Nationalists, which holds rigidly to the Verwoerdian vision of discrete racial and cultural groups with separate destinies. This view is no longer, strictly speaking, conventional, because it is now held by people who do not wield power directly. The conventional discourse, on the other hand, has been modified in certain respects, and there is now some distance between it and the former orthodoxies of apartheid.

But the recent modifications are no more pragmatic, and no more a simple description of the 'real facts' of South Africa, than was the vision from which they stemmed (and with which they still preserve considerable continuity). In conventional terms, the 1980s are a decade of 'reform' in South Africa: great stress is placed on such ideas as 'development' and 'upliftment' for the 'backward' sectors of the population. Much of this argument is summed up in the proposition that South Africa comprises a mix of the 'first world' and the 'third world'. This assumed coexistence of two worlds in one country provides a comfortable explanation of South Africa's current prob-lems, and marks, by an easy analogy, both its tragedy and its challenge.

Such an argument is very flexible, since the boundaries of the 'two worlds' can be formulated in various ways as circumstances demand: both racist and avowedly non-racist positions can find succour in its ambit. This means no more, however, than that it is a clever representation of South Africa; it does not mean that it is a simple description of its real nature. The latter point is difficult to see, precisely because the 'two worlds' argument in South Africa has very strong links with conventional thinking on an international scale. The representational nature of the discourse of domination was most clearly visible when the racism which it openly espoused was out of step with conventional thinking in the rest of the world. The desire to re-establish apparent conformity with the international vision was, indeed, a very powerful stimulus to the most recent modifications to this discourse in South Africa. The extent to which these modifications have succeeded in this respect is marked by the extent to which they are seen to embody a new willingness to be 'pragmatic'.

The structure of this book

The previous section suggested that there are three discernible phases to the discourse of domination in South Africa in the twentieth century. Each phase is associated with a central concept: first 'race', then 'ethnic group', and finally 'first and third worlds in one country'. This argument underlies the organisation of the material in this volume: these main concepts are examined in the order of their historical appearance, and each is linked to other terms which are closely associated with it, and which support or amplify the vision the core concepts convey.

(i) *'Culture', 'tradition' and 'community'*. These three concepts are hardy perennials within the discourse of domination in South Africa. Because we regard their conventional understanding as fairly constant over time, and as having underpinned many of the continuities across the three phases in the discourse, these notions are discussed first. Thornton examines the development of a mode of thought in Europe which conceived the phenomenon of human culture only in the diversity of separate 'cultures', and he shows the lasting influence this view has had in South Africa. Spiegel and Boonzaier discuss the way in which, in the same mode of European thinking, 'tradition' was opposed to 'modernity', and the manner in which the world was divided by this binary classification into 'traditional' and 'modern' societies.

In discussing the vexed issue of 'community', Thornton and Ramphele raise a question which is touched on in several of the other chapters. They note that mechanical attribution of the label 'community' to diverse collections and categories of people is characteristic not merely of the discourse of domination in South Africa, but also, in some measure, of the discourse of the dominated. Even in the latter context, many claims are made in the name or on behalf of 'the community', as if it were readily apparent who was included within this designation. When reference is made to 'the community of the townships', for instance, there is clear presumption that the inhabitants of these areas are of one mind on any given issue. In some cases this assumption may be quite legitimate, but in others it is likely to be misleading and dangerous. If two very different 'community' organisations both claim to speak on behalf of the same constituency, at least one must be wrong and liable to do the people for whom it acts a disservice.

(ii) *'Race' and 'tribe'*. For reasons explained above, the term 'tribe' is placed alongside the notion of 'race'. Anthropologists have a special interest in the way that 'tribe' has been used in popular mythology because their discipline carries a heavy responsibility for its popularisation. In his chapter Skalník discusses the use of the term in South Africa specifically, but also examines the history of the idea within anthropology itself. He comments critically on the tenacious grip it has had on the imagination of the subject's practitioners.

(iii) *'Ethnic group' and 'nation', 'population group' and 'ethnic national citizenship'*. There has also been prolonged discussion of the concepts 'ethnicity' and 'nationalism' in anthropology and other social sciences. Sharp examines some of the developments in this field over time, showing how changes in the understanding of 'ethnic groups' and 'nations' have presented problems to the discourse of domination under apartheid. He also discusses various interpretations of the history of Afrikaner and African nationalism in South Africa.

'Population group' is a peculiarly South African term, invented in and for the apartheid era. The fact that it was custom-made, and not appropriated from an existing discourse, meant that it was free from wider connotation. West shows how this characteristic made the term extremely useful as a means to link the earlier idea of 'race' with the newer notion of 'ethnic group' with a minimum of complication. The meaning of 'population group' was the meaning given to it in the Population Registration Act of 1950; changes to its meaning are defined, with greater or lesser precision, in subsequent amendments to the Act. Outside the Act the term has no logical meaning whatsoever; its meanings within the Act are legalistic constructions, based on the conventional South African understandings of 'race' and 'ethnic group', and on the changing requirements of political control.

'Ethnic national citizenship' is also a South African portmanteau, having no specific meaning beyond the Citizenship Acts pertaining to the various homelands. Its definition within these Acts turns on the conventional understanding of the link between ethnicity and nationalism, and in practical terms it provides an exceedingly flexible measure for allocating people to 'groups' in an arbitrary fashion.

(iv) *'First and third worlds', 'development', and 'informal sector'*. The notion that South Africa is a unique combination of the 'first' and 'third' worlds 'within one country' is the catchphrase of the moment, and is clearly part of the rhetoric of 'reform'. Its widespread appeal stems from the fact that its terminology is internationally acceptable, and that it provides a more delicate way of referring to the perceived 'realities' of race and ethnic group than has hitherto been available. The fact that this new discourse preserves considerable continuity with the past is evident, as Sharp explains, in the way in which the relationship between the 'first' and 'third world' sectors is conceived in conventional argument.

If there is a 'third world' component within the South African population then, by analogy with the recognised shortcomings of the 'third world' generally, it clearly requires a sustained programme of 'development' to counteract its backwardness. Fischer discusses the history of conventional thinking about development in South Africa, and assesses some of the practical consequences of interventions which have been, and are, made in terms of this thinking.

One of the areas on which 'development' planning is currently focused is the so-called 'informal sector' in South Africa. Van der Waal and Sharp explore the emergence of this term in an anthropological study in the 1970s, its very rapid proliferation into standard development discourse internationally, and the various revisions and reconceptualisations of it in the academic world. Their analysis shows that it is one particular, and now widely questioned, interpretation of the 'informal sector' which has become received wisdom in South Africa.

(v) 'Gender' and 'youth'. There is a danger that a book of this nature can give the impression that the only politically inspired representations which have serious social consequences in South Africa are those dealing with 'race relations'. In order to emphasise that this is not the case, we have included two chapters which show how such apparently objective categories as 'women', 'men' and 'the youth' are, in fact, socially and culturally constructed. Ramphele and Boonzaier argue that an integral part of the discourse of domination in South Africa is a discourse about gender relationships – about the proper way that men should relate to women, and vice versa. They demonstrate, by a case study of the position of African women, that the processes of domination along lines of 'race' and 'ethnicity' have been closely intermeshed with the domination of women by men in the society.

Burman makes a similar point with regard to age and the way that the process of growing up is broken into socially recognised segments. One of her key observations is that the accepted break between childhood and adult status varies according to context and, particularly in the conventional view in South Africa, according to 'racial' and 'ethnic' classification. For example, South African law grants people classified 'white' a longer childhood than others.

Other important concepts

We are aware that there are many contentious terms in popular South African discourse which we have not explicitly addressed in this volume. They would include concepts such as 'peoples', 'politics' and 'democracy'. Our aim, however, is not to provide a comprehensive or exhaustive work of reference, but rather to set out an approach to understanding the interpretative nature of a discourse which claims to deal in the 'realities' of the South African situation. The examples we have chosen to illustrate the argument are, we believe, central to this discourse; they also meet the other criteria for selection spelt out above.

Notwithstanding the limitations of this book, there are three further terms which demand attention. Two of these, 'category' and 'group', are very basic terms; some familiarity with the distinction between them is essential to understand the argument of the chapters to follow, and a brief exposition on this topic is therefore set out in this introduction. The third term in question is 'class'; some of the issues pertaining to this crucial idea are discussed in the conclusion to the book.

'Group' and 'category'. When people talk easily of the existence of 'race groups' or 'ethnic groups' in South Africa, it is not just 'race' or 'ethnicity' which is problematic, but also the notion of 'group' itself.

It can be said, as a general rule, that people frequently tend to see groups in the social world where, properly speaking, only categories exist. This tendency is common in the discourse of domination in South Africa, but is by no means confined to it. It is evident on a world-wide scale, and is as common in arguments from the left as in those from the right in the broad political spectrum. In the former instance, a common failing is the mistaken attribution of a sense of group identity and shared purpose to people who stand in a common relationship to the means of production in society. It is wishful thinking to suppose that all people in a given context who do not own (or, indeed, who do own) the means of production, *must*, by virtue of this alone, form a group. A working-class or bourgeois group may well exist under certain circumstances, but these are always broader than the single criterion of the (non-)ownership of productive means (Giddens, 1973).

At issue here is the widespread confusion of 'group' and 'category'. People who do not own the means of production comprise, in the first instance, a social category. A social category is a set of people who have one or more characteristics in common. Categories are fundamentally arbitrary; one classifies people into a category on the basis of some shared characteristic (they are all male, or have red hair, or are left-handed). It cannot be presumed that the people categorised in this fashion must inevitably share other qualities. Nor, quite clearly, does it follow that the people in an arbitrary category will form a group. The anthropological and sociological literature abounds with attempts to define 'groups'. Amongst the best known, and by now classic, endeavours in this regard were those of Merton (1949) and Homans (1951).

They agreed, broadly speaking, that human collectivities should meet three criteria to merit the term 'group'. First, the members of a group should interact with one another 'in accordance with established patterns'; second, the people who interacted in this fashion should 'define themselves as members of a group'; third, these people should also 'be defined by others as belonging' to a group (Merton, 1949: 285–6). Having set out this argument, Merton observed that 'to the extent that these three criteria – enduring and morally established forms of social interaction, self-definition as a member and the same definition by others – are fully met, those involved in the sustained interaction are clearly identifiable as comprising groups'.

Many subsequent writers would regard this formulation as excessively strict, although there is by no means agreement about which of Merton's criteria can be discarded. Moreover, in the South African context, where the notion of 'group' is generally employed with misleading abandon, there is some merit in maintaining a firm insistence on a stringent definition of the concept. Merton's characterisation therefore provides a useful point of entry to an area of widespread confusion.

Popular attempts to define groups often ignore at least one of Merton's criteria, particularly when the reference is to what are known as 'secondary groups'. Primary groups are groups where members interact on a face-to-face basis; the 'domestic group' is a prime example where members know each other personally and interact continuously in a structured fashion. People in a household group will usually also define themselves as its members, and be defined by others in this way (Keesing, 1975).

Secondary groups, by contrast, are usually much larger than primary ones, and their chief characteristic is that not all of the members know or interact directly with each other. The shareholders of the Anglo American Corporation, for example, most certainly do not know each other personally, and may never interact face-to-face; but means exist whereby they can interact in established ways to achieve certain ends. They all have in common something which is more than an arbitrary characteristic (they own shares in the company, and therefore have a common interest in its profitability), and are precisely distinguished by this from other people. For these reasons they can be said to form a group.

The chief difficulty with secondary groups is the absence of direct, personal interaction. In the South African context, are 'the Afrikaners' legitimately seen as a group? Can 'the Zulu' be viewed in similar fashion?

Clearly all Afrikaners, or all Zulus, do not know each other personally and do not all interact in a face-to-face manner. On the other hand, they are frequently regarded by outsiders as forming groups. This leaves two problematic criteria: can they be said to interact, indirectly, in accordance with established and enduring procedures? And do they regard themselves as a group?

The first question turns on the existence of organised avenues for indirect interaction. Such avenues should be enduring, and the subject of recognised norms and expectations of behaviour. Examples of these organisations could well be political parties or movements, churches, and cultural organisations such as schools, universities or societies. The members of a political party, for instance, clearly form a group of common purpose, even though they do not interact directly.

Here one encounters difficult problems with supposed groups such as 'the Afrikaners' or 'the Zulu'. In the first place, not all Afrikaners ('white' people who speak Afrikaans as home language) belong, or have ever belonged, to the National Party, or to a Reformed Church, or to the *Rapportryers*. In similar fashion, not all Zulus belong to Inkatha. The phenomenon of the *'bloedsap'* (an Afrikaner who supported the old United Party) was well known to National Party organisers of an earlier generation; the question of whether the National Party or the Conservative Party is the true home of Afrikanerdom is a burning issue of the present. Bram Fischer and Breyten Breytenbach are also Afrikaners, by virtue of their origin and their self-identification. Inkatha leaders may claim to speak for all Zulus, but the violence in Natal between Inkatha supporters and others exposes this as an ambition rather than a statement of fact.

This raises the question of self-identification. In recent writing, the issue of self-identification has been given more prominence as a criterion for group membership than the others which Merton mentioned. Thus a common contemporary view is that if people regard themselves as 'Afrikaners' or 'Zulus' they can be said to form a group. This argument is acceptable, provided that one recognises that groups formed in this fashion are of limited social significance. People who reject the recognised associations of Afrikanerdom or Zulu-ness may well have some residual awareness of themselves as members of an Afrikaner or Zulu group. But the fact that people indulge in a very vague self-identification does not entitle one to suppose that the groups in question are all-encompassing, and constitute the one and only identity which their members will acknowledge. The classic error in South Africa is to presume that if people are identified, or identify themselves, as 'Zulu', this label marks the essence of their being, and says all that there is to say about them.

The groups to which people refer here are usually seen as national groups. It is worth remembering that after considering the kinds of difficulties indicated above, Merton actually dismissed the notion of 'nations' as groups out of hand, saying that such usages stretched the meaning of the term 'group . . . to the breaking point' (1949: 299). He argued that while one could think of associations whose members were all of one nationality as groups, the notion of a group formed by the total population of a nation was scarcely conceivable. The members of a nation may, he suggested, share 'common values and have acquired an attendant sense of moral obligation to fulfil role expectations' (1949: 299), but they do not normally interact in any systematic fashion towards a common goal.

Thus one cannot assert *a priori* that 'the Afrikaners' or 'the Zulu' form national groups with common goals. And the extent to which they share common values and a sense of moral obligation is, furthermore, a question for historical inquiry. Not only do Afrikaners not form a 'natural' group, but the degree to which they have manifested collective values and obligations has changed over time (as several authors, notably Moodie (1975) and O'Meara (1983), have argued).

These considerations apply to all the concepts addressed in the chapters which follow, and it is important to reiterate that we are not trying to prove or disprove their validity in absolute terms. We are not trying to undermine these terms in general, or to suggest that they should never be used. Rather, we are attempting to document their use and meaning in the South African context and to examine these clearly. The popular use of the terms discussed in this volume does not stand up to close scrutiny; it is the rule, rather than the exception, for them to be used in an inconsistent way. This has brought great suffering to the majority of the South African population. And this in turn because the conventional meanings of these terms inform the policies and practices of those who hold power.

1 Culture: A contemporary definition
ROBERT THORNTON

Culture or cultures

The title of an article in a recent issue of *South African Digest* (17 July 1987) declares, 'The peoples of South Africa: A kaleidoscope of cultures'. Mr Chris Heunis, the Minister of Constitutional Development, tells his audience in the House of Representatives that 'South Africa is multicultural, and the constitution must reflect this' (*Argus*, 27 August 1987). The South African Tourist Board touts 'a world in one country'. The back of Kellogg's Cornflakes boxes offers instruction on how to communicate across cultures. The Freedom Charter asserts that the different peoples of South Africa will be free to develop their own cultures. Virtually everywhere, from all sides, in law and politics, in the press and from the public channels of communication, we hear that South Africa is composed of many cultures, and that these cultures are the products and properties of different peoples or *volke*. These commonplace notions distort the nature of culture. They need to be corrected in order to understand what culture is and what it does.

One textbook goes so far as to say, '*Soveel volke wat daar is, soveel kulture bestaan daar*' (There are as many cultures as there are peoples) (Coertze, 1973: 61). Another widely used textbook, *An Introduction to Anthropology*, by D. P. Stoffberg, says that culture is 'the expression of an ethnic group's speech, thought processes, actions and aspirations. An ethnic group and its culture develop organically and simultaneously to become an indivisible, homogeneous group' (Stoffberg, 1982: 1).

A. C. Myburgh approaches the issue from the other side by defining 'a people' as 'a human group producing and maintaining a culture' (Myburgh, 1981: 31), while B. V. Levitas in yet another textbook claims that the members of a group 'i.e. a people, possess a common way of life and share a common culture', and goes on to say: 'All South Africans are classified into races . . . [and] . . . consist of many peoples, the Xhosa, Zulu and Tswana, etc., each with a distinct language and culture' (Levitas, n.d.: 19). We find similar views world-wide. Elvin Hatch, for instance, defines culture as 'the way of life of a people' in the 1985 edition of *The Social Science Encyclopedia* (Kuper and Kuper, 1985: 178).

But the assertion of cultural differences distinctive of different 'peoples' or *volke* is apparently contradicted daily by the very fact that the ideology of differences is communicated easily across all of the 'cultural barriers' that we are told exist. In the marketplace and workplace, listening to music or watching television, at homes and in churches, people in fact experience the same desires, profess the same religions, follow the same leaders, and eat the same cornflakes, notwithstanding their 'multicultural' condition!

The problem is the little '*s*' that makes 'cultures' from 'culture'. Most of the textbooks just cited acknowledge that culture is what makes the species *Homo sapiens* specifically *human*, but once this is said, all agree that humanity is divided by its many cultures. P. J. Coertze, for instance, illustrates the idea with a little parable drawn from Ruth Benedict's *Patterns of Culture*, in which she quotes an American Indian 'just-so' story: 'In the beginning God gave to every people a cup, a cup of clay, and from this cup they drank their life. They all dipped into the water but their cups were different.' And he draws out the moral of the story, as he sees it: '*Uit die breë en algemeenmenslike kultuurstroom besit elke volk sy eie besondere gevulde 'kelk' wat die Skepper hom besorg het.*' (Out of the broad and common stream of human culture the Creator has provided each people with its very own full 'chalice'.) (1973: 61)

Coertze does not explain, however, that the old Indian chief quoted by Benedict went on to say: 'But the cup is broken now. It has passed away' (Benedict, 1935: 22). The old chief, Ramon, of the 'Digger Indians' of California, was in fact an active innovator. Although he mourned the passing of particular aspects of culture that he valued highly, 'the old man was still vigorous. . . . He did not mean that there was any question of the extinction of his people.' Coertze, then, has distorted the old Indian's original meaning in order to assert the uniqueness of separate cultures.

For Coertze, as for Benedict and many others, much more than the scientific definition of 'culture' is at stake here. The very act of defining 'culture' is itself a declaration of what it is to be human – that is, a moral statement – and a statement of identity – in other words, a political statement. This is because the attempt to understand and to define culture is also part of culture. Unlike the attempt to say precisely how microbes cause disease or specify the exact composition of a piece of granite, to discuss culture is to be part of culture, to have an effect on it, and ultimately to change the very nature of the 'object' itself. Although this concept is difficult to grasp, it is essential if our understanding of culture is to be more than a restatement in different terms of the moral and political ideas of our times.

The idea of culture and its context

The idea of culture as it is used in the modern period acquired the main features of its meaning in the nineteenth century. It shares a complex intellectual history with the ideas of 'society', 'nation' and 'organism', all of which appeared with their contemporary sense around the beginning of the nineteenth century. They have in common the idea of self-contained and self-regulating *wholeness*. Several intellectual sciences developed around these ideas, and today form the content of the academic disciplines of anthropology and/or ethnology, sociology, political economy and/or political science, and biology. The powerful ideas that these sciences have contributed to the world have transformed it completely in the two centuries in which they have been current.

These ideas have interacted with each other too. The idea of 'culture' has frequently been fused with that of 'society', and they have been used interchangeably to refer to a general social state of affairs or to a more or less clearly recognisable group of people. Ideas about 'cultures' and 'organisms' have also influenced each other in the development of theories of evolution, both cultural and biological. Sometimes people have argued that cultures are like organisms, or even that cultures are a *kind* of organism or 'super-organism'. Such notions have supported the idea that nations are endowed with unique cultures – something like the genetic component of an organism – which must be protected in order to preserve 'society'. Unfortunately, these ideas are confused and contribute nothing to a useful understanding of culture.

Worse still, these ideas have been used to justify repressive and brutal forms of government by arguing that, like an organism, a culture or a nation must defend itself against internal, as well as external, enemies. If the initial premise that cultures are 'owned' by nations is accepted, the activities of repressive state bureaucracies may be justified as a form of political hygiene. But in many cases the apparent similarities that exist between ideas of 'cultures', 'organisms', 'nations' and 'societies' are the result of the historical development of these ideas in a common intellectual and political context, and not the expression of genuine insight into the human condition.

In fact, it is scarcely possible to understand either the meaning or the power of any of these terms without also considering their contexts during the period of their development. For instance, the concepts and practices of the modern state arose in close connection with the intellectual ideas we are considering here, and spread to encompass the entire world. Europe, Russia, China and Japan acquired vast empires, and, in the case of Europe and Japan, lost them again. The boundaries of the 150 or so countries that we draw on the map today began to take their modern form at the beginning of this period and the process continued until the 1950s. Technological changes have also been important. Accurate clocks, today only slightly more than a hundred years old, have harnessed human life to a strict temporal regimen throughout the globe, and make it possible to locate literally every place in the world in terms of a single global grid of latitude and longitude. Modern medicine and biology acquired fundamental knowledge of genetics and physiology and developed methods to control many of humanity's oldest ailments. Mass communications, the popular press and popular culture developed on a world scale. New art forms such as the novel and movie were invented, and new ways to understand 'the meaning of life' were offered. Science changed from a gentleman's pastime to a core institution, a way of life, and for many, replaced formal religion as the primary means of understanding the world. Powerful standing armies were formed, unprecedented amounts of money poured into armaments, and unprecedented numbers of lives lost in international wars and other smaller conflicts.

These momentous events form the context in which ideas about culture were formed. They also changed the very nature of culture itself. In South Africa, as part of the world-wide trend of empire-building, intense political and economic interactions between 'the British' and 'the Zulu' were instituted virtually overnight by people from distant parts of the globe thrust suddenly into contact in large numbers and during times of extreme social stress. Although there is, objectively, a relatively smooth continuum of cultural ideas and practices spread across the large land-distance that separates Britain from southern Africa, when large armies are suddenly put down beside one another it is not surprising that they can see only each other's differences. Social stress and warfare increased the perception of social distance, and at the same time increased the internal coherence of each society – British and Zulu – to levels they would not have displayed in the absence of the colonial context. Finally, when books were written about 'the Zulu', 'the Boer', and 'the Briton', these local perceptions of difference became fossilised in the most highly valued – and thus most influential – form: the written word (see, for instance, Duminy and Ballard, 1981). The apparent gulf that separates the different cultures of South Africa is, then, an historical product. In other words, the cultural differences are themselves created by cultural processes which span and encompass these very differences. This is part of what culture does.

The idea of culture has a history

The intellectual history of the era in which ideas about culture developed falls under the labels of Romanticism and Modernism. These apply roughly to the nineteenth and twentieth centuries, respectively. We can trace relatively clear Romantic and Modernist theories of culture, and see how they are connected to other ideas and events of this period.

Roughly sketched, the Romantic idea of culture is that it is the *organic* product of a people or nation. The idea owes much to the German poet Goethe and the philosopher Hegel. Hegel, especially, was interested in the emergence of a German-speaking 'nation', and hoped to justify the formation of a pan-German-speaking state under the leadership of his own province, Prussia. Linguists, like Jacob Grimm, recorded the 'folk stories' (*Hausmärchen*) of the German-speaking peasants. People like Goethe and Grimm did for the German language what authors and ethnologists working in southern Africa and elsewhere did for languages like Zulu, Sesotho and Afrikaans: they recorded a literature which could henceforth be regarded as the 'natural expression', the 'folk-wisdom' or 'genius of the people'. Poets like Wordsworth or Coleridge, who derived inspiration from the German Romantic movement, and historians like T. B. Macaulay, did much the same thing for English.

The impact of these ideas on South Africa was as direct as any intellectual impact could be. Sir George Grey, governor of the Cape Colony from 1854 to 1861, was one of Romanticism's most avid students. These ideas were never far from his mind when he negotiated the settlement between President Boshof of the Orange Free State and Moshoeshoe of the Sotho legions massed at Thaba Bosiu; or participated in the settlement of the political conflict between Theophilus Shepstone, leading official of Natal, and Mpande, King of the Zulu; or defeated Sandile, paramount chief of the Xhosa-speaking Rharhabe, and fixed the border of the Eastern Cape. His assistant and librarian, Wilhelm Bleek, a Prussian intellectual whose kin, mentors and friends included many of the greatest figures of the German Romantic period, coined the term 'Bantu', distinguished clearly the 'Hottentots' from the 'Bushmen', and regularised the usage of words like 'Zulu' (rather than Zoeloe, or Sulu). The vocabulary and the geographic map of South Africa today document the Romantic ideas of culture that these men, and others like them, contributed to the history of southern Africa.

In parallel with the development of the Romantic idea of culture, the so-called Enlightenment contributed a second stream of ideas. For thinkers influenced by the Enlightenment the word 'civilisation' performed much the same functions as the word 'culture' did for the Romantics. According to this view, however, civilisation was the result of rational thought which led to the general improvement of life. These ideas had their roots in Classical antiquity, and as the word 'civilisation' suggests, implied a clear distinction between the people of the cities (*civitas*) and those of the rural areas (*rus*). The former were 'civil', that is they displayed the wealth, manners and cultural attainments of the urban dweller, whereas the people of the countryside lacked these virtues. The division between the 'civilised' and the 'un-civilised', originally founded on the social and economic organisation of Ancient Greece and Rome, was applied to the larger world. Nineteenth-century Europeans were educated in the 'classics', and encouraged to believe that what was right for Ovid or Plutarch was right for their own times. They believed themselves to be 'civilised' – just like the urban Romans – while the rest of the world was 'uncivilised' – just like the conquered rural provinces which provided the urban areas of Classical antiquity with their food and materials.

The anthropologist Edward Burnet Tylor brought these two streams of thought together in his definition of culture published in 1871. 'Culture or civilisation', he said, 'is that complex whole . . . acquired by man as a member of society.' He listed a number of things which culture included, such as 'knowledge, belief, art, morals, law, custom', among others. His definition of culture as a 'whole' which was 'acquired' by humans was a significant intellectual achievement. Among other things, he meant that it was not something people were born with, but something they gained through normal social interaction. This was, for its time, a genuine anthropological concept of culture. Its most important effect was to show that all humans possessed it, and that it was precisely this that made them human. But the history of the word 'culture' continued to suggest to many that culture belonged to specific nations, and that it consisted primarily of positive attainments and achievements.

In the twentieth century, the Modernist idea of culture retained the notion that culture is uniquely associated with a single society or nation. But unlike the Romantic notion, it asserts that culture functions to maintain society (or nations), and that culture is historical and changes over time, often in relation to (or determined by) changes in 'society' (or economy). Because culture – in the form of myths, political speeches, religious beliefs, ideologies, histories and traditions – is held to have a social function, the theory requires that each 'culture' exists as a *whole* within a 'society'.

Anthropologists who wrote according to this concept of culture often spoke about groups of people living on islands, or isolated from others by forests or mountains. Even where the people they wrote about were not isolated in any physical way, simply the fact that they were written about in a book, usually titled something like *The Life of a South African Tribe* (H.-A. Junod, 1912), *The Bantu-speaking Tribes of South Africa* (Schapera, 1937), or *The Pedi* (Mönnig, 1967), suggested their uniqueness and boundedness. The boundaries of so-called national states reflect, in many cases, the limits of a nineteenth-century dictionary which defined a 'language' (such as Tswana), or the designation of map-makers who, from the vantage point of Cape Town, distinguished between 'this side' (*cis-*) and 'that side' (*trans-*) of the Kei River. Elsewhere, culture has been written directly into legislation, administered by bureaucracies, and enforced by armed intervention. Indeed, in South Africa, it is often the history of ethnological *publications*, rather than the real history of South African people, that has had most influence in the shaping of political boundaries.

Recent thought, however, has indicated a number of flaws in these earlier concepts of culture. Most notably, earlier definitions included only positive aspects of culture. Thus knowledge was part of culture but not secrecy, morality but not evil, reason but not madness, tradition but not innovation, law but not disorder, government but not revolution. Nevertheless, secrecy, evil, madness, invention and revolution all display patterns, have histories, and are practised or believed or held as much as knowledge, morality, tradition and law. They must also be part of culture. The difference is often a matter of the perspective of the observer.

One of the factors that determines the perspective of the observer most forcefully is the distribution of wealth and power among the people the observer observes, and this is precisely what most earlier concepts of culture left out – or rather left for others to consider. Since the study of culture takes place in the discipline of anthropology, and the study of power, economy, and biology is pursued by other disciplines, part of the problem is the history of disciplines themselves.

The fact that the observer must also be part of the social situation that is observed was left out of earlier descriptions of 'cultures'. This created the effect of 'cultures' existing by themselves, the objects of scientific and disinterested observation. In fact, there are many reasons why observers observe and writers write about peoples' culture. But in order to write about the differences between people, observers must be *there*. No matter how different they may seem to themselves or to those they describe, observers must look and listen, sometimes understanding and sometimes misunderstanding. They must buy, sell, negotiate – in short, interact in a human and social way. The fact that books which detail all the *differences* of 'cultures' can be written at all negates the idea that cultures are *fundamentally* different.

Many anthropologists now feel that we have come to the end of an age. Some call it post-Modernism, for lack of a better term, to indicate that we have now entered an intellectual age that can dispense with some of the ideas on which the oppressive weight of the modern state rests. It is clear, too, that many concepts that have been fundamental to the sciences which appeared and grew during this age – biology, sociology, anthropology, and others – have changed. The concept of culture, one of the most politically and intellectually powerful ideas of the Romantic and Modern times, is also changing.

Culture is a resource

Today, culture is best thought of as a resource. Like other resources, such as energy, sunlight, air and food, it cannot belong exclusively to any particular individual or group of individuals. All groups and individuals must have access to at least some of these resources to survive. Similarly, culture is the *information* which humans are *not* born with but which they need in order to interact with each other in social life. It must be learned during the long process of education, socialisation, maturing and growing old. Like other kinds of resources, culture can be – and is – controlled by the environment, which places limits on what can and cannot be done. But the physical environment can never determine the content of culture. Unlike other physical resources, however, culture is never 'used up', but can only grow, change or even disappear in use. It is people who create cultural resources and control access to them.

Although culture is an essential resource, this does not mean that all people have equal access to all of culture, or even access to all of the cultural resources that they might need or desire. Indeed, secrecy, lying, misrepresentation, cheating, and misunderstandings are also part of culture! For the most part, earlier theories about culture assumed that everyone had more or less the same degree of access to the cultural resources that their particular social environment provided. Today, we see that this is not true – and believe that it was probably never true, even of the so-called 'egalitarian' or 'tribal societies' which were once thought to be completely homogeneous. It is these limits to access to cultural knowledge and resources, as much as the nature of those resources, that concern contemporary thought about culture.

If we think of culture as a resource, however, then we must include our own ideas *about* culture as part of the resources that culture provides. This is particularly true in South Africa since the concepts of 'different cultures' and 'own culture' have become central to the political thought of most South Africans. For the most part, these political uses of the word 'culture' are not about culture at all, as we shall use the term here, but rather about culture*s*. In this case, it is the final '*s*' that makes all the difference. For while there are differences in the way people behave and think and live, this reflects their differing access to cultural resources, as well as their use of these resources to make statements to each other and about themselves.

One such statement, perhaps the most significant for our understanding of the concept, is the statement about identity and group membership. Wearing a safari-suit or a tee-shirt and beads, participation in a rugby team or a dance band, represent choices made from a selection of cultural resources that comprise a statement about identity. Culture, however, is more than this: it is whole assemblages of safari-suits and tee-shirts, Zulu dance and *sakkie-sakkie*, Afrikaans, English, *gamtaal* and slang – together with all of the ways of using and expressing these and many other material and conceptual resources which our human environments present to us. The claim to 'one's own culture' and the apparent multitude of 'different cultures' in South Africa are therefore also part of the idioms or usages of culture-in-general. An everyday or political use of the term 'culture' must not be confused with an accurate *understanding* of what culture is and what it does.

An understanding of culture, then, is not simply a knowledge of differences, but rather an understanding of how and why differences in language, thought, use of materials and behaviours have come about. There are certainly cultural differences, just as there are differences in climate or personality or the various batches of the same colour of paint – but those differences have meanings, functions and histories. Contemporary cultural studies look at these meanings, functions and histories in order to understand the differences; they do not use the apparent 'fact' of differences to explain history, politics and beliefs.

Culture changes

Since cultural resources are controlled and limited in many different ways by social and environmental factors, culture changes. Over the *very long term* we can talk about the evolution of culture. Evidently, the resources that humans have employed to cope with each other and with their environments have undergone a dramatic evolution from simple stone and wooden implements, primitive drawings, and simpler languages (although we have no record or evidence of these now) to the complex forms we see everywhere today. It is clear that no single region or regional population is more or less responsible than others for the most important changes in the evolution of culture. It is also clear that the evolution of culture and the evolution of the human physical form and racial characteristics are completely unrelated. In fact, physical anthropologists agree that the human body ceased to evolve once humans became fully *human*, that is, when they no longer interacted directly with the environment with their bodies and sensations, but indirectly through the use of tools and concepts. From the dawn of our species, *Homo sapiens*, it has been culture which has evolved in order to provide the knowledge, tools, habits, and beliefs that permitted humans to adapt to changing environments. In fact, humans create their own environments rather than live directly in the natural physical environment. Even the broad vistas of most of the world's landscapes are man-made. These changes have proceeded at more or less the same pace, *over the long term*, everywhere.

In the shorter term, however, it makes little sense to talk about more-evolved or less-evolved cultures, since all but a very few humans possess at least the minimum necessary cultural skills to permit their survival and the full expression of human social and emotional life. The exceptions, where they exist, have nothing to do with 'evolution', but rather with specific social relationships of political power, economic exchange and control of cultural resources that have led to cultural deprivation, poverty and powerlessness of some people relative to others. It has been tempting to explain these differences in terms of the ideas of biological evolution of species – another of the great ideas of the modern age – but the fabric of culture is cut from very different cloth than the genes and organic substance of an organism. Although tempting, the metaphor of evolution drawn from biology is little suited to the task of understanding culture.

What culture does

Part of the problem that besets our current efforts to understand culture is the desire to define it, to say clearly what it is. To define something means to specify its meaning clearly enough so that things which are like it can be clearly distinguished from it. Clear definitions are an essential part of any successful science, or of good speech and clear thought. In fact, defining words, ideas, things, and groups of other people is an important part of what culture *does*.

We all live our lives in terms of the definitions, names and categories that culture creates. A large part of the study of culture involves discovering how and what definitions are made, under what circumstances, and for what reasons. These definitions are used, change, and sometimes fall into disuse. The idea of culture is not different in this respect from other human ideas. In fact, there are a number of competing words that have meanings and uses similar to 'culture' in some contexts. The list might include 'tradition', 'customs', 'way of life', 'civilisation', and even 'race', 'nation' or 'folk-ways', among others. For contemporary anthropology some of these terms have useful and well-defined meanings; others are part of the history of the discipline and have no legitimate usage today.

In fact, there is not much point in trying to say what culture *is*. This is not a failure of anthropology, or even of science and reason. Indeed, to know what can't be known – either to know the limits of a particular science, or to know the limits of knowledge itself – is also *knowledge*. What can be done, however, is to say what culture *does*, and how it does it.

One thing that culture does is to create the boundaries of class, ethnicity (identification with a larger historical group), race, gender, neighbourhood, generation, and territory within which we all live. Boundaries are created and maintained when people observe, learn, and finally internalise the rituals and habits of speech, the dispositions and dress of their bodies and modes of thought to the extent that they become entirely automatic and unconscious. These boundaries come to seem uniquely real and permanent. Their creation through cultural means is only obvious when we step outside of our normal day-to-day interactions.

The borders of states provide a good illustration. In crossing an 'international boundary' we involve ourselves in a complex political ritual which includes elaborate signposts, people wearing austere uniforms with obscure insignia (which only the initiated are permitted to understand fully), gates and narrow corridors. There is always an element of risk, of interference with personal freedom, even death if the formalities of this particularly powerful political ritual are not acknowledged and complied with. The boundaries between countries, in fact, exist only in the imagination. They are created through speech, text and gesture, and are enabled by the complex calculation of latitude and longitude which accurate clocks have made possible. We may see the power of culture in the political boundaries of states – a special kind of cultural category-making – for which most of us today are willing to risk all in modern warfare.

Boundaries between classes and races are similarly maintained by habits of language, postures of deference and domination, dress, differential access to both cultural and economic resources, and patterns of residence. The fact that these are automatic and in many cases unconscious does not make them less cultural. They must be learned. They can be brought to the level of consciousness through speech, text, art, drama and gesture, and thus un-learned. They can be changed. In fact, individuals in South Africa do change their class position, their racial classification, their ethnicity and nationality, even their gender. Although time decrees that we cannot change our age, culture makes the expectations and capabilities of different-aged people changeable as well.

The existence of boundaries and the fact that they are created by means of culture, then, present us with a kind of paradox. Boundaries divide individuals and groups of people, but they can only do so if the groups so divided share a common belief about what criteria and what rituals constitute a boundary. People must believe that it is important to 'be a South African', to 'be an elder', to 'be a man'. It seems that being human guarantees that some set of identities will always be important in this way. These identities overlap and often conflict with each other. They almost never correspond with other identities, however, in a way that would justify the belief that each 'people' has a uniquely different culture.

Cultural categories such as 'a nation', 'a community', and 'a society' are political entities only when they act together in some way (for example, when a nation goes to war, or the Lions Club makes a street collection). Otherwise, they are merely categories based on some criterion or set of criteria (for example 'the coloured people', 'the residents of Hillbrow'). Such categories are properties of thought. They provide a means of classifying and coping with the complexity of life. They are not cultural *groups* in any sense, unless they believe themselves to be so, and act together as a consequence of these beliefs.

The idea that each *volk* or people 'belongs to' or possesses a different culture is itself a part of the cultural processes of establishing political and personal identities. When seen in historical perspective, these ideas emerge clearly as products of their times (*our* times), which will themselves change. Societies, political groups, nations, and so on have boundaries. Their edges are often very easy to perceive and to define. This is what culture does. But the boundaries that are created, we can now see, are at the centre of culture, not its edges.

2 The quest for community
ROBERT THORNTON and
MAMPHELA RAMPHELE

'Community' is a political term – perhaps *the* political term. Communities may be claimed as constituencies in establishment parliamentary politics. In revolutionary movements, they become the ultimate justification for the destruction of the establishment. In the pursuit of justice – either that administered by formal state authorities, or that of the informal 'people's courts' or vigilante squads – 'the community' is the ostensible audience which must 'see' that justice is done, and whose mandate is assumed when executing the sentence imposed. 'Communities' may also be the objects of legislation which determines access to resources such as housing, wealth, jobs, literature, and perhaps even a sense of identity.

'Community' is the ideal for the future, the structure of utopia, the expectation of heaven, the legitimate goal for a truly democratic politics. At the same time it provides the vision of what we have been deprived of in losing the wisdom of the past, the 'way of our forefathers', the 'customs of the tribe'. The church, synagogue, and mosque are public symbols of the community of believers who enact their commitment to community regularly within them. The private prayer or the sacrifice of a beast to the shades is an act of community with the saints, God or the ancestors.

But the term is also used to describe loose entities like the 'international community' or the 'business community'. These usages imply that 'community', so designated, is static and wholly distinct from other social entities. If 'community' is *the* political term today, it is also one of the most stereotyped and obscure. But when all the uses and abuses of this term are taken into account, several features emerge.

First of all, it is often used by the South African government today as a euphemism for 'race', a term which is at least as ill-defined as community. It is also used to designate the targets – or victims – of government-planned 'community development' programmes which at best are often ill-conceived (though sometimes well-intentioned), and at worst vicious and destructive.

Secondly, 'community' is used to designate a following for political action, and an audience for political rhetoric. This usage is common to both the right-wing *Afrikaner Weerstandsbeweging* and to the left-wing United Democratic Front, among other political organisations.

In all these cases, the use of the term does not guarantee that a 'community' actually exists: there may in fact be no audience, no willingness to cooperate, no coherent social organisation, no sense of belonging. Nevertheless, we often assume that 'the community' exists and that it will agree, cohere, follow or listen. Politicians, development experts, and scholars ask what is wrong with 'the community' more often than they ask what is wrong with their assumptions.

There are probably as many good reasons not to belong to a community as there are to do so. It all depends on factors which may not be clear, which are unknown, or not even knowable at the time. Communities do exist, but they cannot be assumed. Claiming them in order to legitimate a political programme or to support a plan of action does not create them.

'Community' in South Africa

In South Africa, as elsewhere, the term 'community' is used to denote aggregations of people who have something in common, such as common residence, geographic region, and shared beliefs, or who claim membership in a common lineage structure, or who are distinguished by similarities of economic activity or class position. The Minister of Constitutional Development, Mr Chris Heunis, in discussing his government's plan for 'reform' through methods of co-optation, negotiation and consultation with co-opted representatives, declared that sharing of beliefs in a 'community' was essential, and that this justified his methods: 'Democracy can only work in a community which agrees on basic common values and among those who have been exposed to the institution of democracy over a long period' (*Argus*, 27 August 1987).

Government usage ranges from generic labels for official racial categories like 'Indian community', 'Coloured community', 'White community' or 'Black community', and extends to include administrative or regional entities, such as 'Lebowa community', which coincide with official labels for 'ethnic groups'. It thus uses the term interchangeably with 'race', 'ethnic group', 'nation' or 'peoples', and in doing so, appears to justify its insistence that since each is a distinct 'community' it must develop 'separately'.

The key to the success of the *Afrikaanse Taalbeweging* (Afrikaans language movement) in the Cape which began during the last half of the nineteenth century was the sense of community it fostered among a relatively powerless rural constituency. A similar constituency was in part responsible for the National Party's election victory in 1948. Although the constituency has changed radically and shifted away from National Party policy in various directions, the key to current government efforts to co-opt support for its policies from among those people whom they have specifically excluded from actual participation is still sought in the appeal to 'community'. 'Community participation' and 'community leadership' are apparently thought to be natural and more or less immediately available on demand.

There are a number of aspects that belong to government usage of the term, and the ideas and practices that go with it. These include (i) the justification of co-opted and appointed 'leaders', (ii) the appropriation of the term itself from other, less tainted contexts, and, perhaps most important, (iii) the restriction of access to resources of housing, education and medicine.

'Community leaders' and 'democratic' organisations

Community organisations declare that their intention is to give power to the powerless so that 'people's power' can be used against the oppressive power of the state. Often, however, these organisations replicate and reinforce the very same power structures that they intend to oppose. This is most clearly demonstrated by the composition and style of leadership: usually male-dominated, with the educated and relatively wealthy being most visible in the leadership ranks.

The need to have 'community participation', not only in the implementation of projects, but also in their planning and evaluation, has encouraged and often sanctioned the emergence of 'community leaders' who may have dubious qualifications other than concern for their own personal and family interests. Johnson Ngxobongwana, the 'mayor of Crossroads', is a case in point. He worked himself gradually into a position of *de facto* mayor of Crossroads and was accepted as such by a small circle of supporters. Later, government officials of the Department of Community Development, in search of a 'leader of the community' with whom they could deal, formally appointed him to the office. One of the residents described his rise to prominence:

We first noticed Ngxobongwana because he used to have a small bakkie and did odd jobs for people. One thing he did was to help take the schoolchildren on outings. One day we asked him how much we should pay him for his help. But he refused. So we thought to ourselves, 'Hey, this man can be useful to us.' It was then that we elected him onto the Noxolo School Committee as a secretary and how he came to be on our Committee. He wasn't elected. We just put him there. Unlike a lot of us he didn't go to work. Even Mr Mdayi wasn't always around because he was a security guard. So Ngxobongwana was the person always around in the community. Slowly lots of things, like the reports on things happening in our absence or messages from the authorities, used to get left with him. In this way Ngxobongwana got to be more and more powerful. (Cole, 1987: 44)

As chairman of the Western Cape Civic Association, his position was further strengthened by an alliance with the UDF. 'Those who were less trusting of Ngxobongwana or had been targets of his economic exploitation and repression inside the community, watched from the sidelines with a certain amount of cynicism. But in 1983, Ngxobongwana was a "popular leader" in the eyes of the leaders of most UDF affiliates' (Cole, 1987: 44).

In what could be called a take-me-to-your-leader syndrome, the same errors are committed by well-meaning people throughout the country; in their eagerness to get involved in 'the community' they end up establishing relationships with the most visible people who tend to be very articulate as spokespersons (mostly spokes*men*) of 'their people'.

There is a difference, however, between visibility and genuine political representation. When there are large power differentials between two or more groups in interaction, visibility may serve as a strategic substitute for representation. In rural areas, teachers, medical doctors and other professionals are often asked, or take it upon themselves, to lead 'communities' simply by virtue of their social visibility associated with better education and high economic and social status (Chambers, 1983: 18).

At a more overt political level, the concept of community is used to describe people who by common calamity share a particular geographic locality for purposes of political control. For example, the African townships were placed under the control of 'Community Councils' after the 1976 upheavals. Some community councillors were elected with percentage polls as low as one per cent. Nevertheless, they are still considered 'representatives of their communities' by the government. It is the large difference in social power between the government and the local population, however, which supports their claims to represent, rather than a genuine political process taking place within the community itself. Indeed, the supposed 'communities' are often little more than legislated categories. They cannot be distinguished from other putative 'communities' either by their differences or by any sense of similarity or common identity within them. They are not 'communities' in any meaningful sense of the term.

Appropriation of the term by government

The South African government has been especially adept at co-opting international jargon to justify the pursuit of its long-standing policy of 'divide and rule'. Thus the potential political significance of the increasing international popularity of concepts like 'community development' and 'community participation' was not lost on the government administrators responsible for naming departments and implementing apartheid policy.

For example, in 1961 the name 'Community Development' was given to the department concerned with development of white (mainly Afrikaans-speaking) 'communities', and the removal of all others from areas designated 'white' under the Group Areas Act. In terms of the 1985 constitution, which gave recognition to so-called coloured and Indian 'communities', the old Department of Community Development was partitioned among the three 'communities' as these were defined by the Group Areas and Population Registration Acts. Africans, on the other hand, are not yet administered under the rubric of 'community', and they are only recently being called 'communities' by government.

Whatever its name, however, the policy of 'development' has been ruthlessly applied to many 'communities' within the government's jurisdiction. Among the most notorious acts of the Department of Community Development was the destruction in 1965 of District Six, a dense suburban neighbourhood that bordered the central business district of Cape Town. This diverse neighbourhood had achieved a high degree of community awareness and cohesiveness. The area was one of the oldest residential areas in Cape Town, and consequently had developed a dense network of economic and social relationships that sustained its residents, who were mainly labourers, tradesmen and small commodity dealers. The destruction of the neighbourhood, in the name of 'community development', broke the web which held this community together.

As the familiar social landmarks of the closely grained working-class communities of the old city were ripped up, a whole culture began to disintegrate. The culture included maps of meaning which made life intelligible to its members. These 'maps' were not simply carried around in people's heads, they were inscribed in the patterns of social organisation and relationships through which people became social individuals. These patterns tended to involve three elements: the extended kinship network, the ecological setting of the neighbourhood and the structure of the local economy . . . this is a web of interlocking mutual interest.

The effect of the Group Areas removals was thus ' . . . like a man with a stick breaking spiderwebs in a forest. The spider may survive the fall, but he can't survive without his web. When he comes to build it again, he finds the anchors are gone, the people are spread all over and the fabric of generations is lost.' (Pinnock 1984)

The cruel irony of the destruction of District Six was that a recognisable community was destroyed in order to accommodate the ideology of 'community' held by government administrators serving their white constituency. People who have been victims of such 'community development' actions are too numerous to list. The result is illustrated by the remains of Sophiatown outside of Johannesburg, now renamed 'Triomf' (Triumph), which has been rezoned for the 'white community'.

Appropriation and control of resources
In another use of the term, government policy claims to 'ensure that

the various communities use their own resources to help themselves'
(De Beer, 1984: 75). The present tricameral parliament, which rigidly
separates responsibility for different 'communities' along the lines of
officially decreed 'population groups', is a strategy which seeks to
apportion resources according to 'community'. In the legislation and
administration of the 'own affairs' departments of education, health,
and other services, legislated *categories* are deliberately confused with
'communities'.

The term 'community', applied at a national level, is used to divide
resources into 'own' and 'general', thereby disadvantaging the poor
and legitimating existing inequalities. These inequalities are most
evident in the area of basic needs where historical neglect and
cumulative deprivation are reinforced by further maldistribution. If
each 'community' has to provide for its own needs, it follows that
those with the least resources will be most hard pressed to contribute
to sorely needed facilities, whereas those who have been favoured in
state allocations in the past will have no difficulty in providing a
relatively small proportion of their income for 'community facilities'.
The paradigm of a separate 'third world' and 'first world' will thus
control the distribution of resources in South Africa.

This is especially so in the field of education and health where the
'community' is supposed to take responsibility for its own services
and facilities. Thus 'community schools' have been for years a popular
way of forcing rural villagers to contribute one Rand for each Rand
spent on education by the government. The 'community' contribution
must be demonstrated before the government puts in its share. This
has inevitably delayed the provision of urgently needed facilities.

Health services in many rural areas are organised in a way that
extracts the maximum contribution from users. The building of
'community' clinics depends heavily on special levies which are
controlled by the local 'tribal authorities'. The 1977 Health Facilities
Plan gave further impetus to this tendency by encouraging private
doctors to use local 'community health centres' while continuing to
charge standard fees to residents (de Beer, 1984: 36–41).

It is fashionable to ensure 'community participation' in development projects, whether government-initiated or non-governmental.
This notion often makes the exploitation of already exploited people
seem justified because it is done in the name of progress. Development
projects world-wide have been known to reinforce inequalities in the
countries where they have been initiated, by not paying sufficient
attention to the patterns and problems of existing social relations. For
example, those who actually carry the burden of child-care and who
make decisions on health-care issues are often ignored in favour of
'leaders', usually males, with special interests of their own (Chambers,
1983: 18–22).

Women are particularly vulnerable to being further disadvantaged by 'community' development projects. Whenever there is a need for voluntary community action it is the women, who are already over-burdened, that have to give their often non-existent leisure time for communal efforts like village health work, building toilets, promoting literacy, etc. The 'community development' or health workers who motivate these women to sacrifice for the 'common good of their community' are often well paid by development agencies which represent interests external to the community. Moreover, it is usually men who are placed in paid supervisory roles, such as village water-pump guards, and may therefore wield enormous power over the women who volunteer their time (Weiss, 1986: 129).

Community and liberation?

Professionals, such as doctors, social workers, or academics who desire involvement in relieving the plight of the underprivileged also use the term to designate the object of their concern. Thus 'community health programmes', 'community development', 'community education' and general 'community organisations' have become of very considerable interest. Some of the ventures originate amongst the underprivileged themselves as they struggle to survive in a harsh environment. The proliferation of community projects and organisations is a phenomenon of the late 1960s, which has accelerated a great deal in the 1980s.

The Black Consciousness movement of the 1970s popularised the use of the word 'communities' to refer to wide socio-political groups like 'black community' (which included all those classified as African, coloured and Indian) or, even more loosely, 'the community' to describe residential entities such as the townships (themselves the product of earlier administrative decisions rather than joint action of the residents themselves). This usage was fully in keeping with the trends in the rest of Africa at the time. The assumption was often made that a community of purpose always existed and that people representing a 'community' would act for the common good. This was believed to be particularly so of communities which had suffered oppression, or which had been economically, socially or culturally deprived (Biko, 1987). In fact, however, many projects have failed in both urban and rural areas as a result of the assumption that communities did in fact exist. The community of wealth, of purpose or of responsibility that was meant to drive the project and ensure its access to resources was simply not there (see e.g. Hyden, 1980: 98–101).

By contrast, other South African liberation movements have resorted to an appeal to 'the nation' (or *isizwe* or *sechaba*) alone or in combination with an appeal to a pan-African community. Recent mass political actions aimed at shifting the present balance of power in South Africa have raised interesting questions about democratic processes and the legitimacy of actions by leaders in the name of 'the community'. Organising political action in a repressive political environment where the flow of information, consultation and free expression of ideas are severely limited, undermines the foundations of democratic processes. Nevertheless, there are clearly discernible approaches to this difficult task with qualitatively different political outcomes.

The first is a slow and painful process of politicisation, such as occurred in Cradock in the mid-1980s, which resulted in the formation of well-organised structures of control by the local residents. The sense of 'community of purpose and action' was demonstrated by the successful actions taken by these residents. The local schools boycott organised in response to the transfer of a popular teacher, Matthew Goniwe, is a good example of political action originating from issues that a community felt strongly about. Port Alfred also provided a model of well-organised, democratic community action in the form of a consumer boycott that forced traders to facilitate negotiations with local government on rents, public amenities and police action (*Work in Progress* 49, 1987).

The second approach is that of national and regional leaders who impose forms of mass action on local residents without due regard to existing conditions and adequate consultations. In the mid-1980s national organisations, in their eagerness to sustain and increase the momentum of countrywide resistance, often by-passed existing local structures. This was a source of bitterness and conflict in some areas where, for example, it was reported: 'Initiatives . . . came from UDF regional leaders who tried to call consumer boycotts without the necessary organizational infrastructure. They also posed general rather than specific local demands. Additional problems included profiteering by township businessmen and the difficulties involved in organizing huge townships.' (*Work in Progress* 49, 1987: 31)

In Cape Town the attempt at consumer boycotts in 1986 involved many of the problems identified here. The final irony was the widespread use of posters and stickers declaring support for the boycott by the traders who most benefited from the exploitation of the resultant captive market – 'the community'.

Background to the term

The idea of 'community' and its practical applications in South Africa are part of a larger concern with the term, which has a considerable and complex history. Much of the history of Western political theory and practice in the last three to four hundred years can be seen as the search for a definition of community that would underpin the structures of the state. More recently, the history of anthropology and sociology shows the same concern, the same search for 'communities' and the structures which create and sustain them (see, for instance, Nisbet, 1967: 47; Bell and Newby, 1971; Guyer, 1981; Cohen, 1985).

The contemporary sense of political community derives primarily from the medieval Christian religious communities, which owe their existence to St Augustine's notion of religious communion and fellowship, expressed in the 'Rule' of these orders. The religious community was held to represent in social form the communion of spirit celebrated in the Mass and Eucharist (see Bloch, 1961: 113–117). Although the Christian ideology of religious communities stresses the voluntary commitment of individuals to the community, none of the medieval religious communities could have survived the intense and protracted warfare of the period without the guarantee of security provided by the patronage of powerful nobles and kings. In return, the European religious communities served as secure repositories of wealth and provided religious justification and legitimation for political authority. Wherever such religious communities existed, from Ireland to Siberia and Ethiopia, they offered a model of political community that was subsequently elaborated by Russian tsars, Amharic kings, and European conquerors and republicans. When communists replaced Tsar Nicholas II in Russia and Haile Selassie in Ethiopia, they justified their actions by appeal to the common history of 'community', though now expressed in a different political idiom.

At the beginning of the nineteenth century, the originally religious concepts were secularised and employed in a radical restructuring of European polity. In England and Europe strong socialist or communist movements developed around the so-called Revolution of 1848 when the remains of the feudal order fell apart, and were replaced by nationalism and republicanism. In a different sphere, churches organised community 'Sunday schools', and mission movements sent communally organised missionaries 'out into the world'. As a consequence of this, in southern Africa as elsewhere, mission stations became models for collective political action that eventually led to the overthrow of colonial domination by Africans educated in the precepts of Christian community and familiar with its practice (Etherington, 1978).

The European movements, and their manifestations in Africa and elsewhere, generated an overriding sense of common identity and common purpose on a new and much larger scale than ever before. It is important not to forget, however, that this also depended on the growth of powerful forces of social coercion and power.

Today, for instance, the churches in South Africa provide an institutional support for well-established communities which are bound together by shared beliefs and material resources held in common. There is little scope for personal or private ownership of property. It is this 'community' that is celebrated and symbolised in 'the Holy Communion' that all practising Christians share. This form of community approximates the ideal community. It is reinforced by a system of rules and regulations that binds the participants together in pursuit of the common good. Such 'ideal' communities are rare, however, and are virtually never the object of government-initiated 'development' or administrative action. Indeed, the more groups approach the ideal of community, the less they are treated to 'community development' or 'community organisation'!

Conclusion

Communities do exist. People believe in communities, desire community, and act as if they exist even when they don't. The word 'community', then, refers in a self-contradictory way to a belief and practice. The problem is that we cannot infer the practice from the existence of the belief; that is, while the belief may be real enough, the reality may not reflect it.

On the one hand, 'community' can best be understood as an 'image of coherence', a cultural notion which people use in order to give a reality and form to their social actions and thoughts. Its history lies in religious concepts, and its political usage is relatively recent.

On the other hand, the sociological existence of communities is founded on more or less intense social interaction among their members, which inevitably produces social boundaries defining them and giving them identity. Sometimes, the 'community spirit' is engendered by the threat of war or violence. Even so, it is contingent on the moment (although it may be a long moment). When the threat passes, the spirit may also pass on.

The boundaries of communities are symbolic and exist by virtue of people's belief in them. Only rarely and under unusual social conditions, such as warfare or long-distance travel, are these boundaries marked by simple physical differences. These differences must be converted into symbols of difference which are asserted through ritual, speech, and in other ways if they are to last as genuine boundaries (Cohen, 1985: 97).

Communities are dynamic, and are always in a constant state of flux, even when they are apparently most stable. Primarily because of the tremendous increase in historical and sociological knowledge of society in Africa, it is difficult to believe, now, in wholly static, wholly history-less 'tribal' or 'primitive' communities (Guyer, 1981: 125). Community is the unpredictable product of history, and the product of people. It is not the same thing as the category created by government or statisticians for reasons of their own. It must not be confused with 'society' for this is always much larger.

Thus, it is clear that communities are made, enacted and believed in. Appeals are made to them which depend on the belief of most people that communities ought to exist, and that they are the legitimate goal of all political action. While we may aim at the achievement of community, we must face the painful truths that communities are the result of complex political processes and exist *in* history, not above it.

3 Promoting tradition: Images of the South African past

ANDREW SPIEGEL and
EMILE BOONZAIER

In a limited sense, 'tradition' refers to the transmission of culture – the repeated handing down of ideas, conventions and practices which humans need in social interaction. Popular understanding of the term goes beyond this neutral sense. Thus when people are told something is 'tradition' they will assume that it is age-old and unchanged since its inception. Any behaviour which is thought to have originated long ago and to have been handed down from generation to generation is thus placed in the category 'traditional'. Formal graduation gowns are described as 'traditional academic dress' because academics have worn such robes for many generations. Similarly, when a style of artistic expression becomes established, it is labelled as 'a tradition'. For example, we speak of the 'Cape Dutch tradition' of architecture.

But 'tradition' and its derivatives ('traditional' and 'traditionalism') are seldom used without subjective, value-laden implications. The past can either be heralded as the source of unquestioned legitimacy as in 'the traditional sanctity of marriage' or 'the traditional value of free speech', or it can be used to suggest other people's backwardness or conservatism as in 'traditional farming practices' or 'traditional medicine'. 'Tradition' can therefore have contradictory or ambivalent connotations, implying either duty and respect or dismissive disdain.

Both connotations provide a resource for people intent on gaining, maintaining or challenging existing power and privilege. For this reason, one often finds 'traditions' being invented (Hobsbawm and Ranger, 1983) or becoming the subject of struggles as to what constitutes *real* 'tradition' (Keesing and Tonkinson, 1982). These processes lead people to confuse the reality of the past with recreated images of the past. We need to question any reconstructions of 'traditional' lifestyles that we may discover in books, films and on television. In many instances, a belief that something has been unchanged for generations will not withstand close scrutiny.

'Tradition' is also very vague about time. On the one hand, there is the implication of infinite timelessness stretching beyond recorded history, as in the phrase 'traditional hunter-gatherers'. On the other, it is possible that 'traditions' may have been established very recently. One cannot specify that practices or ideas must have existed for a certain minimum period or number of generations in order to qualify as 'tradition'.

The fact that people use the term in a variety of ways suggests that its meaning is not self-evident. Nor is it obvious to which sets of people or phenomena the labels 'tradition' or 'traditional' may legitimately be applied. It is precisely this vagueness which permits the term to be manipulated and thus used to promote or justify political ideals.

Anthropological use of the notion of 'tradition' has been equally vague and general, despite the idea's centrality in much academic writing. Most scholars seem to assume that the meaning of the term is either self-evident or immaterial (Boyer, 1987: 49), with the result that the notion has seldom been exposed to explicit discussion or rigorous definition (however, see Eisenstadt, 1972, and Shils, 1981). Nevertheless, as Boyer (1987) points out, the term 'tradition' carries with it a set of common but tacitly held assumptions. These assumptions, which Boyer identifies for anthropological discourse, closely mirror those in the lay use of the term – for example, the idea that 'traditions' are handed down from past generations in essentially unchanged form.

Boyer also draws our attention to the assumption that what we call 'traditions' are *caused* by 'traditionalist' or 'conservative' thinking. Such a 'traditional' outlook or world-view is moreover associated with particular populations ('peoples', 'groups' or 'societies'). It is this aspect that forms the key element in the use of 'tradition' in the dominant political discourse in South Africa.

Tradition in South Africa

In South Africa the term forms part of the political argument that Africans are *still* 'traditional' in outlook and can therefore not be incorporated into the 'Western' (that is, white) political system. Evidence of this outlook is supposedly to be found in the persistence of certain 'traditions', such as bridewealth or *lobola*, initiation rituals, the authority of chiefs, belief in ancestors and the resort to 'traditional' healers or diviners ('witchdoctors').

The term 'traditional' has long been used as a euphemism for the labels 'uncivilised', 'primitive', 'pre-literate', 'tribal' or 'non-Western'. In fact, until recently many anthropologists world-wide spent most of their time studying 'traditional' societies and describing the 'traditions', 'culture' or 'customs' (in this context these three terms are used interchangeably) which were assumed to control the behaviour of people in this category. In the social sciences in general, 'tradition' has been contrasted to the notions of 'reason', 'rationality' and 'science' (Shils, 1981). Thus the lives of 'traditional' people are seen as 'bound by the cultural horizons set by [their] tradition', in contradistinction to 'modern' people who are conceived as 'culturally dynamic, oriented to change and innovation' (Eisenstadt, 1972: 1).

This distinction between 'traditional' and 'modern' is particularly suited to the representation of South Africa as a society comprising two separate parts. Thus the *Official Yearbook* argues that 'the White and Black segments of the South African population have different cultures' (South Africa, 1985: 95), and that 'traditional economics among the Black peoples of South Africa is based on a subsistence rather than profit philosophy. The concept of overproduction in specialised fields for distribution by free marketing is foreign to traditionalist thinking.' (South Africa, 1985: 94) This is followed by a discussion of conceptions of time in order to highlight 'the differences in values between African and Western economics'.

Nowhere is subsistence-based thinking so obvious as in traditional African conceptions of time. In contact situations involving subsistence-oriented personalities and the products of industrialised society, there are often conflicts in regard to time and its significance, each group ethnocentrically applying their own values and adding to the general confusion. Differences are exaggerated and similarities disregarded or misunderstood. To the African traditionalist and the industrialised Westerner, time is a commodity, to be used according to the demands of their respective societies; but for Western man it must respond to the laws of supply and demand. Traditional Africa, on the other hand, uses as much or as little of it as it needs. (South Africa, 1985: 94)

The image conveyed here is of a 'traditional' African culture which is unchanging, homogeneous and communal, as opposed to a 'modern' white culture which is dynamic, diverse and individualistic. Used in this way, 'traditional culture', 'traditional economics' and 'traditional conceptions' are clearly not mere descriptive labels. They form an argument that seeks to account for the marked discrepancies in wealth between blacks and whites in terms of the supposed obstacle presented by 'traditional' beliefs and practices to 'development'. They are also used to explain Africans' increasing rejection of the capitalist system, as when the SABC daily editorial argues that because 'a large group is barely emerging from a traditional culture of collectivism, and moreover feels itself to be disadvantaged, the apparent panaceas offered by socialism are a powerful attraction ... and it is not surprising that many black people tend to favour socialism above free enterprise' (SABC Comment, 10 June 1986).

A picture of Africans as 'traditional' serves to mystify the crucial political and economic processes that have led to the inequalities between whites and blacks. For those concerned to perpetuate the status quo in South Africa there is much to be gained by such an image. Indeed, this is the most prominent usage of 'tradition' in the present South African political discourse.

It is true that in all societies there are 'traditions' which continue, on the surface relatively unchanged, into the present. And there are many examples of life-styles which might be described as 'traditional' in that they differ significantly from, or are isolated from, those we call 'modern' or 'Western'. But in South Africa today the term is used to label an entire category of people whose behaviour and thinking are portrayed negatively. They are seen as 'conservative', 'backward', 'pre-rational' and therefore fundamentally unable to compete with 'modern', 'progressive' or 'developed' people. This usage is entirely compatible with discriminatory ideas which refer to racial differences and inferiority. 'Traditionality', however, has the advantage of being ostensibly neutral and thus more acceptable.

One further aspect of this usage is that, for many, the argument that Africans are backward and impoverished because they are still 'traditional' provides its own (albeit circular) substantiation. For those who hold to this view, ample 'evidence' of Africans' inherently 'traditional' outlook can be found in the fact that they are still 'poor' and 'backward' (for example, see du Preez, 1984). Further support is obtained from the apparent persistence of particular 'traditions', often highlighted in the media, which are interpreted as being common to most, if not all, Africans.

The persistence of 'traditional' practices

A clear example of 'the persistence of custom' relates to the widespread popularity of 'traditional African healers' (diviners or 'witchdoctors'). Discussion of 'traditional' healers usually begins from the premise that Africans are 'irrational' and 'superstitious', but that these characteristics will wane under the influence of 'scientific' medicine.

There has been a tendency in the past to take for granted that education in general, and scientific training in particular, can wipe out traditional beliefs widely held in African cultures. With the growth of Western-type education in Africa it was generally assumed that as people began to distinguish between 'true knowledge' and 'superstitious beliefs', scientific investigation would supersede the worship of gods and of rain and harvest, that the aetiology of disease would be traced to viruses and microbes rather than to witchcraft, juju and evil spirits. (Elliot, 1984: 109)

The assumption is thus that, as Western medicine becomes available to 'undeveloped' populations, 'traditional' or 'indigenous' healing will disappear. Writers therefore express surprise that 'far from decreasing in numbers and influence with the expansion of [Western] health services, the reverse is actually happening, with increasing numbers of traditional healers setting up practice' (Karlsson and Moloantoa, 1984: 43).

This apparent dilemma is explained in terms of the resilience of 'traditional' African beliefs relating to witches and ancestors (see, for example, Elliot, 1984), and medical journals contain many articles referring to 'traditional' African 'cosmology', 'world-view' and ideas about 'disease causation' (see Swartz and Foster, 1984 for a discussion of this literature). Few of the authors of these articles are anthropologists, but they draw heavily on anthropological works written before the 1950s, with scant regard for any changes which have taken place since then.

Sadly, some anthropologists have done little to dispel notions about an unchanging 'pre-scientific' African 'world-view'. One professional has claimed:

The first thing to grasp is the fundamental difference in ideas of causation between Western man and the African. . . . Among all Bantu-speakers all misfortune, and all illness and death, except that from extreme old age, is sent by supernatural beings. There are two possibilities and only two. The misfortune can be caused by ancestral shades or by a witch/sorcerer. (Hammond-Tooke, 1975b: 25–26)

The psychiatrist Vera Bührmann attempts similarly to reconstruct 'the world of the traditional'. Like many early anthropologists, she selected a remote rural area to conduct her research with a small group of 'traditional Xhosa healers' (*amagqira*). On this basis, however, she feels free to comment on the 'world' of the Xhosa, and of Africans in general, typifying it as 'primarily intuitive, non-rational or oriented toward the inner world of symbols and images', in contrast to 'the Western world which is primarily scientific, rational and ego-oriented' (Bührmann, 1984: 15). According to the back-cover blurb of her book, these revelations are necessary 'for anyone interested in the social, political and psychological realities of southern Africa'. This is surely because they can readily be used to understand in what ways Africans are really *different*, displaying differences which are manifested in their continuing to consult 'traditional healers'.

It is of course true that certain beliefs relating to ancestors and witches are still prevalent amongst some Africans. But one must note that the kinds of 'explanations' for the continued reliance on 'traditional' healers we have summarised above, fail to address the political and economic dimensions of the issue. For example, one can question the assumption that Western medicine is readily available to the majority of Africans in South Africa today. Estimates of the doctor–patient ratio for Africans indicate a figure of 1:40 000, which contrasts sharply with the figure of 1:400 for whites. Moreover, while the majority of whites belong to medical aid schemes, fewer than 5 percent of Africans do. Africans have limited access to telephones and private transport, and thus to Western doctors. They also share the typical burden of disease associated world-wide with poverty and poor living standards – conditions not amenable to 'cure' by Western medicine. As patients, their experiences of Western doctors (almost invariably white) involve attending crowded state-run hospitals and clinics, long waits, and an impersonal atmosphere (van Selm, 1984).

Finally, one must emphasise that all patients make rational decisions about which healers to consult, and when to do so. People consult so-called 'alternative' healers *in addition to* (and not instead of) Western doctors. Availability, cost, and perceived efficacy (in treating certain types of conditions) are major factors which influence choice of healer world-wide, and more and more people in Europe and North America are consulting chiropractors, homeopaths, acupuncturists and movement therapists to deal with the increasingly apparent inadequacies of Western medicine.

Therefore, given the negative experiences of many African patients in their encounters with Western medicine, it often makes perfectly good sense to consult so-called 'traditional' healers. In their quest for therapy, patients are simply maximising their chances of being cured. Were their choice simply determined by their 'traditional' outlook, African patients would *never* seek assistance from Western medicine.

Anthropologists and 'traditional' societies

Anthropologists have been responsible for creating and perpetuating a picture of 'traditional' life-styles, and of 'peoples' who existed, and continue to exist, in pristine isolation.

Early anthropologists set themselves the specific task of studying 'others' – people who were obviously not 'Western', 'literate' or 'industrial'. This meant that they deliberately sought people in remote and isolated areas of the world. They undertook long voyages from Europe to the distant Torres Straits, and the Andaman and Trobriand islands, in search of isolated populations. This provided the model to which later generations of anthropologists aspired.

Early anthropologists in South Africa also focused their attention on remote rural areas and concentrated exclusively on indigenous communities. Winifred Hoernlé was the first social anthropologist to carry out fieldwork in South Africa. When, in 1912, she undertook an arduous trip to north-western Namaqualand, the 'most inaccessible corner' of the Cape, her stated aim was to search for 'the few pure Hottentot who to-day lead the life that we know traditionally to have been led by their ancestors of old' (Tucker, 1913: 4).

However, one must not assume that all anthropologists disregarded the significance of change. For example, Hoernlé cited early nineteenth century reports listing some of the dramatic changes that had already affected the indigenous population of the area, and concluded that 'it is certainly with many misgivings that any attempt to reconstruct the past can be undertaken' (Tucker, 1913: 4). Her aim, moreover, was not to create a picture of 'traditional' societies as existing into the present, but rather to provide comparative ethnographic material, in the firm belief that 'primitive societies . . . offer simpler conditions to work with . . . [and permit one] to separate the inherent from the borrowed, to trace the effect of cultural fusions, and finally to define the modes of inner growth and of assimilation from without' (1913: 13–14).

There are many other examples of anthropologists being at pains to emphasise that they have described 'a life that no longer exists' (Hunter, 1979: xiv). Yet this does not mean that we can use these examples to whitewash anthropology. Indeed, a frank assessment of many of the ethnographic texts up until the 1950s is that they did convey a picture of static 'traditional' societies, and highlighted those aspects of social life which the informants said had existed before contact with 'Western' influences.

Moreover, in the view of these early ethnographies, each aspect of social life described had a clear function to fulfil in the culture or society in question – to meet the basic needs of individuals, or to ensure the society's continued existence. Therefore, each society was presented as if it comprised a coherent and self-perpetuating system. In terms of these systems, people's behaviour was seen as perfectly rational, however bizarre it might seem from a European perspective. The convention of describing social institutions and associated practices in the 'ethnographic present' – with the ethnographic texts written in the present tense – was a product of this approach. With hindsight we can see that it has had most unfortunate consequences because, wittingly or not, it created the impression of unchanging societies existing into the present.

Notwithstanding such criticism, the 'traditional' existences portrayed in early ethnographies do have legitimate uses. Treated with sufficient caution, they provide us with some insight into the past in the sense of 'a more or less hypothetical baseline, a reconstruction of traditional society which is contingent on our relative ignorance of pre-colonial conditions' (Murray, 1980: 139). But any attempt to use early ethnographic descriptions as a source of information about the *present* is obviously flawed and easily criticised.

It is more difficult to disprove the assumption that certain practices and beliefs, which resemble those of the past and which can be demonstrated to exist at present, are evidence of unchanging life-styles and inherent and irrational conservatism. Everyone knows that bridewealth, 'witchdoctors', chiefs, belief in ancestors, and manhood initiation rituals are all contemporary social phenomena. Since these resemble pre-colonial forms they are often designated as 'traditional'. These descriptions are then interpreted as signifying the 'traditional' mentality of those who sustain the practices and beliefs.

As in the case of 'traditional healers', these interpretations reveal a lack of concern to locate the practices in their political and economic contexts. Moreover, they show a very superficial grasp of the contemporary social significance and meaning of these 'traditional' institutions. The section which follows discusses some alternative interpretations, offered in more recent anthropological work.

'Traditional' practices as accommodative responses

Far from supporting the view that certain people are 'traditionalist', many anthropologists in recent times have been at pains to understand the apparent persistence of 'traditional' beliefs and practices as a dynamic response to changed circumstances.

One example is the transformation in function of bridewealth payments in rural Lesotho. Murray has emphasised that 'marriage with cattle', although 'deeply rooted in the Sesotho tradition' (1981: 125), has undergone significant change between the mid-nineteenth and the late twentieth century. He points out that in many cases the monetary value of transfers from the groom's family to the bride's has actually increased in the late twentieth century; that cash has replaced cattle as the means of payment; and, most important, that young men have come to obtain this bridewealth (known in Sesotho as *bohali*) from their labour on the mines, rather than from the elders of their family. These changes in the form of the institution raise questions about the contemporary significance of bridewealth transfers.

In the past bridewealth payment signified the transfer of a woman's reproductive, productive and sexual services from her family to her husband's. It served to legitimate and incorporate her children into their father's family, and also provided elders (who controlled cattle) with a means of control over young men.

In the twentieth century, however, men were forced by economic and political circumstances to become labour migrants and to leave their wives and families at home. Paying *bohali* emerged as a major mechanism whereby people coped with the exigencies of migrant labour and the repeated absence of breadwinning husbands, fathers and sons for periods of up to two years at a time. On the one hand, it enabled the senior generation to gain some access to the earning capacity of young migrants. *Bohali* transfers came to be an important source of income for the heads of women's natal households, and the senior generation therefore had an interest in continuing the practice. On the other hand, migrants 'also have an interest in substantially fulfilling their *bohali* obligations, for their long-term security is best assured by establishing access to legitimate dependants within a rural household' (1981: 146–147). Moreover, the knowledge that their wives might leave their marital homes to spur their parents on to demand further *bohali* instalments was a reminder and incentive for men to remit money home for their families' support.

The insights provided by this analysis clearly refute the notion of stubborn 'traditionalism' or backwardness. Not only did the institution of bridewealth undergo subtle but significant change, but it also became a vital mechanism for survival under the system of migrant labour. The analysis also shows, as Murray points out, that one should guard against juxtaposing the individual migrant's 'rational' economic interests and 'irrational' adherence to custom (1981: 148).

The question of rationality has long occupied anthropologists working in 'traditional' societies. In the past a distinction was drawn between individual and social structural rationality. It was argued that individuals in 'traditional' societies may well have behaved irrationally when they acted in accordance with the dictates of 'tradition', but that those actions had a function which made sense when seen as part of the way their cultures worked. People acted rationally to fulfil the 'traditional' demands placed on them. More recently, anthropologists have argued that apparently 'traditional' practices are in fact rational responses, at both individual and structural levels, to wider political and economic constraints. The rationality of custom is apparent from the perspective of the broader social system of which the individual is part, and of particular individuals themselves. In Lesotho, the broader context is the history of years of underdevelopment, resulting in the country's almost total dependence on the export of labour to South Africa. Given progressive impoverishment and the necessity for men to remain absent from their homes while they earn meagre wages, *bohali* became 'a mechanism by which migrants invest in the long-term security of the rural social system, and by which rural kin constitute claims over absent earners' (Murray, 1981: 148).

Imposed 'traditions': continuity with the past?

No 'traditional' practice can ever claim to be an exact replication of an earlier one. 'Traditions', like everything else, change. Sometimes the changes are obvious – for example, the incorporation of Santa Claus into today's 'traditional' Christmas represents a radical change in the form (and meaning) of the celebrations. On the other hand, changes can also be subtle or apparently insignificant, as we have seen in the example of changes in the monetary value of bridewealth payments, and the change from cattle to cash.

Although people recognise that change takes place, it is often assumed that where there is some resemblance to earlier forms, the new forms still represent a continuity with the past – a natural process of adaptation by which outmoded practices respond to changed circumstances. However, this is not necessarily the case. There are many instances of contemporary institutions which are said to be 'traditional', but which, on closer inspection, turn out to have been imposed from outside. They have a semblance of continuity with the past only by being described in similar terms: the institution of chieftainship in South Africa's homelands is one such example.

A chief in Qwaqwa is still called *morena*, the word used to describe nineteenth-century political leaders whose authority derived from their ability to maintain their followers' allegiance, as well as from their descent from particular lines. Today, however, chiefs' roles and the sources of their authority have been radically modified (Quinlan, 1986). They now act as bureaucratic administrators rather than autonomous legislators and mediators, and they are all appointees of a central government which pays scant attention to the wishes of the administered people as to whom they would like to rule their lives for them. The situation of chiefs in the Transkei has followed a similar pattern.

Chiefs and headmen in the Transkei

There is much evidence that in pre-colonial times a significant proportion of the southern African population was organised into political groupings with centralised authority vested in hereditary leaders known as chiefs. The size of these groupings varied considerably – from hordes and clans with a few hundred members, to large 'tribes' and chiefdoms with up to 15 000 followers. Commenting on leadership in some of the larger nineteenth-century groupings, Murray has written:

The chief was the ultimate source of all authority. He embodied the material and spiritual welfare of his people. As custodian of the land, he controlled its distribution. The prerogatives of his office – tribute, court fines, his command of labour and regulation of grazing – enabled him to accumulate vast numbers of livestock. . . . Subject to the advice of his counsellors, the chief decided questions of public policy, introduced legislation and judged all serious crimes and disputes. He regulated the sowing and harvesting of crops. He was responsible for making rain on behalf of the tribe. (Lye and Murray, 1980: 96)

Successive colonial and post-colonial governments recognised the institution of chief as an important political instrument. They could, and did, lend support to chiefs and thereby gain control over the population. At the same time, they could withhold support from particular chiefs by recognising or appointing others in their place. And they could also remove certain rights, such as control over the distribution of land or the right to impose fines, by transferring these to centrally controlled bureaucracies. The result has been a radical change in leadership roles, which occurred at all levels of administration.

What occurred in the Transkei provides a good case in point. Colonial annexation of the various chiefdoms in what became the Transkeian territories took place in the period 1879–94. The boundaries of the chiefdoms were abandoned and the whole area was redivided into districts and locations, administered by white magistrates and by location headmen. The aim was to destroy the autonomy of existing chiefdoms, and to break the power of the chiefs and their subordinates who were feared as dangerous foci of resistance to colonial rule (Hammond–Tooke, 1975a: 77–8).

The new position of location headman revealed the extent to which 'traditional' offices were supplanted, even at the local level. Headmen came to be 'commonly regarded as instruments of alien control, and earned themselves the title of *isibonda*, or "poles" supporting the colonial administration' (Southall, 1982: 89). They and their councillors were 'described as being venal: they were "simply put in the inside pocket of the jacket" of government' (Bundy, 1987: 217).

This form of direct rule remained until the 1950s, when the Nationalist government began to implement its apartheid policies. Ironically, the Bantu Authorities Act of 1951 tried 'to re-establish the power of the chiefs and the integrity of the old chiefdoms' (Hammond–Tooke, 1975a: 2). The government gave various reasons for this, including the argument that the existing system of direct rule left the chiefs, the 'true leaders' of the people in the Transkei, out of all decision-making, and that 'the people generally had "sat in the sun" and expected the government to do everything for them' (Hammond-Tooke, 1975a: 203).

What actually happened was that people who could demonstrate genealogical claims to chiefship were drawn into the existing system and inserted into the administrative hierarchy between location headmen and district magistrates. There was, indeed, a scramble for chiefly status by people with conflicting genealogical claims to it, and the government ethnologist was called upon to arbitrate (Hammond-Tooke, 1975a: 207).

A new tier of regional authorities was also introduced, supposedly based on old chiefdom clusters and paramount chieftainships. Its functions were not, however, fully clarified for some years, and it was only after the Transkei gained constitutional 'independence' from Pretoria in 1976 that the chiefs who dominated the legislature reinforced their own power by giving the regional authorities judicial powers equal to those held by magistrates' courts. 'Traditionality' had been a means of legitimating a racially discriminatory system; it now became a resource used by those Africans who stood to benefit from the apartheid system.

The situation by which Transkeian chiefs had been turned into bureaucratic administrators is well summarised by Streek and Wicksteed:

Direct control of the tribal authorities and the chiefs is fundamental to the system of government. This has been the case ever since the Bantu Authorities system, inaugurated by the South African government in 1951, was introduced in the Transkei in terms of Proclamation No. 180 of 1956. It transformed chiefs – theoretically at least the guardians of the interest of their people – into loyal, government-paid officials. They became key functional elements of the system of government. Not only were they paid by the government, but were also dependent on that same government for their survival in office – predictably they could be removed. (1981: 18)

It must be obvious that with such radical restructuring, 'the whole structure, above the tribal authority level, has no counterpart in the traditional system' (Hammond–Tooke, 1975a: 208).

'Traditional' headmen in town

Over the years the colonial office of headman became part and parcel of the local political and administrative landscape in the Transkei and other homelands. Thus 'headmen' are part of a successful process of 'inventing tradition', and the idea that their presence is necessary to good rural administration is widely accepted.

The 'traditionality' of headmen is further demonstrated by the way in which the office has been brought to town. There is some evidence that people in urban squatter areas accept particular individuals as their 'headmen'. 'In the struggle to adapt to a rapidly changing social environment, . . . people . . . chose familiar structures' (Cole, 1987: 19). Squatter areas have few imposed administrative structures, and there are openings for men with guile and resources to carve out personal fiefdoms, and to demand payment from prospective residents in need of a site and 'protection' (Cole, 1987: 83ff). Outsiders who attempt to assist squatters often reinforce the perceived need for these 'headmen', in order to have leaders with whom to work.

In the Cape Town squatter camp of Crossroads, the first attempts to organise collective resistance to the impact of influx control regulations were made by women (Cole, 1987: 12–15). Both men's and women's committees were established, but the women were more in touch with grassroots affairs because they spent more time in the squatter area itself. Nonetheless, when the women sought assistance from an outside organisation – the Athlone Advice Office run by the Black Sash – the men's committee appointed one of their members to 'act as a link between the community, the lawyers, and the Athlone Advice Office' (Cole, 1987: 13). Moreover, as Ramphele (1986: 23–4) points out, the lawyers, church people and others who were active in assisting the people of Crossroads also became party to the subordination of this women-based grassroots resistance. Their desire to work through a clearly identifiable, orthodox leadership blinded them to the implications of looking to *headmen* as the leaders of Crossroads. It also strengthened the perception that Africans, whether in the homelands or in town, cannot manage their affairs without 'traditional' chiefs and headmen.

When so much of Crossroads and its satellite camps went up in flames during 1986, it was these very headmen who acted as conduits through which the state effected direct and brutal control; they emerged as the kingpins in the process of relocating those people whose presence in the area did not accord with government plans. In the early effort to organise themselves, the people of Crossroads called on 'traditional' structures, which were 'male-dominated and modelled . . . on the "invented tradition" of bantustan structures' (Cole, 1987: 19). In this way they unwittingly laid the groundwork which was eventually used 'to further the exploitative objectives of the state and certain individuals in the community' (cf. Ramphele, 1986).

Traditionalism – conservatism or resistance?

The use of 'traditional' institutions does not always lead to the destruction of popular movements. Indeed, 'tradition' may provide an important focus of resistance. Keesing has observed:

> Faced with massive external threat, some peoples made conservatism a stance for survival, a way of preserving cultural and individual identity. With traditional social systems breaking down, they have sought to preserve central rites and symbols. . . . Subjected to extreme pressures by the onslaught of European power, and forced to reject their centrality in the scheme of things, tribal peoples often came to view their culture as a 'thing'. The customs, values, and rites that . . . had been taken for granted as part of human life came to be seen from an external point of view: a people's *culture* could become a *symbol*. Once this external view was taken, the old ways could symbolise a golden age of past glories and freedoms. (Keesing, 1981: 406)

This insight is invaluable in explaining a range of persistent 'traditional' practices and beliefs in South Africa today. In many instances 'conservatism' is the only viable means of expressing opposition to white domination.

The rapid rise of African Independent Churches has long been recognised as a reaction to political domination. These churches represent a rejection of white-dominated churches. Two 'types' are commonly identified. The 'Ethiopian' churches began as a breakaway from the established mission churches; they have an all-black leadership, but retain the basic Christian teachings. The 'Zionist' churches also rejected white hierarchies, but incorporated 'traditional' African beliefs and practices, notably the belief in spirits and ancestors.

Although Zionist churches are regarded as 'syncretic' (a blend of Christian and 'traditional' elements), they are no longer seen as a cultural throwback to 'traditional' beliefs. For example, West criticises Sundkler's early claim that 'the syncretistic sect becomes the bridge over which Africans are brought back to heathenism' (cited in West, 1975: 172); he emphasises, instead, that they are 'a positive synthesis of western and African elements', and not 'a nativistic phenomenon'. Moreover, Comaroff (1985) has drawn attention to the political dimension of the Independent Church movement; she argues that the movement as a whole is a form of political resistance, and that its rituals and symbols are implicit statements of opposition to white domination in church and society.

Mayer made a similar point in discussing African manhood initiation rituals in East London. He argued that Xhosa initiation practices are 'to be ranked with *lobola* (bridewealth) as a major customary complex which has survived the transition from country to town, as well as impacts of christianisation and school education' (1971: 8). Why, he asked, do people continue to practise initiation rituals? What reasons do they give for the persistence of this custom?

Although initiation continued to be carried out 'in nearly traditional form' in East London, many informants doubted whether this was appropriate to urban circumstances and acknowledged that the rituals were not entirely successful in producing the desired effects – disciplined, responsible and considerate adult males. This 'failure' was generally attributed to the fact that the ritual was no longer performed 'properly' (in the 'traditional' manner), and to the impossibility of maintaining the social distinction between 'men' and 'boys' at places of work where all were treated the same.

Despite these reservations, nearly everyone continued to support the institution in principle. Mayer reported widespread agreement that initiation contributed to the personal development of young males, which Western schooling did not serve adequately.

But it was also clear that continuation of the initiation ritual reinforced group identity. Although it was closely associated with Xhosa tribalism in the rural areas, it also served as a powerful symbol of African nationalism, particularly in urban areas. 'The generally upheld idea is that though Xhosa initiation may not be universally African, it is still African as distinct from European. Thus sentiments of African nationalism and Xhosa tribalism are not felt to be mutually exclusive in this context' (Mayer, 1971: 15).

These examples illustrate that there are few institutional complexes which persist without undergoing significant change in form or function, or both. Such change raises serious questions about whether one should continue to refer to these as 'traditional' practices at all. What is more, the examples refute the idea that certain societies or peoples are fundamentally conservative and resistant to change.

It can be seen that 'traditions' (or culture or custom) constitute an adaptable resource for coping with contemporary situations. We have shown how certain customary institutional complexes are modified to meet contemporary needs. One can consider this as a 'normal' and 'spontaneous' process of *social* adjustment to changed circumstances. There is also, however, a different, and more deliberate, way in which 'traditions' are used as *political* resources.

'Traditions' as political resources

We have seen how government-controlled media manipulate the notion of 'tradition' to present a picture of Africans today as 'backward', and how the idea of 'traditional chiefs' is used to legitimate imposed political structures in the homelands. Such political manipulation – appealing to the past to give legitimacy to contemporary practices – should alert us to another political usage – appealing to the past and invoking 'traditional' symbols in order to mobilise resistance and foster feelings of group identity. Mayer argues that 'traditional' manhood initiation serves this latter end, but there are many other examples of this process. Indeed Mayer's (1980) discussion of the apparently 'conservative' life-style of some areas in the Transkei and Ciskei deserves mention.

On the coastal plain near Willowvale and Elliotdale in the Transkei, one finds people who have resisted the introduction of Christianity and who, on first appearance, seem to have resisted incorporation into the capitalist industrial complex of South Africa. In their religious, agricultural and local political activities, they have evolved forms of behaviour which they claim represent the 'real' Xhosa way as practised since pre-colonial times. As a result of their use of red ochre to colour their blankets, they have come to be known as the 'Red Xhosa' (*amaqaba*).

Research has shown, however, that the people of these areas are as much involved in the system of labour migration as those in other parts of the homelands (McAllister, 1980). Their apparent 'conservatism' is explained as an ideological expression of their rejecting white domination. Mayer refers to the 'Red' world-view as an ideology of resistance, a way of demonstrating rejection of an economic and political system which both draws them into its ambit and simultaneously marginalises them. It provides a way of incorporating the hardships of enforced involvement in labour migration into the life-style they have chosen to adopt. The 'Red' ideology strives, at the cognitive level, to transform the experience of harsh discrimination into something positive: people turn their backs on the wider society which rejects them.

Another example of the use of symbols from an assumed common past can be found in the rise of Afrikaner nationalism. This process involved the deliberate use of 'tradition' as a political strategy of resistance to imperial British rule. For example, Afrikaner nationalists developed an elaborate mythology surrounding the Great Trek and presented an idealised picture of the Voortrekkers as *volksvaders* (fathers of the nation), in order to create an Afrikaner identity and mobilise resistance to the British. Monuments were erected, public holidays created, and even individual items such as the *ossewa* (oxwagon) and *kruithoring* (gunpowder flask) became powerful symbols of Afrikanerdom. Somewhat ironically, the 'traditional' British Boy Scouts were used as the model for the *Voortrekker* youth movement, established during the Depression years. As founder member C. R. Swart (later State President) explained: 'With youthful zeal, enthusiasm and idealism for and faith in our individual identity as Afrikaners with our own language, culture and view of life, we decided to bring about something of our own for our youth' (quoted by Jansen, 1981: 35, 37).

Appealing to 'tradition' is clearly not the monopoly of any one interest group. In fact, one finds opposed interests in contest with one another in their efforts to define what constitutes 'the traditional' and thereby to mobilise people for their different political ends. It is true that the state has used notions of traditionality to create and bolster the homeland system, but that does not mean that the power of 'tradition' must be written off as a reactionary force. Indeed, both the ANC and the Zulu national cultural movement, Inkatha, constantly use appeals to 'tradition' to attempt to mobilise support for their different political programmes. Moreover, the differences which separate these organisations are also reflected in their respective and competing struggles to establish a commanding representation of the past.

This contest is evident in the pages of the ANC's official organ, *Sechaba*, which has repeatedly attacked the way in which 'tradition' is represented by the leader of Inkatha and chief minister of KwaZulu, Gatsha Buthelezi. On occasions such as the recently created Shaka's Day, Buthelezi adorns himself in leopard-skins and rehearses his genealogical links to both Cetshwayo, the last independent Zulu king, and to Cetshwayo's prime minister. *Sechaba*'s response has been to attack his use of 'traditional' regalia, arguing that Buthelezi's political antics contradict the heritage of Shaka as a brave warrior (editorial, Nov. 1985). It contends that Buthelezi, despite his 'traditional' status as chief, has long turned his back on the strong and proud 'tradition' of all Africans – including the Zulu, whose loyalty and support he falsely claims. It is, thus, under the heading 'The Tradition Betrayed' that *Sechaba* berates Buthelezi's participation in the homeland system and, by extension, his support for apartheid (Sep. 1984: 4–5). Clearly *Sechaba*'s editorial writers feel it is important to wrest from Buthelezi his assumption of the right to decide what constitutes 'the traditional', so that it can be appropriated as a resource by the ANC.

Members of the trade-union movement are similarly engaged with Inkatha in a contest over what constitutes the 'traditional'. In recent years there has been a resurgence in the practice of praise poetry, the singing by bards of the praises (and in the past, the faults) of rulers and their antecedents. Inkatha now has its own *izimbongi* (praise poets) who are called upon to praise the organisation and its leaders at various public gatherings. They glorify the present chieftainship in heroic terms, portraying it as the product of a long history of rule by consensus, in which special attention was always given to the interests of the followers (Harries, 1987).

The trade unions have also spawned a number of *izimbongi* from amongst their members and supporters. These poets have begun to use 'traditional' techniques to lionise their organisations and draw attention to the democratic principles on which they are organised (Gunner, 1986). Their poetry is meant to confront the hierarchy and exploitation found on the shopfloor, in the homeland administrative structures, and in the daily lives of working-class people. Writing about one of the foremost of these poets, Mi S'Dumo Hlatswayo, Sitas argues that he 'is *consciously* transforming tradition propelled by a future he longs for as opposed to the *izimbongi* of KwaZulu (and thus Inkatha) who are attempting to *preserve* social hierarchy by linking it to the past' (1986: 54–5; emphases in original). Not only is a 'traditional' form being used to contest an imposed definition of what is legitimate, but the very form which 'traditional' practice takes is being consciously changed. Precisely what constitutes 'the traditional' is thus a subject of struggle.

This notion of 'tradition' as a resource from which ideas for dealing with contemporary situations can be drawn is crucial, in that it directs our attention away from the neutral conception of 'tradition' as culture in transmission. Instead we are faced with the need to analyse those situations where the process of transmission is actively pursued, that is, situations where it may be useful to those individuals or groups who transmit and receive the ideas comprising any particular 'tradition'. Indeed, the fact that some 'traditions' are discarded, and others made anew, reveals the active agency of those perpetuating 'traditions'.

The normative prescriptions implied by the idea of 'tradition' derive from the ways in which people appeal to an image of the past to give legitimacy to presently preferred beliefs and practices. It is especially powerful for political mobilisation, either to create and hold together militant and self-aware groupings, or to create political, administrative and other structures which provide for, or justify, institutions of social control.

This is the reason why the idea of 'tradition' has proved so resilient in the rapidly changing discourse of South African politics. Those presently in power are able to justify their policies by appealing to their 'traditional' characteristics; those in the vanguard of resistance can be expected, increasingly, to appeal to 'tradition', and to point to assaults on, and betrayals of, 'tradition', as a means of mobilising support for their cause.

It is therefore important to realise that when practices are termed 'traditional' this is never simply a statement of objective historical fact. We refer to them as 'traditional' precisely because we believe, or want others to believe, that something in the present resembles or is associated with our image of something in the past.

4 'Race' and the race paradigm
EMILE BOONZAIER

. . . race is not a real, hard fact of nature; it is an idea (Fried, 1965)

'Race', it is often remarked, is a concept used to classify or categorise humans according to *physical* characteristics – and thereby help us bring order to the chaotic range of human physical variation. 'Race' is, however, much more than this. If it were simply a way of ordering human physical variation 'race' would be of little significance to anyone outside the narrow disciplines of physical anthropology and anatomy. Instead, we find that the term 'race', when applied to humans, is essentially social and political in meaning and reference, rather than biological. In South Africa, more so than anywhere else in the world, 'the political, economic and social status of every individual is conditioned, if not predetermined, by his race. Indeed, the whole pattern of every individual's life – from the cradle to the grave – is circumscribed by his race'. (Suzman, 1960: 339) The term is part of our ordinary, everyday vocabulary. We hear it used on radio and television, we read it in newspapers and magazines, and we use it in daily conversation. And even when 'race' is not explicitly used, it is clear that ideas and assumptions about innate racial differences permeate much of our thinking.

Much of the recent literature on 'race' attempts to separate the supposedly scientific and objective classification of *Homo sapiens*, based exclusively on physical criteria, from social discrimination or racism, which is seen to stem from misunderstanding or ignorance of the 'scientific facts'. Such an approach credits the scientific enterprise with undue autonomy and, by restricting the discussion of 'race' to physical features, tends to overlook the basic ideas and assumptions underlying the concept. This set of ideas – the *race paradigm* – was clearly apparent in both popular and academic thinking until the Second World War, and this chapter uses the work of the South African historian G. M. Theal (1837–1919) to identify its key elements. Furthermore, it is argued here that 'race' has consistently been conflated or confused with cultural or other non-physical characteristics and that the demise of the term itself has not been accompanied by a fundamental revision of the assumptions of the race paradigm, many of which continue to thrive under new guises.

The race paradigm in South Africa – G. M. Theal

The idea that the human population could readily be divided into a number of relatively discrete and stable groups, each with its own distinctive physical, cultural and intellectual characteristics, gained widespread acceptance during the nineteenth century. It provided Europeans of the slavery and colonial era with a neat and simple way, not only of categorising human populations, but also of explaining a wide range of social differences and thus justifying their own superior position. In southern Africa, as elsewhere in the 'newly discovered' world, this race paradigm permeated nearly all of the social literature of this period and in turn influenced the emerging social configuration.

It is instructive in this regard to look in some detail at the work of the South African historian George M. Theal, whose influence on social thought went unchallenged in the first decades of this century. Not only does his writing exemplify the idea that physical characteristics of different races are directly tied to cultural and mental traits, but it also encapsulates, in concise form, all of the core ideas about race which were prevalent not only in South Africa or during the last century, but throughout Western thinking until the 1940s. His numerous volumes on South Africa were influential and highly regarded both in this country and abroad, and conformed to existing standards of scholarship and objectivity. As he says in the preface to one of his volumes: 'In preparing the book I was guided by the principle that truth should be told, regardless of nationalities or parties, and I strove to the utmost to avoid anything like favour or prejudice' (Theal, 1894: vii).

Theal identified four discrete and unassimilable races in South Africa – 'Bushmen', 'Hottentots', 'Bantu' and 'European' – each with its own distinctive physical, cultural and mental characteristics.

The aborigines of South Africa [i.e. 'Bushmen'] were savages of a very low type. . . . They were pigmies in size, yellowish-brown in colour. . . . Their faces were broad in a line with the eyes, their cheeks were hollow, and they had flat noses, thick lips and receding chins. . . . To the eye of a European no people in any part of the world were more unattractive. . . . The Bushmen had no domestic animal but the dog, and they made no effort to cultivate the soil. They lived by the chase and upon wild plants, honey, locusts, and carrion. . . . So weak in frame as to be incapable of toil, they possessed great keenness of vision for detecting objects at a distance, and marvellous fleetness of foot and endurance in the chase. Their weapon of offence was a feeble bow, but the arrow-head was coated with poison so deadly that the slightest wound was mortal. (1894: 1–2)

The main features of the 'Hottentots' were listed as follows:

. . . frame slight but sometimes tall, better formed than Bushmen, but back hollow, head scantily covered with little tufts of short crisped hair . . . hands and feet small, colour yellow to olive; weapons assagai, knobkerie, bow and poisoned arrow, shield; pursuits pastoral and to a very limited extent metallurgic; government feeble; habitations slender frames of wood covered with skins or reed mats; domestic animals ox, sheep, and dog; demeanour inconstant, marked by levity; language abounding in clicks. (1902: 8)

It is clear that Theal saw innate mental characteristics ('the constitutions of their minds') as providing the link between race and culture. 'The cranial capacity, or size of the brain of each [race], is given by Professor Flower as: Bantu 1485, Hottentot 1407, and Bushman 1288 cubic centimetres. The average brain size of a European is 1497 cubic centimetres.' (1902: 7) He was therefore able to rank the four races on a scale from 'barbarism' to 'civilization', freely commenting on the innate potential of each.

These nearly naked people [the 'Hottentots'], living in idleness and filthiness indescribable, were yet capable of improvement. During the last century a vast amount of missionary labour has been concentrated upon the natives of South Africa, and though to the present day there is not a single instance of a Bushman of pure blood having permanently adopted European habits, the Hottentots have done so to a considerable extent. They have not indeed shown a capacity to rise to the highest level of civilized life, but they have reached a stage much above that of barbarism.
... [the 'Bantu'] were certainly of mixed blood. ... proof of a mixed ancestry of very unequal capability is afforded by the fact that most of these people seem unable to rise to the European level of civilization, though not a few individuals have shown themselves possessed of a mental power equal to that of white men. (1894: 4–5)

Theal was also insistent that the various races constituted distinct and separate categories even though he was not unaware that at least the 'Bushmen' and 'Bantu' did not originate from pure 'stock' or 'blood'. For example, although he discusses physical differences between 'Hottentots' and 'Bushmen', he does acknowledge 'several points of resemblance' and observes that 'all of this seems to point to the supposition that at a time now far in the past an intruding body of males of some unknown race took to themselves consorts of Bushmen blood, and from that union sprang the Hottentot tribes of Southern Africa' (1894: 4). Nonetheless, although the 'Hottentots' were not *originally* of 'pure stock', this did not detract from his premise that the contemporary 'Hottentots' in South Africa were quite distinct from the 'Bushmen'. 'Some have supposed that they [the 'Hottentots'] sprang originally from Bushman stock, others that the Bushmen were simply Hottentots who became degraded by the loss of their domestic cattle, but neither of these theories is now tenable' (1894: 3). Similarly, 'another branch of the human family', 'the Bantu', were recognised as 'certainly of mixed stock' and 'of mixed ancestry', but still constituted a distinct category with clearly identifiable physical features (1902: 8).

Theal's writing was typical of South African social thought and literature of the era before the Second World War, and the same basic set of assumptions and premises about race could be found in local newspapers, in school textbooks, and in popular thinking. What is important to stress, however, is that this thinking was not confined to South Africa, but was prevalent throughout Europe, its colonial empires and North America. Additionally, there was a congruence of thought between 'scientists' and laymen – at least insofar as 'laymen' are generally taken to be males drawn from the ranks of the most 'civilised races'.

Scientific racism

Many scholars have deemed it necessary to distinguish between 'popular' and 'scientific' conceptions of the term. Indeed, this idea is incorporated in the common distinction drawn between 'race' and 'racism': when scientists use the term they are referring to the objective concept of 'race'; when laypersons use the term they are indulging in 'racism'. Physical scientists study 'race'; social scientists study the social phenomenon of 'racism'. Scientists apply the concept of 'race' exclusively to physical characteristics; the general public confuses 'race' with 'culture' or mental traits or both. Unfortunately the facts do not support such clear and consistent distinctions.

Carl Linnaeus, often identified as the first scientist to apply the concept of race to subdivisions of the human population, did not base his classification exclusively on physical characteristics (1758). In fact, when classifying humans he focused his attention primarily on behavioural or personality traits. For example, the typical traits of *europaeus* were identified as 'light, lively and inventive', while those of *afer* (Africans) were 'cunning, slow and negligent'.

Nonetheless, scientists gradually began to develop and accept the idea that it was possible to classify various human types exclusively on the basis of physical characteristics, and 'race', used in this restrictive sense, was appropriated to serve this end. However, while the physical and the mental or cultural might well have been separated at a conceptual level, many scholars continued to collapse the two when applying the concept to actual populations. Thus Seligman's *Races of Africa* (first published in 1930, but revised and reprinted several times during the next three decades) acknowledges that while 'it is obvious that questions of race should first and last be determined by the study of physical characters . . . the somewhat mixed classification adopted' by him (1961: 1–2) suggests that racial and cultural categories coincide.

More significantly, however, much 'scientific' effort was directed at demonstrating that while mental characteristics were conceptually distinct from the physical ones, there was indeed a causal relationship between them. For example, craniometry (the measurement of skulls) and eugenics (the regulation of breeding in human populations to promote certain traits) were both based on the assumption that mental traits are inherited. And in the twentieth century, intelligence tests, by ostensibly facilitating the direct measurement of *innate* mental ability, simply lent a new dimension to the argument that certain races were inferior to others.

Race and science after 1950

The 1950s marked a turning point in the scientific publications on race. In the aftermath of the era of colonisation and particularly as a result of the shock realisations thrust upon the world by the atrocities of Hitler's applied eugenics, many scientists attempted to dissociate themselves from the race paradigm. Most of the scientific publications on 'race' which appeared in the 1950s and 1960s tried to do just this. Explicitly or implicitly it was argued that science would reveal the truth and therefore allow us to overcome the myths and fallacies associated with the use and abuse of 'race' in popular thought. For example, the foreword to UNESCO's 1951 publication, appropriately titled *Race and Science*, clearly states:

Race hatred and conflict thrive on scientifically false ideas and are nourished by ignorance. In order to show up these errors of fact and reasoning, to make widely known the conclusions reached in the various branches of science, to combat racial propaganda, we must turn to the means and methods of education, science and culture. . . .

A great many introductory texts on the concept of 'race' reflect these same motives and follow a standard format. They begin with a section on the scientific concept of 'race' and end by arguing that these 'facts' are ignored by laypersons, who continue to be guilty of racial prejudice or racism (see, for example, Alland, 1971; Tobias, 1972; and Kuper, 1984). The 'scientific facts' presented generally address three questions: What is race?, Are there pure races?, and Are some races superior to others?

The scientific concept of race, it is pointed out, refers exclusively to physical characteristics, which include such diverse features as head shape, facial form, nasal structure, skin colour, hair texture, and blood group. The important point is often made that, by definition, this list of traits excludes social or cultural characteristics. Races cannot be classified by the criteria of religion, nationality, culture or language. Consequently, it is incorrect to speak of the 'Jewish race', the 'German race', the 'Zulu race' or the 'Afrikaner race'.

Another closely related point often made in these publications, is that race does not refer to mental characteristics, such as personality or intelligence. Criteria like these are most certainly not used to categorise races; nor has it been scientifically demonstrated that certain races are innately associated with specific personality types or levels of intelligence. The validity of intelligence test results as indicators of *innate* mental ability is also questioned, since the tests tend to favour certain populations at the expense of others; moreover, it is impossible to separate the innate from the acquired component of intelligence.

The final point generally made is that race is a statistical aggregate. That is to say, a 'race' is defined as a population which is separated from surrounding populations by the frequency with which certain physical characteristics occur. For example, one might find that the blood groups A, B and O are represented in all three major human races (Caucasoid, Mongoloid and Negroid), but the frequency with which they occur varies from one race to another. It therefore follows that there can be no such thing as a 'typical' representative of any given race, nor can there be any 'pure' races.

These were all powerful arguments, which were rapidly accepted by mainstream scientists and intellectuals in Europe and North America, with dissenters such as Burt, Eysenck and Jensen being severely criticised and often ostracised by their colleagues. Even physical anthropologists accepted the dangers inherent in the concept of race and by the late 1970s were desperately searching for a more acceptable alternative. However, the general public was not as quick to respond to these new perspectives.

This was partly because the racist paradigm, dividing the human species into relatively stable, bounded entities, each with distinctive cultural as well as physical characteristics, is quite easy to understand. . . . In addition, the racial paradigm satisfied the European and white American sense of identity, self-esteem and self-interest. (Thompson, 1985: 196)

South Africa since the 1950s

There is therefore some truth in the claim often made by white South Africans and avidly seized upon by the government-controlled media that racism and racist thinking still thrive in North America and Britain. However, the validity of the implied comparison with South Africa can be questioned.

In the aftermath of the Second World War, at the very time that Europe and North America were beginning to challenge it, the race paradigm was being entrenched in South Africa. The ideology of apartheid and its associated legislation were clearly based upon the assumption that the South African population consisted of a number of discrete and unassimilable groups. Indeed, it was the legislation that ossified these populations and rigidified the boundaries between them, so that the statutory groupings and the resultant very real differences in income and status, simply served to reinforce basic assumptions about the existence of racial groups and innate differences. School textbooks and the media equally helped to spread these underlying notions, while avenues which might have permitted them to be challenged at a political level were also closed. Most important, the race paradigm provided white South Africans with the means to justify the existing differences in power and wealth.

We should not lose sight of the fact that it was the 'race paradigm', rather than the concept of 'race' as such, which formed the basis of and the justification for the political structures that emerged in South Africa. There is little point in attempting to chronicle the explicit use of the term 'race' and the prevalence of purely 'racist' ideas in the South African context. 'Pure' racial assumptions, categorisations and arguments seldom, if ever, occur. For example, close scrutiny of even the Population Registration Act reveals that non-physical characteristics, such as 'general acceptance', are taken into consideration when determining what 'racial' category a person belongs to. Today we seldom come across blatant examples of racist thinking typical of the Verwoerdian era: 'We send this message to the outside world and say to them . . . that there is but one way of saving the white races of the world. And that is for the White and non-White in Africa each to exercise his own rights within his own areas. . . . ' (H.F. Verwoerd, cited in de Klerk, 1976)

Nor does specific terminology necessarily reflect underlying assumptions and thoughts about the nature of human groups and innate differences. Today the negative connotations associated with 'race' are universally recognised, but in South Africa this has merely resulted in 'race' being replaced by euphemistic substitutes such as culture, ethnic group, nation, population, people, community or *volk*. The work of P. J. Coertze, a prominent anthropologist who has had a significant impact on the discipline at Afrikaans-medium universities, illustrates this point. For example, although he distinguishes between the concepts 'race' and *volk*, emphasising that the former is biological while the latter is socio-cultural, and warns against the confusion of the two terms (1973: 6), it is clear that physical features play a major role in his distinction between 'the Afrikaner *volk*' and 'the Coloureds' (1983). In his work he also develops the notion that the genetically determined criteria of race include psychological attributes such as intellectual ability (*verstandelike vermoëns*) and personality (*geesteshoedanighede*) (1983: 34).

At the other extreme, the terms 'white' and 'black' are often employed without any racial (that is, physical) implications. For example, Vera Bührmann, in *Living in Two Worlds* (1984), uses 'black' and 'white' to refer to cultural, and not physical, differences. Similarly, the term 'black' – as in 'black power' or 'Black Consciousness' – is generally used to define the common victims of oppression, rather than a 'natural' category sharing common physical characteristics.

It has moreover become common practice for people to use the terms 'white', 'coloured' and 'black' to signify official legal categories while at the same time dissociating themselves from the racist basis of such classification. Unfortunately this is generally done only by implication and few authors are as explicit as West when he cautions: 'It should be pointed out here that many people classified as Colored reject the classification and all that it entails. . . . I share the view that rejects the concept of classification, and use the term Colored in this text only to refer to the legal category.' (1987: 7)

Finally, the explicit use (or avoidance) of the term 'race' in written sources, broadcasts or speeches does not necessarily convey the full picture of underlying thinking or motives. Similarly, the pronouncements or utterances by politicians tell us little about how their audience interprets them or what they read into them. There has been surprisingly little research into how laypersons (as opposed to politicians or academics) understand race, and such work as has been done invariably utilises existing population categories which might therefore be construed by subjects as being racial, cultural or socio-economic, or any combination of these.

All of this simply serves to reinforce the general confusion that exists about 'race' and the difficulty of separating racial from other forms of prejudice or group formation. However, this might help us answer the question whether race refers to a special form of stratification or to a special criterion of stratification. If we are unable to find much evidence of 'pure' racism in the one country where it is most likely to exist, this suggests that it can hardly be a significant or distinct form of stratification. Much more plausible is the view that innate physical characteristics are one of the many sets of criteria that might be utilised in the process of stratification. In South Africa in the early 1960s there was a relatively rapid shift from racial to cultural rhetoric, and from race to ethnicity. Although it is true that for many people this simply meant a change in terminology, it did represent a gradual conceptual shift. The basic system of differentiation and inequality has, however, remained intact through this transition, which suggests that race might be the means, but certainly not the sole motive, for group formation.

Science and society

The concept of 'race' and the racist paradigm provide us with perhaps the most emphatic illustration of the interrelationship between science and society. The race paradigm is a complex idea which has both a history and a motivation. It has influenced science and has in turn been influenced itself. Like religion, it has the ability to create moods in the minds of humans and to provide justification for action.

In discussing the relationship between science and society (ideas and 'external' reality), sociologists and historians of science have generally tended to imply the primacy of social reality. That is to say, society determines knowledge, rather than the other way around. This is hardly surprising if we consider the context of the general approach taken by the sociology of knowledge whose main aim, initially at least, was to establish that science was not simply an independent and objective enterprise moving inexorably toward the creation of an ultimate truth. In Marxist terms it also makes sense to emphasise the determining role of social or economic relations. But, as Stocking has commented, scientific ideas of 'race' are worthy of more rigorous treatment than simply relating them in a general way to 'European expansion' or 'capitalism' (1982: 271).

In South Africa the racist paradigm emerged without direct recourse to the intellectual justifications of scientific racism. Similarly, the demise of scientific racism had little impact on popular assumptions about racial difference and superiority. For example, Dr. W. W. M. Eiselen, one of the architects of apartheid, as far back as 1929 acknowledged that there was no scientific basis for arguing that some races were intellectually inferior to others (1929: 4). On the other hand, Tobias feels justified in claiming: 'It can be recorded that no South African physical anthropologist was involved in providing scientific underpinning for the government's race classification practices' (1985: 32).

Far from assuming that science offers the voice of reason in an unreasonable world, writers such as Stephen Gould argue that racial prejudice and racism may be as old as human history itself, but scientific justifications simply 'imposed the additional burden of intrinsic inferiority upon despised groups and precluded redemption by conversion or assimilation' (1981: 31). Furthermore, the nineteenth-century scientific theories did provide the underpinnings for popular ideas about classification, bounded and static populations, and social evolution and hierarchy. And these underlying ideas have survived despite their demise in the scientific literature on 'race'.

In most parts of the world attention seems to have shifted away from the concept of race and the nature of racial differences. But the issue of nature and nurture, innate and acquired, heredity and environment, continues to command much attention. The popularity achieved by the pseudo-scientific writings of Desmond Morris and Robert Ardrey, the widespread interest shown in the Margaret Mead–Derek Freeman debate, and the heated responses to E. O. Wilson's 'new' sociobiology, highlight the contemporary significance of the nature–nurture theme. 'Race' is however no longer unequivocally the central arena within which the battle is being waged. For example, in many contexts 'sex' has become the new battleground for those who propose or oppose making 'nature herself an accomplice in the crime of political inequality' (see, for example, Sayers, 1982).

'Cultures' or 'ethnic groups' similarly continue to provide fertile terrain for the perpetuation of many of the underlying notions associated with the race paradigm. Like 'race', 'culture' can be used as a unit to classify people and thus rank them in some hierarchical order. And when 'cultures' are viewed as relatively static, bounded and homogeneous entities, or when ethnic groups are seen simply as fixed populations carrying around such permanent cultural 'luggage', the idea of 'inherited culture' is reinforced rather than challenged (La Fontaine, 1986).

5 Tribe as colonial category
PETER SKALNÍK

The concept of 'tribe' is no longer crucial in South African political discourse. But up to the 1960s 'tribe' was widely used as a device to disaggregate the African population. This was also the period in which the term 'race' was held to be of great significance in South Africa, and the two terms were closely linked in official and public perception. 'Race' supplied the broad division of the country's population; 'tribe' was used to indicate the subdivisions within the African 'race' specifically.

'Tribe' has been largely supplanted, in recent years, by the notion of 'ethnic group'. The latter term preserves some of the earlier meanings of 'tribe', of course, but it has also acquired several new meanings consonant with the changing political environment of the second half of the twentieth century. 'Tribes' are no longer thought to be of any great political significance, so that when the term is used in the public media, it is generally in the context of labelling African cultural curiosities (for example, tribal dancing or manhood initiation).

Nevertheless, it is still assumed, especially by white observers, that every African belongs to a tribe, at least for cultural purposes, and that tribal boundaries mark out age-old hostilities and rivalries which may slumber beneath the surface of daily life, but are not forgotten. The general public in South Africa shows a remarkable facility for assimilating all manner of conflict within the African population into the 'tribal' paradigm, and they appear to assume that if virtually any outbreak of violence is labelled a 'tribal' or 'faction' fight, there is no need to seek for further explanation in contemporary circumstances. The underlying idea is that tribal animosities run deep, and are based on 'natural' divisions; therefore they are bound to surge to the surface in times of tension.

We can identify three distinct usages of the notion of 'tribe'. First, there is the idea that the human population can be divided into two broad categories – those who are 'tribal' ('tribesmen' or 'tribal peoples') and those who are not. Implicit in this distinction is the idea that the former are *still* tribal: they represent an earlier stage in human social evolution when people belonged to 'tribes' rather than to modern nations. Iliffe's comments on the situation in colonial

Tanganyika have a much broader relevance:

The notion of tribe lay at the heart of indirect rule in Tanganyika. Refining the racial thinking common in German times, administrators believed that every African belonged to a tribe, just as every European belonged to a nation. The idea doubtless owed much to the Old Testament, to Tacitus and Caesar, to academic distinctions between tribal societies based on status and modern societies based on contract, and to postwar anthropologists who preferred 'tribal' to the more pejorative word 'savage'. (Iliffe, 1979: 323–4)

Secondly, 'tribal people' are seen as members of – they all 'belong to' – distinct and separate units called 'tribes'. There has been much confusion about the criteria which might be used to identify these 'tribes', and attempts to define the term more precisely by restricting its usage to *politically* defined units have generally been unsuccessful. Instead, we find that the use of 'tribe' persists precisely because it implies significant additional dimensions such as culture, language, territory and even race. Again, Iliffe's comments usefully summarise this usage:

Tribes were seen as cultural units 'possessing a common language, single social system, and an established customary law'. Their political and social systems rested on kinship. Tribal membership was hereditary. Different tribes were related genealogically, so that Africa's history was a vast family tree of tribes. Small tribes were offshoots of big ones and might therefore be reunited. Whole tribes migrated in *Völkerwanderungen* recalling places of origin and routes of migration. (Iliffe, 1979: 324)

Thirdly, 'tribalism' and 'tribal conflict' have become popular labels to describe a broad range of phenomena that are assumed to result from basic 'tribal identities'. These identities are regarded as ancient and powerful, and not open to amelioration, so that animosity and tension arise whenever and wherever members of different 'tribes' come into contact with each other.

This chapter traces the historical origins and changing usage of 'tribe' and shows how the term was incorporated as a key concept in anthropological thinking. Recently, however, the concept has been sharply criticised by a range of writers who have pointed out, above all, that it is a colonial category which has been imposed on indigenous populations and is therefore not a valid analytical tool. In southern Africa, the absence of clear cultural or linguistic boundaries and the fluid nature of political groupings have rendered the notion of 'tribe' – conceived as a static, separate cultural-political unit – particularly inappropriate.

Notwithstanding such criticism, the concept has proved to be particularly resilient – in anthropology, for the general public in the West, and for the people to whom the term has been applied. It has been internalised by the latter and has become a powerful idiom for their expression of political affiliation and difference. This phenomenon of 'tribalism' should, however, be understood as a secondary phenomenon, and in no way detracts from the refutation of 'tribes' as objectively definable, 'natural' units.

'Tribe' in historical perspective

The original usage of 'tribe' in early historical times was not pejorative. The Roman citizenry was divided into three *tribes* (sing. *tribus*). According to some etymologists, the word was derived from *tria* or *tres* meaning three. In a similar way, the Bible records that ancient Israel was divided into twelve tribes (Hebrew: *shevet*, pl. *shevatim*). It was only later that the term was used for the subjugated peoples who had to pay *tributum* or tribute to the Romans (*Webster's Third New International Dictionary* 1976: 2440–1). Eventually, 'barbarians' and outsiders of other sorts came to be viewed as 'tribal', and thus 'uncivilised' when compared to the great civilisations of Europe, the Middle East, India or China. This meaning of 'tribe' became very common during the nineteenth century, when anthropology was establishing itself as a scholarly discipline.

Eventually, 'tribe' (with derivates like 'tribal' or 'tribalism') emerged as one of the few professional terms which anthropology managed, wittingly or not, to implant in the minds of almost everyone, both in the West and elsewhere. Most people in the West use the term synonymously with 'primitive', 'traditional', 'savage' or 'backward'. Perhaps more politely, 'tribal' could today be used as synonymous with 'less developed', 'underdeveloped' or 'developing', although some additional nuances may exist in the usage of such terms. On the other hand, many people living in the interiors of Africa or Amazonia have also internalised the term and might tell anyone visiting them that their 'tribe' does this or that, while a neighbouring 'tribe' does something else.

Conceptually opposed to 'tribe' and 'tribal' are the categories of 'nation' and 'civilisation'. Both these evolutionary levels are thought to be achieved when opposition or disunity among various 'tribes' has been overcome. Similarly, 'tribalism' (the ideology of division into 'tribes') is superseded by 'nationalism' (the quest for the political independence of nations). 'Tribe' is also often juxtaposed to 'state'. In popular understanding 'tribes' are by definition not 'states', since they are neither 'nations' nor 'civilisations'. For example, if a South African were to ask visiting Europeans from which 'tribe' they came, the question would be interpreted as amusing or insulting. One would probably be informed that Europeans have 'nations', and only the less developed people in the 'third world' are organised into 'tribes'.

Anthropologists' concern with 'tribe'

This viewpoint is not limited to people in the West. Other 'civilisations' also distinguish between themselves and 'tribal' populations on their margins. For example, a large section of the population of India is still generally viewed as being 'tribal'. At the Tenth International Congress of Anthropological and Ethnological Sciences in New Delhi in 1978, the then Prime Minister, Morarji Desai, argued in his opening speech that India hosted the congress as the first developing country because many 'tribals' live within her boundaries and because Indian anthropologists have done a great deal of research on these 'tribals'. The *Times of India* reported:

Mr Desai recalled his association with tribals and their welfare activities for over two decades and remarked that the tribals were very brave.

'The tribals are not afraid of wild animals. They meet them with courage. But they are terribly afraid of the so-called civilised man, the educated man, who has exploited them,' said Mr Desai. The tribals knew no tricks, which the latter knew. They were innocent. (11 December 1978)

The president of the Tenth ICAES, Indian anthropologist L. P. Vidyarthi, expressed a similar view: 'There is, again, increasing interest in the study of tribes in the historical and archaeological context as the functional-structural approach has failed to bring out the correct appraisal of tribal situations in India' (1978: 5).

Vidyarthi's assertion and uncritical acceptance of the term were very dated, because in international anthropological circles the concept of 'tribe' and its derivates had for some time been criticised and even rejected outright. The rule of the 'tribal paradigm', which had climaxed in the publication of the collection *Tribes Without Rulers* (1958), Sahlins's article on the segmentary lineage (1961), and Service's *Primitive Social Organisation* (1962), seemed to be over.

As early as 1966, Morton Fried lectured and wrote on the concept of 'tribe' and 'tribal society' in a critical way (Fried, 1966). In 1967, Fried arranged a meeting of the American Ethnological Society devoted solely to the 'problem of tribe'. The proceedings were subsequently published (Helm, 1968) with Fried's 1966 paper reprinted as the leading chapter of the book. The contributors agreed that there was wide disagreement about the meaning of 'tribe'. One of the participants, the Africanist Elizabeth Colson, claimed that the term had outlived its usefulness as an analytical tool even though 'our fellow social scientists and the public at large believe' that tribe exists as a 'distinctive' phenomenon (Colson, 1968: 201).

Colson's view was echoed by Aidan Southall, who argued that the concept of tribe was an 'illusion' as it did not represent any empirical reality (1970). A similar idea was expressed by Archie Mafeje, even though he did acknowledge that 'tribes', narrowly defined as relatively undifferentiated and locally autonomous units, might have existed in Africa during the pre-colonial period (1971: 258).

Notwithstanding such criticisms, the more general usage of 'tribe', especially insofar as it is associated with distinct and isolated cultural units, has positively refused to leave the heads of many scholars. For example, the French Marxist anthropologist Maurice Godelier, in his article 'Tribu' published in *Encyclopaedia Universalis* (1973; in English 1977), signalled that the concept was in crisis, but in order to remedy the situation he suggested a reformist solution. He urged that 'there is an urgent need, both theoretically and practically, to get to the root of the evil and redefine it in order to criticise and evaluate its significance' (1977: 72). Godelier warns that in order 'to determine the scientific aspect of the concept of "tribe" or "tribal society,"' it will be necessary to 'stop studying societies out of context, considering them as entities in relation to neighbouring tribes' (1977: 93). His voice was nevertheless little heeded. He himself, in a recently published monograph on the Baruya of Papua New Guinea, uses the term 'tribe' on many pages in exactly this closed sense of the term (Godelier, 1986).

These criticisms we have discussed refer specifically to the concept of 'tribe'. There has also been widespread criticism of the evolutionist thinking implicit in the 'tribal paradigm' and in the view that societies could be ranked in terms of a hierarchy from primitive 'tribes' to modern civilised 'societies'. It has been argued moreover that 'tribes', at least in colonial and post-colonial situations, do not exist in any observable form; there are no such objectively determinable groupings in which linguistic, cultural, political and economic boundaries coincide neatly. This, it has now been realised, applied even in the pre-colonial period.

Strangely enough, some of the South African government ethnographers, such as Van Warmelo, long ago recognised this problem and therefore sought to define 'tribes' in southern Africa solely as political entities, rather than as cultural-political groupings. 'There is', Van Warmelo said, 'in each tribe a ruling sib, namely that of the chief' (1935: 5–6). Van Warmelo's successor, Jackson, is very specific: 'Tribe . . . refers to a chiefdom, i.e. a body of people ruled by a chief' (1975: 1). These definitions recognise a non-correspondence between political and cultural boundaries, but they actually make the use of the term 'tribe' redundant. Therefore, by continuing to employ 'tribe', with all its added connotations, their discussion of the nature of pre-colonial political groupings in southern Africa loses all clarity.

The study of 'tribalism'

'Tribalism', on the other hand, is a product of colonialism and exists objectively as an ideology of dividing people into 'tribes'. In other words, tribalism refers to the process whereby people in contemporary contexts use the 'tribal' idiom to mobilise group loyalties in situations of competition or rapid social change (cf. Mitchell, 1960). Similarly, in *The Notion of Tribe*, Fried argues:

The most massive and familiar phenomena of tribalism occur as a consequence of the impinging on simple cultures of much more complexly organized societies. I regard the tribe mainly as a 'secondary' phenomenon. While some of its manifestations go back five millennia or more to the appearance of the earliest states, the major locus of tribal formation has been in the period of European colonialism and imperialism. The 'pristine tribe', on the other hand, is a creation of myth and legend, pertaining either to the golden ages of the noble savage or romantic barbarian, or to the twisted map of hell that is a projection of our war-riven world. (1975: 114)

Colson, while rejecting the notion of 'tribe', views 'tribalism' as a 'creation' which reflects

the influences of the colonial era when large-scale political and economic organisation set the scene for the mobilisation of ethnic groups based on linguistic and cultural similarities. . . . Tribalism in Africa today does not represent the continued acceptance of ancient loyalties or the thrust forward into the present of outmoded social forms. (Colson, 1968: 201–2)

In other words, tribalism has come to be viewed as similar to ethnicity. As Ronald Cohen (1978) perceptively asked, is 'ethnicity' not just a new name for 'tribe', introduced at the time when those whom anthropologists study began to find the word invidious when applied to themselves? This indeed seems to be the case, especially when we observe that for many members of the public and also quite a few anthropologists, the use of 'ethnicity' instead of 'tribe' is just another handy excuse for continuing with the same style of thinking and doing. The schizophrenic dichotomy of 'primitive' and 'civilised', 'progress' and 'backwardness' or 'tribe' and 'nation' is thus allowed to remain. (It must not be forgotten that as late as 1971 Cohen and Middleton edited an influential volume, *From Tribe to Nation in Africa*.)

Gwyn Prins in an article on 'Tribe' published recently in the prestigious *Social Science Encyclopedia* (1985: 870) suggests that 'there was a strong trend in scholarship to reject the terms and concepts of tribe principally because of their tainted connections'. The author explains:

'tribe' has been an invention of the dominator. It was a 'false consciousness' without any indigenous root, fostered in order to divide and rule. Those, like anthropologists, who had adopted it into their perspectives, were deluded and thus became, consciously or not, the agents of oppression. In its place there should be substituted a class-based analysis, that would more effectively expose the full dimensions of exploitation upon which colonial society rested.

And finally Richard Fardon, reporting on the 1987 Association of Social Anthropologists conference on history and ethnicity, can be quoted in similar vein. He remarks that sociologists 'subsumed terms of differences, like race and tribe, which had become uncomfortable to sustain because of their biological·and evolutionary overtones . . . . perhaps ethnicity has become a safe haven for ideas we would rather call racist.' (Fardon, 1987: 15–16)

'Tribes' in South Africa?

This critical discussion of 'tribe' raises fundamental questions about the term's applicability to actual social situations. Instead of merely accepting the existence of 'tribes', we need to ask whether and in what sense they can be said to exist (or have existed).

There is a widespread belief that the pre-colonial African population in southern Africa consisted of a number of discrete cultural-linguistic-political units and that these units have continued, unchanged, into the present. These 'tribes', it is further assumed, coincide with the modern African 'nations' – Swazi, Zulu, Xhosa, Venda, Tswana, Ndebele, etc. – associated with the various 'national states' within South Africa.

Southern African history, however, does not lend itself to such neat and static classification. Scholars now commonly recognise that the early African population was not culturally or linguistically homogeneous. But this does not mean that it consisted of a number of discrete cultural or linguistic groups. Culture and language displayed a continuum of variation, rather than a set of discrete and bounded entities. Similarly, such political units as can be identified in history were small and highly variable. They ranged in size from clans with a few hundred members, to chiefdoms numbering several thousand. However, even the latter were 'micropolities' by subsequent standards (Webb, 1979: 136) and were a far cry from the 'tribes' so readily identified today.

Taken individually, neither culture nor politics provides us with a valid criterion for defining 'tribes'; taken together, they make even less sense. Even if one accepts the possibility of cultural and linguistic boundaries, it is clear that these did not coincide with political ones. The broad division made by scholars into two 'cultural groupings' – Nguni and Sotho – has no counterpart in political divisions. Likewise, for example, Xhosa-speakers were divided into a number of independent chiefdoms of which the Xhosa (as a politically defined group) was merely one among many (West, 1979: 111).

The rapid rise of very large political groupings (kingdoms) associated with the *Mfecane* of the early nineteenth century, provides further evidence of the flexible nature of cultural and political boundaries. Essentially, this was a period of incorporation whereby small chiefdoms, through conquest or amalgamation, were rapidly subsumed within the large superpowers such as the Zulu, Swazi, Sotho or Ndebele kingdoms. Within the space of a few decades previously minor chiefdoms had expanded to include hundreds of thousands of 'new' members from disparate cultural, linguistic and political origins (Webb, 1979). The history of southern African 'tribes' is therefore one of rapid change and incorporation, rather than of static and bounded units. The 'tribes' which were to emerge by the end of the nineteenth century were colonial phenomena, the product of new forces such as pressure on land and expansion of trade. Conflict and warfare between these political groups should similarly be seen in these terms and most certainly cannot be said to involve ancient loyalties or animosities resulting from cultural differences between them.

The newly emergent political forms of the nineteenth century were therefore very much a consequence of new historical forces associated with colonialism. At the same time as these processes were occurring on the ground, the model of rigid and static 'tribes' each with their own distinctive language and culture was being developed to interpret this emergent social reality. In both senses, therefore, 'tribes' were the creation of the colonial era.

We can thus conclude that 'tribes' are not natural or immutable social groups. They represent, instead, a particular way of ordering and grouping certain human populations. Interestingly enough, this point is succinctly illustrated in existing South African legislation:

The Governor-General [State President] shall be Supreme Chief of all Blacks in the Union [Republic of South Africa]. . . . The Governor-General may recognize or appoint any person as a chief of a Black tribe. . . . [the] Governor-General may define the boundaries of the area of any tribe . . . divide any existing tribe into two or more parts or amalgamate tribes or parts of tribes into one tribe or constitute a new tribe, as necessity or the good government of the Blacks may in his opinion require. (Native Administration Act 38 of 1927, as amended)

Although the Act had been amended 32 times up till 1986, this particular aspect still remains in force. It refers exclusively to 'Blacks' (by implication the 'tribal peoples' of South Africa) and clearly shows that 'tribes' can be 'divided', 'amalgamated' and have chiefs 'appointed' to them. In short, the legislation shows that 'tribes' are created.

'Tribalism' and 'tribal conflict' in South Africa
We have noted that the terms 'tribe' or 'tribal' are today less commonly used than they were before. However, South Africa is one of the most exemplary socio-political fields where rhetorical shifts often occur without fundamental perceptual reorientation. Neither the general public nor anthropologists and ethnologists have totally discarded the underlying notion that South Africa has a 'tribal' population which is naturally divided into 'tribes'.

This is best illustrated in the continuing reference in newspapers and on television to 'tribal clashes' between 'tribal factions'. The picture conveyed is one of basic and ancient tribal differences that inevitably result in 'tribal conflict'. It is all too seldom that reporters move beyond such primordialist assumptions by investigating the deep causes of conflict – such as competition for land or other resources – which would explain why periodic outbreaks of violence should occur. Instead, the observation that the conflict is expressed in 'tribal' terms is deemed to constitute its own explanation.

Our understanding of 'tribal clashes' in one particular area – Msinga, in Natal – has been deepened by Clegg (1981) and Robbins (1984), who go a long way towards analysing the underlying causes of conflict. They both reveal that the ceaseless fighting among different factions in Msinga can be understood only as a function of pressure on land combined with efforts to regain lost independence, first of all from Shaka's Zulu state, and later from the colonial state. They refer to overpopulation and overstocking as well as unemployment and the negative consequences of migrant labour. Out of all this, serious armed conflict has arisen.

Clegg explicitly addresses the assumption of conventional wisdom that so-called inter-tribal faction fighting is continuous with ancient tribal or clan animosities. Not only does his evidence show that the conflict occurs between districts of the *same* 'tribe', but also 'between sections within a *single* district within the *same* tribe ruled by the *same* clan' (1981:164). The existing factions and the 'ideology of vengeance' therefore cannot possibly stem from loyalties associated with either pre-colonial clans or post-colonial tribes. In fact, they form 'an aberration and perversion of the political and territorial organisation of the Zulu' and can be understood only as a new social phenomenon associated, above all, with the problem of insufficient land. That the 'ideology of vengeance' did gain its own momentum should also be related, Clegg argues, to the shortage of land, as well as to the striving for lost independence:

a certain degree of satisfaction was obtained by the feuders in that for once the Government was in a position of total impotence and ignorance and their inability to terminate feuding emphasised their lack of authority and legitimacy in the eyes of warring parties. In the last instance, feuding is an assertion of autonomy and the commitment to maintain at all costs the control over land and the frail infra-structure of a rural economy – the last vestiges of a dream of independence. (Clegg, 1981: 194)

Quinlan (1986) also questions the existence of ancient tribal loyalties, but from a very different angle. He shows how, in the 'homeland' of Qwaqwa, the 'tribal paradigm' has been a powerful force in contemporary politics. However, he demonstrates to what extent the 'tribal paradigm' has been skilfully manipulated in order to legitimise the present ruling class. This was achieved primarily by appealing to the leaders' purported descent from 'tribal chiefs' of the past. Qwaqwa leaders also used colonial categories such as 'tribe' to create modern political structures which enabled them to rule in a more authoritarian fashion than had any chief in the pre-colonial period. 'Ancient' tribal loyalties and identities could therefore be created; but they could also be modernised when circumstances demanded. In this regard Quinlan shows how, in recent times, these artificial 'tribal' affiliations have been subsumed within the 'broader ideology of ethnic nationalism', thereby accommodating the enforced 'ethnicity' of the government's policy of national states (Quinlan, 1986: 31–2).

Conclusion

The shift in terminology whereby 'tribe' (or 'race' or 'tradition') has been superseded by 'culture' or 'ethnic group', is endemic to the South African situation. Government, the broad public, opinion-makers and anthropologists continue to stress differences, and all of these concepts serve this end well. As Amselle and M'Bokolo observe, 'the Apartheid regime perfected this manipulation: to reduce African societies to tribes does not only mean to proclaim their irreducible "difference" from white society . . . but also to assert that they are in permanent conflict among themselves and to legitimise the policy of systematic division' (1985: 9, translated).

We observe that the term is still sometimes used to help explain difficulties which South Africa is experiencing in the process of political 'reform'. For example, Mr Chris Heunis, Minister of Constitutional Development, claimed on 26 August 1987 (as reported by the SABC) that national unity is impeded by the existence of 'tribal, religious, linguistic and cultural groups'.

Writers of anthropology in South Africa have unfortunately also not been able to liberate themselves fully either from the loose usage of the term, or from the consequences of woolly thinking associated with the idea of 'tribe'. For example, Ben Levitas, in the preface to South African Tribal Life, perpetuates the dualist tribal–Western view of the population:

Tribal life today is in a state of flux and of transition. Traditional established ways, based on tribal experience, are no longer adequate or capable of providing satisfactory solutions to problems now being encountered by detribalized people, particularly those who have moved away from their tribal lands. A breakdown of tribal bonds is affecting all the Bantu-speaking people, whether they live in the homelands or in the urban areas. This process of change and of urbanization has dislocated the lifestyle of the ex-tribal person, and left him in a transitory state with two value systems, one tribal, the other western. (1984: 5)

For Martin West, author of *Abantu. An Introduction to the Black*

People of South Africa, 'the tribal people of Southern Africa have ceased to exist as such' (1976: 7). Nevertheless, he presents a picture of nine distinct linguistic and cultural 'groupings': *the* Zulu, *the* Tsonga, *the* Ndebele, and so on. Thus without using the contaminated term 'tribe', the impression of Africans being divided into discrete 'tribal' units remains in his book.

What is peculiar about the term 'tribe' is that, irrespective of serious criticism, it reappears again and again in writing (as it stays in general public consciousness) either unchanged or under different names such as 'ethnic group', 'culture' (plural, 'cultures') or 'people' (plural, 'peoples'). The reason for this is probably that the concept of 'tribe' has been crucial in all directions of anthropology, be it evolutionist, diffusionist, structuralist, functionalist, Soviet-Marxist or neo-Marxist. World-wide it has fulfilled a role in coping with the evident plurality of custom and social structures. Concepts like 'tribe', however, tend to reify the objects of study, to bound them as if they were strictly delimited units. To strip anthropology of such a fundamental concept is to expose its theoretical nakedness.

Governments and the public do not care much for the anthropologists' dilemma with 'tribe'. They will continue to use the concept because it is a useful simplification. The task of anthropologists is not simply to show themselves and others that there is a serious problem involved in using the term, but also to formulate better concepts whose usefulness could be tested in understanding and explaining social processes, to the benefit of both science and public life. Of utmost importance, then, is the requirement that this be done in constant conversation with what is happening on the ground.

6 Ethnic group and nation: The apartheid vision in South Africa
JOHN SHARP

The definition of 'ethnic group' and 'nation'

The apartheid vision, propounded most fully in the 1960s, saw South Africa's population as divided into a series of 'ethnic groups'. Each ethnic group had, or was meant to have, its own territory where it would develop its inherent potential and become a sovereign 'nation'. This ideological vision came to maturity only during Verwoerd's leadership of the National Party (Adam and Giliomee, 1979: 42). In the 'reform' period of the 1980s the notion of a separate territorial state for each ethnic group has been modified by the government (although not by opposition parties further to the right); but the principle of discrete ethnic groups remains enshrined in the new constitutional dispensation.

The apartheid vision involved a particular interpretation of the terms 'ethnic group' and 'nation'. It held that ethnic groups differed from each other by virtue of objective cultural differences. The members of an ethnic group spoke one language, held to a distinctive set of practices, and shared a common system of beliefs. Because of these objective characteristics, it was argued, the members of the group shared common interests, and would naturally unite in order to propagate and defend their interests. At some point in an ethnic group's history, attempts to further common 'ethnic' interests might well take the form of a striving for political autonomy from others. It was assumed that when this point was reached, the 'ethnic group' in question had graduated to the more sophisticated stage of being a 'nation'.

These underlying ideas about 'ethnic groups' and 'nations' were not confined to early proponents of the apartheid vision. They were widely held. Indeed, in the 1950s and 1960s, ideas which were recognisably similar formed the dominant argument in much international academic writing about these concepts. As the anthropologist Fredrik Barth observed at the end of the 1960s, the conventional view amongst sociologists and anthropologists was still that 'ethnic groups' were simply cultural groups which had developed their distinctive features by virtue of their original (and enduring) isolation from each other (Barth, 1969). The common assumption was that when these groups were brought together in the modern era their boundaries were obvious and clear-cut. Moreover, these boundaries were, supposedly, the prime cause of the social problems of the 'developing' world, because people were suddenly required to interact on a much larger scale than had hitherto been the case. People from different ethnic groups had difficulty in understanding and adapting to each others' ways and values. Hence, in the 1950s and 1960s, there was a rash of literature dealing with the supposed problems of 'culture contact', 'intercultural communication', and of fitting 'old societies' into new states (Geertz, 1963).

Much of this thinking, it is now realised, was misplaced. As Barth observed, ethnic boundaries are not the result of the isolation of groups from each other. On the contrary, where they exist, ethnic boundaries result from the process of social interaction itself. Ethnic boundaries are not sustained, moreover, because of traditional *cultural* differences, but because of political differences. Ethnicity is a political process by which people seek to form groups, and to differentiate one set of people from another, by appealing to the *idea* of ineluctable cultural difference. The question of whether the cultural differences which mark ethnic boundaries are actually 'traditional' or not is a secondary issue, because people can readily invent cultural differences if it is in their political interest to do so. Ethnicity is the pursuit of political goals – the acquisition or maintenance of power, the mobilisation of a following – through the idiom of cultural commonness and difference.

This introduces a most important idea, which has become much clearer in academic writing of the 1970s and 1980s. It is that both 'ethnic groups' and 'nations' are fundamentally constructs of the human imagination rather than entities with a concrete, practical existence in the social world. (Anderson, 1983)

Both 'ethnic groups' and 'nations' differ, in this respect, from 'states'. States do have a practical existence: a state *is* the territory enclosed by a series of border posts; it *is* parliament, the law courts, the police and army, and the bureaucracy which control and administer the lives of the inhabitants of the territory in question. By contrast, both 'ethnic groups' and 'nations' are ideas in people's minds. They may be ideas which only some people in a given situation hold, or they may be shared by many.

One clearly cannot assume that 'ethnic groups' or 'nations' exist when only some of their putative members acknowledge their existence. Welsh and Basque nationalists believe passionately in the existence of their respective 'nations', and cite all the familiar arguments about 'tradition', ineluctable cultural difference, and divine right to bolster their claims. But the majority of people who should, in the nationalists' view, be members of these groups do not at present support the idea of Welsh or Basque separatism. One can certainly say, in such instances, that separatist movements exist, but one cannot claim a practical reality for the Welsh or Basque 'nation'.

Furthermore, even if Wales and the Basque region were to be granted political autonomy tomorrow, they would form states in which many people who were not Welsh or Basque would live alongside those who were. Therefore the inhabitants of such a state would not form a state *after the image propagated by nationalist rhetoric*. Wales would still not be 'for the Welsh' unless those who had not been Welsh up to that point decided to change their identity and take on a new cultural allegiance. Such a switch is not inconceivable. It is what has happened in many of the nation-states of Europe, and elsewhere, in the last two hundred or so years: nationalist sentiment has become widespread amongst people whom various accidents of history placed together within the arbitrary boundaries of states. This process, however, illustrates precisely the fact that 'nations' are products of the human imagination rather than facts of nature. Over time people have come to accept an identity – as members of the British, French, or American 'nation' – which was by no means self-evident at the outset (and which, as the existence of irredentist nationalisms shows, is not self-evident to *everyone* even today).

'Nation' and 'ethnic group' are ideas which people in the modern world use to confirm or challenge the legitimacy of states (Saul, 1979). Sometimes these attempts are made by a few people, sometimes by many; sometimes the few succeed in mobilising the many to support the cause, sometimes they do not. Since 'nations' and 'ethnic groups' are imaginary constructs, one cannot ask what their real characteristics are. One can only ask who believes in them and acts as if they were real. How many are these people? Who leads nationalist or ethnic movements? Why do they do so? Under what circumstances do they succeed or fail in mobilising support for their vision?

These, it is now recognised, are some of the important questions to pose in studies of ethnicity or nationalism, and it is these that one must ask in relation to the apartheid vision of 'ethnic groups' and 'nations' in South Africa.

The apartheid vision was not a simple description of the nature of South African society. It was an attempt by some people to represent the nature of this society to themselves and others. It was part of a complex ideological discourse which, as Posel (1987: 439) has said, embodied

a set of [Christian Nationalist] principles and standards according to which the moral and social meaning of apartheid policies was interpreted and justified, and the identity of white subjects was constituted. Political, economic, social, cultural and sexual segregation were cast as divinely ordained, historically vindicated and the foundation of a just and harmonious society. 'Being white' meant being socially and culturally distinct, politically and economically privileged and physically segregated from those who were not.

Many white South Africans would have denied, and will still deny, the representational nature of this vision. But this illustrates no more than the success with which the apartheid ideology has spun a web of meaning around the interests, aspirations and fears of white South Africans, to the extent that this vision of society appears as part of their 'common sense'.

Its representational character is made apparent, however, by two considerations. Firstly, the fact that certain aspects of the apartheid vision have been subject to (limited) 'reformist' redefinition means that it was never a literal description of an unchanging reality. Secondly, and more important, the same conclusion follows from the fact that the apartheid vision has always been contested: the majority of people in South Africa have never accepted the premises on which the vision was constructed. Indeed, as Greenberg says, 'apartheid ideology spoke of the integrity of national aspirations and of the essential equality in separation. Such tenets resonated in white politics ... but for African workers, who were a growing and dominant presence in South Africa's capitalist order, such tenets must have seemed archaic and irrelevant' (1987: 390). Moreover, part of the reason for the current programme of 'reform' is precisely that the majority have acted out, in numerous overt and covert acts of resistance and defiance, their total rejection of this vision.

If the apartheid vision was not a simple description of a self-evident reality, how did it come to exist? What historical factors brought it about, and ensured its tenacious hold on the minds of most white South Africans? One answer to this question (although not the only one) lies in the historical fact of Afrikaner nationalism. As Posel says (1987: 433): 'The ideology of apartheid was historically and conceptually bound up with that of Afrikaner nationalism.'

The origins of the apartheid vision

Afrikaner nationalism embodies a particular kind of nationalist ideology. There have certainly been different emphases within Afrikaner nationalist thought, and its premises have developed and changed over time. But there is a set of core beliefs which is present in most, if not all, of the different interpretations (cf. Van Jaarsveld, 1964). These core beliefs can be summarised in three propositions:

(i) A strong sense of group attachment (*groepsgebondenheid*) is a fundamental characteristic of Afrikaners, and always has been since the time of European settlement at the Cape in the seventeenth century.

(ii) The fact that this sentiment has always existed is evidence of the long-term existence of the Afrikaner *volk* itself. (Some proponents of the doctrine recognise that the *volk* has passed through several, increasingly complex manifestations in the course of time since 1652; others do not, and seem to imply an absolute continuity of *volkswees* from the start to the present.) The fact that the *volk*, or some manifestation of its essence, has always existed is what has generated enduring group (or nationalist) sentiment amongst Afrikaners.

(iii) The *volk* has always existed because nature, or destiny, or God (that is, some force outside of human history) willed its existence.

Of course, to Afrikaner nationalists (and to others elsewhere who hold to the same kind of nationalist ideology) the moving force outside of history created not merely one fundamental group, or *volk*, or proto-nation, but many. Therefore all humanity is, and always has been, compartmentalised into a series of these groups. Each of these original, primordial groups is destined for political autonomy and eventual nation status; its members will struggle to advance from being a group of common culture (an ethnic group) to a group of common political will (a nation), and will strive to give territorial expression to the inalienable sovereignty of the group to which they belong. This vision is often termed 'ethnic nationalism' (Smith, 1976).

Afrikaner nationalism represents a prime example of the ethnic nationalist vision. The ethnic nationalist argument is, moreover, the ideological link between Afrikaner nationalism's vision of itself and the apartheid vision in South Africa.

Other nationalisms (such as territorial nationalism) reverse some of the terms of the ethnic nationalist argument; it is not that people who are united by a common culture should have a shared political destiny, but rather that people upon whom history has thrust a common political destiny (whether it is political autonomy or subjugation) should have a common culture to give expression to their shared experience. This difference between these two forms of nationalism is, in one sense, entirely trivial; but in another sense it has great significance. I return to this point below in discussing other forms of nationalism in South Africa.

The three premises outlined above are, from any logical perspective, nonsensical, as Gellner (1983) observes in discussing nationalism in general. He also argues, however, that the fact that nationalist ideology is nonsensical has no bearing whatever on the question of its popular appeal under certain conditions. A logical rejoinder to the three premises would stress the following:

(i) The Afrikaner *volk* has not existed since the beginning of time. Indeed, the way in which nationalists define the *volk* (as a community of common culture and political will, to which all white Afrikaans-speakers without exception are bound to belong) actually demonstrates that the *volk* has *never* existed as anything other than an idea and an ideal.

(ii) It is not the prior existence of the *volk* which produced Afrikaner nationalism, but Afrikaner nationalism which preceded, and made possible, the idea of the *volk*.

(iii) Afrikaner nationalism is not a generic characteristic of Afrikaners, but a political philosophy with a specific history.

There has been considerable historical inquiry in recent years into the specific circumstances in which the ideology of the *volk* appeared, and appealed to a wide audience in South Africa. It has also been shown that the *volk* idea was articulated by individuals in a particular social category, rather than by Afrikaners in general. Indeed, it was the articulation of the *volk* idea which slowly, and with considerable difficulty, constituted certain people in South Africa as 'Afrikaners' in the first place. Moreover, recent inquiry shows that the people who invented and articulated the philosophy of Afrikaner nationalism had specific purposes in mind; for them the creation of the *volk* was not simply an end in itself, a fulfilling of God's design for history, but also a means to an end.

What is the historical evidence for these arguments? Various historians have explicitly set out to avoid the stultifying idea of 'a deeply rooted organic "Afrikaner identity" which rumbles through South African history and mysteriously unites all Afrikaners into a monolithic *volk*' (Hofmeyr, 1987: 95). They argue that neither the political nor the cultural unity of 'Afrikaners' can be taken for granted in the way that nationalists do (Du Toit, 1985; Giliomee, 1987a, 1987b; O'Meara, 1983).

The absence of political unity

The lack of political unity is easy to demonstrate. Even avowedly Afrikaner nationalist historians admit to its absence during most of the nineteenth century. Scholtz (1970), for example, remarks on this, and on the lack of national consciousness amongst 'Afrikaners' until the 1850s. On the other hand, he does insist that a mature national consciousness had developed by the 1880s; but many historians now have difficulty with this argument.

Firstly, until a unified South Africa was created, the Afrikaners-to-be were divided between two British colonies and two Boer republics. This had severe implications for concerted political action (as was evident during the Anglo–Boer War), and for the growth of widespread national consciousness. Secondly, the mineral discoveries, and the beginning of industrial development in South Africa after 1870, served to heighten regional and class differentiation amongst Afrikaans-speakers.

Trapido (1978) writes of the increasing tensions between large landowners, small farmers and landless *bywoners* in the rural Transvaal as early as the 1880s. The burgeoning Witwatersrand market stimulated the commercialisation of agriculture, and motivated large landowners to accumulate wealth at the expense of others. Small landowners and tenant farmers were dispossessed both before and after the Anglo–Boer War. Van Onselen (1982) has described the circumstances of those who were driven into the working class on the Witwatersrand *before* the turn of the century. This is important evidence, because it counters nationalist insistence that the 'poor white' problem (the movement of impoverished Afrikaans-speakers from rural to urban areas) was caused solely by British depredations in the countryside during the war (implying that there were no earlier divisions amongst the *volk* itself).

Dispossession caused much resentment against fellow Afrikaans-speakers. Hofmeyr (1987: 101) cites the bitter comment of one struggling landowner in 1905: 'These rich farmers, these selfish, self-righteous bloodsuckers! . . . Even our great generals who make such nice speeches, oppress the poor in private and enrich themselves from the impoverished.' Such hostile views were widely held, suggesting that the existence of a homogeneous Afrikaner community was by no means self-evident to many who should, in nationalist terms, have been its members. Political differences amongst Afrikaans-speakers were not buried in 1910, or in 1914 when Hertzog founded his National Party. Many continued to support Smuts, with his strong 'English' connections, until the 1940s.

One can, of course, discount this evidence of political disunity by referring to the divisions as 'unnatural' (cf. Van Jaarsveld, 1979: 118). But this is special pleading: the divisions were only 'unnatural', and an unfortunate indication of human irrationality, if one starts by assuming that there ought to have been unity in the first place. O'Meara (1983) and others have shown, however, that Afrikaans-speakers divided their support amongst the political parties of the day in entirely rational fashion, because their material circumstances and political interests were not uniform. Why should struggling Transvaal landowners, or the poor whites in the urban areas, have supported the generals' *Het Volk* Party in the early twentieth century, when it clearly represented the interests of mining capital and wealthy agriculturalists? Why should wealthy Transvaal agriculturalists have supported the National Party, given that its anti-imperialist rhetoric seemed to be aimed at mining capital, which was the direct source of their growing affluence?

The invention of tradition

One can also argue that despite political disunity, Afrikaners were bound together at the more fundamental level of common values, symbols and deep-seated aspirations. Scholtz has suggested that the Boers were united by a common culture by the end of the eighteenth century, and that this formed the basis on which, despite all subsequent tribulation, their political unity as Afrikaners was eventually established. But even this is highly contentious. Was the absence of a common language not indicative of a profound lack of shared understanding concerning values, symbols and aspirations?

The Boers did not speak one standard language during the nineteenth century. Hofmeyr (1987) reminds us that, in both the Cape and the Transvaal, the affluent, 'respectable' population spoke Dutch, while others spoke a variety of regional dialects which, although derived from Dutch, also displayed the influence of Malay and Portuguese creole, Khoisan and African languages, and English, French and German. These regional patois were despised by the 'respectable' Dutch-speakers, not least because they were also spoken, as home language, by people who were not white.

The idea that 'Afrikaners' ought to have a common language emerged only towards the end of the nineteenth century, espoused by such organisations as S. J. du Toit's *Genootskap van Regte Afrikaners*. The *Genootskap* attempted to create one standard version out of the diverse dialects, to free it from association with 'non-whites', and to persuade Dutch-speakers that they ought to adopt the new Afrikaans. To do this, they had to elaborate an idea of an exclusive group to whom this language should properly belong. The *Genootskap*, and similar bodies, were instrumental in spelling out the nationalist vision of a *volk* that should be the bearer of the culture they were busy inventing.

They built on attitudes which were already widespread, such as the deep-seated race prejudice of many Dutch settlers, and their antipathy towards British domination. But they combined these into a new, nationalist package, which no-one had ever conceived in its entirety before. The new ingredients were precisely those which the nationalists attributed to the distant past: the notion of original cultural unity, of both racial and cultural exclusivism combined, and of an inescapable, shared political destiny.

Historians who draw attention to these attempts to invent tradition in the late nineteenth century are indebted to the insight of Max Weber, who wrote about the nature of ethnic groups and nations in general. Weber suggested that 'ethnic membership (i.e. membership of a category displaying some common cultural trait) does not constitute a group; it only facilitates group formation of any kind, particularly in the political sphere. On the other hand, it is primarily the political community (no matter how artificially organised) that inspires the belief in common ethnicity.' (1965: 306) Even if the Afrikaners had spoken one language for generations this would not, in itself, have constituted them as a group. People do not form ethnic groups or nations simply because they come from the same place or speak a common language. But if people want to form a political community, then the question of their cultural difference from others may attain great significance. If necessary they will invent a shared past; for if, as Swift observed with customary sarcasm, it is important to invent a tradition about the proper way their forebears opened eggs (at the big end or the little end), nationalists will very likely do so.

Nationalist movements create a vision of a unity which they claim is long-standing. This is not a statement of historical fact, but an attempt to legitimate their vision, by having it recognised as 'traditional'. Nationalists may dwell on events and circumstances of the past (such as the Great Trek, Blood River, and British colonial domination) but they present them in a new light. The Great Trek becomes in this vision a symbol of the whole *volk* in rebellion against foreign domination; Blood River a symbol of its covenant with God. The story of nationalist movements is the story of their struggle to get others, to whom these meanings are not immediately self-evident, to accept their vision as reality.

The mobilisation of the volk

Many of the people whom the *Genootskap* addressed, regarded its initial efforts with undisguised contempt. As Hofmeyr says (1983: 98), the wealthy Cape farmers of the Afrikaner Bond 'had little taste for du Toit's vision of an organic nation, and scoffed at his schemes to promote the "brabbeltaal" of the disreputable populace above the glories of Dutch'. Even President Paul Kruger seems to have been unmoved by Du Toit's ideas (Du Toit, 1985), and it is certain that poor Afrikaans-speakers on the Witwatersrand, who were flirting with socialism early in the twentieth century, would have found much of his vision incomprehensible. Why should wealthy agriculturalists and the new urban poor have responded to an argument that they were both bound to the same fundamental interests? The vision of the *volk* took a long time to gain a firm hold on popular consciousness.

But the vision was carefully nurtured by a specific category of people. Who were these people, and why should they have campaigned so assiduously on behalf of a *volk* which did not exist?

Hofmeyr notes that the members of the *Genootskap* were a closely knit group of Dutch-speaking professionals – clerics, teachers, lawyers and journalists. 'This concentration, even overproduction, of educated men was a common feature of Cape social life where commerce and government were British dominated' (1987: 97). The Dutch-speaking intelligentsia at the Cape were placed in a difficult situation, in the late nineteenth century, by the combination of capitalist economic growth and British political control. They lacked the resources which enabled both Dutch and English agriculturalists to profit from the Cape's links with the imperial system; they could not advance in government service because they were not English; and their education made them acutely alive to the indignities which British domination inflicted on the whole category of Dutch/Afrikaans-speakers.

Their nationalist vision was an attempt to reach out to others in this category, and was linked to efforts to formulate a populist political programme, by calling for 'the establishment of small banks, boycotts of "foreign" traders and more funds for Dutch education' (1987: 97).

These goals revealed their own particular interests, because small finance and trading were the sorts of enterprises which they, with their limited material resources, could hope to command. Expansion of Dutch educational facilities was of direct concern to teachers who were threatened by the 'anglicisation' of schooling. On the other hand, they were also an indication of genuine concern for ordinary people, who were vulnerable in their own way to capitalist transformation and British domination.

Part of this programme involved the establishment of popular newspapers and magazines to propagate the Afrikaans language, and instil in ordinary people a pride in being Afrikaners. These endeavours, and particularly the literary one (for which the intelligentsia had the requisite resources), met with some success from the 1880s onwards, and might have advanced very quickly to widespread prominence had the nationalist movements been able to command political power in society at large. But this did not come about for a long time. Wealthy agriculturalists, who valued the British connection, soon came to dominate the Afrikaner Bond in the Cape; and after Union, mining capital and progressive agriculture (the alliance between 'maize' and 'gold') dominated national politics. This domination persisted even when Hertzog's National Party came to power; and was one of the reasons for the long history of *broedertwis*, of splits and realignments amongst Afrikaans-speaking voters. The nationalists sought a combination of interests which would give them access to decisive power in the state.

Advancement of the ideals of Afrikaner nationalism was a slow and uncertain process. In the early twentieth century it was the intelligentsia, small landowners, and small business people who held most steadfastly to the *volk* ideal, because it remained in their interests to do so. Their efforts to propagate the idea bore fruit slowly, as their message became more widely known, and as they organised themselves more effectively to mobilise people in terms of their vision. O'Meara (1983) discusses the numerous fields in which Broederbond intellectuals, and other members of the 'petty bourgeoisie', organised the structures of a popular nationalist identity in the 1930s and 1940s –

in trade unionism, the economic movement, school, church, family, and political party.

These efforts were assisted by contingent events – the crisis in international capitalism in the late 1920s, and Smuts's fateful decision to take South Africa into the Second World War without consulting the electorate. These events undermined established political loyalties, and made large numbers of people available for redefinition, via the diverse structures of the nationalist movement, as members of the *volk*.

O'Meara's interpretation of Afrikaner nationalist history has been condemned by some fellow historians (Giliomee, 1983; Greenberg, 1983; Yudelman, 1983) because of its economism, its apparent determination to reduce the issue of support for Afrikaner nationalism to one of material interest. This seems to be just comment, insofar as the modern ideal of the Afrikaner *volk* dates as far back as the 1870s, and gained some popular appeal long before the 1930s. It is not as if the organisations of the economic movement (such as the *Reddingsdaadbond*) were solely responsible for foisting a completely new identity on thousands of unsuspecting people in the post-Depression years.

But O'Meara is correct to insist that the vision of Afrikaner nationalism was given real substance only well into the twentieth century, after many false starts and detours. Any useful analysis of ethnicity or nationalism ought not to confuse the idea of the group with its practical realisation, nor assume that once the group has been 'thought' it must inevitably become real. The so-called economic movement, set in motion after the Broederbond-inspired *Ekonomiese Volkskongres* of 1939, was indeed one of the decisive processes in the development of Afrikaner nationalism. It used the *volk* idea to persuade Afrikaners of all classes to support mass economic upliftment. As the *Reddingsdaadbond* stated in 1944, 'a volk which finds itself in ... a state of economic dependence cannot be rescued by other nations, *but by itself alone*' (cited by O'Meara, 1983: 139, original emphasis). Therefore the savings of ordinary Afrikaansspeakers, urban and rural, many of them poor, had to be mobilised, and their buying power concentrated in support of Afrikaner businesses.

One result was that, during the 1940s, many aspirant entrepreneurs did achieve their own particularistic goals: they acquired the resources to begin capital accumulation for themselves (which was what they had aimed at since the 1880s). Moreover, the *volk* idea made credible their assurance that what was good for them was good for all; and it was, at least in part, the mobilisation of thousands of Afrikaansspeakers through the economic movement which brought Malan's National Party to political power in 1948.

Once in power, the National Party did reap material rewards for its supporters, Afrikaners in general, and whites as a whole. But, as subsequent events have shown, it did not fulfil the *volk* ideal. It did not do away with class divisions amongst Afrikaners; it did not turn all Afrikaners into a perpetual community of common political will. It did not create a future in the terms of the nationalist image of the past.

But the fiction that it had done so, because it was the embodiment of the will of the *volk*, made possible the whole ideological exercise of projecting the presumed characteristics of the Afrikaner *volk* onto other South Africans. As Posel says, Afrikaner nationalism made the apartheid ideology conceivable.

The creation of apartheid policy

But Afrikaner nationalism was not responsible for all details of apartheid policy. Apartheid displayed many continuities with the earlier policy of segregation, and the process of dividing Africans, conceptually and practically, into discrete groups had begun long before, in the colonial period.

This is not to say that there were no boundaries, cultural or political, dividing the African population in the pre-colonial era. Africans were not a homogeneous mass, on whom all boundaries were imposed by white settlers. Different languages were spoken in the subcontinent; there were differences in custom; and people were grouped into different political entities, a series of states and chiefdoms, which varied in their internal organisation and geographical extent.

But there is abundant evidence that the white settlers misunderstood (and often wilfully misconstrued) the nature of these cultural differences and political boundaries. As Skalník explains above, the notion of 'tribe' which the settlers deployed, involved a presumption that cultural and political boundaries always coincided and were always clear-cut. This view of pre-colonial African groupings stemmed directly from European notions about the constitution of society (notions which reflected nationalist ideology within Europe itself) and were quite inaccurate when applied to the flexibility of the African situation.

Dutch settlers were by no means the only ones who viewed African society from the vantage of European thought. The same approach was adopted by English settlers and authorities in southern Africa and elsewhere, and by all the colonial powers in Africa. It was expressed in, and reinforced by, the actions of administrators, who wanted convenient units of people in order to facilitate their task, and by missionaries, who standardised clusters of dialects into single languages, and then identified neat groups of people who supposedly spoke them (Harries, 1988).

Afrikaner nationalism did not invent the division of Africans into discrete 'tribal' or ethnic groups; nor did it create the reserve areas which were subsequently to become their 'homelands'. The policy of reconstructing 'traditional' authorities to administer the reserve areas was also begun long before the National Party came to power in 1948. As Lacey (1981) explains, the decision to recreate the system of chiefly authority, which had been significantly undermined in the Cape, Transvaal and Free State reserves, was taken in the 1920s, as part of the Pact government's refusal to contemplate the further extension of common political rights to Africans and its attempt to undermine these rights for those (in the Cape) who already had them.

Even the notion that whites should act as trustees of African political interests, helping them to develop along their own lines, emerged as early as the 1930s. The policy of trusteeship involved the idea that limited amounts of land would be made available to extend the area of the reserves beyond the limits of their demarcation in 1913. The decision to do this involved a compromise between Smuts and Hertzog over the best way to secure a cheap labour force for different segments of capital in South Africa, and agreement on trusteeship was one of the main factors which made the fusion of the National Party and the South African Party in 1934 possible. In other words, the post-1948 National Party, which made trusteeship an important element of the apartheid policy, took over an idea that the United Party had fostered assiduously.

The originality in the apartheid vision involved the idea that the reserves could be styled 'homelands' (subsequently 'national states'), and that their populations were not merely 'tribes' but ethnic groups, which were proto-nations and could be led through various stages of constitutional development towards the attainment of sovereign independence. This notion did not mature until the 1960s, when Verwoerd reacted to growing international condemnation of his government's policies by attempting to apply the vision which Afrikaner nationalism had of itself, and of its own genesis, to the situation of others in South Africa. If Afrikaners had striven for political self-determination because of their primordial unity, surely it was reasonable to assume that others, who must be divided into similar groups, would do the same? And since the Afrikaner *volk*, mindful of its own bitter struggles, was willing to continue in the role of trustee, and to guide Africans towards political sophistication, the challenge of attaining self-determination would be made as easy as possible for the various African 'ethnic groups'.

Why the apartheid policy could never succeed

It is sometimes argued that the idea of ethnic nationalism in the apartheid policy could not have succeeded because it was based on incorrect and irrational premises. This view claims that, contrary to the ethnic nationalist vision, Africans in South Africa did not comprise a series of separate primordial groupings. This is true, but such argument is largely beside the point, and certainly begs the question of why any nationalism should ever be successful (since, as we have shown above, all primordial groups are invented).

Much more important was the fact that the vast majority of the African population was simply never prepared to participate in the government's plans to foster the separate development of ethnic national groups. In order to understand why this was so, it is necessary to consider two issues: the full scope of apartheid policy, and the existence of African nationalism.

The scope of apartheid

The reserves in South Africa were long thought to provide employers, and in particular the mining industry, with a source of cheap labour. This does not mean that capital initially created the reserves in order to be a source of cheap labour, or that labour from the reserves was initially the cheapest available (Lonsdale, 1983; Harries, 1982). But after the reserves had been formally proclaimed in 1913, mining capital certainly impressed upon Botha and Smuts's South African Party the importance of maintaining the reserves, and of seeing that they did not decline into absolute stagnation.

There is some disagreement in the literature about how the cheap labour system actually worked, but one influential argument (Wolpe, 1972; Meillassoux, 1980) holds that labour from the reserves was cheap because the workers' dependants remained behind in the rural areas. This made for significant saving on the requirements for urban infrastructure, which was an advantage to the state. Capital, or private employers, also derived advantage from the fact that the workers' dependants contributed to their own subsistence, by practising subsistence agriculture on the land available to them. Subsistence agriculture made possible the payment of lower wages to workers than would have been the case if their dependants had been forced into total reliance on wage income. Moreover, subsistence agriculture made it possible for workers to support themselves when they were ill, or between jobs, or too old to work for wages.

Maintenance of this system of cheap labour depended on two considerations. Firstly, as mentioned above, it was important not to let the reserves slip into decline as a result of overpopulation and neglect. Mining and other industrial employers had most interest in this issue, and they supported the South African Party's policy of adding land to the reserves (in terms of the recommendations of the Beaumont Commission of 1916). Agriculturalists, on the other hand, were not interested in this issue, since they wanted Africans to remain on their farms rather than move off to the reserves in order to enter industrial wage employment. Hence agriculture was firm in its support for the policies of Hertzog's National Party, which blocked (and even attempted to reverse) the recommendations of the Beaumont Commission for twenty years. As noted above, the two parties finally struck a compromise in the 1930s, and the United Party which emerged from the fusion supported the maintenance of the reserves and their gradual expansion to an extent that would secure the cheap labour advantages they offered. The second important consideration, which formed the other leg of United Party policy, was to attempt to compartmentalise the African labour force, by preventing farm workers from leaving the farms easily, and by preventing migrant workers from the reserves from settling in urban areas permanently.

In fact, however, the United Party did not succeed to any marked extent in either of these policy objectives. The reserves did decline, despite attempts at conservation and agricultural betterment, and people from the reserves did move to the towns and settle there permanently. This was partly owing to the relaxation of influx controls during the war years, and partly because the controls themselves were piecemeal and not very efficient. Farm labourers also left farms in large numbers during the 1930s and 1940s, much to the dismay of the farmers. Indeed widespread dissatisfaction with the United Party's attempts to control African labour was one of the major reasons for its election defeat in 1948.

During the early 1950s a main goal of the National Party's apartheid policy was to tighten up considerably on these controls over African labour. To this end it introduced a battery of new legislation, and established the means to police the new system of labour control and allocation effectively. Influx control was applied uniformly countrywide, a new system of pass laws was introduced, and African women were made to carry passes like their men. In time a complex system of labour bureaux came into operation, which channelled workseekers into jobs where they were needed. The result was to divide the labour force into separate segments much more efficiently than had hitherto been the case. Although there were significant exceptions to the rule, many Africans were confirmed in the status of migrant workers, as very temporary sojourners in the 'white' areas.

The ideals of ethnic nationalism were simply imposed, in the 1960s, on these draconian measures of control. Indeed, they came to form a vital part of the latter, because they provided some kind of legitimation, at least in the minds of white South Africans, for the extensive programmes of population relocation in the 1960s and 1970s: the 'endorsing out' of the unemployed and the aged from the urban areas, the clearance of so-called 'black spots' in the 'white' countryside, and the massive relocations of redundant farmworkers

(Surplus People Project, 1983). In the consciousness of most white South Africans, these people were merely being sent 'home', in order to participate in the grand exercise of nation-building.

One cannot possibly say that apartheid was really about the goal of granting self-determination to others, and that somehow, and very unfortunately, this noble intention succumbed to the human failings of self-interest, greed and the desire for power. Apartheid, as both policy and practice, was always about the whole of its overt and covert agenda. The desire for white political control and security, and for optimum growth in the capitalist system through the enforcement of a cheap labour system (long after small-scale agriculture's contribution to rural subsistence had totally collapsed) were as much integral parts of the apartheid policy as any overt concern with self-determination. And the victims of the policy, liable to influx-control arrests in urban areas, to relocation to distant and barren 'homelands', and to the endless hardship of the contract labour system, could hardly have failed to see it for what it was.

African nationalism

Moreover, the ethnic nationalist vision was not unveiled in a political vacuum. The principle that Africans comprised a series of primordial groups which should aspire to separate self-determinations flatly contradicted another existing, and important, vision of the constitution of African society in South Africa.

The African nationalist movement was about as old as Afrikaner nationalism, and its original proponents occupied much the same social positions as the early Afrikaner nationalists. They too were teachers and clerics, and other 'representatives of the emerging educated class' such as court interpreters, traders and small businessmen (Odendaal, 1984: 47). In the late nineteenth century, these people argued that they were different from the mass of 'tribal' Africans by virtue of acculturation, and that, having proved their merit and their attainment of 'civilisation', they should be allowed to assimilate fully into colonial society. This was particularly true of the Eastern Cape, where there was a pronounced difference between 'Red' and 'School' ideologies concerning the appropriate African response to the imposition of the colonial social order (Mayer, 1980). Moreover:

The non-racial political system of the Cape Colony provided an outlet for these ['School'] aspirations and, in turn, stimulated African political consciousness still further. In time this system, although not free from criticism, was widely accepted by Africans as making reasonable provision for the expression of their political aspirations, and was regarded as being a model for African participation in multi-racial societies. (Odendaal, 1984: 4)

When diamonds were discovered in the northern Cape, a significant number of these people moved to Kimberley to take advantage of the new prospects and the greater sophistication and cosmopolitan character of the new settlement. Willan (1982) provides a fascinating account of the way in which Sol T. Plaatje and his fellow members of the educated elite pursued the social life of Victorian England (complete with formal tea parties and cricket clubs) and saw themselves as members of a great British empire.

People with such aspirations as these consciously discounted, and sought to put behind them, the 'tribal' divisions of pre-colonial Africa. Plaatje's own account of his marriage to a Xhosa woman (he himself was a Rolong from Thaba 'Nchu) is most instructive in this regard:

My people resented the idea of my marrying a girl who spoke a language which, like the Hottentot language, had clicks in it; while her people likewise abominated the idea of giving their daughter in marriage to a fellow who spoke a language so imperfect as to be without any clicks. But the civilised laws of Cape Colony saved us from a double tragedy in a cemetery, and our erstwhile objecting relatives have lived to award their benediction to the growth of our Chuana-M'bo family which is bilingual both in the vernaculars and in European languages. (Plaatje, 1916; cited in Couzens, 1978: 3–4)

The response of white society in Kimberley to the elite's 'pretensions' was an early sign that the goal of assimilation would not be achieved easily. Plaatje and some of his colleagues moved on to the Witwatersrand after the gold discoveries, and here they soon encountered the unabashed and inflexible racism of the Transvaal Republic. Many of them were prominent in the establishment of the South African Native National Congress in 1912, the forerunner of the ANC (Lodge, 1983).

Broadly speaking, the leaders of the SANNC and the ANC clung to their assimilationist vision, the idea that Africans should be selectively permitted to participate in a non-racial democracy in South Africa, for quite some time into the twentieth century. But these attitudes began to change, as the ANC leaders became more closely involved in national and local politics, and were forced to reassess their position in the light of white intransigence regarding their aspirations. As they saw it, Britain had betrayed their interests in 1910, by allowing white domination within the Union of South Africa (cf. Plaatje, 1916). Moreover the ANC leadership was radicalised in the 1920s, in consequence of their involvement in the strike by African mineworkers on the Witwatersrand (Bonner, 1982).

Gradually a more broadly based nationalism began to take hold within organisations such as the ANC, although it is argued that the ANC itself lapsed from this commitment in the 1930s, and 'functioned almost exclusively as a disorganised organ of petty-bourgeois protest' (Karis and Gerhart, 1977: 154). A vision emerged of all Africans, urban and rural, workers and peasants, as members of one nation, the bearers of a common subordination and a shared dream of freedom. Like their Afrikaans-speaking counterparts, the members of the educated class turned to the creation of a populist following, as a counter to their prolonged exclusion from access to political and economic power. But, partly as a result of their earlier assimilationist aspirations, their populist vision was an inclusive one, quite different from the narrow ethnic exclusivism of the Afrikaner nationalists.

White South Africans believed, and still like to believe, that the African nationalist vision was the preserve of a tiny educated minority, isolated from the continued ethnic loyalties of the African masses (and now in forlorn exile). Nothing could be further from the truth: although it was presented in many different forms, the African nationalist message made significant, albeit highly uneven, inroads into popular consciousness in both urban and rural areas. The Industrial and Commercial Workers' Union (ICU) and the Garvey movement (Hill and Pirio, 1987) were important in the widespread dissemination of a broad nationalist philosophy; and even localised episodes of rural resistance showed some imprint of nationalist ideology from the 1920s onwards (Bundy, 1987a; Beinart and Bundy, 1987).

This is not to say that local or 'tribal' loyalties were immediately swept away by a tide of nationalist sentiment. But it does mean that the apartheid vision, which involved the transformation of some of these situational loyalties into cast-iron and overriding boundaries between people, had no chance of resonating with African political aspirations.

Situational identities

All nationalisms, as Tom Nairn has said, are dangerous. It is impossible to distinguish between intrinsically 'good' and 'bad' nationalisms, as if the latter represent the 'accidental aberrations or excesses' of modern history (Nairn, 1981: 347). The danger of all nationalisms lies in the nationalist propensity for zealotry.

Nationalism is a key feature of the modern age. The historical evidence of the last 150 years shows, as Nairn says, that nationalism 'was simply incomparably superior' as a means of mass mobilisation 'to what was contained in a still rudimentary . . . class consciousness'.

The superiority was not accidental – a sort of unfair advantage temporarily won here and there, but soon to recede before the truth. It derived from the very structure of [the] 'modern' societies cast out of uneven development. There never was any chance of the new universal class which figured in Marxist doctrine emerging *as* 'proletarians', rather than as 'Germans', 'Cubans', 'Irishmen' and so on. (Nairn, 1981: 354)

Nairn makes a dramatic point. But he also overstates his case here, because he endorses a grand opposition between class and nation:

people are either 'Germans' or they are 'proletarians'. National identity has certainly tended to predominate in recent history; and many, perhaps most, nationalist movements have tried to argue that national unity eliminates class division. But that is precisely why they are dangerous – because they argue for, and act as if there were, a homogeneity of identity which does not actually exist. Nationalist rhetoric explicitly proclaimed the death of class division amongst Afrikaners. In the 1940s, at the height of the economic movement, Afrikaner nationalist spokesmen created a fleeting impression that this was so; but this did not last, as the present turmoil amongst Afrikaners shows clearly. But the ideology of Afrikaner nationalism has never recognised the contingent nature of the unity it proclaimed: from its perspective, Afrikaners can never be 'workers' but only 'Afrikaner workers'; never 'teachers' or 'parents', or even 'lovers', except that the prefix 'Afrikaner' is added to them.

Afrikaner nationalism is therefore a dangerous phenomenon, which has instilled a lasting political immaturity into its followers. All other nationalisms, including African nationalism, have the capacity to do this, by virtue of the circumstances of their origin and development. The danger is that they will overlook the fact that people have different identities in different situations. They can be workers in one context, and Africans or Afrikaners in another.

This is a point which anthropologists have sought to argue since the 1950s. In a classic study, Mitchell (1956) showed that Africans who lived in the Copperbelt towns of (then) Northern Rhodesia placed great stress on 'tribal' divisions in their day-to-day interactions amongst themselves, but refused to recognise these boundaries when they were imposed by employers in the workplace. He concluded that 'tribalism' was an urban adaptation of rural identities, and that it was used as a means of classifying people for the purpose of social interaction in an impersonal environment. By labelling other individuals as 'Bemba' or 'Lozi', one had a means of knowing how to behave towards them as members of a social category. This knowledge, Mitchell stressed, was acquired in the urban area itself, and had little to do with any cultural or other differences which might have existed in the rural area.

On the other hand, these categories of interaction were not relevant in the workplace. Since the major employers in Northern Rhodesia were colonial whites, African workers saw themselves as *Africans* who shared a common lot of subordination and exploitation. This did not mean, however, that in other contexts, urban Africans were unaware of the existence of class differentiation within their ranks. Mitchell showed that one of the characteristic forms of cultural expression in the urban areas – the so-called Kalela dance – was a complex symbolic commentary on all dimensions of the situational identities of town life (although colonial whites regarded it as mere 'tribal' dancing). By performing these dances, urban people expressed and clarified for themselves the subtle shifts involved in being, simultaneously but for different audiences, members of putative rural groups, and Africans in general, and members of the urban working class.

Amongst South African anthropologists, Mayer has been the most diligent in seeking to exemplify some of the insights of Mitchell. He has shown (1971; 1975) that Africans have remained interested in, and concerned with, the specificities of regional or 'tribal' practices, without subscribing to the apartheid vision of primordial ethnic groups. He has shown that many Africans combine their interest in such particularisms with a deep attachment to the cause of African nationalism. He has also shown, moreover, that the same 'traditions' and customary practices are used to express both particularistic and national identities.

These were, and remain, extremely important arguments. They emphasise that as far as ordinary people's experiences are concerned, there is no grand opposition between 'ethnic group' or 'nation' and class. Building on all of these insights, Beinart (1987) has recently shown that people's experience of 'class' or 'nation' is often mediated by, and reached through, the other ways in which they define themselves. He argues that workers from rural areas in South Africa are often enmeshed, in the workplace, in informal groups which have their roots in the rural particularisms of locality and ethnicity. These groups, which include compound gangs and mutual aid associations, are nonetheless forms of worker organisation, which can be shown to have played a considerable role in worker resistance, and in the development of worker (and possibly also working-class) consciousness. They also form a bridge between the individual and the African nationalist movement, helping to translate the message of the educated elite, which has long dominated the movement, into terms that resonate with the lives of the mass of rural people.

Earlier in this century, the ANC had some difficulty in reaching out to this mass of people, particularly to those in the rural areas. The leaders of the movement were a highly educated elite, who were also predisposed, by virtue of the theories of nationalist mobilisation current at the time, to underestimate the political potential of rural people. Events such as the various rural rebellions of the 1950s and 1960s brought about a reassessment of this potential, and a growing awareness within the nationalist movement of the way in which situational identities could be incorporated into the nationalist struggle.

Given this experience, it is most unlikely that African nationalist leaders will approach the question of national identity from the same narrow-minded perspective that Afrikaner nationalists adopted in the

1930s and 1940s. When the African nationalists achieve power in South Africa they will do so in a different era, and under very different circumstances from those which pertained at the 'triumph' of Afrikaner nationalism. They will inherit a vastly different society, and will have had a much longer period of struggle in which to clarify their vision of the nature of the 'nation'. For these reasons they are unlikely to demand the same subservience to a single identity as did the Afrikaner nationalists. In a more mature society, people will not be called upon to choose, irrevocably, between the dictates of nation and class.

7 Confusing categories: Population groups, national states and citizenship
MARTIN WEST

Citizenship is a means whereby states commonly regulate access to rights and resources. Citizens, for example, normally participate in the political process, have access to land, have the right to education, and enjoy mobility within their country. Non-citizens, on the other hand, do not participate politically, and their access to other resources is controlled. They are usually subject to some form of alien control legislation.

In contrast, South African citizenship of itself confers few general rights of the sort mentioned. Moreover, the citizenship legislation as such makes no distinction between citizens on any discriminatory basis (Boberg, 1977: 48). Instead, differential access to resources, and differential rights, are determined by a system of population classification based ostensibly on 'race'. Rycroft has commented succinctly on this modified form of citizenship:

Exactly what sort of citizenship a person enjoys in South Africa hinges precisely on racial classification. One's race determines what land one can buy, where one can live, in what school one can be educated, the amount of one's pension and so on. This concept of citizenship – one that permits different classes of citizen – diverges from international norms to such an extent that the continued use of the term 'citizenship' appears at times to be wholly inappropriate, if not deceptive. (Rycroft, 1987: 209)

In addition, since the 1960s, people classified as black have had a form of dual citizenship imposed on them (of South Africa and of a 'homeland'), and subsequently South African citizenship has been removed from millions of black people as some homelands have been declared independent, turning the people involved into aliens.

In this way population classification and citizenship have been increasingly linked in a dual system of control. It will be the purpose of this chapter to examine some of the assumptions underlying this dual system by contrasting popular perceptions with the changing legal categories which have underpinned them.

Defining the indefinable
The system of population classification in South Africa is often

referred to as 'race' classification. Opponents and supporters of this classification regularly refer uncritically to 'race' as the guiding principle, arguing that the system divides South Africans on the basis of colour and other physical features. In fact, while stereotypes are likely to be concerned largely with physical characteristics, in practice both formal and informal classification is on the basis of several factors – appearance, descent, acceptance, language, behaviour, and so on. Race classification is therefore not based exclusively on physical features of race.

Official literature and rhetoric, plus much general opinion, place South Africans, as a result of the system, into a number of bounded 'population groups'. These groups are deemed officially to have separate, identifiable interests and characteristics which distinguish them from other groups. The existence of these 'population groups' is by no means universally accepted, with many rejecting the categorisations stemming from the classification system and others denying the existence or the significance of the groups thus created. While South Africans, for political or other reasons, may affirm or deny the existence of such groups, they have a special significance in that the system forces people into structured inequality by virtue of their classification.

It is also clear that the categories created are not 'natural', bounded groupings. Were this the case, there would have been no necessity to define them in law and to provide for procedures for reclassification and appeal. The legislative attempts to define population categories are instructive, for they demonstrate very clearly what Arthur Suzman refers to as the attempt by the legislature to 'define the indefinable' (Suzman, 1960: 367).

The Population Registration Act

The key to the current classification system lies in the Population Registration Act of 1950, as amended. In its current form, the Act lays down three basic definitions, black, coloured and white, in Section (1). A black (previously Native, Bantu) is 'a person who is, or is generally accepted as, a member of any aboriginal race or tribe of Africa'. The legislature has never been able to define the coloured category, other than negatively. A coloured person is therefore part of a residual category: 'a person who is not a White person or a Black'. Most elaboration, however, has gone into the definition of a white person, which nevertheless remains, as Boberg says with considerable understatement, 'less than crystal clear' (Boberg, 1977: 99). A white person is: 'a person who (a) in appearance obviously is a White person, and who is not generally accepted as a Coloured person; or (b) is generally accepted as a White person and is not in appearance obviously not a White person'.

The definition of a white person then goes on to exclude any person, despite the foregoing, who 'freely and voluntarily admits that he is by descent a Black or Coloured person, unless it is proved that the admission is not based on fact'.

The problems with these definitions will be discussed below, but it is also important to note that the Act has been regularly amended (no fewer than fifteen times between 1956 and 1986) and that various riders have been attached to the definitions to assist in classifying people who do not fit neatly into the preordained categories.

Thus the following clauses have been added to clarify how to classify a white person. In deciding whether a person is 'in appearance obviously a White person', Section 1(2)(a) lays down that 'habits, education, speech and deportment and demeanour in general shall be taken into account'. The question of 'general acceptance' is dealt with in Section 1(2)(c) as follows: 'a person shall not be deemed to be generally accepted as a White person unless he is so accepted . . . at any place where he (i) is ordinarily resident, (ii) is employed or carries on business, (iii) mixes socially or takes part in other activities with other members of the public.' In addition, he must also be accepted as a white person 'in his association with members of his family and any other persons with whom he lives'.

A further modification was added in Section 5(5) of the Act, which stressed the importance of descent over appearance or general acceptance (Girvin, 1987: 6). This section rules that notwithstanding the previous definitions a person shall be classified white if both natural parents were classified as white, and may not be classified white if one natural parent was classified coloured or black. In the same way a person must be classified coloured if both natural parents were classified coloured, or if one parent was classified white and the other coloured or black. And where a person is the child of one black and one coloured parent, his or her classification will follow that of the father.

Section 5(1) of the Act also allows for people classified as coloured or black to be further divided by proclamation into 'ethnic or other groups'. This was done in 1959, and amended and made 'court proof' in 1967 following a Supreme Court finding that the original proclamation was void for vagueness (Boberg, 1977: 99n). The seven sub-groups created for the coloured category were: Cape Coloured, Malay, Griqua, Chinese, Indian, Other Asiatic and Other Coloured. Membership of these sub-groups is to be determined by the classification of the natural father, or by being 'in fact' a member of the group, or by being 'generally accepted' as a member. The definitions of these groups refer to membership of a 'race, class or tribe', and in the case of Indian, Chinese and Asiatics to a 'national home' outside South Africa (Boberg, 1977: 109n).

A farrago of imprecision

The system of classification, then, far from being based solely on physical characteristics, involves a mishmash of indicators, most of which in themselves are highly problematic and contentious. A survey of the legislation already mentioned reveals the following undefined terms: 'race', 'class', 'tribe', and 'ethnic or other group'. In deciding on classification, such loose and undefined phrases as 'in fact is', 'generally accepted as', and 'obviously is', are freely used – leaving it to the courts to decide, what (if anything) they mean. And finally, we should note that – if descent fails – such vague characteristics as 'habits', 'education', 'speech and deportment' and 'demeanour in general' can be taken into account.

There can be few, if any, pieces of legislation in South Africa which are phrased so imprecisely, and in which such a range of problematic criteria is used. But this is of course necessary precisely because the population cannot be fitted neatly into the defined 'population groups'.

Changing classification: the present

It is also possible to change one's classification in South Africa. There exists a Race Classification Board *(sic)*, and the right of appeal to the Supreme Court. The best indication of the problems of classification raised by the legislation is to be found in the cases of people who have been dealt with by this Board. It is beyond the scope of this chapter to detail such cases here, but a series of examples can be found in Boberg (1977: 98–129).

Each year a list is published by parliament which documents the number of people in the preceding year who have changed their classification. The details appear in Table 1 below. In 1986, 1 624 people applied for reclassification, of whom 1 102, or 72 per cent, were successful. The majority of those applying – 79 per cent – were asking for reclassification between the major categories of black, coloured and white; 61 per cent were successful. The rest were seeking to move between the sub-groups of the coloured category, and 91 per cent were successful. It should be noted that the 1986 figures for applicants were considerably in excess of those for the period 1983-5, which ranged from 707 to 908 (Girvin, 1987: 8).

It is also possible for a person to be classified in more than one way at the same time. Boberg explains this as follows: 'Since definitions of racial groups vary from statute to statute, it is possible for a person to be a member of one race for a certain purpose and a member of another race for another purpose' (Boberg, 1977: 127). The main statutes with their own definitions were until recently the Group Areas Act, the Prohibition of Mixed Marriages Act and the Immorality Act. The last two no longer apply to population classification, having been repealed in part or in whole, but the Group Areas Act remains with its own system of classification which 'does not follow or incorporate the classification of the Population Registration Act' (Schoombee, 1985: 78).

Table 1: Reclassifications, 1986

	Applied	Successful	Unsuccessful
White to Cape Coloured	9	8	1
Cape Coloured to White	506	314	192
White to Malay	2	2	–
Malay to White	14	9	5
Indian to White	9	4	5
Chinese to White	7	7	–
Griqua to White	1	1	–
Cape Coloured to Black	40	35	5
Black to Cape Coloured	666	387	279
Cape Coloured to Indian	87	81	6
Indian to Cape Coloured	65	63	2
Cape Coloured to Malay	26	25	1
Malay to Cape Coloured	21	21	–
Malay to Indian	50	43	7
Indian to Malay	61	53	8
Cape Coloured to Griqua	4	4	–
Griqua to Cape Coloured	4	2	2
Griqua to Black	2	2	–
Black to Griqua	18	16	2
Cape Coloured to Chinese	12	10	2
Black to Indian	10	9	1
Black to Malay	2	2	–
Black to Other Asiatic	5	1	4
Indian to Other Coloured	2	2	–
Other Coloured to Indian	1	1	–
Total:	1 624	1 102	522

The Group Areas classification system

The Group Areas Act controls ownership, use and residence of land in terms of a system of population classification. The main categories are black, coloured and white, and again there is provision for the further sub-division of the coloured and black categories. The basic definitions of population classification employed in this legislation are therefore similar to those of the Population Registration Act. But there is a significant difference relating to the issue of where people who are married or cohabit can live, or own property, in the event that they are classified differently. Thus a white partner, male or female, takes the classification of the other partner, whether black or coloured, for the purposes of the Act. In relationships between people classified coloured and black, however, the woman takes the classification of the man.

This aspect of the Group Areas Act recognised and made provision for 'mixed' couples who had been living together prior to the introduction of the Prohibition of Mixed Marriages Act and Immorality Act (which forbade whites from marrying or having sexual relations with people classified differently, and prevented, at least in theory, further occurrence of such 'mixed' couples). The recent repeal of these two Acts therefore does not affect Group Areas legislation in any way.

For Group Areas, therefore, the white group includes 'any person who in appearance obviously is or who is generally accepted as a White person, other than a person who, although in appearance obviously a White person, is generally accepted as a Coloured person', and excludes any white person married to, or living with, a person classified as black or coloured.

The black group includes 'any person who in fact is, or is generally accepted as, a member of an aboriginal race or tribe of Africa'. It includes white men and coloured or white women married to, or living with, black partners. It excludes black women with coloured partners.

The coloured group includes 'any person who is not a member of the White group or of the Black group', and includes white men and black and white women with coloured partners. It excludes coloured women with black partners.

It is clear, then, that with the exception of blacks, classification for the purposes of Group Areas does not depend on descent: 'membership of a group does not, except in the single case of an aboriginal African, depend solely on blood or descent. As a general rule it is a question of habits and mode of life – of acceptance' (Van Reenen, 1962; rev. 1967: 125). Van Reenen refers to the criteria for assessing 'general acceptance' in the courts. These have included accepted use of facilities segregated for a particular group (transport, hotels, restaurants, schools), voter registration, and – in the case of would-be whites – working with or over other white people (Van Reenen, 1962: 122).

It can be seen from this that it is possible to be classified, say, as coloured in terms of the Population Registration Act (by descent, if one of your parents was not white, irrespective of appearance or acceptance) and as white in terms of the Group Areas Act (through appearance and acceptance, irrespective of descent). More simply, you could be classified white in terms of the Population Registration Act but classified coloured or black for the purposes of Group Areas in terms of the classification of your marriage partner.

In addition to these broad classifications, the State President may, by proclamation, 'define any ethnic, linguistic, cultural or other group of persons who are members of the Black group or of the Coloured group' (Section 12.2). He may declare these groups to exist either generally or for particular residential areas. This has in fact taken place for the coloured category. At present the sub-groups created are Indians, Malays and a 'residual' coloured group. The Chinese sub-group became white for the purposes of the Act in 1984 (Schoombee, 1985: 108n). The extent of the proclamation varies – Indians do not 'exist', in terms of the Act, in the Orange Free State, Malays occur only for the purposes of the Schotsche Kloof area of Cape Town, and there is even a sub-sub-group (from the Indian sub-group) of Zanzibari Arabs, for areas in Durban and Pinetown in Natal (Schoombee, 1985: 108n).

The same arguments that were made about the Population Registration Act definitions can be made for Group Areas: the terms are vague ('ethnic, linguistic, cultural or other group', 'race or tribe', 'generally accepted') and the categorisations are arbitrary. This is particularly true for the Group Areas Act, where categorisations can be made to apply to small areas of land.

Finally, it should be pointed out that although the Group Areas Act may be applied to blacks, it has not been used for this purpose – there being much other legislation under which the lives of black people have been controlled. It should be noted, however, in the context of the repeal of influx control regulations, that the Group Areas legislation remains in place and can be applied to blacks.

Black classification, national states and citizenship

It remains to examine the ways in which black people have been further classified in South Africa, particularly in relation to citizenship. The basic official premise on which black people have been subdivided in South Africa is conveniently summarised in the preamble to the Promotion of Black Self-Government Act (46 of 1959) which states unambiguously that: 'the Black peoples of the Union of South Africa do not constitute a homogeneous people, but form separate national units on the basis of language and culture. . . . ' On the basis of this policy a number of groupings were identified, into which all black people in South Africa were compulsorily placed, with these groupings being formally associated with what Robertson (1987: 108) refers to as 'ethno-geographic units' ('homelands', 'national states', 'Bantustans', etc.). In theory each of these geographic units was to be the putative political home of each grouping: Lebowa (North Sotho), Basotho Qwaqwa (South Sotho), Bophuthatswana (Tswana), Venda (Venda), KwaNdebele (Ndebele), Gazankulu (Tsonga), Kangwane (Swazi), KwaZulu (Zulu), and Ciskei and Transkei (Xhosa).

Two points need to be made at the outset about this system. Firstly, the categories created by this legislation do not in fact reflect discrete cultural or linguistic units. While it is true that the African population is not culturally homogeneous, like all populations it defies absolute cultural categorisation. Southern African prehistory was one of intense interaction between people, and such cultural differences as might have existed between populations represented the consequences of isolation and adaptation to different physical environments, rather than absolute cultural divisions. Linguistic boundaries, on the other hand, do exist. But these are recent creations which have resulted from outsiders' (usually missionaries') efforts to codify a continuum of linguistic variation into a number of discrete languages. The contemporary reality of change resulting from the penetration of Christianity, capitalism, and Western medicine and education further underlines the impossibility of subdivisions based on supposedly 'traditional' African cultural differences. At most, such objective cultural differences as might exist between North Sotho and Tswana South Africans are no more significant or absolute than those between South Africans of English and German origins. In this context it is significant to note that for political purposes the former set of differences is judged by the South African government to be of crucial significance, whilst the latter set is not.

Secondly, even if one accepts that such categorisations have some validity, the populations thus defined do not fit neatly with the national states created. For example, 'Xhosas' are formally split between Ciskei and Transkei, despite the absence of any linguistic or cultural grounds for this. At the same time both 'Xhosa' and 'Sotho' may be found in Transkei, although it is officially associated with the Xhosa category. However, although it has not been deemed necessary to create a separate unit for 'Sotho' now resident in Transkei, there has been a relatively recent decision to create a homeland – KwaNdebele – for 'Ndebele' who had been attached to other homelands.

It is clear that the populations in any of the national states are not culturally or linguistically homogeneous (Lye and Murray, 1980: 99–103). This situation is compounded for the urban population where millions of black people of various backgrounds interact, and where linguistic or cultural factors are by no means necessarily seen as of primary importance.

The designation of specific national states, then, is largely a matter of political convenience. There is a need to preserve the official view of the black majority in South Africa as a set of national minorities and to see that no national state becomes too large numerically in comparison with the white population. The classification is also partly determined by the availability of black leadership in certain areas who would be willing to go along with the system.

The embryo national states created by the homelands policy did not contain homogeneous populations. This is abundantly clear from the legislation which attempted to define citizenship of these areas. The National States (formerly Bantu Homelands) Citizenship Act of 1970 conferred compulsory dual citizenship on all black people: South African citizenship (primarily for 'international' purposes) and citizenship of a national state. The latter citizenship was conferred on people by virtue of birth, domicile (the 'normal' criteria for citizenship) or by a set of supremely vague criteria, including speaking any black language or dialect used by the population of a particular area, or being 'identified' or 'associated with any part of such a population by virtue of . . . cultural or racial background' (Section 3).

As the official policy progressed, Transkei, Bophuthatswana, Venda and Ciskei were declared independent of South Africa, and their citizens lost their South African citizenship. Millions of people living outside these territories became instant foreigners, and subject to legislation dealing with and controlling aliens. The definition of citizenship was established in a set of 'Status' Acts – for example the Status of Transkei Act of 1976 – which laid down criteria similar to the legislation already discussed. Citizenship of Transkei, for example (in terms of Schedule B of the above-mentioned Act), was to be by birth, domicile, language, or being 'related to', 'identified with', or 'culturally or otherwise associated with' the Transkei population.

This legislation is, if possible, even more vague than that discussed above. One might ask, for example, what it means to be 'otherwise associated' or 'identified' with a population, or what a 'racial or cultural background' could conceivably mean.

In 1986, in a modification of policy, legislation was introduced to allow the restoration of South African citizenship to certain categories of people permanently resident in South Africa (Rycroft, 1987: 220-4). In terms of control over people, the granting or removing of South African citizenship, rather than ethnic labelling, is now clearly of much more significance for people classified as black.

Conclusion: changing legislation

A study of the legislation which categorises and divides the South African population confirms that South Africans cannot be easily pigeonholed into 'population groups', 'races', 'tribes' or 'cultures'. The population, as it has always done, moves, interacts, and intermarries, and therefore changes and denies rigid classification schemes.

We have shown that the legislation in one sense has of necessity had to be extremely imprecise. In another sense, though, it can be argued that it has been directed at precise ends. This is best illustrated by returning to the Population Registration Act, to examine how it evolved and to suggest certain reasons for this.

It appears from perusal of the various House of Assembly debates on the Population Registration Act and its amendments that the overriding interest of the legislators was to define the white category to the exclusion of others. Firstly, everybody had to be classified. As senior National Party M.P. Mr S. F. Kotze said in 1969, ' . . . we cannot evade our responsibility of determining the race of people in this country . . . ' (Assembly Debates, 17 March 1967, col. 3176). Secondly, the Act was crucial to the system of apartheid. The Minister of the Interior (Mr S. L. Muller) put this quite clearly in 1969: 'I know that on many occasions it is not pleasant to administer this Act, but I also know that it forms the corner-stone of our policy of separate development, and that we have to give effect to it, for the eventual benefit and in the interests of all our various race groups' (Assembly Debates, 12 June 1969, col. 7875).

The debates, however, reflect changing white interests over time. The earliest form of the Act allowed people to be classified white by appearance or by general acceptance. It was not desirable to go into the question of descent. Speaking in 1962, the Minister of the Interior (Mr J. de Klerk) said:

If the community takes into consideration the two factors I have mentioned here, namely acceptance and appearance, then it is not necessary to delve deeply into the question of the person's descent to ascertain whether he has a few drops of non-white blood in his veins, dating back to the second or third, or perhaps even an earlier generation. That is not necessary, neither was it ever the intention of the Act. (Assembly Debates, 26 April 1962, col. 4436)

It would appear to have been necessary *not* to have included descent as a critical factor in the early phase of the system, for this would have put the classification of many whites at risk. The fact that many whites were of mixed descent (see Heese, 1984) was accepted tacitly by the Minister, and more openly by others. As Mr Japie Basson M.P. said in parliament in 1967, amid interjections, 'If people are to be classified on the basis of descent, there are very few people in this House who would be classified as whites' (Assembly Debates, 20 March 1967, col. 3268).

During the 1950s and early 1960s, then, the main object of the exercise was for the 'white' population to be classified and consolidated on a broad basis. With this initial task completed, it would then seem, as the 1967 debates show, that the next stage was to restrict further entry to white ranks. By this time, presumably, most 'generally accepted' whites had been thus classified. In the debates in 1962 and 1967, the legislators focused on 'coloured' people being classified as white on the basis of acceptance. The Minister of the Interior (Mr P. M. K. Le Roux) argued in 1967: 'This provision was interpreted in such a way that a person who was a full-blooded non-white person could be classified as a white person in terms of that definition if he could prove that the community accepted him as such' (Assembly Debates, 17 March 1967, col. 3172). Parliamentarians cited examples of people who were obviously not white in appearance, or by descent, who were reclassified simply by getting whites to testify that they were generally accepted as white. Recognising this as a problem, the Minister said: 'there are whites in our society at the present time who are capable of doing anything [providing guarantees of acceptance of others] in their attempts to eliminate the colour bar' and introduced an amendment to the Act to 'put an end to creeping integration' (Assembly Debates, 17 March 1967, col. 3175-6).

The amendment 'closed the door' by adding the descent rule (Section 5 of the Population Registration Act, referred to above). This was not, of course, descent in any proper sense, but simply referred to the classification of parents. People previously classified white (based on appearance and/or acceptance and irrespective of descent) would have their children classified the same way; people not classified white could no longer produce children (irrespective of appearance or acceptance) who could be classified white.

At the same time, the retention of the definitions in the Group Areas Act served to maintain the 'purity' of white group areas after the repeal of the Immorality and Mixed Marriages Acts, as whites marrying people of another classification would lose the right to live in white areas.

Much confusion has been apparent: the legislators have changed their minds (as when Chinese became white for Group Areas purposes, or when Japanese became 'honorary whites' in the 1960s) and their labels (as when Natives became Bantu and then blacks). Despite this one can see that the legislation has been directed clearly at dominant interests. The legislation remains a corner-stone of the apartheid system. And one should also note that while the crude discrimination based on the distinctions of the Population Registration Act is being modified – as in the case of the abolition of influx control measures – in some important ways it is being replaced by controls over citizenship which have much the same effect. The new aliens, for example, have even fewer rights than when they were citizens subject to influx control.

I return then to the point made at the beginning, that the system does not exist simply for the purposes of classification in itself. The classification of the population is neither based simply on physical features of race, nor inspired simply by racist assumptions of innate difference and inferiority. The system exists to divide and control in terms of access to political rights and economic resources and thereby to maintain white power and privilege.

8 Two worlds in one country: 'First world' and 'third world' in South Africa
JOHN SHARP

Description and politics

One often hears the argument that South Africa is a combination of the so-called 'first world' and 'third world'. Many people use these labels with descriptive intent, because they seem to capture the contrast between the sophistication of the country's metropolitan areas and their inhabitants, and the apparent backwardness and simplicity of its isolated rural regions, particularly the so-called 'homelands'. The terms describe things that people see and experience: on the one hand the high-rise buildings, hi-tech industries, high-speed freeways and efficient services of the cities, and on the other the rudimentary dwellings, pitted roads, and inefficient bureaucracies of the 'homelands'.

'First world' and 'third world' are not, however, neutral or simply descriptive terms. Their use has political implications, in large measure because the way they are used always implies a certain relationship between the regions and the segments of the population thus designated. This underlying presumption, which specifies the way in which the two 'worlds' came to be as they are, is frequently opaque to many who use the terms. People as a result end up saying a great deal more than they mean when they use 'first world' and 'third world' as a convenient, descriptive shorthand.

The purpose of this chapter is to examine the political implications of the various uses of the 'first world–third world' terminology. It begins with a case study, which details the rise to prominence of the terminology in South Africa and its specific use by the South African Broadcasting Corporation (SABC). This section shows that the terms have been appropriated from an international discourse about problems of world-wide socio-economic development, and discusses the specific use to which they are put in the local context in official and semi-official discourse. The second part of the paper deals in more general terms with shifts in the discourse of domination in South Africa over time; it shows that the relatively recent introduction of the 'first world–third world' metaphor to this country bears certain parallels to an earlier attempt to 'modernise' the ideological justification for white rule.

The final section argues that there is more than one way to conceptualise the relationship between 'first' and 'third worlds'. The dominant usage sees their co-existence as accidental; an alternative view makes the underdevelopment of the 'third world' a consequence of the development of the 'first'. The alternative view, it is argued, makes better historical sense, in that it involves a more accurate depiction of the terms of the relationship over time. On the other hand, however, it too is a simplification of complex social processes, and it can be used, and certainly has been used, to the detriment of the people whose misfortune it purports to explain.

The rise of the 'first world–third world' paradigm in South Africa

There are various constraints on reform in South Africa. . . . The Deputy Director General of Health and Population Development, Dr G. S. Watermeyer, stated that the transition from tribalism to Western-style democracy is a historical process that demands a historical time scale. . . . It requires a critical mass of knowledge and skills. . . . In South Africa these must be drawn from the relatively small First World component of the population. Individually and collectively they make up the dynamo that keeps the country going. (SABC Comment, 11 March 1987)

The free enterprise system has proved itself to be by far the more effective generator of wealth. But in a country in which a large group is barely emerging from a traditional culture of collectivism, and moreover feels itself to be disadvantaged, the apparent panaceas offered by socialism are a powerful attraction. South Africa is such a country in which First and Third World co-exist, and it is not surprising that many black people tend to favour socialism above free enterprise. (SABC Comment, 10 June 1986)

The SABC's 'Comment' programme is far from being the only user of 'first world–third world' terminology in South Africa. It is very widely employed in the other media, including respected journals such as *Financial Mail* and *Finansies en Tegniek*, in academic circles, and in popular discourse.

The 'Comment' programme is, however, a useful source for the purpose of the present discussion. This is not simply for the obvious reason that it has an influential role in shaping public opinion, but also because its daily transmission provides a continuous flow of opinion and interpretation, which can be examined for evidence of shifts in dominant concerns and forms of expression over time. The programme is also disarmingly frank about the reasons for the use of different forms of expression.

A rapid escalation in the use of the 'first world–third world' terminology can be dated with some precision in the sequence of 'Comment' programmes. Although there were isolated instances of their use in earlier years, the terms have come increasingly into vogue since 1983. Before then the favoured terms for describing diversity within South Africa were 'ethnic group' and 'nation', and the programme frequently invoked the 'ethnic factor' as sole cause for internal strife not merely in South Africa itself, but also in other states such as Cyprus, India and Sri Lanka. The purpose of these forays into the analysis of conflict in other areas was clear: the ostensible universality of ethnic loyalties and divisions justified their institution-alised enforcement in South Africa.

1983 marked a transitional year in the programme's forms of expression. On the one hand, and in earlier idiom, it still doggedly maintained that to understand South Africa, one 'must recognise the existence of a diversity of Black nations – nations which have a primary allegiance to their own people, language, culture and political aspirations' (SABC Comment, 10 October 1983).

On the other hand, and as harbinger of arguments to come, it announced: 'A government so exclusively preoccupied with ethnicity that its blind response is a determination to entrench the power of the group it represents at the expense of the others, is destined . . . for authoritarianism, political strife and economic stagnation' (SABC Comment, 28 July 1983).

After 1983 'ethnicity' was handled with greater circumspection than had hitherto been the case. It remained an important factor in the SABC's analysis of South African 'realities', but was also subordi-nated, particularly in references to Africans outside the 'national states', to a vision of a 'third world' population in the process of developing modern values. The reason for this shift in emphasis was explained in the programme itself:

In earlier years it was believed that the national states could be developed at a rate that would turn them into true heartlands – not only cultural but economic and political – of South Africa's Black nations. However, in spite of the most strenuous efforts of the state . . . that ideal has proved impossible of attainment. (SABC Comment, 23 April 1985)

The 1985 quotation is taken from a programme devoted to the topic of 'Black Citizenship', which sought to explain the government's decision to return South African nationality to selected categories of the citizens of Transkei, Bophuthatswana, Venda and Ciskei, the four 'independent homelands'. This decision was part of a broader process of 'reform' in which the government admitted that the political aspirations of Africans in 'white' South Africa could not be fully met within the confines of ethnic, 'homeland' structures. This admission was manifest in the appointment of a special cabinet committee 'to investigate the political role of the urban African', and in some of the provisions of the Black Local Authorities Act of 1982 (SAIRR, 1983: 252–3). The committee was appointed, and the Act came into effect, in 1983. This was precisely the time at which the SABC modified its earlier insistence on the absolute salience of ethnic divisions.

The 'first world–third world' terminology provided a splendid medium by which to represent some of the shifts and continuities of the politics of 'reform'. Identification of the African population as the third world 'sector' of South Africa did not preclude its disaggregation into 'ethnic' components in contexts where this was still deemed necessary. On the other hand, the third world designation provided a means of aggregating the African population in other contexts, without in any way implying that a lesser emphasis on ethnic differentiation necessarily involved a relaxation of the boundaries maintained between black and white.

If political participation by urban Africans could not be channelled into 'homeland' structures, there was little point in maintaining the fiction of fundamental ethnic diversity in planning a dispensation for them. On the other hand, identifying them as part of a 'third world' sector within South Africa justified their continued separation from the people who made up the 'first world'. In this sense, of course, 'first' and 'third worlds' were simply new euphemisms for the old racial categories of white and black, but they possessed the advantage of widespread respectability. The language of 'race' has long been discredited, but 'first world–third world' terminology is part of current international discourse about problems of development.

Another advantage of the new terminology is its flexibility, since there is no intrinsic reason why 'first world' and 'third world' have to be defined in 'racial' or 'ethnic' terms at all. On the contrary, it can be argued that people in the 'third world' are merely undeveloped or underdeveloped, and that appropriate assistance and motivation can change their situation. In this view 'first world' status is the highest step in a meritocracy, a goal which the most able members of the 'third world' sector may ultimately achieve. The power of the 'first world–third world' terminology, and its attractiveness to official opinion-makers, lie precisely in its ability to accommodate a range of political viewpoints, from the avowedly racist to the ostensibly reformist. It can, therefore, be presented and assimilated as *common* sense.

These arguments about the functions of the new terminology explain only that some modification to the established language of ethnic diversity was necessary, to accommodate the state's vision of reform. They do not explain the specific appeal of 'first world' and 'third world' in this context. It appears, however, that the rise of this particular discourse was closely linked to the founding of the Development Bank of Southern Africa (DBSA), and to the prestige accorded its operations and analysis of the South African situation. The DBSA was established in 1983, and took over many of the functions performed by the Corporation for Economic Development (formerly the Bantu Investment Corporation) (SAIRR, 1983: 368–71).

The latter body had acquired a suspect reputation, even in the eyes of 'homeland' leaders and aspirant entrepreneurs, for its willingness to subordinate the requirements of economic development to precepts of Verwoerdian apartheid. Part of the rationale for the establishment of the DBSA was, therefore, to 'depoliticise' development in the interests of 'reform', and the Bank has accordingly tried to project an image of neutrality, professionalism and technical competence.

In pursuit of a technicist image, the DBSA has modelled itself on the World Bank (the International Bank for Reconstruction and Development), and has taken over the latter's favoured discourse about the problems of international development and their causes and resolution. Here one refers not simply to the 'first world–third world' terminology, but also to the World Bank's characteristic concern, since the 1970s, to refurbish an outmoded concentration on the criterion of overall national economic growth with alternative strategies of 'growth with redistribution' and 'the satisfaction of basic needs'. All of these themes have enjoyed high prominence in the DBSA's journal *Development Southern Africa*. The DBSA can therefore claim a respected precedent for its central preoccupations and modes of expressing them. The vision of reform which it and the South African government espouse can be seen then as a local variant of an extensive international endeavour to bring development to 'less developed' countries and people.

In some ways, of course, this is precisely what it is. Williams (1981) has shown that the World Bank's activities are animated by a view that people in 'third world' countries are incapable of their own development, and that this process must therefore be instigated and guided by the 'first world' and its development agencies. 'Third world' peasants 'are more or less rational and efficient within their traditional environment, which is seen as static, but when faced with new opportunities are conservative, traditionalist and unable to respond rationally' (Heyer, Roberts and Williams, 1981: 8; see also World Bank, 1975).

This inability to adapt to social change is taken to be particularly acute in countries, such as those in Latin America, which incorporate great diversity in levels of development. In Latin America millions of poor people stream from the countryside to the modern cities, and congregate in notorious urban slums. As Perlman (1976) has shown, the common view, held by both Latin American governments and international development agencies, has long been that the slum-dwellers bring 'traditional', rural values with them to town; consequently they are socially, culturally and economically marginal to, and parasitic upon, the progressive, urban environment.

This is exactly the import of the first quotation from the SABC (above), which argued that people in the 'third world' sector of South

Africa are still mired in 'tradition' and 'tribalism', regardless of whether they are in the 'homelands' or the cities. They therefore need the 'first world sector' to act as 'the dynamo that keeps the country going'. Both the international argument and its local version ignore the fact that top-down programmes for economic or political development fail principally because they are misconceived by their planners rather than because the people at whom they are directed cannot understand their advertised benefits. They also ignore the findings of researchers such as Perlman, who demonstrated that Latin American slum-dwellers are far from marginal to the urban environment. In fact, she argued, they are closely integrated into it, but on such menial terms that they can never escape their poverty. Theirs is 'a marginality of exclusion and exploitation rather than one of low motivation and parochialism' (1976: 161).

There is, says Williams, a studied avoidance of these conclusions by agencies such as the World Bank. Despite ostensible revisions to its programmes over the years, the World Bank remains firmly attached to the vision of a static 'third world' which is unable to help itself, and a dynamic 'first world' which, by virtue of its own state of development, has both a duty and a right to tell the other segment of humanity what is good for it. This conclusion is represented in the second quotation from the SABC: the 'first world' segment of South Africa is living proof of the superiority of the capitalist system; if people in the 'third world' sector reject free enterprise, this must be a delusion brought on by their ignorance and helplessness. The fact that they have experience of a century of exploitation under a system of racial capitalism, involving innumerable constraints on their economic, political and cultural ambitions, is curtly explained away.

The purpose of this thinking, and indeed of the whole conceptual division of the world, or South Africa, into exclusive segments – one dynamic and the other static – is to justify control of the one by the other. As Williams says, these views inform attempts by the World Bank, via its development assistance, to secure a greater involvement by 'third world' people in the markets and other institutions controlled by the 'first', and to undermine their capacity to resist their co-optation.

The point which is missed by those who use the 'first world–third world' terminology without due reflection, is that the descriptive content of the two segments is highly malleable and not particularly important. It does not matter whether one conceives the 'third world' within South Africa in racial, ethnic or meritocratic terms. The key issue is that by using the terms after the fashion prescribed in official and SABC usage, one lends support to their idea of the nature of the relationship between the two 'worlds'.

The changing discourse of domination

The rapid rise of the 'first world–third world' paradigm suggests that official perception of South African 'realities' is undergoing a certain modification, with one set of ideas about the essential constitution of the society in process of being supplemented with, although not wholly replaced by, another.

The current modification to the discourse of domination is not without precedent. In an earlier period, references to 'race' in official parlance were partially supplanted by the language of 'cultures' and 'ethnicity'. In the first half of this century South Africa's population was seen to comprise different 'races'; thereafter, for the next thirty years, greater emphasis was laid on cultural differences and 'ethnicity' as factors responsible for diversity in the country's population, particularly the African population (Thompson, 1985). In the 1980s, however, some of this former diversity is being subsumed within a dualist paradigm, which sees the main divide between a developed sector of the population and an undeveloped and undifferentiated one.

These shifts in the discourse of domination are not random events. In the case of the first switch, the term 'race' fell into international disfavour in the aftermath of the Second World War, because it had been used in Nazi Germany to justify the persecution of Jews and other minorities. In South Africa it was partially supplanted by a term which had widespread respectability. To have maintained the argument that South Africa's social problems resulted solely from the co-existence of different 'races' would have contributed to the country's growing isolation, given a post-war world which was keen to demonstrate that 'race' had no social implications. Adopting the language of 'ethnicity', on the other hand, was an argument that South Africa's internal problems were a local variant of a world-wide dilemma: in the era of expanding mass communications and enhanced geographical mobility, the barriers supposedly resulting from fundamental cultural differences were a topic of major international concern. Much interest was also shown, in the 1950s and 1960s, in the problems of nation-building in colonial and post-colonial states that incorporated diverse 'cultures' and 'ethnic groups' within their boundaries (Geertz, 1963; Cohen and Middleton, 1971).

It is not necessary to suppose that there was a general conspiracy to replace 'race' with 'ethnicity' in South Africa in an attempt to secure international understanding for the unfolding system of apartheid. In selected instances the shift was, undoubtedly, deliberate and instrumental, undertaken with a view to selling an otherwise unpalatable policy. Most people, however, adopted the new terminology because it seemed to them to be self-evidently true. 'Ethnicity' avoided the pitfalls and opprobrium associated with 'race', but allowed people to maintain the commonsense perception that South Africa's population comprised a series of disparate groups. The new revelation was simply that the source of the social disparities lay in cultural rather than physical differences.

In the thirty years in which 'ethnicity' spearheaded the South African discourse of domination, the initial argument about the salience of primordial cultural differences has been widely questioned in the international debate. Ethnicity is no longer seen as a simple matter of unchangeable and unbridgeable cultural differences, and it is recognised that people do not form groups simply because they possess common cultures. On the contrary, it is now widely realised that ethnicity is a political phenomenon, that ethnic groups are formed to unite people from different classes for political purposes, and that cultural differences themselves are as much a result as a cause of processes of political competition.

Recent thinking on ethnicity has, therefore, undermined some of its usefulness as a justification for apartheid policies, because the latter rely heavily on the earlier assumptions about its primordial character. The argument that cultural differences are not immutable, and that ethnic groups are social constructions rather than natural units into which humanity is divided, serves to expose the extent to which the South African government has forced a system of classification and grouping onto the country's inhabitants. It has become clear that it is coercion, rather than voluntary association, which sustains the officially demarcated 'ethnic groups' within South Africa.

The most recent shift in the discourse of domination rehearses the earlier switch from 'race' to 'ethnicity' in several ways. In the first place, adoption of the 'first world–third world' terminology in official discourse is a new search for international legitimacy, another attempt to link South Africa's internal problems to issues of world-wide concern. Secondly, like 'ethnicity' before it, the new terminology appeals to the commonsense understanding of South African diversity. In many ways, however, the prolonged discussion of 'ethnicity' since the 1950s has rendered the concept too difficult and too vague to encompass the apparently simple contrasts of everyday experience.

Hence the rapidity with which the 'first world–third world' terminology has proliferated in the public media and consciousness in South Africa. It offers a way out of the growing doubts which beset the older language of domination, makes concession to international opprobrium directed at the enforced 'ethnicity' of apartheid, but still reaffirms, in new and supposedly respectable terms, the fundamental division of the South African population along lines which have little or nothing to do with the ways in which the majority of people have actually experienced the country's social order.

Finally, the terminology is useful as a means to represent and explain recent policy changes within South Africa. 'Race' was the language of segregation, and 'ethnicity' the language of apartheid; 'first world–third world' is, as shown above, a suitable discourse for the politics of 'reform'.

The dangers of 'underdevelopment'

The dominant vision of a benign 'first world' carrying the benefits of progress to a benighted 'third world' has long been challenged in international debate. One of the most powerful alternative arguments has simply inverted the orthodox depiction of the 'first world–third world' relationship, claiming that the developed countries have achieved their current standing by means of long-term and ruthless exploitation of the rest of the world. In this argument, poverty and backwardness are not original conditions, but disabilities which have been visited on the 'third world' by the terms of its historical relationship with the 'first'. The characteristic term used to express this interpretation of the relationship is 'underdevelopment' (Frank, 1971; Leys, 1975; Palmer and Parsons, 1977).

The theory of underdevelopment has successfully challenged many of the cherished conceits of the orthodox position, and has stimulated a number of important insights which can readily be applied to South African history. For example, this perspective has been used to reveal the fictional nature of the customary depiction of the Bushmen or San in the Kalahari as members of a traditional society which has long been isolated from the modern world (Gordon, 1985). The evidence actually points to the opposite conclusion, namely that the so-called Bushmen were once spread over the whole of southern Africa, that they were virtually exterminated in the process of colonisation of the subcontinent, and that the people in the Kalahari today are refugees from this devastation. They survived in the desert because the colonial pastoralists could not make use of this environment; and their way of life, which has been romanticised by such respected authors as Van der Post, is an adaptation to these harsh conditions, rather than a timeless re-creation of an untouched past.

In similar vein, it has been shown that poverty in South Africa's 'homeland' areas is a product of their inhabitants' involvement in the development of the capitalist system since the late nineteenth century (Bundy, 1979). It is the outcome of measures such as the Land Act of 1913, the institutionalisation of labour migration, and policies of mass relocation, all of which are responsible for the underdevelopment of the 'homelands'. The counter-assertion, that poverty is an original condition in these areas, is a wilful denial of the weight of this empirical evidence.

The 'underdevelopment' thesis has brought many positive results, not the least of which is that it has restored a measure of dignity to the downtrodden in farflung places. Study after study in different parts of the world has shown not merely that they were always part of mainstream historical development, but also that their vital role in progress has been systematically denied to them as part of the subjugation of the 'third world' by the 'first' (Wolf, 1982). It is the people in those parts of the world which have been defined as 'backward', as having always been 'outside of progress', who have, in fact, learnt the basic skills of mining, commercial agriculture, and export manufacturing; and it is by their rapid acquisition of these skills and by their vast expenditure of effort that the wealth has been generated to sustain progress elsewhere.

In South Africa, the African population has played an essential role in the genesis of a modern industrial society: they have acquired not merely technical skills, but also those of communication. Many Africans can speak both English and Afrikaans, as well as several indigenous languages, with facility, whereas a large number of whites struggle in anything other than their natal tongue. In this crucial respect, then, it is the whites, rather than the Africans, who have evinced a narrow, 'traditionalist' outlook: the former have, in Perlman's words, been 'isolated by their own "urbane" provincialism' (1976: 137).

The major weakness of the theory of underdevelopment is, however, that it endorses the notion of the two 'worlds' (Palma, 1981). It is a reversal of the terms of the orthodox argument, rather than a complete challenge to its basis. It preserves the dualist simplification of the dominant discourse, the sense of 'us' and 'them' which lies at the root of the discourse's capacity to mislead the unwary. At a popular level, it redefines who 'we' and 'they' are, so that the 'them' in the one view becomes the 'us' in the other.

But the problem is that neither 'world' contains an undifferentiated 'us' or a uniform 'them'. *The* 'third world' comprises a vast array of different countries, from the oil-rich states of the Middle East to the destitute countries of the Sahel. The population within these countries is also differentiated with respect to their access to resources, wealth and power: a Saudi sheik is different not merely from a rural peasant in Burkina Faso, but also from the vast majority of his own country's inhabitants, who are forced to expend their labour in various ways to provide the surplus which maintains his position. In both 'first' and 'third' worlds there are many gradations of wealth, prestige, status and power. Therefore all claims to speak on behalf of one or other of these 'worlds' as a whole are suspect.

This does not deter some leaders from doing so; nor, indeed, does it deprive their efforts of all credibility. Libya's Qadhafi is an apposite example of a ruler who maintains his domestic position by means which are anything but democratic, but is widely seen as a champion of various 'third world' causes. The fact that his claims in this regard do considerable violence to the diversity of interests in the 'third world' in general is often ignored. Worsley (1984) explains why this should be so, suggesting that the idea of '*the* third world', and its appeal as a device to present a façade of unity between repressive rulers and those whom they command, are a reaction to the indignities inflicted by the glorification of the 'first world' by people in the developed countries. But, as he insists, in the final analysis this reaction cannot be seen as anything other than a further assault on ordinary people's freedom.

The 'third world' future

One use of the 'first world–third world' terminology in South Africa is clearly intended to glorify the 'first world segment' of the society, presenting it as 'the dynamo which keeps the country going' in spite of the dead weight of the other sector. There is considerable danger, as Worsley suggests, that this conceit will, in due course, simply beget its opposite, as reaction to it. In some senses this process has already begun in South Africa: one sees 'homeland' leaders advertising their concern for the impoverished masses over whom they preside by claiming to share their 'third world' plight with them. Given the fact that these leaders are well rewarded for their loyalty to Pretoria, live in considerable luxury, and have ample opportunity for accumulating personal wealth, these claims to a kinship of experience with the poor are quite without substance.

If one could be certain that the use of these rhetorical devices was limited to the leaders whom the present South African government nurtures and supports, there would be little cause for long-term concern. But ways of thinking about the constitution of society and the nature of political authority in it become deeply ingrained with the passage of time. Even in post-revolutionary situations, the new discourse about the nature of society may owe a great deal to the vision it replaces. It is for this reason, as well as for the others mentioned above, that one contemplates the current proliferation of the 'first world–third world' terminology in South Africa with considerable disquiet.

9 Whose development? The politics of development and the development of politics in South Africa
AT FISCHER

This chapter opens with a case-study of a development project in the Mhala district of Gazankulu, the 'homeland' for Tsonga-speakers in the eastern Transvaal. The purpose of this case-study is to illustrate the discrepancy between the conventional rhetoric of 'development' and the actual consequences of its implementation. This rhetoric serves, as the chapter argues, to shield not simply the general public, but also the development agencies and experts involved from recognising the consequences of their actions.

Thereafter the chapter proceeds to inquire into the historical reasons for the present situation in Gazankulu, by examining the relationship between the planning and practice of 'development' on the one hand, and changes in the political order in South Africa in the twentieth century on the other. It also deals with the more general issue of the similarities and differences between development policies and practices in South Africa and the rest of the world.

Development and land use in Gazankulu:
a case study in Mhala district

Gazankulu was created as a 'homeland' for Tsonga-speaking people between 1969, when the Machangana Territorial Authority was established, and 1973, when self-government was granted by South Africa. Gazankulu is composed of four administrative districts, consisting of four geographically dispersed areas; Mhala is the southernmost district.

Seville is the name of a small settlement in Mhala district. It is a former white-owned farm taken over by the South African Development Trust in the 1960s; and even in the 1980s, almost all the families living on it had been tenants of the previous owner. During the period of labour tenancy their homesteads had been dispersed and their fields scattered over suitable land within the bounds of the farm. When the Trust took over the land it was planned according to 'betterment' principles. This meant that the people were relocated into a central village, and separate arable and grazing lands were demarcated by officials. The farm was large enough (about 1 600 hectares) for each household to secure both arable and grazing land, and people also had access to other resources (such as fuel and building materials) of the land.

There was a further major development intervention in Seville in the 1970s. It is the aims and results of this project that concern us directly. In 1971 Seville was chosen as the site of a cattle-improvement scheme for the Tribal Authority area in which it is situated. Two hundred hectares of land were fenced in, a predator-proof cattle kraal was erected, and certain livestock-owners in the 'tribal' area were invited to join the scheme. In 1979 the scheme was extended to approximately a thousand hectares and divided into several camps.

In 1984, when the present author was working in Seville, the members of the scheme had free access to a very expensive infrastructure, preferential marketing facilities, registered stud bulls, and the labour of workers on the payroll of the Department of Agriculture. The scheme was soundly managed by (white) officials of this Department; these individuals were also highly skilled in the technical aspects of cattle farming, and their commitment to the task of livestock improvement was abundantly apparent. The members could not have hoped for a better scheme, particularly since they themselves were required to make relatively little contribution to its operation.

The officials were motivated by a number of perceptions about the area in which they worked. They were genuinely concerned about the poverty of the people of Seville and the rest of the Tribal Authority area. They argued that a major cause of poverty was the incorrect and inefficient use of land in the area, and were convinced that the scheme which they tended so diligently was making a signal contribution to improving the situation.

The people of Seville, however, had many reservations about the scheme. In 1979 it was determined that membership of the cattle scheme was to be restricted to 20 members only. Moreover, only those people in the 'tribal' area who owned more than six head of cattle, certified free from brucellosis and meeting strict criteria of 'functional effectiveness', were permitted to apply for membership. These qualifications effectively excluded 99 per cent of the district's inhabitants. In fact, in 1984, because of these strict requirements (and possibly also because of general scepticism about 'development'), the scheme had only 14 members. Between 1979 and 1984, over half of the 120 head of cattle on the scheme belonged, indeed, to one man. This man was the only member of the scheme who was resident in Seville itself and he also owned more than half of the stock which were not part of the scheme. People in Seville pointed out that many members were wealthy even before they joined the scheme. For example, three were civil servants, one was a shopkeeper, and one owned a furniture factory.

The officials who managed the scheme were unperturbed by the notion that their activities disrupted a whole community's subsistence agriculture for the sake of a few wealthy individuals, who, one could plausibly argue, needed no 'development' at all. They countered any such suggestion with the argument that the scheme encouraged the commercial use of land, and was therefore in the interests of Gazankulu as a whole. They also insisted that the scheme would have a demonstration effect, inasmuch as other stockowners in the vicinity would recognise the advantages of scientific management and breeding and would seek to emulate them.

Both of these arguments seem to be highly questionable. How, in the first place, could the officials believe that livestock owners who were desperately poor would copy an innovation which clearly required extensive capital inputs on a continual basis? Secondly, how was it possible for officials to insist that a scheme which deprived ordinary people in Seville of much of their land was good for 'development' in Gazankulu 'as a whole'? What was the nature of the 'whole' to which they referred, and what does 'development' mean in this context?

It cannot be said that Seville's problems were uniformly replicated in the rest of Gazankulu or in other homelands, but they certainly were, and are, not unique. One development project after another in the South African homelands follows broadly the same pattern, and the questions posed above have, therefore, a general relevance.

The meaning of development

At first sight the concept 'development' may appear to be relatively straightforward: according to the *Oxford English Dictionary*, it denotes 'progress' and the idea of 'growth by gradual stages from within'.

In contemporary international usage, however, 'development' refers to relationships between the affluent, 'first world' nations of the northern hemisphere which are generally taken to be 'developed', and the poor nations in the 'third world' which are regarded as 'underdeveloped' (Mair, 1984: 1).

After the Second World War, 'first world' nations competed for the 'loyalties of the emerging nations as well as for their raw materials and markets'. In the process, their governments provided aid and expertise for the 'upliftment', 'modernisation' and 'development' of the poor 'third world' (Robertson, 1984: 35). In the poor nations of Africa, Asia and Latin America, moreover, 'building the state and planning development' became major priorities of many of the regimes which assumed power after decolonisation. Governments have therefore been the major agents in relations between 'aid-giving' and 'aid-receiving' countries. Thus, in its contemporary use, 'development' invariably refers to actions by, and relationships between, states.

During the latter part of this century state-planned (or -approved) intervention in the lives of the poor has become a world-wide phenomenon (Robertson, 1984: 2). There is, however, no natural or given correspondence between the basic meaning of 'development' and the practices institutionalised by states which attempt, ostensibly, to combat poverty and inequality. State interventions have very often not improved the position of the underprivileged; as a matter of fact the positive connotation of the concept 'development' is often employed to provide 'justification for many self-interested actions' (Mair, 1984: 2). This discrepancy clearly indicates that 'development' is at times an abused concept.

Planned development, instigated by the state, was introduced to the black rural areas of South Africa at least as far back as the last decades of the nineteenth century, when the Glen Grey Act was passed in the Cape Colony. It was however not until the reserves were created by the 1913 Land Act and an Agricultural Division was established in the then Department of Native Affairs in 1929, that planned intervention was introduced on a wide scale. Since then, however, development of this kind has become an increasing preoccupation of the South African state.

The term 'development' was first used in the 1930s by the Department of Native Affairs to describe its activities in the reserves. Since then, and particularly in the second half of the century, it has gained much greater prominence. The sequence of names given to this department after 1961 (Bantu Administration; Bantu Administration and Development; Cooperation and Development; and, at present, Development Aid) bears witness to this growing importance. Moreover, in view of the fact that implementing the state's policies towards Africans has been the principal responsibility of this Department, these renamings suggest that 'development' became over time the major instrument for justifying the policies officially.

'Development' world-wide and in South Africa: similarities and differences

Development that is initiated by the state, centrally planned, and dominated by state ideology, is by no means peculiar to South Africa (Robertson, 1984: 97–8). Indeed, the development to which the black population of South Africa has been subjected since the 1930s shares several structural and procedural similarities with development elsewhere.

Since development in any country is often determined by the interests of the state, it is frequently an important mechanism by which the state attempts to exert control over its people (Robertson,

1984: 154). For this reason, 'development' has invariably created conflict between state and people.

In South Africa the state has long used development to extend control over the rural African population. The nature of power relations in South Africa, and the widespread support which segregation and later apartheid were accorded by the (white) South African electorate, allowed the state to proceed with unusual determination to implement its racial policies through development programmes. These have involved massive interventions, including the large-scale relocation of people. Such interventions met with widespread rural resistance, particularly in the 1950s and 1960s, as understandable reaction to centrally planned development which demonstrated extreme disregard for the people who fell victim to its implementation (Beinart, 1984: 80–1). Thus far, however, the power of the state has rendered this resistance largely ineffective.

In the global context, the notion that there is a developed 'first world' and a 'third world' in need of development justifies the actions of powerful and rich nations to bring about 'self-sustained growth' in the poor nations and 'improve the quality of life' or provide for the 'basic needs' of the world's poor. In South Africa this dualist interpretation is used to characterise socio-economic realities *within* a single country, and supplies the basic premise for development interventions by the state.

It is widely assumed that, within South Africa, there exist alongside each other an advanced, modern, industrialised 'first world', dominated by the white section of the society, and an undeveloped, tradition-bound 'third world' centred mainly in the areas for exclusive African occupation. As elsewhere, this dualism provides a pretext for external intervention in the 'third world', in order to overcome the developmental 'obstacle' of traditional culture. The task of the external agents is to supply know-how and expertise to this end. The idea of 'traditional culture' has been, as we show below, crucially important as a justification for planned development in South Africa.

South Africa has followed the rest of the world in the multiplication of experts who are involved in development: at present there are agriculturalists, agricultural economists, economists, development specialists, urban and regional planners, social workers and constitutional experts, all involved in the state departments or state-mobilised institutions which deal in 'development'. These departments and bodies have become a burgeoning industry and a formidable employer.

Since its early days, development in South Africa has appropriated international development discourse and practices with ease (Beinart, 1984; Sharp, 1985a: 137). But development in South Africa also deviates fundamentally from international and regional processes. This uniqueness relates to the specific, 'racial' character of the ideology that has moulded development in South Africa. However, development in this country has not only been determined by the ideologies and policies of the state; it has itself been a major instrument in realising the racial policies of successive South African governments.

Because of this merging of development with the political interests of the state, *'selfstandigheid'* (self-sufficiency) – the achievement of relative political and economic independence by the African areas within the country – has emerged as the overriding goal of development in South Africa. This goal is not entirely different from that which former colonial powers set for their African colonies as they prepared to 'scramble from Africa'. But *'selfstandigheid'* has a distinct South African quality. It is conceived in ethnic terms; and according to official thinking it can only be achieved by means of the separate development of 'ethnic units'. The separate development of ethnic entities follows directly from the 'assumption that South Africa's population can be neatly divided into discrete categories differentiated along lines of culture' (Sharp, 1985a: 135).

'Selfstandigheid' of ethnic units as the main development goal also accounts for an important aspect of planned and directed development in South Africa. Since the 1950s development has not only referred to economic issues, but also to the constitutional interventions which eventually resulted in the creation of ten 'ethnic national' entities in the areas demarcated for Africans by the 1913 and 1936 Land Acts.

Why and how has 'ethnic nationalism' become the dominant framework for development in South Africa? What are the wider goals such 'development' is intended to realise?

The development of politics and the politics of development in South Africa

Development in South Africa has always been tied up with the 'native problem'. This is true both for the earliest, piecemeal interventions by the state to control black farming, and for the present-day comprehensive interventions which aim at restructuring not simply African agriculture, but also the entire socio-economic and political life of the African population.

There has been a remarkable continuity in the way in which fundamental concerns of the white population regarding Africans have been expressed in political rhetoric throughout this century. At the same time, the precise details and direction of development policy have been closely related to changing circumstances in the countryside and the changing needs of the South African economy as a whole.

Between 1870 and 1930 South Africa was a predominantly agrarian society. White settler farmers competed with black farmers for land and for the local markets created by industrial capital in South Africa

(Beinart, 1984: 63). During the last decades of the nineteenth century both white and black farmers responded to burgeoning agricultural markets. Africans experimented with new methods, crops and animals (Beinart, 1984: 66), and black farming entered the most productive period in its history (Davenport, 1987: 393). At the same time, however, white farming was also expanding and in need of black labour.

To allow white farming to expand, severe restrictions were imposed on independent black farmers. These restrictions included the abolition of black share-cropping on white-owned land; the control of other forms of tenancy on this land; and, most serious of all, the imposition of possessory segregation under the 1913 Land Act, which prevented Africans from purchasing land outside the reserves (Davenport, 1987: 391–2). As an inevitable sequel, land within the reserves came to be farmed more and more intensively and by the 1930s there were frequent reports of overstocking and serious soil erosion in these areas.

State policy and interventions to safeguard white farming resulted in conditions in the reserves which required drastic action to 'save the soil' (Davenport, 1987: 393). Further intervention, justified precisely by a pretence at 'saving the soil', became a major instrument for the implementation of the broader 'racial' policies.

The policy of racial separation unfolded through several stages after Union: there was a policy of segregation for much of the first half of this century, and it was followed by a short-lived period of trusteeship, and then by apartheid and separate development. As in the case of the underlying ideology, these different formulations of the racial policy not only influenced development; development was itself a crucial aspect of these policies of domination. As the racial policy unfolded, the development policies of the state were continually adapted, development priorities redefined and development goals altered accordingly.

Segregation, South Africa's colour policy from Union in 1910 until the Second World War, aimed at the territorial separation of black and white in South Africa. The chief segregationist measures, the 1913 and 1936 Land Acts, made land available for separate African occupation. State intervention in these areas (explicitly designated as 'development' only in the 1930s) was intended to provide a livelihood for the African population in the reserves. Attempts at conservation and reclamation were, in part, means to 'save the soil' from further deterioration, but they were also strictly subjected to the ideology and politics of segregation. So also were programmes based on experimental farms coupled with extension and demonstration services, even though their primary aim was to expand and improve peasant agriculture in the reserves (Beinart, 1984: 68). They were all intended to increase the reserves' capacity to accommodate the African population.

By the late 1930s there was increasing concern about the condition of the soil in the reserves, because its deterioration was having palpable effect on the capacity of these areas to support their inhabitants. Smuts voiced this concern when he said that 'erosion is the biggest problem confronting the country, bigger than any politics' (Beinart, 1984). This concern, which was linked in official eyes to the rapid decline in individual land ownership and the increasing prominence of communal tenure on Trust land, 'set in motion the "rescue operation" which came to be known as "betterment" in the 1930s' (Davenport, 1987: 394).

The early Betterment Proclamation of 1939 was intended mainly 'to save the soil' by means of planned settlement and other conservation measures: under the charge of native commissioners residential patterns were to be restructured, pastures fenced, stock limitations imposed on the basis of 'carrying capacity', arable land was to be demarcated, and contour ploughing promoted. Betterment reflected an intention to intervene in the rural areas in much more fundamental and systematic ways than had hitherto been the case. The Second World War put a brake on the implementation of these measures, however (Beinart, 1984: 73). When renewed efforts to apply them were made in the 1950s they met with widespread rural opposition, in part because betterment had come to be administered by the new and unpopular Bantu Authorities (Davenport, 1987: 394).

The social dislocations brought about by the war instilled greater realism in the official mind about the viability of segregation as a policy to address the 'native problem'. In 1942 Smuts, then prime minister, remarked that 'isolation has gone and I am afraid segregation has fallen on evil days too' (*South African Outlook*, 1942). He presented the idea of 'trusteeship' as an alternative formulation of racial policy and emphasised the responsibility of the trustee towards the ward.

Before Smuts fell from power in 1948, his idea of 'trusteeship' had little direct or immediate effect on racial policy in South Africa. But the incoming Nationalist government took up the idea, and combined it with the goal of segregation in the new policy of apartheid. This policy was intended not simply to segregate along racial lines, but also to establish separate black and white communities in South Africa. 'Development' was reformulated to realise this objective: the state, as self-appointed trustee, assumed the responsibility of developing the African community.

'Trusteeship' therefore became a major justification for interventions by the state to implement its racial policy. According to the Minister of Bantu Administration, M. C. Botha, 'development' meant that 'the different [African] nations must be placed in a situation where, by means of appropriate institutions and organisations, they are able to behave in accordance with their best interests as conceived by the trustee' (*Bantu*, 1970: 19, author's translation). An important qualification was added to the notion of 'development': this was the idea of '*eiesoortige ontwikkeling*' (autogenous development). Africans were to be developed '*eiesoortig*' under the guidance of the trustee, according to their particular character and capabilities.

Development continued to include conservation and betterment as key elements; these were, henceforth, mobilised to achieve '*eiesoortige ontwikkeling*'. But the idea included much more than intervention in rural settlement patterns and farming practices.

Apartheid was a political, as well as an economic, solution to the 'native problem'. To maintain white domination it envisaged a dispensation of separate political structures. Constitutional intervention therefore became a dominant aspect of 'development'.

The implementation of apartheid required the creation of alternative political bodies for Africans. After passing the Bantu Authorities Act in 1951, the state embarked with firm determination on a programme of 'constitutional development'. Tribal, Regional, and Territorial Authorities were instituted in the African areas. Over the next thirty years the constitutional status of these areas changed from 'self-management' to 'self-government', and in some cases (though this was not foreseen in the 1950s) to 'independence'. And changes to the constitutional status of these areas affected development priorities.

In the early 1950s the Nationalist government appointed the Tomlinson Commission to make recommendations about the socio-economic development of the African areas to achieve '*eiesoortige ontwikkeling*'.

As embodied in the final report, Tomlinson's central proposals involved the development of self-sustaining small farmers on 'economic units', and the diversification of economic activity to reduce the numbers dependent on the land for a living (Davenport, 1987: 395). These proposals were enormously influential, but the government did not implement them directly, even though Tomlinson's recommendations for stimulating a peasantry were modest. The commission decided that a minimum income from agriculture of £60 per annum was adequate for the average household. Even so, however, the government was unwilling to commit sufficient land for the creation of economic units to permit this outcome.

What it feared was that the creation of a large number of the recommended units would jeopardise the goal of accommodating as many Africans as possible in the existing reserve areas. The land units which were given out continued to be suited to subsistence, rather than commercial, agriculture. In only a few selected places were additional resources, such as irrigation facilities, made available in an attempt to boost the commercial potential of African agriculture. The land which households received (where they received any at all) provided only a marginal income, and most people continued to rely heavily on income from migrant wage labour. As Davenport has said, 'when the government reacted to the [Tomlinson Commission's] report in its White Paper of 1956 what emerged was an ideological preoccupation which seemed more important than any formula for successful farming' (1987: 345).

Another reason for the continued, and growing, reliance on income from migrant labour was the exceptionally low priority the state gave, in the 1950s and early 1960s, to the diversification of economic activity within the reserves. Because it was committed to the establishment of so-called 'border industries' (which meant that industrial developments remained within 'white' South Africa), the government spent only a fraction of the sum which Tomlinson had recommended for this diversification.

In the 1960s apartheid came to embrace the 'homeland' policy. The Promotion of Bantu Self-Government Act of 1959 used the territorial base provided by the Land Acts to establish a new political dispensation of 'ethnically' differentiated homelands. Implementing this homeland policy of separate development impacted on development priorities decisively. Henceforth, the 'guardian' deemed it in the interest of the 'ward' to be developed as separate ethnic units. *'Eiesoortige ontwikkeling'* was further qualified and became *'eiesoortige volksontwikkeling'*. *'Ontvoogding'* (the relinquishing of trusteeship) and *'selfstandigheid'* (independence) emerged as major development goals.

Constitutionally, homelands were 'developed' from self-managing *(selfbesturende)* to self-governing *(selfregerende)* homelands, and from self-governing homelands to self-governing or independent 'national states'. Their changing constitutional status naturally affected economic development. Resources such as land, which had been regarded primarily as public assets for the benefit of the people of the reserves, turned, in official eyes, into resources for the benefit of ethnic units, to provide income for homelands.

For instance, as homelands developed towards self-government, the idea of dividing available land into economic units seemed progressively outdated. The new development goals accorded increasing priority to the strength of homeland economies as a whole rather than the promotion of subsistence farmers.

As the homelands were transformed into 'national states', development became 'national' development. The 'national' interest of 'ethnic national units' became the chief development priority, the development of their 'national' economies the overriding development goal, and the commercial use of their resources the dominant development trend. The scope of 'development' initiatives was considerably broadened: thus commercial farming, industrial development, and tourism were all seen as areas which could contribute to 'national' economic growth. By a similar logic, government buildings, universities and nature conservation were seen as both symbols of national development, and the means for lending credibility to the constitutional status of the 'national states'.

Ethnic nationalism and development in Gazankulu

Development projects in contemporary Gazankulu must be seen as part of the unfolding policy of ethnic nationalism (Sharp, 1985a). Since its inception this policy has had significant consequences for the African population of the lowveld area of the Transvaal. In the early 1960s much of this area was administered from Bushbuckridge. During this decade the Bantu Development Trust bought up large tracts of land which had been earmarked for 'release' (from white ownership to the reserves) by the 1936 Land Act. Much of the land purchased had long been under the control of absentee owners, and there was a considerable African population living as tenants on it. The population was diverse, with Sotho- and Tsonga-speakers intermingled and scattered across the land.

At first the development initiatives did not try to change this distribution of the population. Land was not allocated on an ethnic basis, and limited steps, involving land reclamation, soil conservation and planned settlement, were undertaken in order to develop subsistence agriculture for 'the Bantu of Bushbuckridge area' rather than for specific 'ethnic groups'. It was at this time that the inhabitants of Seville farm were subjected to betterment planning.

In political terms a series of Tribal Authorities was established on the Trust lands in pursuit of the goal of separate development for the African population of the region. But these Tribal Authorities were heterogeneously composed, and were planned as parts of ethnically heterogeneous Regional Authorities.

With the shift to the policy of 'ethnic national development' after the late 1960s, the area was, however, apportioned between two distinct 'homelands' – Gazankulu (for Tsonga-speakers) and Lebowa (for Sotho-speakers). The Tribal Authorities were unscrambled, and Mhala district, in which Seville is situated, became part of Gazankulu. From this point on, ethnic identity (as officially conceived) came to determine access to and control over land and other resources in the southern lowveld. This led to a period of considerable population relocation, because many Tsonga-speakers were made to leave what had become Lebowa and move to Gazankulu, and many Sotho-speakers made the journey in reverse.

When self-government was granted to Gazankulu in 1973, the chief development priority became the homeland's 'national interest'. As indication of this, the Shangaan/Tsonga Development Corporation (STDC) issued the following manifesto: the STDC 'is, first and foremost, an instrument for the implementation of the policy and strategy of the Gazankulu government in pursuit of Gazankulu's national aim and objectives and in accordance with Gazankulu's national interest' (STDC, 1986: 2).

Land in Mhala district is now officially regarded as a national resource, and is commercially planned to be used productively in this interest. In developing land in Mhala, development experts (mainly white) follow the modes and techniques of land use of the white farmers still in the surrounding lowveld area. In consequence the economic circumstances of the people in Mhala, and their patterns of agriculture and land use, are largely ignored.

The 'white' area of the lowveld is generally known as a cattle-farming and game-ranching area, and in development planning cattle farming receives priority over subsistence agriculture. Commercial cattle projects, of which the Seville initiative is one example, are increasingly being introduced. Moreover there has also been a move to copy the proliferation of white-owned game ranches in the surrounding area: in the early 1980s almost 6 000 hectares of Trust land in Mhala were fenced as a game reserve, for hunting and viewing by tourists. About 400 families who had lived on this land were declared squatters, and relocated into a closer settlement – a village without access to land – in order to further the 'national interest' of Gazankulu.

There are other examples of the same process: in the late 1970s a large irrigation scheme in Mhala was replanned so that a number of peasant farmers, who had earlier been given economic units, were relieved of their land. The justification was that these farmers were not using their land productively; the land in question has now been given to the STDC, which farms it as a commercial venture.

Land use and 'tradition' in Seville

The rationale for all of these development projects is the same: land that is managed by the Development Corporation and the Department of Agriculture is used productively, generates an income from the sale of produce which can be used to finance the Corporation's activities, and provides a source of tax revenue for the Gazankulu authorities. On the other hand, it is argued, where the people have access to land it is generally used unproductively, in large measure because it is locked up in an inhibiting system of 'traditional' land tenure and agricultural organisation: 'What has to be realised . . . is the fact that a lot of capital is tied up in this land which is always under-utilised. The people who have the right to use this land pay no income tax to our government because they make no money out of this land that they have removed from productive use.' (Gazankulu Government, 1985: 5)

In this context the notion of 'traditional' land tenure and agricultural practice implies irrationality. Ordinary people, who do not farm their land commercially to generate profits and tax revenues, are being irrational. They are irrational because they are still caught in the thrall of 'tradition', of beliefs and practices which have remained unchanged since the distant, pre-colonial past.

These premises are, however, of doubtful validity. In the first place, the system of land tenure which exists in an area such as Seville has no continuity with the pre-colonial past: as we explained above, before the Trust bought the farm the people were labour tenants of a white landowner, and after the farm was purchased it was subjected to betterment planning, whereby the fields and grazing areas were demarcated which the residents use at present. Control of this land is vested in the local Tribal Authority, a body which was created by the South African government and shows no continuity with any forms of political authority in the pre-colonial past. Seen in this light, the notion of 'tradition' is used as a convenient device on which to pin blame for the poverty of the area's inhabitants.

But the people of Seville (and indeed of most other homeland areas) derive the greater part of their income from migrant wage labour. Given the history of racial separation in South Africa, and of the unequal allocation of land and other resources which this involved, there is no alternative to this source of income for most people in the homelands. If, then, they are poor it is because of their involvement, as migrant workers, in the wage economy. And the way in which they use the land available to them is not in any simple fashion a cause of poverty but, rather, a reflection of it.

The fact that the income derived from migrant labour is low and uncertain means two things to the people of Seville. Firstly, it means that they must cultivate the little land available to them and try to keep whatever livestock they can acquire. The products of these endeavours are vital as a supplement to low wages and as a source of temporary subsistence should the wage income be lost. Secondly, however, their low wage incomes also mean that they have little capital to invest in agricultural activities.

Therefore their activities are designed to minimise the risk to the little capital they can invest. In Seville people attempt to maximise the labour input into agriculture: they try to spread the planting season, to cultivate different soils, and to use a system of intercropping. In doing these things, they make use of skills and knowledge of the local environment which have been handed down from the past. In this sense, these practices are indeed 'traditional', but they are not irrational.

The returns from these activities are certainly very small, when compared to a commercial farming operation, but they are not without significance in a poverty-stricken village. Research shows that the average household in Seville produced six 80kg bags of maizemeal, which (together with the legumes, melons and pumpkins which were planted alongside the maize) made a major contribution to domestic subsistence. Moreover, this contribution came out of a very small capital input: in 1984 each household invested less than the value of one bag of maizemeal in cultivating the soil. The main input was labour, and the point is that the people whose labour was so lavishly expended for so 'small' a return (mainly women, old men and children) could not, in the prevailing circumstances, have done anything more productive with their time and energy.

These are the factors which the development experts who ran the cattle scheme in Seville refused to recognise. They saw a 'traditional' system of agriculture in operation, which was inefficient and wasted a national resource because it produced nothing for the market. They believed that their cattle improvement project would eventually bring widespread benefit, if and when people outside the scheme learnt from their example.

But the people living on what is left of Seville cannot follow their example: they do not have the land or the capital to follow in the experts' footsteps. The commitment and the concern of the development officials on the ground are not to be questioned. But their efforts, and those of the bodies and authorities they represent, have to be interpreted in the context of the unfolding history of racial and development policies in South Africa as a whole. In this context, it is clear that projects such as those in Gazankulu cater, in fact, to the needs of a very small elite in the homelands. The elites are indispensable to the continued existence of these areas as 'national entities', because they form the category from which the 'national' leaders are drawn. It is, however, highly misleading to claim that such interventions in the name of 'development' serve the interests of the majority of people. The people would, in fact, be better off if none of this kind of 'development' took place at all.

10 The informal sector: A new resource

KEES VAN DER WAAL and JOHN SHARP

Not only does development of the informal sector provide employment and the necessary goods and services for the lower-income groups, but both economic activity and skills are developed and stimulated, and future growth is encouraged (Suchard, 1979: 100).

Informal activity 'in general' . . . is carried out – precariously for the most part – in what might be termed the interstices of the capitalist economy and is unified at this level of analysis essentially through its role in reproducing the labour force required by that economy (Wilkinson and Webster, 1982: 5).

The origins of the informal sector

The idea that economies have an 'informal sector' rose to prominence in the 1970s. Discovery of the 'informal sector' implied, of course, the existence of a 'formal sector'. Economies were therefore seen to comprise two parts, with the one being in many ways the antithesis of the other.

What needs to be examined critically about this formulation is, as many writers have stressed, not simply the concept of the informal sector itself, but more particularly the idea that economies are divided into two parts. What is the nature of the relationship between the two parts of an economy? How, in other words, does the informal sector relate to the formal one?

In the 1970s the term 'informal sector' was new, but the underlying argument, that the economy in many countries (particularly those in the so-called 'third world') comprised two discrete sectors, was an old one. Conventional wisdom had long held that the economies of the underdeveloped (or, more positively, developing) countries contained a 'modern' sector superimposed upon a 'traditional' one. This notion of the 'dual economy' was often used to explain the lack of progress in the third world, because the large 'traditional' sector was seen as a drag on the dynamism of the modern.

The informal–formal dichotomy became very popular, in both academic and development circles, because it was widely interpreted as a variant of older dualist arguments. Its popular usage preserved considerable continuity with, and therefore fitted comfortably into, established patterns of thought. But it also added a new, more positive and hopeful dimension to earlier thinking. The 'traditional' sector of the economies of developing countries had hitherto been regarded as an inevitable and inescapable brake on progress; activities within this sphere were seen as antithetical to modernisation, because their tenacious conservatism inhibited innovation, risk-taking, and the application of scientific knowledge. The new wisdom of the 'informal sector' notion was that these self-same activities were, in fact, a key to future economic growth, because they provided people with employment, income, and (perhaps most important) rudimentary training in the skills of the market place. In this way the concept supposedly shed new light on a previously misunderstood phenomenon.

This was good news indeed for development specialists and agencies. After the Second World War, they had pinned their hopes on the spread of industrialisation throughout the developing world. But industrialisation was slow to spread, and even where it did, it failed to generate large-scale employment or reduce income inequalities to any marked extent. Nor did the hopes of development through agricultural or educational stimulation materialise. Development agencies such as the ILO (the International Labour Organisation) focused more and more clearly on unemployment as the major cause of poverty and income inequality, but were brought up against the fact that the possibilities for creating mass employment within the framework of existing economic policies were exceptionally limited.

There was a desperate need for alternatives that offered a prospect of success without revolutionising existing economic systems of the 'free market' type. An ILO survey in Kenya in 1972 was the first study to point to the informal sector of the economy as the key to employment and growth (Moser, 1978). The ILO study drew heavily, and rather inaccurately, on the work of the British anthropologist Keith Hart. Hart had worked on the problem of urban unemployment in Ghana in the late 1960s, and his report on this study to a conference at the University of Sussex in 1971 drew considerable interest.

Hart set out to challenge the idea that the very large number of people, in cities such as Accra, who were unemployed or underemployed constituted a passive mass resigned to their poverty and, therefore, parasitic upon the urban society. He showed that official employment statistics were misleading, in the sense that they recorded as employed only those workers who were in stable employment and earned regular incomes. Censuses ignored the very wide spectrum of activities which did not fall neatly into the category of stable, regular wage employment, but which nonetheless provided alternative sources of income to many people. These activities comprised what Hart termed the 'informal sector' (1973: 68).

His list of the activities within this sector has been widely repeated. It included the following: productive and secondary activities (manufacturing by artisans, craftwork, building, subsistence agriculture); distribution activities (street hawking, catering in food and drink); and service activities (transport, shoeshining, backyard vehicle repairing, magic and medical services).

Hart pointed out that while some activities within the informal sector were legitimate (that is, within the law), many were not: thus many of the urban poor attempted to sustain themselves by producing illegal liquor or drugs, or by means of services such as receiving stolen goods, drug pushing and prostitution, or by engaging in illegal transfers such as pickpocketing or petty theft. Sometimes such apparently innocuous activities as street hawking were regarded by the urban authorities as illegal, thereby adding to the difficulties faced by the poor (this list is adapted from Hart, 1973; see also Beavon and Mabin, 1978; and Wilkinson and Webster, 1982).

Hart showed that despite the many difficulties which faced them, the urban unemployed manifested considerable inventiveness, and were actively engaged in diverse strategies to secure a livelihood. He also noted, as further challenge to received wisdom, that they often worked extremely hard and for long hours.

The impact of his contribution lay in demonstrating the income-generating potential of the range of activities outside the formal sector of the urban economy. This stimulated a hopeful exploration by international development specialists of the positive contribution which the informal sector could make towards addressing the problem of widespread poverty (as in the ILO's Kenya report).

It is fair to say that the development agencies saw things in Hart's work which he had not intended. Hart had written specifically of West African cities, where the supposedly unemployed were for the most part relatively recent migrants from the rural interior. These immigrants had been targeted as a political and economic 'problem' by urban authorities, and his argument was a response to this victimisation. He had written, in other words, about a particular context, and did not seek to advertise the 'informal sector' as a universal panacea for unemployment and underemployment. Furthermore, his study made it clear that many who participated in the informal sector remained desperately poor despite the toil and energy they expended.

Most of his qualifications were ignored in subsequent writing. The development fraternity 'discovered' the informal sector as a separate, indigenous phenomenon in the 'third world', and linked this notion to the older idea of the dual economy. They took the separateness of the informal sector for granted and did not question its history and links with its counterpart, the formal sector, in specific instances. In this way, the informal sector was defined as the unofficial, shadow side of the national economy, where entry was easy, training minimal and informal, and where creativity was ubiquitous despite official harassment and other constraints. The 'development potential' of the informal sector was ascribed to its ability to absorb surplus labour and to its provision of entrepreneurial experience:

The informal sector thrives because it makes and services things that the people need. It uses little capital, but much labour, and overheads are very low. The materials used are of local origin or are discards of the formal sector of the economy. Profits made by entrepreneurs are spent locally, so that no money is remitted abroad. In short, the informal sector is in many ways a perfect model of what economists say industry should be in developing countries. (Norwood, 1975: 86)

What had happened, in fact, was that a new idea had been created: the 'informal sector' as a social and economic construct, a new category, to describe that part of the economy which had remained unnoticed by formal economic thinking. But taking note of the informal sector did not mean that it was properly understood in relation to its context and the reasons for its existence. Typical of dualist economic thinking, the economy was still thought to consist of two loosely connected entities. In this sense the informal sector concept reproduced the 'dual economy' idea. The relation between the two hypothetical sectors was seen, in developmentalist idiom, as benign; the sectors were mutually dependent; and the informal sector was open to stimulation to facilitate sector mobility.

In this way informal sector operators became what Bromley and Gerry called a 'target group' for development policy. The diverse category was considered as a homogeneous group, and this led to 'an oversimplification of [its] internally-rooted characteristics and the externally-imposed relations . . .' (1979: 306).

Since the informal sector was apparently thought to absorb labour even under adverse conditions, it was reasoned that encouraging its constituent activities would make a major contribution to overcoming the problem of widespread unemployment. In fact, however, subsequent experience in many parts of the world has shown that it is very difficult to stimulate all informal activities artificially and in isolation from their social and economic context. Some of the reasons for this difficulty are the small scale of many informal operations, the unprofitability of the poor market in which they operate, as well as the lack of educational and commercial background of many informal entrepreneurs. The lack of the necessary infrastructure and facilities needed to compete with factory production is a further inhibiting factor.

The informal sector in South Africa

Optimistic studies on the potential role of the informal sector began to proliferate in South Africa by the end of the 1970s (cf. Rogerson and Beavon, 1980). Most of these studies set out merely to describe the activities in this sector that had hitherto been hidden from official recognition. But these studies made up for their lack of theoretical insight by their unbounded enthusiasm for the promise of the informal sector.

The policy suggestions in these studies were made along two complementary lines. Firstly, they stressed the need for deregulation of the economy in order to create a legal climate more favourable to the operation of the informal sector. In addition to this, they advocated the provision of financial and technical assistance, from both public and private sources, in order to stimulate informal economic activities. It was envisaged that intervention along these lines would contribute to a massive upsurge in productive activity and general well-being.

The argument for deregulation of the economy was quickly taken up by government institutions and policy-makers. This marked a sharp contrast to the long history of suppression and restriction of informal economic activities in this country, and no doubt contributed to the widespread euphoria which accompanied the 'discovery' of an indigenous informal sector. This new deal has been advertised as part of the 'reform' process of the 1980s, and, within that process, as integral to moves to foster the system of free enterprise amongst all South Africans.

There was certainly a great deal to do by way of the removal of restrictions. Many municipal regulations and the South African legal framework in general had made the existence of small-scale economic enterprise extremely precarious. This has to be understood in the historical context of the racial and economic policies of the country. In accordance with the policy of separate development, Africans in the 'white' areas of the country were meant to supply labour; all other economic activities were to be restricted, insofar as possible, to the homelands. Influx control, the Group Areas Act and the policing of economic activities in the urban areas had forced the African informal sector in towns and cities underground. Permission for the legal pursuit of these alternative economic strategies was almost impossible to obtain. People who tried, for instance, to sell goods as hawkers often landed in court, where they faced fines and the confiscation of their stock.

But the shock of the 1976 uprising, and the gradual recognition that the homelands were not going to be self-sustaining, had some effect on official thinking. After Africans were accepted as permanent residents in the 'white' part of South Africa in the late 1970s, 'reformist' policy was able to accommodate the informal sector as a possible ally in the economic system. The earlier harassment and persecution were gradually replaced by acceptance of the reality of these previously invisible and wished-away activities.

But attempts to stimulate the informal sector on a large scale have not been more successful in South Africa than elsewhere. The Small Business Development Corporation (SBDC) is the most important of a small number of organisations which provide financial and technical assistance to the 'backyard entrepreneur', but help of this kind is in general limited to those who are regarded as possible entrants to the formal sector. These are, however, the people who have gained success through their own efforts, and the assistance does not reach the large mass of people in the informal sector who can never hope to join the ranks of the emerging African middle class.

By the middle of the 1980s official thinking was beginning to take account of some of the difficulties of large-scale stimulation of the informal sector, and the exaggerated enthusiasm of the late 1970s was on the wane. This is clearly reflected in a statement by Dr Simon Brand, head of the Development Bank of Southern Africa, the institution created by the state in the early 1980s to speed up 'development':

Trying to 'uplift' each participant in the informal sector to be a small entrepreneur can result only in forcing people beyond their competence, leading to a worse situation than before for them. In this way the functioning of the informal sector can be severely damaged. The approach in this regard should therefore rather be a selective encouragement to those informal sector participants who have proven themselves as potential entrepreneurs by their achievements. . . . [For the rest] a policy of benign neglect is possibly the best road to take. (1986: 18–19, our translation)

Brand's statement is a sober reflection on the limitations of developmental intervention in the informal sector, and it puts forward an argument shorn of all grandiose rhetoric about making significant inroads into the problem of mass poverty and unemployment. Indeed, in many ways, it marks an admission of defeat for a brave, new idea: the best that can be done for the destitute is to offer them 'benign neglect'. In other words, 'development' amounts to little more than selective deregulation of the economy.

There is, however, more to Brand's statement than a sober reappraisal of past enthusiasm. Critics of the conventional development approach to the informal sector would certainly argue that the views he expresses provide a most revealing window on the real intentions of official rhetoric and policy about the state's relationship to the informal sector.

What, in this critical line of thought, are the real intentions of conventional development policy?

The critique of the 'informal sector'

Many critics have pointed out that the basic weakness of conventional thinking lies in its assumption that the relationship between the formal and informal sectors is a benign one:

> Capitalist production is, above all, interested in the extraction of profit, not the provision of employment. This makes it necessary to ask whether the increasing interest of policy-makers in the informal sector is based on a desire to ameliorate the situation or whether they see the development of the informal sector as actually in their own interest. Is it a matter of simply tolerating this sector or is it functional to the whole capitalist system? (Moser, 1978: 1062)

There have been many attempts, in the international literature, to explain how and why the informal sector is 'functional to the capitalist system' (and the interested reader may wish to consult the seminal collection of papers in the journal *World Development*, 6 (9/10), 1978) as a useful point of entry to the debate). We concentrate here on discussion which has taken place in the South African context.

Foremost in this discussion are two papers, by Wilkinson and Webster (1982) and Wellings and Sutcliffe (1984), although it must be said that both have the drawback that their arguments are complex and theoretically sophisticated. This means, we believe, that many of the people who should take note of their line of thinking will find their discourse impenetrable. Our aim is, therefore, to provide a relatively straightforward summary of the basic premises on which their arguments rest.

Their point of departure is that most of the proponents of 'development' for the informal sector have always taken a very narrow, economistic view of its constituent activities. The economism of conventional wisdom lies in the assumption that activities in the informal sector can usefully be analysed by reference to the neo-classical theory of the economic behaviour of business enterprises and of entrepreneurs. This assumption means that, for example, street hawking as an informal activity is appropriately studied by seeking to calculate the volume of turnover, the costs of inputs in labour and stock, and profits from sales for individual hawkers in isolation from their surroundings. Criticism of this approach, as in the two papers mentioned above, does not claim that such calculations cannot be made; it suggests, rather, that they are not useful because they give a false impression of the nature and purpose of informal sector activities.

Such calculations are a self-fulfilling exercise: if one starts by assuming that informal sector activities are so much like formal sector enterprises that methods of analysis appropriate to the latter can be applied to them, then one is bound to see informal sector operators as proto-entrepreneurs. And if one sees people in the informal sector as proto-entrepreneurs, then one is bound also to see the relationship between the two sectors as benign, because (as was explained above) the informal sector is regarded as the formal sector in-the-making.

Wilkinson and Webster reject the imposition of the model of the capitalist firm onto informal sector activities, and begin their inquiry by taking account of the wider political and economic context in which these activities occur. They, and others who have written in similar vein, draw attention to two particular features of this context.

Firstly, it is argued, South Africa has a high unemployment rate which is not responsive to swings in the business cycle: in other words, even when the economy is in a boom period, unemployment remains very high. This situation is, in large part, a result of the way in which the South African economy is inserted into the international capitalist system, and reflects South Africa's dependence on the advanced industrial countries. 'Structural' unemployment is therefore a permanent feature of the national economy (as it is in other, similarly dependent countries), and there are many people who will never obtain secure wage employment irrespective of the efforts they may make to find it.

Secondly, a very large proportion of the population has no representation whatever in the institutionalised political system. Amongst the consequences of this is the fact that there is minimal provision by the state of social security benefits for this section of the population. Thus most poor people who lack regular wage employment also do not have the political means by which to secure significant state benefits in the form of unemployment insurance, grants, or pensions. These people are also affected by the fact that, owing to their powerlessness, the state makes only a meagre provision of items of 'collective consumption' (such as schools, hospitals, or crèches) for them.

Faced with these twin characteristics of the society in which they find themselves, what do the poor who lack access to regular wage employment do? Since they refuse, as Wilkinson and Webster remark, simply 'to disappear, or to suspend the question of how their subsistence needs are to be met' (1982: 6), the diverse activities in which they engage must be seen as strategies for survival. And by asking the question 'what strategies do they engage in?', one opens up a perspective on a much broader range of activities than would otherwise be noticed if one looked merely for evidence of rudimentary economic enterprises. The conventional approach to the informal sector concentrates on the very narrow range of production and service activities which do bear some resemblance to enterprises within the formal sector, and this limitation occurs precisely because of the nature of the assumptions from which the inquiry begins.

In fact, however, informal production and service activities are embedded in a very complex network of *social* relationships, and comprise only a small fragment of the strategies which the poor deploy in order to attempt to survive. These social relationships include the reciprocities of kinship, of mutal aid associations, and of savings clubs. The 'economic' aspect of such relationships might not be immediately apparent to the observer, but they are certainly vital resources for people who must struggle to survive.

Moreover, what unites all of these diverse activities is that they are, in very large measure, mechanisms for the redistribution of income which is earned in the formal sector. This is particularly clear and obvious in the case of services such as prostitution, and transfers such as theft and pickpocketing, but the same logic applies in many informal production and distribution activities. People who brew beer, or practise as herbalists in the townships, are involved not so much in the creation of significant amounts of new wealth, as in trying to gain access to the income of wage-earners who are in regular employment. The most important clients of shebeeners or herbalists are workers who are earning a wage income: because other drinking or health facilities are limited in the townships, shebeeners and herbalists are able to supply commodities and services which the workers need.

But the key argument in the critical response to the proponents of the informal sector is that the phenomenon needs to be looked at more broadly than simply from the vantage of the individuals who take part in the informal sector. This is because their activities, taken in aggregate, have important functions for the economy as a whole and the political order of the society.

In the first place, the informal sector provides people who are in regular wage employment with cheap goods and services, which means that wage levels can, in overall terms, be lower than if the workers had to purchase all their requirements from the formal sector. In countries such as South Africa, it is often more profitable for the formal sector to target its production and distribution on the middle-class market (both local and international) rather than on the poor one.

Secondly, the availability of opportunities within the informal sector to people who are unemployed, and who are never likely to gain secure wage employment in the formal sector, can be said to relieve the state of the duty of meeting needs for certain collective consumption items and social security benefits. We noted above that most informal sector activities actually redistribute income within the working class 'as a whole' (that is, from those who are employed to those who are not). Part of the burden of supporting the unemployed is therefore shifted, via the informal sector, from the state to the shoulders of the working class itself. Thus it is argued that, although the informal sector provides no guarantee that specific individuals will be able to survive in the face of structural unemployment and political powerlessness, it does play a key role in maintaining and perpetuating a highly unequal and discriminatory social order in society as a whole.

The conventional approach does not permit one to see this reality of the informal sector, because it is committed to viewing the informal sector in its individual manifestations – as a collection of discrete enterprises, run by individuals who are proto-entrepreneurs. It is only when one looks at the phenomenon in aggregate that one can see the role the informal sector plays in reproducing the conditions which make the system of racial capitalism in South Africa possible. Wellings and Sutcliffe (1984: 517) spell this conclusion out forcefully: ' "Development" of the informal sector, it is argued, excuses the state from providing more adequate social-welfare services and creating jobs in the formal sector for black South Africans. In this sense the persistence of the informal sector is functional to the state and to the continuation of apartheid.'

This interpretation casts the statement by Simon Brand (cited above) into a very sombre light, and his recommendations take on a significance which was previously hidden. Deregulation of the economy, particularly if it is selective so that established interests are only minimally affected, is cheap in both financial and political terms, and, as Brand makes clear, nothing more is intended for the mass of unemployed who are desperately poor. What deregulation does, in fact, is to make it slightly easier for the process of redistribution of income *within* the working class to take place. On the other hand, only those few people who both aspire to middle-class status and have proved their potential as entrepreneurs, will be given assistance to complete the transition to the middle class. A main aim of conventional 'development' is therefore not to relieve mass poverty, but to strengthen the emerging African middle class, the members of which, it is hoped, can be weaned from any commitment to revolutionary change in the South African socio-political order.

Many people, including those who are personally involved in official attempts at 'development', will recoil from such analysis, and attempt to dismiss it on the grounds that it is 'ideologically motivated'. But this is a poor reason to dismiss the argument out of hand, because it is clear that official pronouncements, such as the one by Simon Brand, are also rooted in a particular vision of what South Africa is and ought to be. The one side of the debate about the informal sector is as ideological as the other. The critical discourse about the informal sector has several very positive characteristics, even for those who are not Marxists or committed to a socialist future for South Africa.

Not the least of these characteristics is that the critical discourse can serve to sensitise the general public to the discrepancy – the credibility gap – between official rhetoric about the development of the informal sector and the likely consequences of practical interventions along these lines. Any success in deflating some of the more fulsome claims which are made is to be welcomed. The important lesson is that there are no instant or painless ways in which to solve the problem of mass poverty in South Africa, and that those who really care about this problem can easily be taken in by the rhetoric of those who do not. And it is certain that in order to make any significant inroads into poverty in South Africa, there will have to be far-reaching and fundamental change in the social order, in the course of which established interests will inevitably be hurt.

Does this mean, however, that no efforts to address the issue of mass poverty can possibly bear fruit until both apartheid and the capitalist order are done away with? A very rigid reading of Wellings and Sutcliffe, and Wilkinson and Webster, might suggest that this was so. If it is true that the informal sector is functional to the maintenance and reproduction of the capitalist system, then surely any attempt to stimulate its constituent activities will have results which are the opposite of those intended. If the roots of poverty lie in the system as a whole, then good intentions must wait until the system has been transformed.

We do not altogether accept that this is so. Our main reason for saying this is that much of the critique of conventional thinking about the informal sector relies very heavily on functionalist premises. It argues that if one can explain the 'function' of some social phenomenon (the role that it plays in the smooth workings of the total social system), then one has somehow defined its *essential* character and said all that can usefully be said about it.

The fact that the informal sector does function to lower the costs for both the state and capital of reproducing the labour force and the working class 'as a whole' seems to us to be a useful insight, for all the reasons outlined above. On the other hand, to suppose that a phenomenon which is so diverse, and in which so many people participate in different ways, has only this one function seems to us to be both a simplification and an unwarranted generalisation. The critical discourse tells us that we must consider the informal sector in aggregate in relation to society as a whole; this is clearly a very necessary step, but one needs also to go on from there to examine the particular manifestations of the phenomenon in specific historical contexts.

The final part of this chapter is a brief attempt at the latter exercise. We examine the various opportunities for survival open to people in Venda and KwaNdebele, two 'homeland' areas in the Transvaal in which one of us has done research (Van der Waal, 1985), and we show how the specific histories and circumstances of these areas have produced different patterns of involvement in informal sector activities. We argue also that if one descends from the abstract discussion of 'society as a whole' to more detailed, regional comparisons of the kind suggested below, one may be able to identify forms of developmental intervention which have some possibility for significant impact and are, at the same time, realistic as to the structural limitations on their outcome.

The informal sector in Venda and KwaNdebele

It is the specific experiences of the process of domination which explain both the real meaning of the informal sector and the differences between its manifestations in KwaNdebele and Venda. Both political groupings were brought under the control of the Transvaal Republic at the end of the nineteenth century by military force. The Ndebele kingdom was subjugated in 1883, its land confiscated and its inhabitants were indentured as farm labourers, whereas the Venda chiefdoms were finally incorporated, with a portion of their lands intact, in 1898. After this, most Ndebele-speakers had a long experience of farm labour on white-owned land, while the people in Venda were soon introduced to labour migration and to administration of their territory by commissioners, chiefs and headmen in the service of a white-dominated government.

Later in the twentieth century the logic of the unfolding policy of apartheid demanded the creation of a separate area for each 'ethnic group' within the African population. For this reason KwaNdebele was established in the late 1950s as a 'national home' for Ndebele-speakers, and in both KwaNdebele and Venda the political structures of an imposed tribalism were used to build administrations which would, ideally and in due course, become 'independent'.

As a result of influx control in the cities, mechanisation and the eviction of 'squatters' on white-owned farms, and the actions of other 'homelands', such as Bophuthatswana, which ejected Ndebele-speakers on the grounds that they were not 'ethnic' citizens, a population of several hundred thousand swarmed into KwaNdebele between the 1950s and the 1980s. In the decade after 1970 alone the population of KwaNdebele grew by over 400 per cent. In contrast to this the population in Venda has been much more stable, and most of the growth over the years has been the result of natural increase.

At one level, the economic circumstances of people in both KwaNdebele and Venda are moulded by a common experience of loss of control over local resources and of forcible incorporation into the growing industrial economy of modern South Africa. But the two areas differ substantially, for historical and geographical reasons, in the availability of local resources, in population density, and in location relative to the industrial centres; because of this the processes of deprivation and incorporation have affected the two areas in different ways.

Income from agriculture is very low in both areas, but higher, in relative terms, in Venda, where more land is available for small-scale farming. KwaNdebele, on the other hand, is situated much nearer to the metropolitan areas of Pretoria and Johannesburg, where most jobs are to be found. The rate of external wage employment is therefore higher in KwaNdebele than in Venda, with the result that in the late 1970s, when the research in the two areas was done, per capita income was nearly 50 per cent higher in the former.

These gross differences are reflected in the patterns of participation in informal sector activities characteristic of each area. For example, in Venda women were very largely confined to agricultural activities. This was partly because there were virtually no opportunities for them in migrant or commuter wage labour, but also because men in the area thought it improper for their women to venture beyond the domestic domain in order to earn income. Men in Venda had much greater difficulty securing external wage employment than did their counterparts in KwaNdebele, in consequence of which they attempted to exclude women from all the more lucrative forms of informal production and marketing of craftwork. In Venda, therefore, the main forms of informal craftwork were dominated by men; there were, moreover, many more young men engaged in these activities, because of the lack of job opportunities for young men in and around Venda.

In KwaNdebele, on the other hand, most of the male craftworkers were the aged and disabled because there was greater scope for wage employment for the able-bodied. Women were also rather more prominent in craftwork in KwaNdebele, partly because there were almost no agricultural activities to which they could be confined, partly because there was less competition from men over involvement in these activities, and also because it was easier for women to gain independent access to markets, in the urban areas, for their products.

The fact that men and women in both Venda and KwaNdebele had differential access to informal craftwork opportunities drew our attention. For analytical purposes one could identify three categories of craft production on the basis of the origin of the crafts and the markets to which they were directed. Firstly there were the local crafts for internal consumption (wood-carving, basket-work, metal-work, skin-work, calabashes, pottery and beadwork). Secondly there were what can be called 'new' crafts, also for internal consumption (these included joinery, sheet-metal work, polythene work and needlework). Finally there were the crafts which were intended for external consumption (which comprised wood-carving, horn-carving, basket-work, skin- and leather-work, pottery and beadwork).

The local crafts are produced mainly with locally available materials and by technologically simple procedures. The products are used for practical and symbolic purposes and are seen by the people to represent a continuing 'tradition'. Women are very prominent in these activities, and, particularly in Venda, there is a limited and diminishing market for the products. A part of this production is distributed on the basis of reciprocity, since it has social and symbolic meaning for the local people and points to the importance of maintaining kinship and other social and political relations. Most of the produce is however sold for cash to supplement household income.

Although the market for these items is limited in Venda, much greater opportunities in this sphere were found in KwaNdebele. The period of diaspora and the long experience of deprivation on white-owned farms led to a heightened sense of ethnic affiliation among Ndebele-speakers. In political terms, this strong sense of affiliation gave the 'tribal' leadership considerable scope to exploit the possibilities provided by the homeland system, with results which were not necessarily beneficial to the ordinary inhabitants of the area. On the other hand, however, craft products (especially beadwork, basket-work and skin-work) came to occupy an important role as ethnic markers in initiation and marriage ceremonies. People who had been scattered over the rural Transvaal for many years, and who had recently managed to find their way to KwaNdebele, proclaimed their new-found sense of 'belonging' by self-conscious adherence to old custom. This meant, fortuitously, that there was a significant demand in KwaNdebele for items which women played a major role in making. In Venda, where people did not have this heightened sense of ethnic identity, craft products did not function in the same way in ceremonial contexts.

Products of the new crafts are made from materials which have been transformed by industrial processes outside these areas. Waste materials are often used in these crafts, showing the poverty of the local market. The products of this second type of craft are all utilitarian, and there is a steady demand in both areas for many of the items produced because they are frequently cheaper and more durable than the equivalent products of industrial manufacture which have to be purchased in the stores. Men predominate in much of this utilitarian craftwork, partly because they had acquired some of the skills of working with plastic and sheet-metal while employed as migrant workers in the urban areas. Where women were active in this kind of production, the activities they undertook tended to be an extension of their domestic skills, such as needlework (cf. Preston–Whyte and Nene, 1984).

Products intended for external consumption are aimed at consumers with a much higher standard of living, and for them local crafts are transformed to provide utensils and 'tribal art' according to need. The demand in the external market for craft products is indicative of the prevailing stereotypes about the inhabitants of areas like KwaNdebele and Venda. So-called tribal art is valued for its depictions of 'traditional life', for instance wood-carvings which show women in submissive domestic roles and men as warriors. Beadwork and wood-carvings, used as decorations by middle-class white tourists and city dwellers, reinforce the prevalent notions about the black rural areas as traditional, idyllic and near to nature. In this way the mostly white buying public are getting what they themselves have created indirectly by setting a demand for stereotyped images. The producers respond by providing items according to these images because it makes economic sense to do so.

Graburn has stressed the political implications of this process:

European and Western society in general, while promoting and rewarding change in its own arts and sciences, bemoans the same in others. They project onto 'folk' and 'primitive' peoples a scheme of eternal stability, as though they were a kind of natural phenomenon out of which myths are constructed. Much as Lévi–Strauss . . . has shown that these peoples use 'nature' as a grid against which to demarcate their experience, so the rulers of the world have used the powerless and the exotic as 'nature' by which to demarcate their 'culture'. (1976: 13–14)

In this way curio outlets, as well as ethnology exhibitions in museums, institutionalise the unequal relations between the producers and consumers of certain craft products and their respective social worlds by emphasising the distance between these worlds as natural and given.

It must also be noted here that the battery of legal restrictions which were, until very recently, intended to keep Africans from the homelands out of the 'white' urban areas, made it difficult for local makers of tourist crafts to market their products directly. This gave a privileged position to middlemen (mostly 'white') who owned curio shops and other outlets in the urban areas, where the craft products were sold at a high profit margin. This arrangement had a particularly severe effect on women in Venda who were craft producers, because they did not have the freedom or means to visit the urban areas. In this way an external market for the type of product Venda women used to produce was never developed. An external trade in curio items was, therefore, mostly dominated by men, some of whom were regularly visited by several private and semi-government (Development Corporation) dealers. A few of these master craftsmen produced on a large scale, employed apprentices (men) and labourers (women), and also sent salesmen to towns and cities to sell the finished goods.

There was some qualification to this situation in KwaNdebele, where the line between the crafts produced for local purposes and for external sale was not wholly clear. This was because KwaNdebele is (relatively) close to the Pretoria–Witwatersrand area. In contrast to craft items made by women from Venda, the beadwork and basket-work made by women from KwaNdebele had become famous over the years for its attractive colour and design. This had happened because many young Ndebele-speaking women were 'domestic servants' on farms and in the cities, where they displayed some of their beadwork. Moreover, a 'Ndebele village' north of Pretoria had been, since the 1950s, a tourist attraction, and glossy tourist and artistic photographs were regularly published in magazines and books depicting 'scenic South Africa' and 'tribal life'. The high demand for these beadwork items led to the manufacture and sale of curio work as well as the sale of used items of clothing and decoration which had symbolic and social use. Women from KwaNdebele were visited, on arrangement, by bulk curio buyers, but they also attempted to hawk their wares directly in the nearby towns and cities. They exploited the white suburbs and business centres, despite harassment by influx control enforcement, for the sale of curio items. They also took advantage of the substantial market in the townships for the sale of items with a more practical or social use.

There are also a number of trends in craftwork activities in general which deserve mention. Craft workers in both areas have become progressively more dependent on external sources for their materials, especially in KwaNdebele. Apart from the fact that natural materials such as wood are now less available because of the high population–land ratio, further restrictions are experienced as a result of the nature conservation policies of these areas. The same authorities who impose these restrictions, however, have large areas of bush deforested for agricultural projects. The result is that producers tend to cut green wood illegally or have to gather materials from far outside their area at considerable cost. Locally, prices of raw materials tend to be much higher than in the urban centres, and people have often to pay now for materials such as pottery clay which were freely available previously. To keep costs down, use is often made of alternative materials, such as scrap iron, leather off-cuts and discarded plastic bags. The gradual loss of control over the natural resources in their areas has made craft producers more dependent on the people who have access to these materials and to transport, both inside and outside of KwaNdebele and Venda.

Most participants generate only a very small income from craftwork. Usually, therefore, crafts tend to be an additional source of income, supplementing wages and pensions, rather than a resource for people who lack all access to other income. Craft production on its own can scarcely be an alternative to other sources of income as a result of the economic insecurity, unemployment and general poverty which are experienced in these areas. This conclusion is supported by Sharp and Spiegel (1984: 10) who have pointed, with regard to

Qwaqwa and Transkei, to the 'crucial importance of a reliable source of cash income (from wage labour or pensions) to domestic groups as the main shield against impoverishment. Other material resources, such as agriculture and other forms of petty production and retailing, are not alternatives to [this].'

Can one develop the informal sector?

There are several implications for developmental interventions in our discussion. In the first place, the experience in Venda and KwaNdebele convinces us that agencies which profess concern about poverty in the homelands would do a great deal better to pressure employers to pay decent wages and the state to make adequate pension provision, than to devise elaborate schemes to 'develop' the informal sector. Having said that, however, it remains true that activities within the informal sector have a useful supplementary role within the gamut of strategies which people adopt in order to survive. It needs to be stressed that people's access to informal sector activities and the income which can be derived from them is by no means uniform.

Close regional comparison of the kind undertaken above helps one to recognise and explain the many factors which structure such access by different categories of people. It is clear that in both Venda and KwaNdebele women, in particular, face adverse conditions in their attempts to generate income from these activities. The reasons for this are both general to the 'homeland' situation and specific to particular historical instances. Developmental interventions which operate with a close awareness of the obstacles that pertain in particular cases, and of the limitations of well-intentioned assistance to the informal sector, may be able to have some beneficial impact on the situation.

At present, however, the reverse is often the case. The Venda Development Corporation, for instance, experimented for some time in the 1970s with the production and marketing of crafts. The shielded workshops of churches and hospitals were taken over in an effort to establish a large-scale, profit-orientated enterprise. In the course of this, disabled workers, who could not cope with expected output, were paid off. Officials stressed that the undertaking was not a charity. The venture eventually collapsed because it did not make the anticipated profit. This left the field open once more to the churches and the South African Institute of Race Relations, which appear to have more success precisely because they provide training and marketing channels to the most needy small-scale producers, amongst whom women figure prominently.

11 The position of African women: Race and gender in South Africa

MAMPHELA RAMPHELE and EMILE BOONZAIER

. . . no man is powerless. However exploited, however stupid, however brutal, however deceived, all men are potent in the realm of reproduction. (O'Brien, 1981: 84)

The issue of gender does not constitute an obvious element in the political discourse in South Africa. It is commonly felt that 'race relations' form the core of the political debate and that concern about gender relationships is either irrelevant or overshadowed by the more pressing problems associated with relationships between different races, ethnic groups, cultures, tribes and so on.

This belief has significant implications for the discussion of gender in this country. Whereas notions such as 'race' and 'ethnic group' have been the subject of vigorous critical debate, the issue of gender has been, and continues to be, a neglected topic. The ground rules of the various debates on which other chapters in this book draw are already established, the issues have been debated at various levels of sophistication, and some attempt can be made to periodise changes in thinking. On the other hand, the debate about gender has scarcely begun. It is not possible to summarise the debate in this country; nor is there much point in attempting to locate it by reference to the heated discussion taking place in other countries. Instead, this chapter seeks to demonstrate that although 'male' and 'female' are in themselves unproblematic categories based on clear-cut biological differences, there are powerful cultural constructions associated with the different positions of men and women in society. These culturally constructed roles have significant social consequences – they define the parameters within which the domination of men over women takes place. But in South Africa they do so in a way that is often reinforced by the system of racial domination.

This point is pursued in this chapter by looking in some detail at a case-study of the dynamics of gender politics in the 'single-sex' African migrant labour hostels in the Western Cape. In particular, it focuses on the way in which these relationships are shaped by the exploitative system of racial discrimination, economic deprivation and the manipulation of 'tradition' as a means to legitimate male domination.

Sex and gender: biological categories and social roles

Gender relationships, universally characterised by the domination of men over women, refer to *social* relationships. Although the protagonists are identified by reference to *biological* differences of sex, this does not mean that such differences determine either the socially constructed roles associated with each of the sexes, or the nature of relationships between them. This issue has been the subject of strong debate between the 'biological essentialists' – who argue that gender relationships are biologically determined – and the 'social constructionists' – who see them as socially and historically determined.

It seems that much of this debate has been misplaced (for thus conceived, the issue can never be finally resolved) and, while we fully accept the significance of the socio-economic determinants of gender inequality, there is a need for reinvestigating its biological (and not only anatomical) roots (Sayers, 1982). Whatever the outcome, however, the debate has crystallised the importance of differentiating very clearly between the biological and the social. *Sexual* differences are something we are born with; they refer to basic and unchangeable biological facts. *Gender* roles and relationships, on the other hand, are socially learned, reinforced and modified by the economic, political and cultural environment in which we live.

From an early age we are socialised into appropriate gender role behaviour. Boys and girls are taught how to dress, sit and talk 'correctly'. Appropriate activities and interests are inculcated and reinforced, often through the medium of gender-specific toys and games. Even certain personality traits – such as assertiveness and aggressiveness or shyness and sensitivity – are conceived of in gender-specific terms. Behaviours that are tolerated and even encouraged in boys are often admonished and ridiculed in girls, and vice versa. We are all familiar, for example, with the way in which 'inappropriate' behaviour is sanctioned by the use of labels such as 'effeminate' or 'sissy', 'butch' or 'tomboy'. All of this serves to emphasise that we are talking about *socially constructed gender roles* and not about *biologically determined sexual differences*.

Patriarchy: a point of agreement between black and white men

Patriarchy, the system of domination of men over women, is universal. It transcends different economic systems, eras, regions and classes. Not surprisingly, it transcends other differences between white and black men in South Africa.

In the authoritative *Kultuurgeskiedenis van die Afrikaner* it is claimed:

This patriarchal tradition of the household is one of the most beautiful national legacies of the Afrikaner. ... As main characteristic of the old farming household we can mention that it was a *community of authority*. In this small community the father was the highest authority. In other words, he was at the head of a specific authority structure. Since every authority structure . . . can have only one head, the woman was under the authority of her husband. . . . The mother, on the other hand, was pre-eminently the loving and understanding party who cared and served in silence. (Cronjé, 1945: 326; translated)

Such sentiments are not too far removed from those expressed in Inkatha's *Ubuntu-Botho: Good Citizenship*:

This respect within the [Zulu] nation is found even among adults. In the family the man is head. The woman knows that she is not equal to her husband. She addresses the husband as 'father', and by so doing the children also get a good example of how to behave. A woman refrains from exchanging words with a man, and if she does, this reflects bad upbringing on her part. (Cited in Mdluli, 1987)

Simply identifying such common ideas in the ideology of male dominance does little more, however, than allow one to repeat the uncontentious observation that patriarchy is universal. Although acknowledging this fact is a precondition for understanding more fully the process of female oppression, in itself it tells us nothing about the specificity of gender relationships in particular contexts, or about the way in which these are generated and perpetuated. Furthermore, a concern with 'universal patriarchy' predisposes one to seek universal 'explanations', which almost invariably centre around biological factors.

Patriarchy, or male dominance, is not a single entity which varies only in degree. It takes on different forms in different contexts, and it is only by looking at similarities *and* differences that one can begin to analyse the highly variable range of factors that impinges upon the process of male dominance.

The politics of gender in Cape Town hostels: a case-study

We turn now to a case-study of gender relationships in the migrant labour hostels in Cape Town. This section is based on data collected as part of a broader study, undertaken during 1986-7, into living conditions in these hostels. Although most of the observations made here would apply to all African hostels in the Western Cape, the statistical data are drawn from a sample of hostels in Nyanga, Guguletu and Langa. Most of the detailed information relating to gender relationships, however, relates to council-built hostels in Langa, where in-depth research was concentrated.

Our discussion largely focuses on the material conditions pertaining to the hostels – the generalised poverty, overcrowding, lack of privacy, legislation (as regards migrant labour and the homelands) and access to employment. But it is also important to understand these conditions in relation to pre-existing male–female relationships, especially as these are exemplified in *ideas* about the position of women in both the domestic and broader social spheres.

There is a widespread ideology of male dominance amongst Africans which emphasises the idea that women pass through the control of different men throughout their lives. It is a system of control that stretches from the cradle to the grave. The father's control operates up to the time of marriage, at which point it passes over to the husband. In cases of children born to single women, the mother's father and brothers assume control. Widowed women fall under the control of a designated brother-in-law who assumes the responsibility of his late brother, including, in some cases, fathering children for him (Hunter, 1936: 210). This system confers the status of perpetual minor on African women, and has been reinforced by legal provisions of successive white governments (Simons, 1968: 281).

A cornerstone of this ideology of control is the system of *lobola* (bridewealth), which is used to secure control over the reproductive powers of women (Lye and Murray, 1981: 119). *Lobola* also plays an important role in the ordering of relations between men, both as individuals and as groups. In the past cattle were not just a symbol of wealth, but an indication of the relative strength of individual men in the system of control. Thus their use as a unit of exchange in *lobola* transactions also symbolised the transfer of control over individual women from one patriarchal family structure to another. Notwithstanding the observations that 'traditional' bridewealth practices have undergone significant change in response to new socio-economic demands (Murray, 1980: 114–15), this symbolism remains relatively intact and continues to provide a powerful means of control over women.

There is a danger, when talking about women's roles or the ideology of male dominance, of implying that all women passively accept or subscribe to these notions of the ideal of womanhood. There is also an implicit functionalist argument that, in any given society, individual behaviour conforms perfectly to the dictates of idealised roles. A growing body of literature has demonstrated the untenability of all these assumptions (see, for example, Obbo, 1981), and changes in the male ideology of domination can be seen in part at least as a function of the success of individual women's struggles against their stereotypical gender roles. Nonetheless, the position of women in the hostels in the Western Cape, we shall argue, renders them particularly powerless to challenge their stereotypical roles. It is in this sense that the hostels serve to reinforce the system of male dominance.

The setting

The hostels in Cape Town are a logical outcome of a deliberate policy, pursued by successive white governments, to discourage urbanisation of Africans, particularly in the Western Cape, and to reserve the area mainly for use by whites and coloureds (West, 1985; Savage, 1984). Africans were only allowed to reside here on a temporary basis and most were housed in single-sex barrack-like accommodation commonly referred to as 'hostels'.

The legacy of this policy is that today there is an acute shortage of housing for Africans in the Western Cape. The hostels, in particular, are subjected to extreme overcrowding with grossly inadequate basic amenities. For example, our survey indicates an average bed occupancy of 2,8 persons; a person to working toilet ratio of 133:1; and a person to tap ratio of 117:1.

Access to accommodation is focused around registered bed-holders (35 per cent of residents), with dependants (65 per cent) acquiring rights via their relationships (mostly as wives, children, siblings or girlfriends) with bed-holders. By definition all of the registered bed-holders are adult males. Some 57 per cent of the dependants are adults (17 years and above), of whom 68 per cent are female. Bed-holders (all male) therefore find themselves in the enormously powerful position of controlling the only viable source of urban accommodation available to dependants (mostly female). In addition, although employment opportunities for all are limited and entirely restricted to low-paying jobs, 71 per cent of the adult males and only 18 per cent of adult females enjoy regular incomes.

A system of discipline, aimed at limiting tensions and promoting cordial relations between residents, is concentrated in the hands of elderly males. This system involves electing one bed-holder from each 'door' (a unit of rooms, usually six, which shares one external door) to act as convener, arbitrator and chairman of disciplinary hearings, which are called whenever a complaint is lodged by one of the residents. Such conveners are called *izibonda*, since their role closely resembles that of men in rural areas who are often used by government authorities to control local villages (Hammond–Tooke, 1975a: 80). These *izibonda* are recognised by local township authorities, and depend on these authorities to enforce disciplinary evictions from the hostels (Thomas, 1987).

Social relationships in the hostels

Access to accommodation, for all dependants, comes via relationships with male bed-holders. Unlike their male counterparts, however, female dependants do not have the same, albeit limited, opportunities to transcend their dependent status. Thus their average age (37 years) is significantly higher than that of dependent males (27 years). It is virtually impossible for them to acquire beds in their own right and they have very limited chances of regular employment.

Like all other African urban migrants, women in the hostels are compelled to enter the urban areas primarily by economic necessity. Given the housing situation and the limited job opportunities available to women, however, access to urban economic resources is likely to be defined in terms of women's relationships with men – either as wives or as 'lovers'.

The majority of female residents (51 per cent) are wives of bed-holders. For many of them the move to Cape Town was an attempt to maintain some personal relationship with their migrant husbands, while at the same time seeking to retain a rural base in one of the 'homelands'. With the lack of adequate housing and the history of African insecurity in urban areas, retaining a rural home is still seen by many as an essential strategy, and thus makes necessary the pattern of male and female oscillation from countryside to town and vice versa.

Some marriage relationships continue to function well in spite of these constraints, but for many wives the move to town involves entering a cold, indifferent and sometimes openly hostile environment where they are seen as intruders by their husbands. These unstable marriage relationships are usually marked by the husband's failure to send regular cash remittances to the wife, and are in turn associated with unemployment, loss of responsibility for the family at 'home', alcohol abuse and extra-marital relationships with 'girlfriends' in town. Many of these wives come to the hostels as a desperate measure to save their families from disintegration, starvation or both.

Most of the unmarried women – widowed, divorced or never married – have children, and come to Cape Town in search of a source of income to support their families. Relationships with men are motivated primarily by the need for accommodation, although other considerations, such as financial support and occasionally affection, also play a part. As one woman put it: 'People have boyfriends mainly because they need a place to stay. Some do it for the sake of being supported by these men, but they are a minority. Most people hate the system of living together [*ukuhlalisana*], but they have no choice because of accommodation problems.'

This dependence on bed-holders places men in an enormously powerful position over women, making the hostels truly 'a man's world'. This power manifests itself in various forms – such as denying women the right to participate in decision-making and placing on them the burden of complete responsibility for domestic chores. But the generalised effect on relationships is that women have constantly to please their husbands or partners. Because of the unequal power relationship which exists, women tend to become submissive. For example, women are unwilling to question certain decisions taken by men, simply because they fear they might invite displeasure. Men justify their insistence on independent decision-making by referring to women's tendency to hesitate, echoing the standard stereotype of women as lacking the capacity for rational thought (O'Brien, 1981: 119). Women are also unable to challenge the double standards of sexual morality which men demand. Irrespective of their own behaviour, men use the risk of 'having children fathered by the open veld' as the main reason for disapproving of extramarital relationships for their wives but not for themselves. Some have gone as far as to prohibit their wives from using contraceptives in order to control their sexual activities. As one of the men commented: 'One has to remove the licence to loose life to avoid one's name being disgraced in the village during one's absence.'

Unmarried women in the hostels find themselves in a particularly difficult position. Besides being denied the social respectability associated with marriage, their relationships with male bed-holders are by definition much more fragile as they face constant competition from other unmarried women. There is general agreement amongst both men and women that most of these 'lover' relationships are characterised by mutual abuse and that both partners derive whatever benefit they can, whilst they can. For men the benefit is mainly that of having a 'domestic slave' to attend to their laundry, cooking and cleaning, as well as a sexual partner. The women are constantly reminded that they are dispensable. 'I know the face of my wife,' is a common saying of married men to their girlfriends whenever there is an argument. They are also disadvantaged by the stiff competition for males who will support them, which limits their ability to bargain for a better deal: for they know that there are countless other desperate women waiting to replace them.

Relationships between women are marked by intense competition – both between married and single women and amongst single women. Married women tend to see unmarried women as potential or current objects of their husbands' attentions and consequently as a cause of their husbands' neglect of family responsibilities. Unmarried women, on the other hand, resent the lack of respect which married women display towards them and feel strongly about being blamed for the irresponsible behaviour of married men. There are numerous instances cited by informants of physical fights between women over these issues, which in rare instances even end in death. One such case involved a wife who arrived in the hostels in the early hours of the morning, having received a tip-off from another woman who had been visiting her own husband. Her husband was on night duty, but she found his girlfriend asleep in his bed. She had come prepared for a showdown and was armed with a knife, but in the ensuing struggle the girlfriend got hold of the knife and stabbed the married woman to death. Cases such as these, and numerous others that emphasise the frequency with which families have broken down under the stress of triangular relationships, are simply grist to the mill of those who see single women as destructive elements in the hostels.

Animosity between single women centres around competition for the attention of potential partners. In this context physical attractiveness becomes a matter of survival, and women do everything in their power to make themselves attractive to men. One of the unfortunate consequences of this is the widespread use of skin-lightening creams. Failing to use such preparations is seen as suicidal: 'You are regarded as a woman who doesn't care about her appearance and you are dumped in favour of those women who are nice and pink.' When questioned on the problems of long-term skin damage, a typical retort was: 'Let that day come when it comes. As for now I can't stop and take the risk of losing out . . . in any case it might happen when I am too old to bother about my looks.'

The detrimental consequences of the use of skin-lightening creams serves to illustrate the common theme of the sexual objectification of women's bodies, but it also highlights the way in which notions of 'beauty' are influenced by the racist environment in South Africa. Lightness of skin colour is equated with higher socio-economic status and beauty – a widespread association that is also vigorously promoted in advertising.

Relationships between men, on the other hand, are not marked by such intense competition. Kinship links are a particularly important source of support and are utilised to find new workseekers accommodation, food and placement in jobs. People from one home village also help and support each other, especially in times of major life crises (such as death and sickness) and major life events (initiation ceremonies and marriages).

Age, however, is an important stratifying device, and young males (especially those who have not gone through initiation rituals) also find themselves in a relatively powerless position. The *izibonda* system, in particular, is monopolised by older men who should be revered and consulted on all important matters where wisdom is needed. This pattern of interaction is a recipe for conservatism, and while the older men have a vested interest in perpetuating a system that gives them so much power, there is no evidence of a concerted attempt by younger men to challenge this system either.

Coping strategies

This brief description of social relationships in the hostels inevitably conveys a picture of generalised competition and conflict, domination and subservience. Without detracting from the main thrust of these observations, we should emphasise that some (albeit isolated) marriages *are* warm and trusting relationships, and even some couples living together enjoy 'satisfactory' relationships where the parties live together in relative dignity and where they encourage each other to continue to fulfil their respective responsibilities to their rural families. One woman involved in such a relationship went so far as to say that her lover's wife was eternally grateful to her for the positive contribution she has made to their married life.

There are also many instances of cooperation and mutual support between women. These relate mainly to periods of distress or illness. For example, when someone is ill and unable to help herself, other women in the 'door' will assist with nursing care. There is also significant support given to the mothers of newborn babies in the form of providing warm meals, washing laundry and running small errands. Interestingly, this is also a period during which the husband's or partner's support is readily given. In addition to sharing the limited bed space with the mother and newborn baby, the man has to ensure that hot water is available for washing, breakfast is cooked for the mother, and, in cases where the woman is unwell, to wash the nappies.

Women also rally to the support of others during times of grief, sickness of relatives, and assault by male partners. When assaults occur, some women will alert other people, especially males, to restrain the offender. According to residents, disturbing the peace, rather than the assault of women, is punishable by fines ranging from R10 upwards, with significantly higher fines for multiple offenders. Some men therefore take their partners to the open veld where they assault them without running foul of the disciplinary code. However, only the unknowing women fall prey to this, and most women would refuse to go out after an argument, or threaten to scream if forcibly dragged out.

It is also clear that women do not merely accept their subservient roles passively. Faced with the circumstances within which they have to exist, women try to manipulate the system of male dominance to suit their own aims, developing strategies to circumvent some of the restrictions, or merely scoffing at those aspects about which they can do nothing.

We have just seen how women learn to exploit an instrument of male domination, the *izibonda*, for their own protection, and how women close ranks and forget their competitive stances temporarily to protect victims of assault. Much more common, however, are various strategies which are resorted to *within* the system of male dominance imposed by the hostel situation. For instance, wives often adopt pretexts for leaving their rural homes and coming to the hostels. The most frequent is to plead illness, either of the woman herself or one of her children. Informants express the view that there is no way in which a man can escape his responsibility of caring for sick members of his family. One's wife and children are an obligatory responsibility, and there are rituals and healing ceremonies that simply cannot proceed without the man of the house. In addition, inequalities in health-care services between urban and rural areas justify the move to Cape Town. The following case-study, although ultimately unsuccessful, illustrates how this strategy operates:

Since his arrival in Cape Town in the early 1960s, Dlamini used to send money regularly to his family in the Transkei. This stopped after 1980, at which time he also ceased to visit his family during the December holiday period. When his teenage daughter [our informant] came to seek him out in 1984, she found him living with another woman. Although this woman treats her well, she hates her and blames her for her family's problems. She had come on this visit because she had developed *mafufunyane* (a temporary mental illness said to be brought about by evil forces) and her mother had sent her so that her father could take responsibility for her treatment. However, although Dlamini has taken the responsibility of caring for his sick daughter, he has not responded to the implicit pressure to return home or to remit money.

This case should be seen in the context of possible alternative strategies for coping with errant husbands. For example, the wife could sue the husband for maintenance. However, the costs of embarking on this route far outweigh its uncertain benefits. In addition, the ability of courts in South Africa to enforce compliance in the event of successful claims is questionable (Burman and Barry, 1984). The wife could also sue for divorce, but this would require that she return to her natal home. It is unlikely that her family would accept her back, since they would then have to face the inevitable demands, from the husband's family, for the return of bridewealth. Finally, she could seek direct confrontation with her husband by coming to Cape Town herself. This is a risky option, requiring courage which some women cannot muster, especially when there has been a long period since the husband last communicated with his wife; he is more likely to throw her out of the hostel and force her to find her own way home.

Some women, however, choose the confrontational route. They take the risk and come to town to demand support. In some cases it pays off, but generally it is a struggle which only the most persistent can win. One such woman comes regularly to get money from her husband, who abuses alcohol and remits money irregularly. She times her visits to coincide with bonus month (November). She acknowledges that it is not easy and that she is sometimes assaulted in the process, but thinks that it is well worth the effort in the end.

Most women recognise that they are more likely to get what they want out of marriage if they are seen to possess the 'traditional' female virtues of modesty and deference. They are acutely aware of the fragility of men's egos and the need to make these men feel like 'masters of their own domains'. For example, the open spaces in most of the hostels are cluttered with old cars in various states of disrepair which men have bought but are unable to maintain. Women see this as a waste of money, but refrain from openly challenging their partners' ill-advised decisions to purchase these wrecks. They simply tolerate these 'corpses of our men's toys'.

Although unmarried women are in many respects particularly disadvantaged, many of them deliberately choose to stay single and exploit to the full the opportunities afforded by their single status. They literally jump from bed to bed to survive, as this case of Sisi Buli demonstrates:

She was widowed in 1978 and left with the sole responsibilities of caring for her four children. In desperation she came to Cape Town in 1982 in search of work. After a short spell as a live-in domestic worker she was fired because she did not have a proper pass. She then moved to the Langa hostel where her sister was staying with her husband. She used to sleep on a sponge mattress on the floor between the beds in her brother-in-law's room, and made a living by selling vegetables from a stand outside their hostel. She soon found a boyfriend, from another hostel, with whom she moved in. She had a child from this man, but had to move out in 1985 when his wife came to stay with him. She moved next door, where she had a relative, but again had to sleep on the floor between beds. She has now secured another boyfriend, a successful shebeen operator, and helps him to run a mobile shop parked outside their window. Her teenage daughter came to join her in 1986, and she put her up in the same block in a bed which had been left to her by a retrenched man from her home village. She did not seem perturbed by her daughter's pregnancy (which occurred a few months later) and even expressed satisfaction at the turn of events. Her youngest child is thriving and the only one of her children who has not suffered from malnutrition. She sums up the situation as follows: 'I feel that relationships with men are a matter of convenience. One takes what comes and moves on when the time is right. There is a lot of competition amongst women for men's attentions, and once involved with one, you must ensure that you keep their attention.'

Sisi Buli is one of the many women who have elected to stay single after the end of her marriage. She initially tried the 'respectable' way of earning an income – domestic work is one of the few avenues open to poor African women – but the ruthlessness of the pass laws put a stop to it. Her story also shows the importance of some of the networks operative in the hostels, which have provided her with entry into this supposedly male preserve. Direct relatives, acquaintances from 'home' and friends all serve, at some stage or another, as helpful contacts. Men are seen in this context as a useful resource, thus making competition inevitable. The manipulation of sexual and reproductive capacities, by both herself and her daughter, is part of the survival kit utilised.

Notwithstanding these individual attempts to resist the system of male dominance, the women in the hostels have thus far been unable to organise effectively as a group in order to fight for a better deal. Several factors are relevant here. Although they spend much time together while most men are at work, the divisions of age, marital status, length of stay in Cape Town, and degree of economic deprivation, are stronger than the ties of common oppression. Furthermore, these divisions delineate their differential capacity to manipulate patriarchy for their own ends (Cole, 1986). There is also the fear of taking risks, which is a feature of most exploitative systems and a determinant and outcome of unequal power relations (Biko, 1987). Finally, the totality of oppression conditions the oppressed to believe that their best interests are served by acquiescing in the demands of the oppressors (Brittan and Maynard, 1984: 218). The outcome is that when women do resist, they tend to do so in ways that reinforce their nurturing roles and not in those that promote their interests as people in their own right.

The situation in the hostels is a complex one which merits fuller discussion than the scope of this chapter permits. Nonetheless, it raises several issues and illustrates various themes which need to be made explicit.

Like all social situations, the case described above is unique. At the same time, it highlights many universal themes in the politics of gender relationships. Many of the issues raised are not peculiar to the hostels, but apply more broadly both to South Africa and internationally. However, they assume great intensity and importance in a situation of deprivation, and are compounded by the legislative framework which has forcibly separated men from their wives and created an environment which has limited the space for the development of mutual trust and respect between men and women.

We have seen, for example, how men in the hostels adhere to the common stereotypes of women and their role. The idea that women do not think rationally, the double standards of sexual morality, the sexual division of labour, and the importance attached to women's physical appearance, are widespread and well documented in other contexts. Similarly, women elsewhere also respond to the male need for docile and deferential women. As one of Obbo's informants in Kampala remarked: 'What men want is a softly spoken woman, who can kneel at their feet while serving them. I have many pairs of stockings worn through kneeling. I don't know why I do it.' (1981: 104)

It is also clear that many of the general observations made in the literature about patriarchy are directly relevant to the situation in the hostels. For example, Mary O'Brien has argued that gender politics should be viewed in a dialectical way as power relationships between men and women with reproduction as a central focus, in the same way that production is at the centre of capitalist class relations. She also points out that the capacity of the ruling class to exercise power over others derives from their ability to exploit the domination of men over women so as to fulfil the exploited workers' psychological need for power.

> There are obvious psychological ramifications of this situation which ruling classes can exploit, giving, for example, to wretched male labourers dingy homes which are none the less private castles. The determinants of power do not, quite clearly, lie within the realm of social relations of production, where most men have been powerless for a long time. They lie in the sphere of reproduction, and just as the labour process is the fundamental determinant of economic and technological development, reproductive process is the key to the mysteries of the potency principle and the forms which male supremacy takes. (O'Brien, 1981: 133)

These observations have a direct relevance to the situation in the hostels and raise important questions about the relationship between race and gender in South Africa.

Finally, the hostels provide a particularly good illustration of the way in which 'tradition' – a reconstruction of the past that is unchallengeable – is used to support the system of male dominance. The institutions of bridewealth, *izibonda* and male circumcision rituals all serve to reinforce control over women. Even the 'traditional' practice of barring women from the cattle kraal in deference to the departed who might be buried there has been transplanted to the urban environment. In one hostel in Guguletu women were barred from the common room during certain periods, on the grounds that it was *ebuhlanti* (the kraal) which men used for discussions and meetings.

Besides appeals to 'Xhosa tradition', it would appear that men can also freely invoke other 'traditions' as their needs require. One of the hostels adopted a policy of excluding all women (including wives), except as day-time visitors. This was justified in terms of their commitment to a 'clean Christian life' and their desire to maintain a spirit of 'brotherhood'. Allowing women to sleep over would threaten this moral purity, create points of conflict between the men, and set a bad example for younger residents. All residents of this hostel are said to be 'born-again Christians' and thus subscribe to this approach. Such selective conservatism – the selection of beliefs or practices which serve ends fully congruous with the old order (Hunter, 1936: 548) – manipulates the Christian values of 'purity' in conjunction with the worst elements of African 'traditionalism'.

Conclusion

The debate about the primacy of race and class over gender in resistance politics rages on, and in this country it has become a highly emotive issue. Accusations of introducing divisive issues into an already complicated political environment are very appealing to both men and women engaged at different levels in the struggle for a better future. *Umtapo Focus* goes so far as to claim: 'Black men are powerless and subsequently are incapable of oppressing and exploiting their women' (November 1987: 12).

The data presented here suggest that this is not the case. As Brittan and Maynard have commented: 'Oppression is multi-dimensional, because its operation in the one domain is easily transferable to another. ... One form of domination serves as a paradigm for another.' (1984: 217)

The social and political order in South Africa impacts on working-class black men in a way that brings out the worst kinds of chauvinism in them. Black women present the only cushion against their complete powerlessness, and any suggestion of equality between the sexes is a real threat to their egos. The oppression they suffer in the wider society acts as a paradigm for their domination of women, which is reinforced by an appeal to 'tradition' to justify practices that are said to be central to 'African culture'. The resultant ideology of male dominance, although subject to change over time, has the capacity for developing its own momentum and is therefore unlikely to disappear naturally along with other forms of oppression.

12 Defining children
SANDRA BURMAN

At first sight 'children' may seem an unsuitable category for examination in this book. If its function is to study the use and abuse of ambiguous terms for political purposes, why discuss an unambiguous term like 'children'? After all, everyone knows what a child is and, no matter what population classification South African children receive or in what activities they may participate, they remain 'children'. Or do they? This chapter questions such assumptions and examines the uses of the term in South Africa.

It is not, of course, disputed that a rich range of words exists to describe humans in the period between birth and adulthood. Of these, 'child' is probably the most commonly used in legal, official, and academic documentation. But it is argued here that childhood and its related words have meant very different things at different times, that they carry with them a range of hidden connotations and assumptions, and that they are categories which are manipulated in South Africa for administrative and political purposes.

Circumscribing childhood

Even the socio-biological definition of childhood as the period from birth to adulthood is in fact very ambiguous. Whether and, if so, at what stage a foetus counts as a child varies in different societies and in different periods. For example, until as late as 1915 a stillbirth was not registrable in England (Rose, 1986) as no person was held to have come into existence. Similarly, what constitutes the attainment of adulthood varies greatly in different societies, in the same society over time, or even within one society at the same time. In societies where children begin work very early and life expectation is short, childhood as a stage in a person's life may be almost or completely defined out of existence. The historian Phillippe Aries (1962), for example, believes that 'there was no place for childhood in the medieval world'. In the past, a prolonged period of training and protection in the early years of a person's life was a luxury many societies were not able to afford for any of their members. Today this luxury is most commonly denied to the poor.

Where childhood – or minority – is legally distinguished from adulthood, as in South Africa today, the mark of transition between the two states varies widely for different people and even for the same person. According to the civil law in South Africa, for example, it is normally on reaching the age of 21 that persons attain the full legal powers of adults, able to make contracts without the assistance of their guardian (who must be an adult). But should they marry at an earlier age, they will immediately acquire those powers – though they may be limited by the nature of the marriage contract or by an earlier legal declaration of prodigality. Should the marriage end in divorce (but not annulment) before either spouse reaches the age of 21, the spouse or spouses freed by matrimony from guardianship do not revert under it. Thus, according to the civil law, a person can attain adult status by reaching a given age or by marriage. This change of status may be at 21, or as young as 18 for boys and 15 for girls – or even earlier if the permission of the Minister of Home Affairs is obtained. In addition, but much more rarely, persons who have reached at least the age of 18 may attain adult status by applying to the Supreme Court for such an order, primarily on the grounds that their interests would be best served by anticipating their majority (Boberg, 1977).

But people may also become adults by some other *rite de passage*. For example, a Jew becomes classified as an adult after his *barmitzvah* or her *batmitzvah* at the age of 13, a ceremony of reception as a full adult into the Jewish community. In this case the contradictory definitions of the Jewish 13-year-old's status generate no practical problems. It is clearly understood by all concerned that this reception into adulthood pertains only within a religious context, and claims to be treated as an adult in any other context are given short shrift. However, where the scope of the *rite de passage* is not so closely circumscribed, the status of adulthood it confers can lead to collisions with the civil law system. For example, African boys who have undergone initiation ceremonies are generally regarded as men and may no longer be disciplined by women, irrespective of the boys' physical age. Some are as young as 6 years of age; many are in their mid-teens. Yet, apart from such exceptional cases as children who leave home and take to the streets, there is no question of most initiates becoming financially or legally independent of their families. They remain at home, under the control of the head of the family. However, an increasingly prominent feature of South African society is the number of *de facto* female-headed households, with migrant labour making this a particularly strong trend in African households. Simkins (1986) cites figures of almost 60 per cent in rural homeland areas, and 30 per cent in metropolitan South Africa. The result is that the heads of households are often legally responsible for 'adults' whom they cannot control but whom the civil law still defines as 'children' under their control.

The connotations of 'childhood'

Children remain under adult control because the civil law assumes them to be incapable or only partially capable of responsible judgement. They therefore cannot be held responsible or fully responsible for their actions and must be protected from society. Under the age of 7 children have no active legal capacity at all. They cannot be held responsible for any wrongdoing. Thereafter, until the age of 21, children can incur civil and criminal responsibility for wrongdoing in certain circumstances and have limited active legal capacity. The age of 18 marks the end of 'childhood' for the purposes of those provisions of the Child Care Act 74 of 1983 which seek to protect children against exploitation, ill-treatment, neglect and other abuses of the parental power. Various other legal provisions give children increasing responsibility for and control over their lives with increased age, though not necessarily in obviously logical sequence. From the age of 10 children's consent is required for their adoption; at 12 years a girl can validly consent to sexual intercourse; between the ages of 7 and 14 children are presumed not to be criminally responsible and this presumption must be rebutted by the state in order to convict the child accused, but at 14 years children lose the advantage of the rebuttable presumption that they lack criminal capacity; from that age they are also competent to witness a will; at 16 years children become competent to make wills and may also be members of or depositors in a building society; at 17 males classified as white become obliged to render compulsory military service; and at 18 those children of both sexes classified as white acquire the franchise and become able to insure their lives. But, unless they marry or are expressly declared to be majors, they cannot, unaided by their guardians, enter into contracts or administer their own property until they attain 21 years. What this reveals about society's attitudes to the control of property as against, for example, control of the military mechanisms to kill people, is not the subject of this discussion. Rather, its aim is to focus on the way that the distinctions drawn between different phases of childhood and between children and adults reflect – and probably add to – the host of hidden connotations attached to the word 'child' and its related terms.

Children are seen as weaker, less developed, with less judgement, less able to take responsibility; therefore to be protected, controlled, circumscribed. The word 'child' carries all these connotations with it. 'Youth', on the other hand, frequently tends to have connotations of adolescence and deplorable irresponsibility. 'Youngster' generally carries connotations closer to those of 'child'. Sometimes 'minors' or 'juveniles' is used when the word 'children' would carry too many unwanted connotations, or when 'youngsters' would be too informal. For example, 'altogether 209 juveniles had been killed and 703 injured in police action taken during unrest from January 1985 to February 10 this year, Mr Vlok replied to an NRP question' (*Cape Times*, 19 February 1986).

Media reporting of criminal and unrest incidents, or undesirable social conditions, can be highly manipulative simply by omitting the information that the offenders were young children, or by the choice of noun in describing the perpetrators or victims of the incident. A 14-year-old sleeping rough on the streets is usually described as a child, or possibly as a boy or a youngster, but if that same 14-year-old snatches a bag, he tends to become a 'youth', except to those protesting about his subsequent imprisonment in police cells, who will usually describe him as a child. Nor is the term 'youths' necessarily confined to teenagers. Reports of crime tend to stretch the category to embrace all the miscreants, such as: 'an elderly man who has been a regular at the shopping centre for two years, said the youths – who ranged in age from 9 to 12 years old – were responsible for thefts of handbags and break-ins of vehicles' (*Cape Times*, 17 July 1986).

Similarly, the scope of a category may be deliberately circumscribed to avoid as much undesired sympathy as possible. Thus the *Star* reported:

The Johannesburg Child Welfare Society (JCWS) has criticised recent official reports on the detention of children for referring only to those under 15, saying the legal definition of a child [under the Child Care Act] is any person under 18 years old. . . . The constant talk of the release of children under 15 might lull the community into believing that children between 15 and 18 were adult and could be treated as such, Dr Thomas said. (1 September 1987)

On the other hand, even where older teenagers are the victims, battering by parents is always described as child battering. And though the *batterer* may well be legally a child – the statistics show that teenage parents are the most likely to batter their children, and that many such parents are unmarried – reports that describe the batterer as a child are so rare as to be almost non-existent. At most, the parents may occasionally be described as 'hardly more than a child', the implication being that they are therefore less blameworthy because they are too young to be able to cope. This is not to suggest that every use of these terms is deliberately manipulative. Sometimes the selection of the various terms simply reflects insensitivity to their nuances, or is determined by the journalistic need to avoid repetition, but a survey of the newspapers over the past five years leaves no doubt of what readers are expected to think in various situations.

Further, a subtle development of this manipulative use of terms is to be seen in the occasional reporting of offences committed by young children – such as car stoning – in such a way that the stress is placed squarely on the consequences of the children's actions. While the age of the child may be omitted because it is not known, in some instances the omission appears to be less innocent. On other occasions the age of the child is used to imply that the child must be depraved to have behaved so badly so young. Such accounts have the effect of distracting attention from the legal principle that a child under 14 is presumed to be without criminal intent to commit a misdeed unless the contrary is proved. The law in fact punishes either *intention* to commit forbidden acts or *negligence* as to the consequences of doing so, but the media, by stressing the consequences of the child's action, divert attention to the fact that its *results* were as dire as if committed by an adult. The unspoken argument then runs that, since the action and consequences were the same as if an adult had committed the crime, it is in order to punish the child in the same way as an adult would have been punished.

Putting away childish things

As mentioned above, the recognition of a separate state of childhood, set aside for training and carefree play, is something of a luxury for the very poor throughout the world. Even where legislation exists, as in South Africa, to prevent the exploitation of child labour, the urgent need by the poorest households for additional income tends to produce illegally youthful newspaper boys or child farm labourers. However, in South Africa there is an additional factor. 'Race', in the form of population classification, determines at what age children of each group from poverty-stricken households shall be forced out to work. This is achieved by the use of crucial regulations which, for their purposes, define children of different 'population groups' into adulthood at different ages. Both the existence of these regulations and their rationale are important.

The prime regulations under discussion are those that control the state maintenance grants which are theoretically available as the final safety net to prevent starvation in needy families. The current regulations provide that state maintenance for children classified as white and coloured shall terminate when they reach 18 years of age, while for black children it stops when they turn 16. Welfare officials, when asked to justify this anomaly, explain that children classified as black are not considered dependent at that age. In other words, for purposes of support they become defined as adults. Actual cases demonstrate that even if blacks aged 16 are patently not self-supporting and unable to become so, being unskilled in an over-supplied market for unskilled labour, the state maintenance grant still stops. The criterion given for defining them out of the category of children is therefore either applied despite overwhelming evidence that it is based on a fallacy, or is not the actual reason (Burman, 1987).

A related example is provided where a family applies for a state grant or pension and has children living at home who are over 16 years of age. A means test is always applied when assessing whether a family qualifies for assistance, to ensure that the income already being received is not above a set limit. Income received from lodgers may be included in the calculation. In the case of families classified as white, coloured, and Indian, 'lodgers' is defined to exclude members of the family living at home, whether married or single. But for that section of the population classified as black the term includes children of the family who are working or even capable of working. Thus, black children over the age of 16 living at home can be defined as lodgers *and* wage-earners, thereby becoming an additional liability for poverty-stricken parents. This regulation reinforces their eviction not only into the labour market but out of the parental home at an age when children of other population categories are still treated as dependent children. Nor does proof of the 16-year-old's actual unemployed status force the rent officer to reassess a classification as a lodger; the officer can fix a 'reasonable amount' as the supposed rent supplied from the child's non-existent wages (Black Sash, 1985).

There are obvious short-term fiscal advantages to any ruling group in curbing welfare payments to the poorest section of the population, which in every country is also the largest. However, electoral considerations usually impede this course of conduct to some extent. In South Africa the section which is most disadvantaged does not have the vote, and the sensibilities of voters are not such as to prevent different scales of payments being made to populations classified differently by 'race'. This is usually rationalised on the grounds that the cost of living varies greatly between the different groups. The advertised aim of the government since 1948 has been to provide equal but separate facilities for each group. It remains the ideological ideal, even if honoured more in the breach than in practice. Children – sweet, helpless, and dependent – are an emotive issue, and the announcement that, since there are so many African babies, they should be supported for a shorter time than other groups, would be liable to give rise to an outcry. A far simpler solution is to define them out of that embarrassing category for the purposes of state payments.

But unfortunately for policy-makers, reality has a way of ignoring neat definitions, if not turning them on their head. In South Africa the children being most readily defined as no longer dependent may absorb the import of the message, as the schoolchildren's revolts since 1976 have demonstrated. As they also showed, a refusal thereafter to treat those same children as adults capable of negotiation is to lay bare the contradictions in state policy and to reinforce mistrust of all state-sponsored solutions. In the long term, therefore, defining childhood differentially for different population categories may prove to have been far more of a hindrance than a help to South Africa's development, whatever the short-term advantages. The children now having independence forced upon them may well in the years ahead play a major role in determining the country's future, and their frustrations could permeate the shape of things to come. As Wordsworth pointed out, 'the Child is father of the Man'.

Afterword
EMILE BOONZAIER

Readers may feel that the preceding chapters have been excessively critical of the terms addressed. There is, seemingly, an emphasis on the way in which they should *not* be used, and little attempt has been made to provide constructive alternatives. Some might ask: 'If all of these terms are problematic, which are the satisfactory ones?'

Before proceeding to discuss some of the substantive issues which this criticism raises, it is necessary to reiterate two points which are implicit in all the chapters.

Firstly, the basic aim has been to challenge the widespread assumptions that the categories implied by the various terms – races, tribes, traditional peoples, cultures, children, third world, and so on – simply describe an objective reality or a natural state of affairs. This was done by showing that these are all constructions or interpretations which have been *imposed* upon that reality. In other words, we are questioning the presumption that the terms depict objective 'truth'. To attempt, at this point, to substitute our version of objective truth for all these constructions would defeat the main thrust of the book and stretch the reader's faith beyond its limits. The same argument applies to the individual chapters, where authors have in fact not attempted to provide 'correct' definitions, precisely in order to examine in greater depth the assumptions on which all definitions ultimately depend.

Secondly, while all the chapters are critical of the way in which terms are used to present a particular version of the South African social 'reality', none argues that the concepts themselves are universally invalid. However, social concepts are seldom, if ever, used in an entirely neutral way, and it is this which the various chapters attempt to highlight. There is no attempt, for example, to deny physical or cultural difference, differences in age or sex, the possibility of communities, or the reality of tribalism and ethnicity. What is denied, however, is the unquestioned validity of the social constructions which are imposed upon this reality. Even 'race', if defined with reference to non-morphological genetic traits (such as the genes for blood groups and for specific proteins), might yet become entirely dissociated from the assumptions of the race paradigm and thus legitimately establish itself as a valid analytical concept in physical anthropology (cf. Tobias, 1985b). Similarly, Thornton argues that the term 'culture' becomes problematic when used to imply the existence of separate cultures associated with naturally discrete populations, without denying its continued analytical usefulness. And Sharp acknowledges the existence and validity of 'the third world' when used simply as a descriptive label, but is highly critical of the way in which its political use promotes the image of two separate and fundamentally different sections of the South African economy and society. In other words, the book's general criticism is directed not at the terms as such, but rather at their use in particular contexts, their implicit assumptions, and, most important, the practical implications of their usage.

These two points are clear from a close reading of the various chapters, but the question of alternative (and less problematic) constructions raises two more substantive issues which we want to discuss briefly. Firstly, why has the notion of 'class' proven to be such an attractive alternative for analysing the South African situation? And secondly, what implications does our critical discussion of the various concepts have for contexts other than South Africa?

'Class' in South Africa

'Class' differs from all the concepts addressed in this volume in one important respect: it does not form part of the dominant political discourse in South Africa. Although this is hardly surprising to anyone familiar with this country, it is instructive to note that 'class' has, in other contexts, proved eminently suited to the task of political manipulation and mobilisation. In addition, 'class', however vaguely conceived, is perhaps the most obvious way of describing the visible differences and divisions within the South African population. In many instances where differences such as white–black, Western–African and first world–third world are referred to, the actual situation often seems to be more accurately and appropriately described as one of social class – that is, rich and poor. For example, the most glaring difference between white suburban residential areas and African townships is one of wealth. Typically, solid and spacious houses, late-model cars and well-kept gardens and roads contrast strikingly with grey, overcrowded residential blocks and makeshift extensions, abandoned car wrecks and unpaved roads. These are the basic differences which all South Africans are aware of, but it is their *interpretation* which is not necessarily agreed upon.

The central argument underlying much of the state's rhetoric is that differences in wealth are the *result* of other basic differences. Poverty is seen as a normal or expected condition associated with the third world, with less developed countries, traditional cultures, tribal peoples and black races. Similarly, conflict is seen as the inevitable outcome of given racial, cultural, ethnic or tribal differences. If these basic premises are accepted, apartheid (or separate development, or multinationalism) not only becomes a morally justifiable way of reducing conflict and inequality, it also becomes the logical, self-evident and most rational response (Posel, 1987).

This logic represents a coherent argument whereby racial, cultural, tribal and ethnic differences are considered to be 'basic' – they are the given reality around which South African society is structured. Differences in wealth and conflict are secondary phenomena resulting from these primary realities. The idea of class, viewed simply as rich and poor, is therefore entirely compatible with this argument and in no way threatens its underlying logic.

The Marxian idea of class, on the other hand, is part of an explanatory framework which provides a fundamental challenge to this whole argument. Within this framework, economic *relationships* are seen to constitute the basic structure of society. Racial and ethnic conflicts are analysed as the manifestations of underlying economic struggles, and differentials in wealth are related directly to economic interests and political power.

Neo-Marxist analysis, which emerged in Europe and North America in the 1960s, proved to be a particularly attractive alternative to understanding the South African situation. Not only did it challenge the very foundations of orthodox wisdom, it also provided new hope for the future. If racial and ethnic prejudices were basic, some form of segregation would offer the only solution. However, if prejudice was seen to be the consequence of economic and political struggles, new solutions, which did not passively accept the 'givens' of racial, cultural, ethnic or tribal differences, could be sought.

Many young South Africans, especially those raised within a liberal tradition, turned to neo-Marxism with vigour. Part of their motivation stemmed from two 'realities' which were increasingly becoming apparent: the policy of separate development had merely exacerbated economic inequalities; and the 'homeland' policy was contradicted by the continuing pressure for African urbanisation, the increasing flow of migrant workers, and the obvious non-viability of the economies of 'homeland' areas.

Neo-Marxist analysis provided a useful alternative to an uncritical acceptance of analytical concepts that predisposed one to see the southern African situation in terms of separate and isolated parts – races, cultures, tribes, economies and worlds. It offered an analytical framework which allowed one to look at the relationships *between* sections of the population in the southern African region as a whole. Units which had previously been regarded as isolated, separate and independent entities became part of an interrelated whole. Different classes were identified essentially in order to highlight the relationships of exploitation which exist between them. For example, migrant labourers were no longer seen as 'men of two worlds' attracted by the 'bright lights' of the cities and oscillating between 'Western' and 'traditional African' cultures (Houghton, 1960). Instead, they became wage labourers who were forced to respond to the needs of capitalism and who could be paid low wages because their families were ostensibly feeding, housing, educating and caring for themselves (Wolpe, 1972). Thus poverty and underdevelopment were understood as a function of the exploitative relationships associated with capitalism, rather than as a natural product of racial and cultural differences (Palmer and Parsons, 1977). Similarly, racism and ethnicity were seen to be motivated by economic and political competition, and not by inherent, primordial differences (Sharp, 1980).

The main and, at the time, very necessary thrust of the neo-Marxist argument was to challenge the assumption of the primacy of racial and ethnic groups and prejudices. This inevitably led to an initial overemphasis on economic relationships without due regard for the way in which these intersect with institutions, identities, prejudices and beliefs. Liberal critics rapidly exploited this weakness. They were quite emphatic that they had never denied the significance of economic relationships, but pointed out that the neo-Marxists had gone too far in stressing their importance (Welsh, 1987). They could therefore claim for themselves the position of reasonable moderates, innocent of all monocausal determinisms. Not surprisingly, much of the criticism by the liberal school was directed towards early attempts at class analysis, and little attention was paid to the more recent critiques of this literature by neo-Marxists themselves (for example, see Bozzoli, 1983).

Although it is tempting to view liberalism as the route towards a reconciliation between the extreme views of racist ideology and Marxian analysis, it is clear that the liberal school has not succeeded in challenging the fundamental assumption of the inevitability of racism and ethnicity in what is still seen as a situation of diverse races and cultures. Most of their critique of the neo-Marxists centres around the discussion of the phenomena of racism and ethnicity and focuses on the question of the primacy – 'Which came first?' – of capitalism or racism. This question is unlikely to be resolved, and, as Sharp has pointed out (1985b), the significance of the question itself needs to be questioned. The issue is not whether ideas about physical and cultural differences gave rise to class differences or vice versa. Rather, it is to look at the way in which ideas about physical, cultural, and other differences are structured to foster and justify sectional economic and political interests.

South Africa and the outside world

This book has focused on the way in which a variety of terms has been used and abused in South Africa. There is a danger, however, of concluding that their usage in South Africa represents a unique and isolated aberration and that the self-same concepts and ideas about society are legitimate and unproblematic in other contexts. A close reading of the various chapters suggests that this is not the case. Rather, the situation in this country can be seen as a vivid illustration, albeit in extreme form, of the potential weaknesses inherent in all of these terms. Since each is associated with a set of ideas and assumptions which is seldom made explicit, their use can be manipulated to suit a range of political interests.

With the exception of 'population group' and 'ethnic national citizenship', which are local creations, all the terms have been appropriated from an international repertoire of notions about human difference. From the South African government's perspective, this has the obvious political advantage that it creates a rhetoric which can resonate with usages in the outside world. But the disadvantage is that such a strategy requires constant revision and modification in response to shifts in international thinking. This is one reason why 'race', for example, has been largely replaced by the terminology of 'cultures', 'ethnic groups' or 'first world–third world'.

The contributors to this book have attempted to highlight these points by tracing the historical development, largely in Europe and North America, of the various terms. They have also emphasised that the use of the terms outside South Africa has not been unproblematic; and they have referred, where appropriate, to international theoretical criticisms.

In other countries it is also increasingly recognised that anthropology has done little to dispel nineteenth century misconceptions about race and that these ideas, at least in Britain and Australia, enjoy continued support under the guise of 'culture' and 'ethnicity' (Street, 1987; Cowlishaw, 1987). The underlying ideas about human evolution, classification, hierarchy and conjectural history have survived the transition from biological categories to sociological ones (Banton, 1987).

The other theme which the contributors to this volume have emphasised, is that they are dealing with *culturally created categories*, rather than with objective or natural phenomena. This observation is also not unique to South Africa, as many writers have recognised in other contexts. For example, commenting on the situation in Australia, Cowlishaw observes that the notions of 'traditional Aborigines' and 'Aboriginal culture' are cultural constructions with significant political implications:

The process of categorisation whereby people of a society are allocated to one or other group which is called a race, or to any other category, is part of the wider process of construction of ideology. The categories created are not a direct consequence of a certain genetic or cultural heritage, but are part of a cultural process of evaluation and bestowing meaning on certain phenomena such as biological or cultural characteristics. . . . [It] is a matter of ideology: a dynamic cultural construction which is part of wider political and economic processes. (1987: 228)

A concern with 'social process, the construction of identities and the symbolizing of boundaries . . . requires problematizing the unit of study, rather than taking it as given' (Street, 1987: 14). Before one can begin to study the popular meaning of the various terms, one has to grasp that they are cultural constructs and not simply reflections of 'objective reality'. This book is a first, but we believe necessary, step towards this broader goal of documenting and analysing the way in which people understand and use the various terms or subscribe to their implicit assumptions.

Calls for a reorientation of focus, usually combined with strong criticism of anthropological concern with the 'essential meaning' of 'given cultures', are increasingly being heard (for example, Asad, 1979). This raises interesting questions about future directions in anthropological research both in this country and abroad.

An anthropological analysis should help expose how such ideas were and often still are linked with conceptions of hierarchy, power and domination. . . . it is now apparent how the 'scientific' theories came to be linked with political ideologies of class, hierarchy and world order. Contemporary anthropologists would argue that race is to be understood in this context rather than as a useful analytical category: they can both suggest alternative ways of making sense of the complexity and diversity of human social life and provide in-depth analyses of the representations, ideologies and discourses in which 'race' is embedded. (Street, 1987: 14)

Street is referring here specifically to 'race', but his argument applies equally to all the other terms addressed in this volume. However, the approach which is being called for is not simply a return to either the 'idealist' approach of the liberal scholars, or the 'materialist' approach of early neo-Marxists.

On the one hand, there is the need to recognise the extent to which ideology (or discourse, or rhetoric) is linked to 'access to real resources in real and shifting historical circumstances' (Street, 1987: 14). One must ask what 'specific political and economic conditions . . . make certain rhetorical forms objectively possible and *authoritative*' (Asad, 1979: 616). On the other hand, it is not only economic resources which are at issue, but ideologies and discourses as well (Street, 1987: 15). Many of the chapters explicitly make the point that ideas are a resource to be manipulated and exploited, and all acknowledge that ideas (beliefs *about* reality) have real social, political and economic consequences. The central questions we should be addressing are therefore how and in what contexts certain ideologies and discourses come to dominate others.

Bibliography

Adam, H. and Giliomee, H. 1979. *The rise and crisis of Afrikaner power*. Cape Town: David Philip

Alland, A. 1971. *Human diversity*. New York: Columbia

Amselle, J. and M'Bokolo, E. 1985. Introduction to *Au coeur de l'ethnie. Ethnies, tribalisme et état en Afrique*. Paris: Editions la Découverte

Anderson, B. 1983. *Imagined communities: reflections on the origin and spread of nationalism*. London: Verso

Ardener, E. 1985. Social anthropology and the decline of modernism. In J. Overing (ed.) *Reason and morality*. ASA monographs no. 24. London: Tavistock Publications

Aries, P. 1962. *Centuries of childhood*. London: Jonathan Cape

Asad, T. (ed.) 1973. *Anthropology and the colonial encounter*. London: Ithaca Press

Asad, T. 1979. Anthropology and the analysis of ideology. *Man*, 14: 607–27

Banton, M. 1987. *Racial theories*. Cambridge: Cambridge University Press

Barth, F. (ed.) 1969. *Ethnic groups and boundaries*. London: George Allen and Unwin

Beavon, K. S. O. and Mabin, A. 1978. *Hawkers in Johannesburg*. Unpublished paper presented to the South African Geographical Society's Urban Studies Workshop

Beinart, W. 1984. Soil erosion, conservation and ideas about development: a southern African exploration, 1900–1960. *Journal of Southern African Studies*, 11 (1): 52–56

Beinart, W. 1987. Worker consciousness, ethnic particularism and nationalism: the experience of a South African migrant, 1930–1960. In Marks and Trapido (1987)

Beinart, W. and Bundy, C. (eds.) 1987. *Hidden struggles in rural South Africa: politics and popular movements in the Transkei and eastern Cape, 1890–1930*. Johannesburg: Ravan Press

Bell, C. and Newby, H. 1971. *Community studies: an introduction to the local community*. London: George Allen and Unwin

Benedict, R. 1935. *Patterns of culture*. London: George Routledge and Sons

Biko, S. 1987 (1978). *I write what I like*, ed. by A. Stubbs. London: Penguin

Black Sash, 1985. *You and your state pension*. Johannesburg: Black Sash

Bloch, M. 1961. *Feudal society*, 2 vols. Chicago: University of Chicago Press

Boberg, P. Q. R. 1977. *The law of persons and the family*. Cape Town: Juta

Bonner, P. 1982. The Transvaal Native Congress, 1917–1920: the radicalisation of the black petty bourgeoisie on the Rand. In Marks and Rathbone (1982)

Boyer, P. 1987. The stuff 'traditions' are made of: on the implicit ontology of an ethnographic category. *Philosophy of the Social Sciences*, 17: 49–65

Bozzoli, B. 1983. Marxism, feminism and South African studies. *Journal of Southern African Studies*, 9 (2): 139–171

Brand, S. S. 1986. Deregulering en die informele sektor. *Aambeeld*, 14 (4): 16–19

Brittan, A. and Maynard, M. 1984. *Sexism, racism and oppression*. Oxford and New York: Basil Blackwell

Bromley, R. and Gerry, C. (eds.) 1979. *Casual work and poverty in third world cities*. Chichester: John Wiley

Bührmann, M. V. 1984. *Living in two worlds: communication between a white healer and her black counterparts*. Cape Town and Pretoria: Human and Rousseau

Bundy, C. 1979. *The rise and fall of the South African peasantry*. Berkeley: University of California Press

Bundy, C. 1987a. Land and liberation: popular rural protest and the national liberation movements in South Africa, 1920–1960. In Marks and Trapido (1987)

Bundy, C. 1987b. We don't want your rain, we won't dip: popular opposition, collaboration and social control in the anti-dipping movement, 1908–16. In W. Beinart and C. Bundy (eds.) *Hidden struggles in rural South Africa: politics and popular movements in the Transkei and eastern Cape 1890–1930*. Johannesburg: Ravan Press

Burman, S. B. 1987. Marriage break-up in South Africa: holding want at bay? *International Journal of Law and the Family*, 1: 206–247

Burman, S. B. and Barry, J. 1984. *Subordination, feminism and social theory*. Carnegie Conference paper no. 87. Cape Town: University of Cape Town

Chambers, R. 1983. *Rural development: putting the last first*. London: Longman

Clegg, J. 1981. Ukubuyisa isidumbu – 'bringing back the body'. Mpofana rural locations, 1882–1944. In P. Bonner (ed.) *Working papers in southern African studies*. Johannesburg: Ravan Press

Coertze, P. J. 1973. *Inleiding tot die algemene volkekunde*. Johannesburg: Voortrekker Pers

Coertze, P. J. 1983. *Die Afrikanervolk en die Kleurlinge*. Pretoria: Haum

Cohen, A. P. 1985. *The symbolic construction of community*. London: Tavistock Publications

Cohen, R. 1978. Ethnicity: problem and focus in anthropology. *Annual Review of Anthropology*, 7: 379–403

Cohen, R. and Middleton, J. (eds.) 1971. *From tribe to nation in Africa: studies of incorporation processes*. Scanton: Chadler Publishing

Cole, J. B. (ed.) 1986. *All American women: lines that divide, ties that bind*. New York: The Free Press

Cole, J. 1987. *Crossroads: the politics of reform and repression, 1976–1986*. Johannesburg: Ravan Press

Colson, E. 1968. Contemporary tribes and the development of nationalism. In J. Helm (1968)

Comaroff, J. 1985. *Body of power, spirit of resistance: the culture and history of a South African people*. Chicago and London: University of Chicago Press

Couzens, T. 1978. Introduction to S. T. Plaatje, *Mhudi*, ed. by S. Gray. London: Heinemann

Cowlishaw, G. 1987. Colour, culture and the aboriginalists. *Man*, 22: 221–37

Crick, M. 1976. *Explorations in language and meaning: towards a semantic anthropology*. London: Malaby Press

Cronjé, G. 1945. Die huisgesin in die Afrikaanse kultuurgemeenskap. In C. M. van den Heever and P. de V. Pienaar (eds.) *Kultuurgeskiedenis van die Afrikaner*, vol. I. Cape Town: Nationale Pers

Davenport, T. R. H. 1987. Can sacred cows be culled? A historical review of land policy in South Africa, with some questions about the future. *Development Southern Africa*, 4 (3): 388–400

De Beer, C. 1984. *The South African disease: apartheid, health and health services*. Johannesburg: Southern Africa Research Service

De Klerk, W. A. 1976. *Puritans in Africa: a history of Afrikanerdom*. Harmondsworth: Penguin

Duminy, A. and Ballard, C. (eds.) 1981. *The Anglo–Zulu War: new perspectives*. Pietermaritzburg: Natal University Press

Du Preez, J. H. 1984. Basic socio-economic elements of a development theory for traditional societies. *Development Southern Africa*, 1 (1): 36–55

Du Toit, A. 1985. Puritans in Africa? Afrikaner 'Calvinism' and Kuyperian neo-Calvinism in late nineteenth century South Africa. *Comparative Studies in Society and History*, 27(3): 209–240

Eiselen, W. M. 1929. *Die Naturelle vraagstuk*. Cape Town: Nasionale Pers

Eisenstadt, S. N. 1972. Post-traditional societies and the continuity and reconstruction of tradition. In S. N. Eisenstadt (ed.) *Post-traditional societies*. New York: W. W. Norton

Elliot, J. 1984. Black medical students and African cosmological beliefs. *Africa Insight*, 14 (2): 109–112

Etherington, N. 1978. *Preachers, peasants and politics in southeastern Africa, 1835–1880: African Christian communities in Natal, Pondoland and Zululand*. London: Royal Historical Society

Fardon, R. 1987. History, ethnicity and pageantry. The 1987 ASA Conference. *Anthropology Today*, 3 (3): 15–17

Frank, A. G. 1971. *Capitalism and underdevelopment in Latin America*. Harmondsworth: Penguin

Fried, M. H. 1965. A four letter word that hurts. In H. R. Bernard (ed.) *The Human Way*. New York: Macmillan Publishing Co.

Fried, M. H. 1966. On the concepts of 'tribe' and 'tribal society'. *Transactions of the New York Academy of Sciences*, 28 (4): 527–540

Fried, M. H. 1975. *The notion of tribe*. Menlo Park: Cummings

Gazankulu Government. 1985. *The economic development of Gazankulu, with special reference to the agricultural sector*, File no. 6/10/1, Department of Agriculture and Forestry

Geertz, C. (ed.) 1963. *Old societies and new states*. Glencoe: Free Press

Gellner, E. 1983. *Nations and nationalism*. Oxford: Basil Blackwell

Giddens, A. 1973. *The class structure of the advanced societies*. London: Hutchinson

Giliomee, H. 1983. Constructing Afrikaner nationalism. *Journal of Asian and African Studies*, 18 (1–2): 83–98

Giliomee, H. 1987a. The beginnings of Afrikaner nationalism, 1870–1915. *South African Historical Journal*, 19: 115–142

Giliomee, H. 1987b. Western Cape farmers and the beginnings of Afrikaner nationalism. *Journal of Southern African Studies*, 14 (1): 38–63

Girvin, S. D. 1987. Race and race classification. In Rycroft (1987)

Godelier, M. 1977 (1973). The concept of 'tribe': a crisis involving merely a concept or the empirical foundations of anthropology itself? In M. Godelier (ed.) *Perspectives in Marxist anthropology*. Cambridge: Cambridge University Press

Godelier, M. 1986. *The making of great men: male domination and power among the New Guinea Baruya*. Cambridge: Cambridge University Press

Gordon, R. J. 1985. Primitive accumulation and Bushman policy in South West Africa. In C. Schrire and R. Gordon (eds). *The future of former foragers*. Cambridge, Mass.: Cultural Survival Inc.

Gould, S. J. 1981. *The mismeasure of man*. Harmondsworth: Penguin

Graburn, N. H. H. (ed.) 1976. *Ethnic and tourist arts: cultural expressions from the fourth world*. Berkeley: University of California Press

Greenberg, S. 1983. Review of D. O'Meara, *Volkskapitalisme* in *Social Dynamics*, 9 (1): 105–107

Greenberg, S. 1987. Ideological struggles within the South African state. In Marks and Trapido (1987)

Gunner, E. 1986. A dying tradition? African oral literature in a contemporary context. *Social Dynamics*, 12 (2): 31–38

Guyer, J. 1981. Household and community in African studies. *African Studies Review*, 24 (1–2): 87–137

Hammond–Tooke, W. D. 1975a. *Command or consensus: the development of Transkeian local government*. Cape Town: David Philip

Hammond–Tooke, W. D. 1975b. African worldview and its relevance for psychiatry. *Psychologica Africana*, 16: 25–32

Harries, P. 1982. Kinship, ideology and the nature of pre-colonial labour migration: labour migration from the Delagoa Bay hinterland to South Africa up to 1895. In Marks and Rathbone (1982)

Harries, P. 1987. Imagery, symbolism and tradition in a South African bantustan: Gatsha Buthelezi, Inkatha and Zulu history. Mimeo, University of Cape Town.

Harries, P. 1988. The roots of ethnicity: discourse and the politics of language construction in south-east Africa. *African Affairs* 346: 25–52

Hart, K. 1973. Informal income opportunities and the structure of employment in Ghana. *Journal of Modern African Studies*, 11 (1): 61–89

Hatch, E. 1985. Culture. In *The Social Science Encyclopedia*, 1985

Heese, H. 1984. *Groep sonder grense*. Wes-Kaaplandse Instituut vir Historiese Navorsing nr. 5: Bellville

Helm, J. (ed.) 1968. *Essays on the problem of tribe*. Seattle: American Ethnological Society

Heyer, J., Roberts, P. and Williams, G. 1981. Rural development. In J. Heyer, P. Roberts and J. Williams (eds.), *Rural development in tropical Africa*. London: Macmillan

Hill, R. and Pirio, G. 1987. 'Africa for the Africans': the Garvey movement in South Africa, 1920–1940. In Marks and Trapido (1987)

Hobsbawm, E. 1983. Introduction: Inventing tradition. In Hobsbawm and Ranger (1983)

Hobsbawm, E. and Ranger, T. (eds.) 1983. *The invention of tradition.* Cambridge: Cambridge University Press

Hofmeyr, I. 1987. Building a nation from words: Afrikaans language, literature and ethnic identity, 1902–1924. In Marks and Trapido (1987)

Homans, G. 1951. *The human group.* London: Routledge and Kegan Paul

Houghton, D. H. Men of two worlds: some aspects of migratory labour. *South African Journal of Economics,* 28 (3): 177–190

Hunter, M. 1936. *Reaction to conquest: effects of contact with Europeans on the Pondo of South Africa.* London: Oxford University Press

Hunter, M. 1979. *Reaction to conquest: effects of contact with Europeans on the Pondo of South Africa,* 3rd, abridged ed. Cape Town: David Philip

Hyden, G. 1980. *Beyond Ujamaa in Tanzania: underdevelopment and an uncaptured peasantry.* Berkeley: University of California Press

Iliffe, J. 1979. *A modern history of Tanganyika.* Cambridge: Cambridge University Press

Jackson, A. D. 1975. *The ethnic composition of the Ciskei and Transkei.* Department of Bantu Administration and Development: Ethnological Publications no. 53. Pretoria: Government Printer

Jansen, H. 1981. 50 jaar van koershou – die Voortrekkers. *Flying Springbok,* 1 (4): 34–37

Junod, H. 1912–13. *The life of a South African tribe.* 2 vols. Neuchatel, Switzerland: Attinger Frères

Karis, T. and Gerhart, G. (eds.) 1977. *From protest to challenge,* Vol. III. Stanford: Stanford University Press

Karlsson, E. L. and Moloantoa, K. E. M. 1984. The traditional healer in primary health care – yes or no? *Continuing Medical Education,* 2: 43–47

Keesing, R. M. 1975. *Kin groups and social structure.* New York: Holt, Rinehart and Winston

Keesing, R. M. 1981. *Cultural anthropology: a contemporary perspective.* New York: Holt, Rinehart and Winston

Keesing, R. M. and Tonkinson, R. (eds.) 1982. *Reinventing traditional culture: the politics of kastom in island Melanesia.* Special issue of *Mankind,* 13 (4)

Krader, L. 1976. *Dialectic of civil society.* Amsterdam: Van Gorcum

Kuper, A. and Kuper, J. (eds.) 1985. *The Social Science Encyclopedia.* London: Routledge and Kegan Paul

Kuper, J. 1984. *Race and race relations.* London: Batsford

Lacey, M. 1981. *Working for Boroko: the origins of a coercive labour system in South Africa.* Johannesburg: Ravan Press

La Fontaine, J. 1986. Countering racial prejudice: a better starting-point. *Anthropology Today,* 2 (6): 1–2

Levitas, B. (with J. Morris) 1984. *South African tribal life today.* Cape Town: College Press

Levitas, B. N.d. *Ethnology: an introduction to the peoples and cultures of southern Africa.* Cape Town: Oxford University Press

Leys, C. 1975. *Underdevelopment in Kenya: the political economy of neo-colonialism, 1964–1971.* London: Heinemann

Lodge, T. 1983. *Black politics in South Africa since 1945.* Johannesburg: Ravan Press

Lonsdale, J. 1983. From colony to industrial state: South African historiography as seen from England. *Social Dynamics* 9 (1): 67–83

Lye, W. F. and Murray, C. G. 1980. *Transformations on the Highveld.* Cape Town: David Philip

McAllister, P. A. 1980. Work, homesteads and the shades: the ritual interpretation of labour migration among the Gcaleka. In Mayer (1980)

Mafeje, A. 1971. The ideology of 'tribalism'. *Journal of Modern African Studies,* 9 (2): 253–261

Mair, L. 1984. *Anthropology and development.* London: Macmillan Press

Marks, S. and Rathbone, R. (eds.) 1982. *Industrialisation and social change in South Africa: African class formation, culture and consciousness 1870–1930.* London: Longman

Marks, S. and Trapido, S. (eds.) 1987. *The politics of race, class and nationalism in twentieth century South Africa.* London: Longman

Mayer, P. 1971. Traditional manhood initiation in an industrial city: the African view. In E. J. de Jager (ed.) *Man: anthropological essays presented to O. F. Raum.* Cape Town: Struik

Mayer, P. 1975. Class, status and ethnicity as perceived by Johannesburg Africans. In L. Thompson and J. Butler (eds.) *Change in contemporary South Africa.* Berkeley: University of California Press

Mayer, P. (ed.) 1980. *Black villagers in an industrial society: anthropological perspectives on labour migration in South Africa.* Cape Town: Oxford University Press

Mdluli, P. 1987. Ubuntu-botho: Inkatha's 'people's education'. *Transformations,* 5: 60–77

Meillassoux, C. 1981. *Maidens, meal and money: capitalism and the domestic community.* Cambridge: Cambridge University Press

Merton, R. K. 1949. *Social theory and social structure.* New York: Free Press

Mitchell, J. C. 1956. *The Kalela dance: aspects of social relationships among urban Africans in Northern Rhodesia.* Rhodes–Livingstone paper no. 27. Manchester: Manchester University Press

Mitchell, J. C. 1960. *Tribalism and the plural society.* Oxford: Oxford University Press

Mönnig, H. O. 1967. *The Pedi.* Pretoria: Van Schaik

Moodie, T. D. 1975. *The rise of Afrikanerdom: power, apartheid and the Afrikaner civil religion.* Berkeley: University of California Press

Moser, C. O. N. 1978. Informal sector or petty commodity production: dualism or dependence in urban development? *World Development,* 6 (9–10): 1041–1064

Murray, C. G. 1980. Migrant labour and changing family structure in the rural periphery of southern Africa. *Journal of Southern African Studies,* 6 (2): 139–156

Murray, C. G. 1981. *Families divided: the impact of migrant labour in Lesotho.* Cambridge: Cambridge University Press

Myburgh, A. C. 1981. *Anthropology for southern Africa.* Pretoria: Van Schaik

Nairn, T. 1981. *The break–up of Britain: crisis and neo-nationalism.* London: Verso

Nisbet, R. 1967. *The sociological tradition*. New York: Basic Books

Norwood, H. C. 1975. Informal industry in developing countries. *Town Planning Review* 46 (1): 83–94

Obbo, C. 1981. *African women: their struggle for economic independence*. Johannesburg: Ravan Press

O'Brien, M. 1981. *The politics of reproduction*. London and New York: Routledge and Kegan Paul

Odendaal, A. 1984. *Vukani Bantu! The beginnings of black protest politics in South Africa to 1912*. Cape Town: David Philip

O'Meara, D. 1983. *Volkskapitalisme: class, capital and ideology in the development of Afrikaner nationalism, 1934–1948*. Johannesburg: Ravan Press

Palma, G. 1981. Dependency: a formal theory of underdevelopment or a methodology for the analysis of concrete situations of underdevelopment? In P. Streeton and R. Jolly (eds.) *Recent issues in World Development*. London: Pergamon Press

Palmer, R. and Parsons, N. (eds.) 1977. *The roots of rural poverty in central and southern Africa*. Berkeley: University of California Press

Perlman, J. 1976. *The myth of marginality: urban poverty and politics in Rio de Janeiro*. Berkeley: University of California Press

Pinnock, D. 1984. *Breaking the web: economic consequences of the destruction of the extended family by Group Areas relocation in Cape Town*. Carnegie Conference Paper no. 258. Cape Town: University of Cape Town

Plaatje, S. T. 1916. *Native life in South Africa before and since the European War and the Boer Rebellion*. London: P. S. King and Sons

Posel, D. 1987. The language of domination, 1978–1983. In Marks and Trapido (1987)

Preston–Whyte, E. and Nene, S. 1984. *Where the informal sector is not the answer: women and poverty in rural KwaZulu*. Carnegie Conference paper no. 235. Cape Town: University of Cape Town

Quinlan, T. 1986. The tribal paradigm and ethnic nationalism: a case study of political structures in QwaQwa. *Transformations*, 2: 31–49

Rabinow, P. and Sullivan, W. M. (eds.) 1979. *Interpretive social science: a reader*. Berkeley: University of California Press

Ramphele, M. 1986. The male and female dynamic amongst migrant workers in the western Cape. *Social Dynamics*, 12 (1): 15–25

Ranger, T. 1983. The invention of tradition in colonial Africa. In Hobsbawm and Ranger (1983)

Robbins, D. 1984. *What's the matter with Msinga?* Carnegie Conference paper no. 55. Cape Town: University of Cape Town

Robertson, A. F. 1984. *People and the state: an anthropology of planned development*. Cambridge: Cambridge University Press

Robertson, M. K. 1987. 'Orderly urbanisation': the new influx control. In Rycroft (1987)

Rogerson, C. M. and Beavon, K. S. O. 1980. The awakening of 'informal sector' studies in southern Africa. *South African Geographical Journal*, 62 (2): 175–190

Rose, L. 1986. *The massacre of innocents. Infanticide in Britain 1800–1939*. London: Routledge and Kegan Paul

Rycroft, A. J. 1987. Citizenship and rights. In Rycroft (1987)

Rycroft, A. J. (ed.) 1987. *Race and the law in South Africa*. Cape Town: Juta

Sahlins, M. 1961. Segmentary lineage: an organisation of predatory expansion. *American Anthropologist*, 63: 322–345

Sahlins, M. 1968. *Tribesmen*. Englewood Cliffs: Prentice–Hall

Saul, J. S. 1979. The dialectic of class and tribe. *Race and Class*, 20 (4): 347–372

Savage, M. 1984. *Pass laws and the disorganisation and reorganisation of the African population*. Carnegie Conference paper no. 281. Cape Town: University of Cape Town

Sayers, J. 1982. *Biological politics*. London and New York: Tavistock Publications

Schapera, I. 1937. *The Bantu-speaking tribes of South Africa: an ethnographic survey*. London: George Routledge and Sons

Schapera, I. 1967. The old Bantu culture. In I. Schapera (ed.) *Western civilization and the natives of South Africa: studies in culture contact*. London: Routledge and Kegan Paul

Scholtz, G. D. 1970. *Die ontwikkeling van die politieke denke van die Afrikaner*, Deel II. Johannesburg: Voortrekker Pers

Schoombee, J. T. 1985. Group Areas legislation: the political control of ownership and occupation of land. *Acta Juridica*, 339–367

Seligman, C. G. 1961 (1930). *Races of Africa*. London: Oxford University Press

Service, E. R. 1962. *Primitive social organization. An evolutionary perspective*. New York: Random House

Shangaan/Tsonga Development Corporation Limited (STDC) 1986. *Philosophy, objectives and functions of the Shangaan/Tsonga Development Corporation Limited*.

Sharp, J. 1980. Can we study ethnicity?: a critique of fields of study in South African anthropology. *Social Dynamics*, 6 (1): 1–16

Sharp, J. 1985a. Development, politics and culture in South Africa: a sceptical comment. *Development Southern Africa*, 2 (1): 134–162

Sharp, J. 1985b. Unit of study, context and culture: towards an historical anthropology. *African Studies*, 44 (1): 65–85

Sharp, J. and Spiegel, A. 1984. *Vulnerability to impoverishment in South African rural areas: the erosion of kinship and neighbourhood as social resources*. Carnegie Conference paper no. 52. Cape Town: University of Cape Town

Shils, E. 1981. *Tradition*. London: Faber and Faber

Simkins, C. 1986. Household composition and structure in South Africa. In S. Burman and P. Reynolds (eds.) *Growing up in a divided society: the contexts of childhood in South Africa*. Johannesburg: Ravan Press

Simons, H. J. 1968. *African women: their legal status in South Africa*. London: C. Hurst and Co.

Sitas, A. 1986. A black mamba rising: an introduction to Mi S'Dumo Hlatswayo's poetry. *Transformations*, 2: 50–61

Smith, A. D. (ed.) 1976. *Nationalist movements*. London: Macmillan Press

Social Science Encyclopedia, ed. by A. Kuper and J. Kuper. 1985. London: Routledge and Kegan Paul

South Africa. 1985. *Official yearbook of the Republic of South Africa.* Pretoria: Department of Foreign Affairs

South African Institute of Race Relations (SAIRR) 1983. *Handbook of Race Relations in South Africa.* Johannesburg: SAIRR

Southall, A. 1970. The illusion of tribe. In P. Gutkind (ed.) *The passing of tribal man in Africa.* Leiden: Brill

Southall, R. 1983. *South Africa's Transkei: the political economy of an 'independent' bantustan.* New York: Monthly Review Press

Sperber, D. 1985. *On anthropological knowledge: three essays.* Cambridge: Cambridge University Press

Stocking, G. 1982. *Race, culture and evolution.* Chicago: University of Chicago Press

Stoffberg, D. P. 1982. *Introduction to anthropology.* Johannesburg: Macmillan South Africa

Streek, B. and Wicksteed, R. 1981. *Render unto Kaiser: a Transkei dossier.* Johannesburg: Ravan Press

Street, B. V. 1987. Anti-racist education and anthropology. *Anthropology Today,* 3 (6): 13–15

Suchard, H. 1979. Informal sector development. *South African Journal of African Affairs,* 9 (2): 98–103

Surplus People Project. 1983. *Forced removals in South Africa,* 5 vols. Cape Town: Surplus People Project

Suzman, A. 1960. Race classification and definition in the legislation of the Union of South Africa. *Acta Juridica,* 339–367

Swartz, L. and Foster, D. 1984. Images of culture and mental illness: South African psychiatric approaches. *Social Dynamics,* 10 (1): 17–25

Theal, G. M. 1894. *South Africa.* London: Fisher Unwin

Theal, G. M. 1902. *The beginning of South African history.* London: Fisher Unwin

Thomas, E. 1987. *Conflicts and their resolution in Guguletu migrant hostels: a study of the role of the Western Cape Hostel Dwellers' Association.* Unpublished Honours thesis, University of Cape Town

Thompson, L. 1985. *The political mythology of apartheid.* New Haven: Yale University Press

Thornton, R. J. 1983. Narrative ethnography in Africa. *Man,* 18: 502–520

Tobias, P. V. 1972. *The meaning of race.* Johannesburg: South African Institute of Race Relations

Tobias, P. V. 1985a. The history of physical anthropology in South Africa. *Yearbook of Physical Anthropology* 28: 1–52

Tobias, P. V. 1985b. Race. In Kuper and Kuper (1985)

Trapido, S. 1978. Landlord and tenant in a colonial economy: the Transvaal, 1880–1910. *Journal of Southern African Studies,* 5 (1): 26–58

Tucker, W. (née Hoernlé) 1913. *Richtersveld – the land and its people.* Johannesburg: Witwatersrand Council of Education

Tylor, E. B. 1871. *Primitive culture: researches into the development of mythology, philosophy, religion, language, art and custom,* 2 vols. London: J. Murray

UNESCO. 1951. *Race and science.* New York and London: Columbia University Press

Van der Waal, C. S. 1985. Die betekenis van die informele sektor: kleinskalige vervaardiging in KwaNdebele en Venda. Unpublished Ph.D. dissertation, Rand Afrikaans University

Van Jaarsveld, F. A. 1964. *The Afrikaner's interpretation of South African history*. Cape Town: Simondium Publishers

Van Jaarsveld, F. A. 1979. *Die evolusie van apartheid*. Cape Town: Tafelberg

Van Onselen, C. 1982. The Main Reef Road into the working class: proletarianisation, unemployment and class consciousness amongst Johannesburg's Afrikaner poor, 1890–1914. In *Studies in the social and economic history of the Witwatersrand 1886–1914. Volume II: New Nineveh*. Johannesburg: Ravan Press

Van Reenen, T. H. 1967 (1962). *Land: its ownership and occupation in South Africa*. Cape Town: Juta

Van Selm, C. 1984. Why the private doctor? *South African Journal of Family Practice*, 5 (5): 136–8

Van Warmelo, N. J. 1935. *A preliminary survey of the Bantu tribes of South Africa*. Department of Native Affairs: Ethnological Publications no. 5. Pretoria: Government Printer

Webb, C. de B. 1979. The Mfecane. In *Centre for African Studies Occasional Papers no. 2: Perspectives on the South African past*. Cape Town: University of Cape Town

Weber, M. 1965 (1947). Ethnic groups. In T. Parsons, E. Shils, K. Naegele and J. Pitts (eds.) *Theories of society: foundations of modern sociological theory*. New York: Free Pess

Weiss, R. 1986. *The women of Zimbabwe*. London: Kesho Press

Wellings, P. and Sutcliffe, M. 1984. 'Developing' the urban informal sector in South Africa: the reformist paradigm and its fallacies. *Development and Change*, 15 (4): 517–550

Welsh, D. 1987. Democratic liberalism and theories of racial stratification. In J. Butler, R. Elphick and D. Welsh (eds.) *Democratic liberalism in South Africa: its history and prospects*. Cape Town: David Philip

West, M. E. 1975. *Bishops and prophets in a black city*. Cape Town: David Philip

West, M. E. 1976. (with J. Morris) *Abantu. An introduction to the Black people of South Africa*. Cape Town and Johannesburg: Struik

West, M. E. 1979. The Bantu-speaking people. In *Centre for African Studies Occasional Papers no. 2: Perspectives on the South African Past*. Cape Town: University of Cape Town

West, M. E. 1985. Influx control: the 1983 statistics. *Regional topics paper*. 85/2. Cape Town: South African Institute of Race Relations

West, M. E. 1987 (1971). *Apartheid in a South African town, 1968–1985*. Berkeley: Institute of International Studies

Wilkinson, P. and Webster, D. 1982. Living in the interstices of capitalism: towards a reformulation of the 'informal sector' concept. *Social Dynamics*, 8 (2): 1–10

Willan, B. 1982. An African in Kimberley: Sol T. Plaatje, 1894–1898. In Marks and Rathbone (1982)

Williams, G. 1981. The World Bank and the peasant problem. In J. Heyer, P. Roberts and G. Williams (eds.) *Rural development in tropical Africa*. London: Macmillan

Wolf, E. R. 1982. *Europe and the people without history*. Berkeley: University of California Press

Wolpe, H. 1972. Capitalism and cheap labour power – from segregation to apartheid. *Economy and Society*, 1 (4): 425–456

World Bank. 1985. *The assault on world poverty*. London: Baltimore

Worsley, P. 1984. *The three worlds: culture and world development*. London: Weidenfeld and Nicolson

Yudelman, D. 1983. Review of D. O'Meara, *Volkskapitalisme,* in *Social Dynamics*, 9 (1): 102–105

Index